Culturally Sensitive
Art Education
in a Global World

About NAEA

The National Art Education Association is the world's largest professional visual arts education association and a leader in educational research, policy, and practice for art education. NAEA's mission is to advance visual arts education to fulfill human potential and promote global understanding.

Membership includes elementary and secondary art teachers, middle school and high school students in the National Art Honor Society programs, artists, administrators, museum educators, arts council staff, university professors, and students from the United States and several foreign countries. It also includes publishers, manufacturers, and suppliers of art materials; parents; students; retired art educators; and others concerned about quality art education in our schools.

NAEA publishes *Art Education*, *Studies in Art Education*, and other professional papers on art education; holds an annual convention; conducts research; sponsors a teacher awards program; develops standards for student learning, school programs, and teacher preparation; and co-sponsors workshops, seminars, and institutes on art education. For further information, visit our website at www.arteducators.org

To order a copy of this book or obtain additional information, contact National Art Education Association: www.arteducators.org or 800-299-8321.

Order No. 332

ISBN 978-1-890160-66-1

Culturally Sensitive
Art Education
in a Global World:
A Handbook for Teachers

EDITED BY

MARJORIE COHEE MANIFOLD
Indiana University

STEVE WILLIS
Missouri State University

ENID ZIMMERMAN
Indiana University

DEDICATION

Together we are dedicating this book in memory of art educator Dr. Kenneth Marantz, who was a founding member and first President of the United States Society for Education though Art (USSEA). We also would like to dedicate this book in memory of Sylvia Marantz for her commitment to supporting images and stories in children's books that enlighten their perceptions of many cultures around the world.

Table of Contents

Section One: Commonalities and Contrasts

Section Two: Knowing and Honoring Self in Local and Global Communities

Section Three: Dialogic Interactions— Looking, Questioning, Listening, and Engaging

Culturally Sensitive Art Education in a Global World:
A Handbook for Teachers

MARJORIE COHEE MANIFOLD

If the future of any nation lies in the ability of its people to interact harmoniously with one another, within and across national boundaries, toward a common good, then the education of that nation's youth must prepare them accordingly. Such an education should enable youth to apply critical thought to any situation they might realistically encounter during the course of their lives (Held, 2007; Noddings, 2005, 2007; Slote, 2007). Importantly, it should cultivate abilities to empathize with and care about others (Gardner 2007; Noddings, 2003; Stout, 1999), since this informs and inspires personal responsibility for ameliorating local conditions and circumstances, which might otherwise culminate in or contribute to conflicts. We, the editors of this handbook, believe culturally sensitive art educational practices should support development of these skills and incline people of many nations toward harmonious and collaborative interactions.

Our interests in culturally sensitive and inclusive art educational practices were differently inculcated into experiences in our formative years. Editor Enid Zimmerman is of first- and second-generation Polish Russian ancestry and grew up in a highly diverse community in the Bronx, New York City. Her interests in the visual art education of students from culturally diverse populations have been evidenced in her many years of research, teaching, and service contributions to the field of art education (Sabol & Manifold, 2009). Steve Willis, who is of Native American heritage, is committed to pedagogical practices that respect the entire being of the student, including those aspects that are distinctively individual, culturally defined, or shared in common with all humanity (Willis, 2012). My understandings about culture were rooted in a White, middle-class, rural Midwestern upbringing. Curiosity about the human aesthetic experience, as a powerful involuntary response to an unfamiliarity erupting from a field of ordinariness, led me to explore how people from many places around the world experience aesthetic responses to visual culture (Manifold, 2000, 2004b). Over the span of our careers as art educators, our understandings about diversity that differently shaped each of our perceptions during our formative years were challenged, confirmed, enlightened, and transformed through interactions with students and peers from many backgrounds in local, national, and international contexts.

Our shared commitments to teaching culturally sensitive and inclusive art education to students living in a globally connected world are mutual, and were motivating factors in our becoming active members of the International Society for Education through Art (InSEA) and United States Society for Education through

Art (USSEA). InSEA as an organization was conceived following World War II by an international group of art educators who believed that all children all over the world should have opportunities to express themselves artistically, and have products of their expression shared among and appreciated by children from other nations and global cultures (Steers, 2001). If children all over the world came to appreciate one another through art, they reasoned, peoples of the world would become more tolerant and respectful of one another. Conflicts born of prejudice, cultural misunderstandings, or fear of unknown peoples would be averted (Marantz, 1978).

USSEA emerged as an affiliate of InSEA and the National Art Education Association (NAEA) in 1977. This was due to a growing awareness in the United States that, as large groups of people were immigrating into the country or migrating from place to place within the nation in search of new economic opportunities or changes of lifestyle, the demographics of schools and communities would become multicultural (Zimmerman & Marantz, 2011). Art teachers who were largely from White, middle-class backgrounds often struggled to understand the cultural experiences of students from other cultures and nations who they taught. Sparks of discord often flared between students or students and teachers, who were unfamiliar, unaccustomed, and sometimes resistant to one another's ways of being or interacting (Manifold, 2004a).

InSEA and USSEA's founders saw a role for art education in bringing students and teachers from dissimilar cultural backgrounds or vastly separated parts of the world to greater understanding of and appreciation for one another's worldviews. However, while art teaching and research that enlightened educators about issues of cultural diversity were recognized by InSEA and USSEA, few guidelines were provided to K-16 teachers about how such goals might be attained in varieties of educational contexts around the world. It was within this context that I approached my friends and colleagues, Enid Zimmerman and Steve Willis, with a proposal that we compile a handbook that would present useful models for teaching art to students from diverse populations in a culturally sensitive way. I wrote the proposal to the National Art Education Association, with input from Willis and Zimmerman, and was notified that the handbook was accepted for publication. Since that time, I have served as coordinator and first editor of *Culturally Sensitive Art Education in a Global World: A Handbook for Teachers.*

Cultural Sensitivity

Since this book is intended as a teacher's resource for developing culturally sensitive art curricula for students in kindergarten through postsecondary grades, it is important to set forth a clear understanding of what we will be referring to when using the term *culture*. The word has several dictionary definitions. A Latin etymology of culture refers to the act of tending, guarding, cultivating, or tilling the land. One branch of this root evolved to signify a betterment or refinement of an individual through education. Thus, the term culture has become synonymous with educated tastes, as, for example, when declaring a person to be a cultured man or woman. When paired with the qualitative adjective *high*, culture refers to the aesthetic products and preferences (i.e., the *high culture*) of an elitist citizenry of socially, economically, or politically empowered patrons, supporters, fine artists, and architects within a particular socionational or regional context. These definitions are exclusivist, insofar as they imply that expressions of people who are not members of an elite class, or whose works have not been sanctioned by some official or institutionalized organization in the art world, might be perceived as of lesser value. Taken to an extreme, this narrowed definition of culture connotes that any aesthetic expression created outside a sanctioned field, along with the people who create or prefer these works, are culturally deficient or of a lesser cultural importance to society. Such a definition or conclusion would be antithetical to notions of cultural sensitivity and inclusion advocated by editors or authors of this handbook.

Throughout this text, we will use the term culture in reference to a group of people who share a mutually constructed and maintained environment; hold similar beliefs, histories, customs, mores, and values; communicate with one another in a common language or symbol system (Adejumo, 2002); and pass on shared knowledge to newcomers and future generations of a particular group. As signifier of a general group, culture implies no evaluative judgment of the political correctness or social value of the group being referenced. It merely affirms that there are many diverse cultural groups whose members are distinguished by commonalities of religion, nation, race, socioeconomic conditions, or interests. One's sense of cultural identity may have been passed down through generations of ancestors and be grounded in the cumulative aesthetic traditions of a particular nation, such as Turkey or South Korea, or in the aggregate experiences of a people, such as the Romani, Hopi, or Sami peoples.

Additionally, culture may refer to people who are drawn together through commonalities of national or local geographies, shared experiences, traits, interests, or activities. Authors of this text address a variety of such cultural communities, from LGBTQ youth to children of migrant workers to students in preservice art education programs. These communal cultures may be understood as subcultures, insofar as they include families or individuals who identify with larger cultural groups, yet also manifest traits, express interests, or experience needs that set them apart from others of a larger group. Subcultural groups may experience isolation within a larger culture, or may find it necessary to cross over or through larger cultural borders in order to participate in a subcultural community.

The authors of this handbook look beyond exclusive or generalized definitions of culture and instructional approaches that focus on learning *about* peoples from unfamiliar cultures; they advocate that students be taught dispositions of being sensitive and empathic with people of other cultures. The essays, suggested strategies, models, units, and activities presented in this book focus attention on the way we address the human experience and how this can lead to openness to the world (Greene, 2003; Hansen, 2008). Samples of possible cultural content are provided, with emphasis on how these lessons encourage student understandings of themselves within diverse and complexly connected societies. Understanding is value-laden and does not evolve from value-neutral cultural content. It is a matter of seeing with the heart (Nussbaum, 1998) and a foundation upon which youth may come to love and embrace their own heritages while being enriched by differing points of view (Nussbaum, 2003). The goal is to cultivate, through education, people who act and think morally and compassionately in interaction with others.

A Global Perspective

Prior to sending out a call for chapter proposals for this handbook, the editors engaged in conversations about the need for cultural sensitivity from a *global* perspective. We evidenced this need in ongoing tensions between differing groups within nations and between nations of the world, and in the proliferation of conversations about incivility, intolerance, and bullying taking place within educational circles and everyday life (Williams, 2012). As technological advances shorten travel time across vast differences, visiting foreign lands becomes a commonplace event for many who have the means to make such trips, but this does not always result in deep appreciation

or respect for differences in cultures. Tourism may fuel stereotypes as easily as inform understandings of what it is like to live in or a be a citizen of a visited community (Molz, 2010; Wiggins, 2010).

Virtual visits to unfamiliar places may also be problematic. For example, although a considerable body of academic literature extols uses of Interactive Communication Technologies (ICT) as a means of connecting people and opening spaces for democratic interactions of people from diverse regions and across nations, we noticed there are places in the world where school children have no access to these technologies. Furthermore, having access to ICT in classrooms neither automatically guarantees that global interactions will occur, nor that, if interactions do occur, mutual appreciation and respect for one another's ideas will result. In fact, there is beginning to be evidence that Internet cyberspaces might provide sheltered, incubational environments for clandestine interests, exclusive fraternities, and bullying activities as easily as they encourage inclusive or caring interactions among various peoples (Hinduja & Patchin, 2011, 2012). To counter this negativity, we included chapters in this handbook by authors who describe ways art teachers integrate digital and communication technologies in order to facilitate sharing, dialogue, and collaborations globally. These authors focus on how students are assisted in becoming agents of democratic teaching and learning by employing technologies as instruments that support positive pedagogical goals and cooperative artmaking processes.

Globalism or Multiculturalism

In an uncomplicated form, global art education would incorporate images and artifacts from around the world as instructional exemplars. This approach alone, however, might trivialize global cultures in the same way that a "heroes and holidays" approach to multicultural education might belittle the culture being presented (Banks, 2008). A simplistic presentation reinforces students'

> false sense of superiority, gives them a misleading conception of their relationship with other racial and ethnic groups, and denies them the opportunity to benefit from the knowledge, perspectives, and frames of reference that can be gained from studying and experiencing other cultures and groups. (p. 195)

Furthermore, introducing students to artifacts created by peoples from differing parts of the world alone contributes little if anything to the dissolution of fixed borders of understanding among cultural groups.

Globalism or *globalization* refers to more than the sum of nations and cultures: It suggests an interconnectedness of peoples within and across world nations and cultures (Fairleigh Dickinson University, n. d.). It implies a collapse and dissolution of borders between once clearly defined groups of people. As distinguishing features of cultural or national groups mingle, they become subject to appropriation or assimilation by others and may morph or be fused into new forms. Thus, debates spark over the fate of traditional cultural identities and expressions. Will the globalization of art education result in a loss of cultural diversity? Will minority cultures eventually submit to influences of a few or a single powerful pan-global culture, or will a plurality of cultures be respected and appreciated throughout the world? These debates are similar to those that have troubled advocates of multicultural art education in the past. In fact, we found that authors of this text often struggled to differentiate between notions of multiculturalism and globalism when addressing issues of cultural sensitivity. A complication is that while multiculturalism, as it applies to education, has been extensively explored through academic literature of the last several decades (Banks & Banks, 2008; Bennett, 2010), globalism remains differently and often contradictorily defined by academics across disciplines. While globalization implies a mutually beneficial interactivity across national or cultural borders, multiculturalism implies the preservation of differing cultural traditions, expressions, and distinctions of peoples within a unified society (Banks, 1986; Baumeister & Leary, 1995). Multiculturalism refers to interactions of people from diverse backgrounds or agendas within the same tangible, regionalized space. Globalism, however, is a worldview that places the interests of the entire world above the interests of a single person, groups, or nations, or it may describe how individuals come to function competently or harmoniously with peoples from different cultural and national backgrounds.

We found the latter definition of globalism most appealing, insofar as interactions among peoples in remote parts of the world require us to become familiar with and negotiate ways of knowing and engaging with one another. We chose authors for this handbook who suggested fruitful ways of bringing students from differing worldviews together through art learning, making, and sharing. In our minds, the purpose of culturally sensitive art education is to "promote understanding, tolerance and friendship among people of all nations, racial or religious groups" (UNESCO, 1974, article 26), and communities that comprise a diverse world. This ideal harks back to goals set forth by post-WWII art educator-founders of InSEA, who believed the arts could play an instrumental role in developing empathic individuals who would seek to live in harmony with one another in the world (Steers, 2001).

Yet as communities worldwide are growing more diverse due to migration of peoples from one geographic region to another, immigration across cultural or national boundaries, or intermingling of people from far-flung regions of the world in cyberspace, we also see value in the preservation of cultural histories. We are in agreement that it is important that students identify with and draw upon familiar stories of their cultural communities as starting points for understanding the larger world. Therefore, although we encouraged authors to consider how models or ideas they presented might be applicable to art education in global contexts, we recognized the importance of honoring multicultural diversity within local communities as a necessary step in becoming open to the larger world.

Additionally, several authors in this handbook consider discovery of personal identity as fundamental to recognizing the complex, multiplicative, plastic, and ambiguous identities of individuals globally. Political scientist Sajed (2005) wrote, "It can be argued that processes of globalization constantly interact with processes of identification" (p. 1). Being sensitive to culture, declares Sajed, requires consideration of "whether the boundaries of identity are mobile or fixed, and whether one can and should even be able to talk about identity as a clearly defined notion, one which awaits our impartial and detached investigation" (p. 1).

As students awaken to Self as a multifaceted construct, they recognize pieces of self that can bridge or be called upon to be a connecting site for coming to know Others. At the same time, they begin to see that no culture is static, and no one person or group of people can be fully recognized or known when viewed through the lens of a single cultural context. Authors in this handbook all begin with the premise that students must not lose sight of who they are even as they lose themselves in respectful explorations of others. It is our hope that the very notion of Otherness—as something apart from oneself—be dissolved without permitting one's self to be absorbed or subsumed by universal sameness.

Organization

The materials of the handbook are organized in three sections, each of which is introduced by one of the editors. As we prepared this text for publication, each editor took principal responsibility for editing the chapters and communicating with the authors of that section. The three editors also read and commented on the revised versions of all chapters. **Section One: Commonalities and Contrasts,** edited by Enid Zimmerman, includes chapters by authors who describe concepts that inspire research and ground pedagogies that are sensitive to cultural differences and similarities. Oppositional ideas focus students' attentions on qualities and phenomena shared by all people, then reveal reasons and ways these universals may be interpreted or experienced differently.

Steve Willis edited the chapters of **Section Two: Knowing and Honoring Self in Local and Global Communities**. Authors of chapters in this section present strategies aimed at understanding and appreciating self, local communities, and their intimate environments as prerequisites for developing empathy for others. Authors also provide models of mindful attention to the cultural contexts of others' lives and empathetic interactions across national borders, and they address the importance of maintaining varieties of cultural aesthetics in a global environment.

I was editor of **Section Three: Dialogic Interactions—Looking, Questioning, Listening, and Engaging**. This section presents chapters that describe strategies for coming to know the world as others know it without having been physically immersed in the everyday cultural experiences of The Other. These strategies involve finding a neutral space where dialogic interaction of people from differing cultures can occur. Authors of this section look at how students may be empowered by being enabled to claim and contribute their own visual narratives of cultural heritage and identity.

In each section, chapters conclude with questions and/or activities "For Further Consideration" that are intended to prod reflection and spark critical discussions about ideas presented or excluded in the chapter. In addition to questions that are focused by the content of each chapter, we offer here some general questions about the aims of culturally sensitive art education and the kinds of student behaviors that might be an expected result of such practices.

General Questions to Consider When Reading Chapters

Throughout this handbook, we present readings with suggested activities or discussion questions that, when offered to students for serious reflection, urge them to look beyond mere formalistic knowledge of art and consider how cultural beliefs and practices inform expression, what human ethics and caring would look like if enacted in local and global settings, and how art teachers and students might take action in order to help bring about changes in the world. As you read through the various chapters, you might consider the following questions and discuss your answers with others.

- What art and culture should be considered? How should cultural topics be approached?

- What strategies are appropriate for art instruction of students who bring a diversity of backgrounds, experiences, and understandings to educational settings?

- Can any lesson about a culture other than one's own provide or represent an authentic experience?

- Toward what ends should visual arts that focus on culture be taught?

- How should these goals be evaluated?

- How might interactive communicative technologies or visual resources be integrated seamlessly and sensitively in an art curriculum?

- How might we assess the success or failure of various culturally sensitive approaches?

- How might a student of successful global instruction behave differently or more competently than one who lacks the benefits of such instruction?

At the conclusion of this handbook is an appendix of Selected Resources that might be useful for teachers when developing comprehensive units of visual art study that are culturally sensitive in a global world.

REFERENCES

Adejumo, C. O. (2002). Considering multicultural art education. *Art Education, 55*(2), 33–39.

Banks, I. A. (1986). Multicultural education: Development, paradigms and goals. In J. A. Banks & I. Lynch (Eds.), *Multicultural education in Western societies* (pp. 1–29). London, England: Holt, Rinehart & Winston.

Banks, J. (2008). Approaches to multicultural curriculum reform. In J. Banks & C. M. Banks (Eds.), *Multicultural education: Issues and perspectives* (pp. 242–264). Boston, MA: Allyn & Bacon.

Banks, J., & Banks, C. M. (Eds.). (2008). *Multicultural education: Issues and perspectives*. Boston, MA: Allyn & Bacon.

Baumeister, R. F., & Leary, M. R. (1995). The need to belong: Desire for interpersonal attachments as a fundamental human motivation. *Psychological Bulletin, 117*(3), 497–529.

Bennett, C. I. (2010). *Comprehensive multicultural education: Theory and practice* (7th ed.). New York, NY: Pearson.

Fairleigh Dickinson University. (n. d.). *Global education vs. globalization*. Retrieved from http://view.fdu.edu/default. aspx?id=263

Gardner, H. (2007). *Five minds for the future*. Watertown, MA: Harvard Business Review Press.

Greene, M. (2003). *Releasing the imagination: Essays of education, the arts, and social change*. Hoboken, NJ: Jossey-Bass.

Hansen, D. T. (2008). Curriculum and the idea of a cosmopolitan inheritance. *Journal of Curriculum Studies, 40*(3), 289–313.

Held, V. (2007). *The ethics of care: Personal, political, global*. New York, NY: Oxford University Press.

Hinduja, S., & Patchin, J. W. (2011). Overview of cyberbullying. White paper for the White House Conference on Bullying Prevention. Washington, DC: Whitehouse Conference on Bullying Prevention. Available at http://people.uwec.edu/ patchinj/cyberbullying/white_house_conference_materials_ Hinduja&Patchin.pdf

Hinduja, S., & Patchin, J. W. (2012). Cyberbullying: Neither an epidemic nor a rarity. *European Journal of Developmental Psychology, 9*(5), 539–543.

Manifold, M. C. (2000). Valuing a rural aesthetic. *Art Education, 53*(4), 18–24.

Manifold, M. C. (2004a). Featured teacher: Ginna Cullen. *USSEA Newsletter, 27*(1), 11.

Manifold, M. C. (2004b). In a Bishonan boarding house: Time, space and the social dimensions of an info-age aesthetic. In G. Diaz & M. B. McKenna (Eds.), *Teaching for aesthetic experience: The art of learning* (pp. 63–84). Cambridge, MA: Peter Lang.

Marantz, K. (1978). The promise of collective action. *Journal of Aesthetic Education, 12*(2), 121–123.

Molz, J. G. (2010, November 30). Tourism, global culture, and transnational diplomacy. *World Politics Review*. Retrieved from www.worldpoliticsreview.com/articles/7144/tourism-global-culture-and-transnational-diplomacy

Noddings, N. (2003). *Caring: A feminine approach to ethics and moral education*. Oakland: University of California Press.

Noddings, N. (2005). *Educating students for global awareness*. New York, NY: Teachers College Press.

Noddings, N. (2007). *Critical lessons: What our schools should teach*. New York, NY: Cambridge University Press.

Nussbaum, M. (1998). *Cultivating humanity: A classical defense of reform in liberal education*. Cambridge, MA: Harvard University Press.

Nussbaum, M. (2003). *Upheavals of thought: The intelligence of emotions*. New York, NY: Cambridge University Press.

Sabol, F. R., & Manifold, M. C. (2009). *Through the prism: Looking through the spectrum of writings of Enid Zimmerman*. Reston, VA: National Art Education Association.

Sajed, A. (2005). Identity. *Globalization and autonomy online compendium*. Retrieved from http://globalautonomy.ca/global1/ servlet/Glossarypdf?id=CO.0061

Slote, M. (2007). *The ethics of care and empathy*. New York, NY: Routledge.

Steers, J. (2001). InSEA: A brief history and a vision of its future role. *Journal of Art & Design Education, 20*(2), 215–229.

Stout, C. J. (1999). The art of empathy: Teaching students to care. *Art Education, 52*(2), 21–24, 33–34.

UNESCO. (1974). The Universal Declaration of Human Rights. Retrieved from www.un.org/en/documents/udhr/

Wiggins, K. (2010). The two-faced world of the "cultural tourism" industry. *Policymic*. Retrieved from www.policymic.com/ articles/1292/the-two-faced-world-of-the-cultural-tourism-industry

Williams, R. B. (2012, July 15). The rise of incivility and bullying in America. *Wired for Success*. Retrieved from www.psychologytoday.com/blog/wired-success/201207/the-rise-incivility-and-bullying-in-america

Willis, S. (2012). Quadratic pedagogy. In L. Campbell & S. Simmons III (Eds.), *The heart of art education: Holistic approaches to creativity, integration, and transformation* (pp. 133–140). Reston, VA: National Art Education Association.

Zimmerman, E., & Marantz, K. (2011). *Interview with Ken Marantz Part I* [Video]. Retrieved from www.youtube.com/watch?v=Mr_0gSeZ9vg

Commonalities and Contrasts

SECTION ONE:
COMMONALITIES AND CONTRASTS

Introduction

ENID ZIMMERMAN

In Section One, the terms *commonalities* and *contrasts* are explained as they apply to similarities and differences people experience within and across diverse cultural, ethnic, racial, gender-related, religious, and other group affiliations. By focusing on *commonalities*, students can recognize attributes that provide an opportunity for harmonious and cohesive interactions among peoples in a variety of contexts. As an equitable introduction to developing culturally sensitive curricula, teachers may find it helpful to highlight commonalities by considering units of instruction, such as those found in Section One, that address: tolerance, caring, lack of prejudice, and empathy; creative integrative arts experiences; human rights education; study of ritual, storytelling, and traditional arts; aesthetic perception; systems of power and social responsibility; and interdependence in a global world.

Use of the term *contrasts* emphasizes differences between beliefs and expressions among groups of people as evidenced in their practices. Attending to contrasts as well as commonalities allows students to sort out and make meaning of complex concepts and ideas. Students can be guided to recognize that people understand or respond to similar experiences in different ways. Art teachers of students of all ages need to address issues of commonalities and contrasts when they challenge their students to consider how artworks represent differing interpretations of common experiences. Curricula based on themes of commonalities and contrasts should require that students question how and why artworks are interpreted within the mores and traditions of the group that created them. Concomitantly, such curricula also should also take into account how similarities and differences with other groups can help expand students' understandings about themselves and the world around them.

In this section, emphasis is placed on pedagogies that are rooted in theoretical frameworks and explained by the authors as integral parts of their own developed teaching practices. In the first chapter, "Increasing Students' Cultural and Global Sensitivities Through Designing Cross-Cultural Curriculum Units," Joanne E. Sowell explores how to present a culture as The Other without homogenizing all cultures and viewing them as the same. In planning a curriculum, commonalities among cultures are thought of as big themes that link cultures, although such themes may not have the same attributes. Therefore it is important to consider that artworks may differ greatly as a result of reasons they were made and differences and connections they engender based on themes the works represent.

In "Port of Entry: Puppetry! An Interdisciplinary Arts Experience," Melanie Davenport and Douglas Stevens describe their collaboration teaching a puppetry art and music course for college level preservice students in which they integrate language arts, social studies, intercultural and global education, and technology. Focus is on creative expression that serves as a window into similarities and differences in beliefs, practices, and adaptive strategies of populations around the globe. In "Using Artifacts to Promote Cultural Awareness in Cyprus Primary Schools," Fotini Larkou offers a human-rights-focused art education curriculum model developed for increasing students' cultural awareness potential through artifact-based pedagogy that promotes commonalities and differences through cultural understandings. The model embeds common aims to eliminate hostilities and misunderstandings and bring people around the world closer together.

In "Exploring Ritual Through Art," Angela M. La Porte explains ritual as directly connecting to secondary and postsecondary students' lives by offering pathways to interdisciplinary and global understanding in a shared world. She offers as an example a unit of instruction where students examine their own and others' rituals to gain an appreciation for similarities and differences among cultures around the world. Laurie Eldridge's focus is on indigenous, traditional arts of Ghana in her chapter, "Learning and Teaching About Traditional Ghanaian Art Forms: Developing Global Perspectives Using Digital Media in Art Education." She presents a curriculum designed for elementary art students in which content, social context, and development of cultural identity are highlighted. This intercultural curriculum provides elementary students with tools to explore, know about, interact with, and appreciate similarities and differences with others and with their own customs, and to see themselves as citizens of the world.

Jonathan Silverman emphasizes the importance of metaphorically stepping into another's shoes as a catalyst for practicing empathy, storytelling, and aesthetic sensibility. In "Becoming Empathic Storytellers: A Curriculum for Developing Cultural Sensitivity," he reports about a literacy project that transcends cultural gaps and empowers students by giving them a voice. This is accomplished through a curriculum in which artistically representing stories of others is shown to enhance aesthetic perception, social responsibility, and global awareness. In Marit Dewhurst and Jen Song's chapter, "Looking, Creating, and Making It Public: Strategies for a Globalized Approach to Arts Education," they emphasize contemporary art practices from a global perspective through focusing on teaching skills for collaborating across socially constructed identity barriers, analyzing how systems of power influence daily lives, thinking creatively about the interdependent nature of the world, and

contributing to creation of a more just and equal society. This global approach to art education moves beyond including artists from diverse backgrounds to one that prepares students to be thoughtful about commonalities and differences in visual arts practices within a complex and interdependent world.

Pamela Stephens presents a case study of an at-risk Navajo student in "The Story of Doris: Cultural Sensitivity in Action." This student is described as successfully navigating complexities of a post-secondary art education program and, in the process, becoming a role model of cultural sensitivity for her peers through shared and diverse interests, encouraging thoughtful listening, and venerating reciprocal compassion. According to Stephens, teachers and students should be willing to learn about traditions and beliefs of other cultures that are similar and different from their own and demonstrate tolerance, caring, empathy, and lack of prejudice. Jennifer Stoopes-Mokamba presents another point of view about global sensitivity and understanding others in her chapter, "Changing Perceptions About Stereotypes of Art Images Through Investigations of Views About Native American Art." She asserts that no one can truly *know* another's culture. Using contemporary Native American art as an example, she demonstrates that when viewing what is perceived as someone else's culture, personal perspectives can influence interpretations. Rather then relying only on outsiders' interpretations, information about an artwork received directly from an artist can aid in understanding, and students then can view people from another culture as individuals living complex lives in communities both similar and different from their own.

Visual arts instruction and developing global sensitivity are of utmost importance and should be an essential component in a variety of teaching and learning contexts including schools, museums, community centers, and other venues where art education is taught. Students need to learn to understand and value diverse perspectives locally, regionally, and globally about similarities and differences within and outside their immediate environments, something that is increasingly important in today's technologically interconnected, global society. The chapters in this section, written by authors from the United States and abroad, present a variety of practical means through which teaching and learning with global sensitivity about commonalities and contrasts among peoples around the world can be adapted in other contexts and flourish.

CHAPTER 1

Increasing Students' Cultural and Global Sensitivities
Through Designing Cross-Cultural Curriculum Units

JOANNE E. SOWELL
University of Nebraska at Omaha

The typical way that art from diverse cultures is taught in K-12 classrooms is to focus on a single culture at a time. While these lessons are often interesting for students, and art productions associated with them can be appealing, I do not believe they significantly increase students' cultural and global sensitivities. After a brief look at some of the problems with implementation of multiculturalism and globalism in the classroom, I will propose a method for designing cross-cultural curricula that address a number of these issues.

According to Lei and Grant (2001), in their history of multiculturalism in the United States, in the 1990s the "popular understanding of multicultural education continued to be and became more solidified as celebratory events and the inclusion of diverse populations in the curricula" (p. 229). In reflecting back on his 1996 book, *Cultural Pluralism*, Chalmers (2009) indicated that he believed that "so-called multicultural art programs" (p. 188) tended to focus on individual cultures, celebrations (often associated with particular times of the year), and making copies of objects from other cultures. "A quick trip to most teachers' resource centers will show that they still largely look this way" (p. 188). Lei and Grant (2001) conclude that in the United States, "mainstream understanding of multicultural education is at a superficial level" (p. 222). This is not only the case in the United States, as indicated by Rizvi (1994), who calls the implementation of multiculturalism in Australia "limited" and states that "in some instances the so-called multicultural activities may have done more harm than good—in reinforcing stereotypical racist representations, for example" (p. 58). Many theorists have long been calling for a more critical form of multiculturalism that not only considers diverse cultures within one country but also includes cultures found in countries around the world, challenges systems of oppression, and calls for schools to become a force for social justice (Chalmers, 2009; Lei & Grant, 2001; Nieto, 2004). As part of this more critical multiculturalism and globalism, culture is no longer seen as bounded, but as contested and hybrid, with mixtures of cultures having significant effects on identity (Mahalingam & McCarthy, 2000). Thus, cultures do not stay the same over time and are constantly influenced by and influencing one another. Chalmers (2009) sees a lack of this critical approach to culture in art education:

Within Cultural Studies the notion of hybridity is rather old, but in school-based visual art education rarely, other than by perhaps looking at the influence of West African masks on Picasso, or the relationship between Van Gogh's work and Japanese prints, do students study such phenomena in schools… It is critical that educators grasp the concept that cultures are both internally diverse and ever-changing. In school, except in a few cases, it has seemed too messy to deal with new hybridized identities, forms and cultural practices, so we have left them alone and instead reinterpreted, diluted and exoticized selected cultures. (p. 193)

If, however, as Chalmers suggests, many theorists writing for educators neglect to discuss how their ideas can be implemented in the classroom (p. 187), then how are teachers supposed to reflect more nuanced notions of culture in their own practices?

One way to begin is to adopt a different idea of the relationships among cultures. Writing in 1993, Ovando and McCarty noted that too many people conceive of cultures as separate islands, each completely distinct from every other. They suggest instead that we use a model of cultures as great circles on a sphere, each of which intersects with every other (see my visual representation of this in Figure 1). This visual metaphor creates a more complex image of cultures and allows for a possibility that one person, as a single point, might belong to many cultures, encompassing a hybrid identity. Then, as Chalmers (1996) suggests, we can focus on the similarities among cultures—the nodes on the sphere—rather than the differences.

This emphasis on similarities among cultures also is contested. Some suggest that a focus on similarities is an attempt to view cultures as the same, in opposition to the affirmation of difference as a key part of multiculturalism (Nieto, 2004). The acceptance of difference, however, does not have to mean defining another culture as The Other which is often done in the name of inclusion and globalization. "Inclusion of traditional marginalized populations in the form of curricular materials, posters on classroom walls, and a multicultural week or month… perpetuates the exoticization and Othering of the populations… [teachers] aim to 'include'" (Lei & Grant, 2001, p. 232). Across the world, emphasis on a right to cultural difference often is seen as particular to the United States and "seems to be opposite to the narrative of inclusion… Difference appears to entail the threat of segregation, balkanization and social schism" (Dussel, 2001, pp. 108–110). In a classroom context, Keating (2007) notes that at times "students assume that difference between themselves, and the various others they encounter are too different—too other, as it were—to have anything of importance in common" (p. 13).

The Cross-Cultural Curriculum

Given these critiques of multicultural implementation, how does a teacher avoid presenting a culture as The Other without homogenizing all cultures to make them the same? Keating (2007) proposes the term *interconnectivity*, which evokes the nodes on the sphere (Figure 1), as a way to negotiate between similarities and differences among cultures. "Commonalities indicate complex points of connection that enable us to negotiate among sameness, similarity, and difference" (p. 33). She finds three reasons to begin with commonalities: they are useful to begin classroom discussions, they encourage students to reexamine their own perceptions and assumptions, and they "prevent students from equating difference with deviation" (pp. 45–46). This third reason seems to be the most important in increasing global and cultural sensitivity. If we distance ourselves so far from another person or group that we see them as deviant or Other, then it is easy to be insensitive to their concerns.

The commonalities among cultures can be thought of as big themes that link cultures without making them have the same attributes. In 2009, Chalmers reflected on his suggestions for the use of big themes in the art classroom:

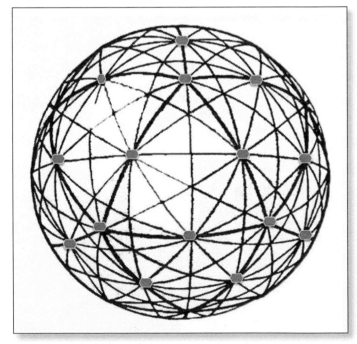

Figure 1. Visual metaphor of cultures depicted as great circles on a sphere where a node represents the intersection of cultures or a hybrid identity.

In Celebrating Pluralism (Chalmers, 1996) I directed attention to the big themes—themes that can address and incorporate transcultural hybridized experience. In exploring these themes, some of this art, studied and made, will strive to perpetuate established cultural values and will support continuity and stability in such aspects as religion and politics. Other art will urge and reflect change. Studio projects will encourage students to tell their own important stories. (p. 188)

Between 2000 and 2010 I taught a cross-cultural art history course for both art teachers and other teachers who wanted to integrate art into their classrooms. In this course, *Celebrating Pluralism* was used as the primary text. Teachers read, reflected on, and discussed Chalmers' ideas, and yet I found that when they began to try to design a cross-cultural curriculum they had difficulty putting his suggestions into practice. To bridge theory and practice I designed a series of steps which follow Chalmers' theories but make actual implementation of his ideas more concrete.

Step One: Start With Why People Make Art

If we are going to deal with the functions of art, we need first to address a culturally based idea that most people who have grown up in the United States share—the idea that art is not made to fulfill any specific function other than to be appreciated visually. This is what Keating (2007) calls a status-quo story that is a culturally based belief we think of as a fact. In order to address this cultural assumption with my students, I do an activity in which I divide students into small groups and give them images from many different cultures (Sowell, 1993, 1996). For example, they look at different types of pottery: a Japanese water jar that has no decoration, a 6th-century BCE Greek amphora decorated with a mythological theme, a Native American pot with animal decoration, a commercial collector's plate from a magazine advertisement, Meret Oppenheim's fur covered cup, and a plate from Judy Chicago's *Dinner Party*. Also included in the images are a Native American skirt woven out of grass, elaborately decorated clothing being worn by African women, a kimono carefully displayed on the wall, a 19th-century quilt, and a story quilt by Faith Ringgold. Other images include an African wood sculpture and a medieval cathedral. Students are asked to divide the works into two categories, Fine Art and Craft, and then to discuss what reasons influenced their decisions. I have done this exercise many times with first-semester college freshmen, with classes of undergraduate students of all levels, with graduate students who are teachers, and with college professors. Always, the determining factor is whether the work of art is considered functional, a feature associated with craft. The Greek amphora is usually put into fine art even though it can be used, because the students focus on the painted narrative decoration or on the early date it was made, which they assume makes it rare. They generally think that no one actually would use such a beautiful pot; hence it is considered fine art. On the other hand, the Native American pot is often considered craft, even though it too is decorated, because the decoration is simpler and the date it was made is 19th century. After a discussion about the works and about the reasons they used to place objects in one category or the other, I ask students which category is valued more. The answer is always Fine Art. I do this activity before we begin a study of Native American art to help students understand their own culturally based assumptions about art. They realize that they may automatically devalue a piece of Native American beadwork worn as clothing without even thinking about it. This activity also helps them understand that art can have many functions beyond being an object of contemplation, even art made in the 21st-century United States.

Later in my courses we do another activity that centers on why art is made. Students are put into groups and asked to come up with ten reasons why people make art. We then compile a mind map based upon their answers (Figure 2). Using images from the Joslyn Art Museum, my local museum in Omaha, Nebraska, I found a number of works that were made to indicate membership in a group, a subset of expressing identity as seen on the mind map. A portrait of a Russian woman wearing peasant dress and a painting of peasants by Jules Breton both indicate particular social classes and express political messages. *Transformations* by Roxanne Swentzell (a sculpture of young Pueblo women getting dressed for a corn ceremony) and an Italian religious painting showing donors with the Virgin Mary both display figures as members of particular religious groups. A Haida (Northwest Coast Native American) button blanket by Dorothy Grant also displays both status and clan lineage. It is important to note that works can have several functions, such as indicating status and displaying membership in a group. By connecting the lines in Figure 2, several of these connections become apparent.

Having identified a number of reasons why art is made, a theme can be developed for writing a curriculum unit. Looking at the mind map (Figure 2) we can pick one of the large themes and then narrow it to make it significant for the students as expressed in their daily lives. For example, if we chose the theme "storytelling," we could write it as the statement, "Artists have made art to tell stories." Then we could narrow to a particular type of story, such as stories of growing up or coming of age. Another example from the mind map might be, "Art is made to display power." This is a very large theme that can connect to social studies and could encompass many works of art. We could narrow our theme of power to "Artists around the world and through time have conveyed the concept of power through representation of human figures." As an example, we now have a theme about power for a cross-cultural curriculum unit. The next step is to choose the works of art we want to discuss in the context of this theme.

Step Two: Find Images That Represent a Diversity of Cultures, Ethnic Groups, and Genders

Now that we have our theme—artists around the world and through time have conveyed the concept of power

through the representation of human figures—we need to pick some images to use in our curriculum unit. Many works of art have been made to represent rulers. I chose an African plaque from Benin City that shows a king riding a horse with attendants holding his arms, a medieval manuscript showing an Ottonian king seated between military and religious leaders, a drawing of a Mayan carved lintel showing two leaders capturing prisoners in war, and a portrait of a Chinese emperor. There are a number of visual features that these works have in common. To express their dominance, the Benin king, Ottonian king, and Mayan rulers are all depicted larger than the other figures in the images. All three have elaborate headdresses that mark them as important. The Benin king and the Ottonian king are both placed facing forward in the center of their compositions. All four rulers are wearing elaborate dress. The Chinese emperor is somewhat different in that he is alone in the image, making it impossible to compare him to other figures. Yet his confident stance and his elaborate clothing suggest that he is someone important. Some of these characteristics are features that we can easily recognize as representing power. Others are more specific to the particular culture, such as the Chinese emperor's yellow robe decorated with dragons, or the fact that the Benin ruler is riding sidesaddle. This

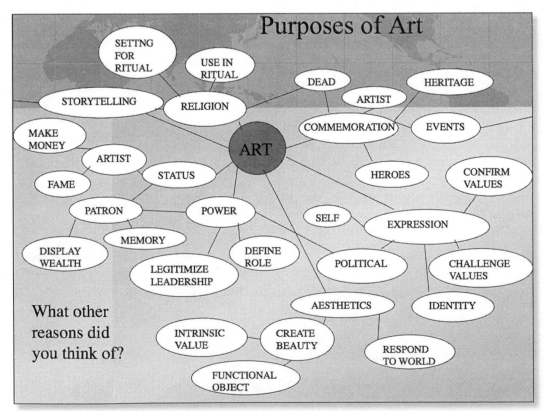

Figure 2. Mind map, created in a college classroom activity, of reasons why people make art.

For Further Consideration

1. Give an example of a work of art that exhibits a hybrid identity or contested culture. Explain.

2. Discuss an example of a multicultural lesson that you think exhibits a superficial understanding of multiculturalism. How would you change it to reflect a more critical understanding of multicultural theory?

3. Develop a theme that addresses why people make art, and which would require students to make connections among diverse works from around the world.

4. Choose works from 3 different cultures that fit your theme (see #3). The selected works should incorporate art media and making processes that are typical or appropriate to the cultures in which they were made.

   • Explain the purpose for which these works were made and the meanings they might hold for people of the cultures that produced them.

   • In what ways do these works differ?

   • Based on your determinations regarding similarities or differences in terms of media use, processes, purposes, and meanings, explain how these artworks relate to your theme.

5. In what ways, other than by making art that is "like" or "in the style of" another artist or group of artists, can art lessons be based on culturally relevant themes?

   • Design an art lesson for students that would require that the artmaking be related directly to your theme, but not copy or imitate the works of other artists or cultural groups.

feature might cause confusion if it were interpreted to mean that the figure was a woman, a meaning specific to 19th-century Western culture.

I also chose some more recent works of art that consider power in a different light. Moroccan-born artist Lalla Essaydi explores gender and power in her photographs of Moroccan women covered in Arabic calligraphy, combining the female art of painted henna designs with the male art of calligraphy. Skin, clothing, and entire environments are covered with calligraphy as Essaydi challenges gender hierarchies in Muslim society. Nigerian British artist Yinka Shonibare MBE explores power relationships in the context of colonialism, post-colonialism, and contemporary globalization in his installations, in which figures are dressed in Victorian costumes made from what is considered typical African cloth. The cloth, which Shonibare purchases in London, is made in Holland from Indonesian batik designs and then is typically sold in Africa. The mixture of Victorian design and "African" patterns in the clothes worn by his models is meant to raise questions of power relationships in terms of race, class, identity, and economics. African American artist Betye Saar, in her *Liberation of Aunt Jemima*, takes a repugnant stereotype of the happy black mammie and

gives her power. In a box lined with images of Aunt Jemima from the pancake mix, Saar creates an assemblage of a stereotypical figure of Aunt Jemima with dark black skin and large red lips. She is holding a broom in one hand and cotton balls are around her feet, but in her other hand is a gun. Below her is another image of Aunt Jemima holding a crying white baby, and in front of that is a black power fist. Saar has liberated Aunt Jemima by giving her symbols of power.

Native American artist James Luna's *Artifact Piece* was an installation and performance piece that he did in 1987 at the Museum of Man in San Diego. He installed three museum cases. In one he placed ritual items from his Luiseño Reservation. In another he placed personal possessions such as his favorite CDs. In the third he lay in a bed of sand with his scars labeled. He challenged the power of the museum visitor with an "artifact" that could look back at them. His work also dealt with the fact that Native Americans have been displayed in museums without their consent (Roberts, 1994). Luna took back power by choosing to force museum visitors to confront this history. All these works represent contemporary artists reclaiming power that had been denied them as members of colonized or marginalized ethnic or gender groups.

Figure 3. Collage created by undergraduate art education student Mandy Vint, reflecting a time in her life when she felt powerless.

Step Three: Design a Performance Task Connected to Students' Own Lives

Continuing with our theme of power, we need to find a way for students, as artists, to convey power in relation to their own lives. There are many ways to do this. One performance task that I have used in relation to this theme asks students to design a collage illustrating a time when they felt either powerful or powerless. I also ask that they focus on at least one visual characteristic that artists have used to represent power, such as size, placement, headdresses, relationship to other figures, and so forth. This exercise allows students to represent something meaningful to them and make the connection to the works of art we have previously discussed. Some examples of topics my adult students have addressed include losing weight, winning a competition, being stricken with cancer, becoming pregnant at age 16, and escaping an abusive marriage. The student who was a cancer survivor focused not on her recovery, but on the powerlessness she felt when she became so ill at such a young age (Figure 3). She represented cancer as a huge figure with a headdress of syringes towering over a falling young woman. When asked why she chose a black male to represent the negative figure in her collage, the student answered that she was focusing on her requirements for a large figure with a menacing look on his face rather than on the race of the figure. She reflected on the fact that she had only one fitness magazine in which to find an image and that if there was a stereotype at work, it was probably

We now have works made in different cultures around the world, in different times, by different ethnic groups in the United States, and by men and women. They also offer an opportunity to talk about power in different ways. As Chalmers indicates, teachers using this method do not need to know everything about a culture before they can use an image in teaching units and lessons (Chalmers, 1996). Teachers should focus on how a work of art connects to the theme they have chosen. In other words, they need to know why the work was made. In this case, focus would be on how the work represents the power of an individual. Now, a connection needs to be made to the students' own lives so that they can view the theme of power as a reason for making art that relates to them.

Figure 4. Collage by graduate student and elementary art educator Staci Simonsen, representing a time when she felt powerful.

BIG THEME Why art is made.	KEY WORK 1 Identification Culture How it relates to themes.	KEY WORK 2 Identification Culture How it relates to themes.	KEY WORK 3 Identification Culture How it relates to themes.	PERFORMANCE TASK Connect the theme to student's own lives.
To convey power Artists around the world and through time have conveyed the concept of power through the representation of human figures.	Benin plaque of Oba AFRICA The plaque would have been nailed to the pillars of the palace to proclaim power. The Oba, who is wearing an elaborate headress, is represented larger than the other figures, and his greater status is indicated by the fact that he is riding.	Maya Lintel #8 MESOAMERICA This image indicates the importance that the Maya placed on recording the activities of their kings both in warfare and ritual. Bird Jaguar is the figure on the right, whose power is indicated by his large size, elaborate clothing and headdress.	James Luna *Artifact Piece* CONTEMPORARY NATIVE AMERICAN Luna places his body in a museum case as if he were an artificat. The shock of Luna's own presence and his ability to confront the museum-goer changes the balance of power.	Students will create a collage to represent a situation in which they have felt powerful or felt disempowered. They will use imagery, words and/or symbols to represent their experience of power in their own lives. They will explain their work to the class and write a reflection on the activity.

PRAIRIE VISIONS 2011, Friday, June 10
Designing Cross-Cultural Curriculum
　　　Start with a reason WHY people make art — BIG THEME
　　　Look for examples from different cultures/ethnic groups — KEY WORKS OF ART
　　　Connect them to children's own lives — PERFORMANCE TASK

Figure 5. Chart used to plot ideas for cross-cultural curricula with an example of the theme of power.

a gender stereotype causing her to look for a male as a figure of power. Another young woman chose to represent a time when she felt powerful. She lost weight in order to keep up on a hiking trip with her husband's family and represented herself on the top of a mountain with the sun creating a halo around her head (Figure 4). Both students created successful collages that powerfully conveyed emotions they felt using visual devices we had discussed in class in relation to historic images.

Figure 5 is a chart I developed to help teachers plot their ideas in developing cross-cultural curricula around themes based on why people make art. In this chart the theme of power is used as an example. In 2011 the Prairie Visions summer professional development workshop for teachers was focused on cross-cultural curricula, and we used my curriculum ideas as a basis for the workshop. This chart was used at the end of the workshop to aid participants in generating lesson ideas for their own themes. One group of teachers used the theme, "Artists create to inspire environmental healing." They chose three images that exemplified their theme: Neukom Vivariuman, an environmental work focused on renewal by Mark Dion; a Zen garden meant to create feelings of harmony; and a Lakota Sioux shirt for the Ghost Dance, meant to heal both the people and the earth. They designed a perfor-

mance task asking students to create a healing environment made from natural or recycled objects. Another group working with elementary children chose the theme, "Artists explore the meaning of heroes/heroines in a cross-cultural American society," and chose artworks representing Cesar Chavez, Rosa Parks, and Ben Kuroki as heroes. The performance task they designed was to draw a superhero's cape and use symbols and imagery to represent a person they chose to be their superhero. This could be a family member, public figure, peer, or someone from the past.

This last example was a modification of another sample lesson that teachers experienced at the Prairie Visions Institute. The theme for this lesson was, "Artists around the world and through time have portrayed cultural ideals through their heroes." We looked at works of art from many different cultures that portrayed heads of state as heroes, mythological heroes, sports and celebrity heroes, and ordinary people as heroes. We then considered whether artists could be heroes, looking at self-portraits by Albrecht Dürer and Yolanda Lopez and works by Chicana/Native American artist Carmen Lomas Garza, who was the keynote speaker at the Institute. Each group was given information about a contemporary female artist. They were asked to read the information and look

Figure 6. Place setting for Elizabeth Catlett as a cultural heroine (and detail of a plate) made by a group of participants at Prairie Visions Institute, June 2011.

at the illustrated artworks and decide what made their female artist a cultural hero and what symbols and imagery they could use for her representation. After looking at Judy Chicago's *Dinner Party* and discussing how she and others created place settings for heroic women from history, each group was asked to create a place setting for their chosen artist. Figure 6 includes the place setting made for Elizabeth Catlett and a detail of the plate. While this performance task does not focus directly on the student's own personal life, it does ask the student to engage with information from contemporary culture as he or she considers an artist's life and works.

Conclusions

These three steps allow a teacher to design a cross-cultural curriculum that affirms both differences and connections. The art that is chosen will most likely differ greatly; it can be in different media and styles and represent different perspectives. The works are tied together through the reasons they were all made: to convey status, to indicate membership in a group, to record important events, to tell a story, to display power, and so forth. It is important that in choosing works of art, a teacher thinks about different perspectives on the theme the works represent. Are perspectives included that challenge widely held assumptions about art or society (Grant & Sleeter, 2007)? For example, James Luna's *Artifact Piece* challenges a number of assumptions about museum display and power relationships, and raises issues about how Native Americans have been displayed and how culture is understood. Finally, if the performance task asks students to convey their own relationships to a theme, then they should be able to express their own perspectives and perhaps recognize that they have some of the same concerns as artists from many places and times. It is this sense of connection, while including many differing perspectives, that can increase cultural sensitivity and prevent students from equating difference with deviance.

In conclusion, this three-step method for designing cross-cultural curricula addresses some important criticisms of current multicultural curricula. It allows for a more hybrid notion of cultures in a variety of global settings, and encourages teachers to incorporate the art of a variety of cultures and ethnic groups throughout their curricula, rather than focusing on a single culture or country at a time. By using themes based on why people make art, this approach encourages students to see connections among other cultures worldwide and their own culture, while still affirming diversity. Students, rather than seeing difference as deviation, can see the commonalities they have with artists from around the world.

REFERENCES

Chalmers, F. G. (1996). *Celebrating pluralism: Art, education, and cultural diversity*. Los Angeles, CA: The J. Paul Getty Trust.

Chalmers, F. G. (2009). Celebrating pluralism six years later: Visual transculture/s, education, and critical multiculturalism. In K. Freedman (Ed.), *Looking back: Editor's selections from 50 years of studies in art education* (pp. 185–197). Reston, VA: National Art Education Association.

Dussel, I. (2001). What can multiculturalism tell us about difference? The reception of multicultural discourses in France and Argentina. In C. A. Grant & J. L. Lei (Eds.), *Global constructions of multicultural education* (pp. 293–114). Mahwah, NJ: Lawrence Erlbaum.

Grant, C. A., & Sleeter, C. E. (2007). *Doing multicultural education for achievement and equity*. New York, NY: Routledge.

Keating, A. (2007). *Teaching transformation: Transcultural classroom dialogues*. New York, NY: Palgrave MacMillan.

Lei, J. L., & Grant, C. A. (2001). Multicultural education in the United States: A case of paradoxical equality. In C. A. Grant & J. L. Lei (Eds.), *Global constructions of multicultural education* (pp. 205–237). Mahwah, NJ: Lawrence Erlbaum.

Mahalingam, R., & McCarthy, C. (2000). Rethinking multiculturalism and curricular knowledge for the twenty-first century. In R. Mahalingam & C. McCarthy (Eds.), *Multicultural curriculum: New directions for social theory, practice, and policy* (pp. 1–11). New York, NY: Routledge.

Nieto, S. (2004). *Affirming diversity: The sociopolitical context of multicultural education* (4th ed.). Boston, MA: Pearson.

Ovando, C. J., & McCarty, L. P. (1993). Multiculturalism in U. S. society and education: Why an irritant and a paradox? In J. Q. Adams & J. E. Welsch (Eds.), *Multicultural education: Strategies for implementation in colleges and universities*. (Vol. 3) (pp. 53-70). Macomb: Western Illinois University.

Rizvi, F. (1994). The arts, education and the politics of multiculturalism. In S. Gunew & F. Rizvi (Eds.), *Culture, difference and the arts* (pp. 54–68). St. Leonards, NSW, Australia: Allen & Unwin.

Roberts, C. (1994). Object, subject, practitioner: Native Americans and cultural institutions. In National Museum of the American Indian. *In Native American expressive culture* (pp. xi, 3–4, 22–29). New York, NY: Akwe:kon and National Museum of the American Indian.

Sowell, J. E. (1993). A learning cycle approach to art history in the classroom. *Art Education, 46*(2), 19–24.

Sowell, J. E. (1996). A cross-cultural survey of art history: Challenging assumptions about art. In J. Q. Adams & J. E. Welsch (Eds.), *Multicultural Prism: Voices from the field* (Vol. 2) (pp. 137–150). Macomb: Western Illinois University.

CHAPTER 2

Port of Entry: Puppetry!
An Interdisciplinary Arts Experience

MELANIE DAVENPORT
DOUGLAS STEVENS
Georgia State University

Imagine diverse groups of students, preparing to teach elementary school in an urban environment, productively engaged in learning about cultures from around the world through puppetry arts. While one group focuses upon writing their script, another group is building their characters. In another room, five or six students are using what they have learned about landscape painting to create scenic murals as backdrops, while others use sculpture techniques to create fanciful props. Later in the day, they utilize authentic instruments and technology to compose original soundtracks to help tell their stories, which are based upon their extensive research into traditions and contemporary settings of distinctive global populations (Figure 1).

The course we co-teach for Early Childhood Education (ECE) majors at Georgia State University (GSU) provides an opportunity not only to introduce these future teachers to the Arts, but also to expand their worldviews through the Arts. Davenport is the visual art instructor and Stevens teaches the music portion of the curriculum. For the past several years, we have collaborated in teaching an art and music course for 160 to 250 ECE students per year, exposing them to methods for integrating visual arts and music into their curricula. We focus on creative expression as a shared human trait that serves as a window into the beliefs, practices, and adaptive strategies of populations around the globe. The main project of this course is an exploration of puppetry arts resulting in final productions that incorporate language arts, social studies, intercultural education, and technology, as well as visual arts and music. Puppetry arts are a particularly happy marriage of visual and musical arts, as they employ the dimensions of time and live performance into an interdisciplinary process, avoiding reliance on a static and insular view of art and knowledge. In this chapter, we explain the philosophy that guides our work, the processes and resources we employ, the outcomes our students achieve, and their reflections on this learning experience. We have found that puppetry arts can be a welcoming port of entry into arts integration for ECE students.

Many others have found this to be the case as well, through different projects with a similar aim of utilizing puppetry arts to explore the world. As Smith (2009) suggested:

> From the magic of the Shaman bringing dead things to life to the violent, dangerous slapstick of Punch and Judy, there is a rich history of puppetry in a myriad of cultures. Throughout this history, puppetry has remained at the boundaries of performance between the popular and the artistic… at the borders of cultural activity. (p. 69)

Figure 1. To portray a story from the Huichol community of central Mexico, students created scenery, puppets, and props inspired by their research into the environment, music, and material culture of this population.

Wheeler (1999) concurred, stating that "puppet the-ater contains within it the opportunity for more than commentary on single events… [it] offers a chance for sweeping coverage and analysis of long spans of human history, and beyond that, for… structure analysis" (p. 19). Bodmann and DeArment (1997) likewise remarked that puppetry can "encourage creative ideas that lead toward understanding the global and environmental aspects of society" and can "generate dialogue about social and political issues," as well as foster "cultural connections" through a combination of "ritual, lesson, and entertain-ment" (cited in Asher, 2009, p. 6).

Our collaboration has been successful due to our shared commitment to the belief that elementary teachers should:

- Develop confidence in themselves as beings capable of creative self-expression;

- Value the ways that the Arts enrich individual lives, communities, and civilizations;

- Make meaningful connections between the Arts and other subject areas in the elementary curriculum;

- View creative projects as valuable means for perfor-mance-based assessment of student learning; and

- Learn and teach about the world through the Arts.

Focusing upon this last item, we structure the course so that students spend a significant portion of the semes-ter immersed in cultural research, visual and musical production, and ultimately in the presentation of a pup-pet show with original props, scenery, and soundtrack

inspired by folk stories, music, and material culture of distinctive subnational populations around the globe.

In what follows, we will describe the structure and spe-cific assignments of our course and provide information about teaching puppetry arts, learning about indigenous language populations, and integrating art and music into the curriculum, while suggesting resources for imple-menting a cultural research project through puppetry arts with younger learners.

Structure of the Course

Every semester, 40 or so students enroll in the course, which is divided into two groups, each of which receives instruction from both of us as the art and music teach-ers. In the art section, students begin by learning about children's art development with a global focus. Davenport screens a video, "Windows on the Mind" (Open Univer-sity& Sachs, 2003), which offers a view of how culture impacts children's visual arts through a comparison between youngsters in Dundee, Scotland and in Yuen-dumu, an Australian Aboriginal community. In music class, students consider that human expression did not begin with theory and notation, but rather through the cultural acts of singing, dancing, and playing. As Asher (2009) explained, "puppetry has been and continues to be a medium for passing on an oral history of a culture to the next generation. It creates a story through auditory and visual elements" (p. 8) (Figure 2).

Through this combined music and visual arts course, we manifest our shared belief that aesthetic expression is central to human existence. We have collaborated closely to develop a course that demonstrates both literally and

Figure 2. In this Maori tale, a soft-sculpture whale interacts with a rod puppet created from an empty soda bottle.

For Further Consideration

For younger learners, an adapted version of the cultural research aspect of this project could be a complement to any unit on diversity, social studies, human history, or local traditions. Puppetry arts can be utilized with children across disciplines to express, validate, and assess learning. Many resources are available to teachers, including those listed below.

Websites for Cultural Research

National Geographic for Kids
http://kids.nationalgeographic.com/kids

Kids Online Resources
www.kidsolr.com/geography/index.html

Multicultural Learning Resources for the Promotion of Indigenous and Multicultural Global Education (Australia)
www.globalkidsoz.com.au

Websites for Global Music

Mama Lisa's World: International Music and Culture
http://mamalisa.com

Traditional Folk Songs
www.folklyrics.net

ChoralWiki
www1.cpdl.org/wiki/index.php/Traditional

The Musical Instrument Collection at Edinburgh University
www.miayf.org

Websites for Puppetry Arts

Center for Puppetry Arts Resource Page
www.puppet.org/edu/resources.shtml

Creative Drama.org
http://digitaldjs.info/joomla/index.php/puppetry

Global History of Puppets
http://library.thinkquest.org/07aug/00659/history.html

Legends and Lore Puppet Resource Center
www.legendsandlore.com/teacher resource.html

Puppets Now, History of Puppets
www.puppetsnow.com/history-of-puppets.html

Shadow Puppet Lesson Plan
www.yaneo.org/what/attachments/_lesson-plans/YALP_Shadow-Puppet_Deb-Wuliger.pdf

Sample Journal Publications

Ashby, J. B. (2009). Bridging the gaps: The Puppets Up! International Puppet Festival. *Canadian Theatre Review, 138*(Spring), 33–38.

Asher, R. (2009). Radical puppets and the language of art. *Art Education, 62*(3), 6–12.

Badenhorst, Z., & Axmann, M. (2002). The educational use of videoconferencing in the arts faculty: Shedding a new light on puppetry. *British Journal of Educational Technology, 33*(3), 291.

Brown, S. (2004). Building character through shadow puppetry. *Art Education, 57*(6), 47–52.

Butler, J. H. (1942). A point of view on puppetry. *Western Speech, 6*(2), 18–21.

Church, E. (2001). Using puppets as language-building partners. *Early Childhood Today, 16*(2), 45.

Contreras, G. (1995). Teaching about Vietnamese culture: Water puppetry as the soul of the rice fields. *Social Studies, 86*(1), 25.

Crumpecker, C. (2003). Puppets with personality. *Arts & Activities, 134*(4), 18.

Duprey, R. (2008). Create a character! Puppetry as a tool in teaching narrative fiction. *Puppetry Journal, 59*(4), 24–25.

Levin, R., & Hines, L. (2003). Educational television, Fred Rogers, and the history of education. *History of Education Quarterly, 43*(2), 262–275.

McLennan, A. (2007). A snapshot from the integrated classroom. *Mask, 30*(2), 56–57.

Oaks, H. R. (1977, August 14–17). *Puppets as an Intercultural Communication Tool.* Paper presented at the Annual Meeting of the American Theatre Association, Chicago, Illinois. (ERIC Document Reproduction #: ED163552).

Peck, S. J., & Virkler, A. (2006). Reading in the shadows: Extending literacy skills through shadow-puppet theater. *Reading Teacher, 59*(8), 786.

Podlozny, A. (2000). Strengthening verbal skills through the use of classroom drama: A clear link. *Journal of Aesthetic Education, 34*(3/4), 239–275.

Servizzi, K. (2008). Fixing puppets so they can talk: Puppets and puppet making in a classroom of preschoolers with special needs. *Early Childhood Research and Practice, 10*(2). Retrieved from http://ecrp.uiuc.edu/v10n2/servizzi.html

Welty, K. (2004). Puppets, prose, plays, and patterns. *Technology & Children, 8*(3), 9.

Video

Malkin, J., Malkin, M., & Campanella, J. (2001). *Puppetry: Worlds of imagination* [DVD]. New York, NY: Speckled Koi Productions.

Books

Blumenthal, E. (2005). *Puppetry: A world history.* New York, NY: Harry N. Abrams.

Hunt, T., & Renfro, N. (1982). *Puppetry in early childhood education.* Austin, TX: Nancy Renfro Studios.

Kennedy, J. (2004). *Puppet mania!* Cincinnati, OH: North Light Books.

Moore, J. E., & Evans, J. (2000). *How to make puppets with children.* Monterey, CA: Evan Moor.

figuratively how the Arts can be the glue that brings together disparate disciplines within the public school curriculum. Not only do we use a single shared textbook, *Arts Integration* by Merryl Goldberg (2011), we also have developed a common calendar, in addition to the puppetry project, that results in similar assignments given in both classes.

Students see arts integration in practice, and participate in studio activities to develop confidence in their abilities to utilize the power of the Arts to benefit their learning. By the third week of the semester, they have formed into groups of ideally four to six students who work together the remaining weeks on various assignments, culminating in a final project. The focus is on global education, cultivating in these future teachers a deeper understanding of their world, its peoples, and the rich, diverse forms of expression that encode and communicate human experiences.

Students typically group themselves by their shared curiosity about particular cultural populations, based upon personal interests or selected from a United Nations list of language groups around the world. The focus is not on a nation-state, but on populations that predate and often overlap arbitrary political boundaries, including, for example, such distinctive peoples as the Sami, Tuvans, Quechua, Hmong, Wirarika, Buryat, Igbo, Hopi, Akan, Navajo, and Maori. We also find students interested in exploring populations such as Cajuns, Romani, Gullah, Celts, and even contemporary urban youth culture. We encourage students to make their own selection and emphasize research into these populations with the intent that as future teachers they will begin to recognize distinctions between nationality, ethnicity, and culture.

Students conduct research into the environment, economy, and other factors, such as colonization or hybridity (blending of diverse cultures or traditions), that have historically helped shape worldviews, languages, and adaptive strategies of these groups. They then investigate current political status, struggles, and efforts of these groups to survive and thrive in the contemporary world. We direct students to find examples of music, art, architecture, stories, and other forms of expression illustrative of resource-use, worldviews, idea diffusion, traditions, or other distinctive characteristics of these groups, and to present this information in class to their peers.

We encourage our students to engage in intercultural learning, that is, learning *about* each other *from* each other, by seeking primary sources of information. For instance, one group studying reindeer herders of northern Finland discovered that the Samis (Lapplanders) have their own Facebook page where they share stories, videos, and other resources. Several communities within the Navajo nation publish their own online newspapers and use other web resources. Although not every indigenous language group has found their voice through global media discourse, we encourage students to find information as close to firsthand as possible, rather than relying on second- or third-hand accounts of these populations.

Each group of students selects a folk tale or other interesting story about or from this population to enact through puppetry. Next we describe each phase of this intensive, interdisciplinary project in detail. After a number of weeks learning basic skills and information in art and music to empower them on this journey, we embark on an in-depth exploration of puppetry arts.

Urban Resources

Central to this project is a field trip to the Center for Puppetry Arts in downtown Atlanta, an engaging cultural site with a strong educational mission (www.puppet.org). Students recognize familiar characters from Sesame Street and the Muppets, who provide a nonthreatening point of entry into the world of puppetry. After touring the Jim Henson exhibit, students also explore the Center's museum, which houses an impressive collection of puppets from around the world, including Chinese opera puppets, shadow puppets, and African full-body ceremonial puppets, as well as robotic and ventriloquist characters. Handouts with specific questions help guide their inquiry as they move through exhibits of contemporary, abstract puppetry, to shadow puppets from different countries, to puppets used in religion and ritual, to significant historical representations. The collection includes examples from virtually every puppetry tradition and all inhabited continents, as well as contemporary artistry and animatronics. Students see how puppetry has contributed to the history of human communication, from simple story telling to education and socialization, to ritual and ceremony, to aesthetic and social experimentation. We find this experience increases our students' enthusiasm for their projects and their expectations of themselves.

The Center is not just a museum, but also a performing institution with a full complement of writers, musicians, performers, and technicians—creating new productions, revisiting old ones, and serving as a venue for visiting performing artists and puppetry videos. Students enjoy a

Chapter 2: Port of Entry: Puppetry! An Interdisciplinary Arts Experience | Davenport and Stevens

17

Figure 3. A student experiments on a djembe as part of her group's instrumental improvisation.

behind-the-scenes tour of the puppetry and scenic workshops, visit the education department, and sometimes sit in on a rehearsal—all of which inspire and motivate them to dive into their own productions.

It is crucial for these future teachers to be aware of and take advantage of cultural offerings and the educational programming their community has to offer. Fenech (2003) suggested that engaging students with "museums can broaden understanding and equip them with alert and inquiring minds, helping them to deconstruct the intended and accidental meanings of the experience of visiting these arenas of cultural knowledge" (p. 50). Educators who may not have access to local resources can still engage their students in puppetry arts through online and print publications, such as those listed in the For Further Consideration section of this chapter.

The diverse urban student population at GSU contributes fundamentally to the success of the class. Anthropologist Wax (1993) described historically significant cultural centers in terms of the fact that "human growth and creativity tended to occur not within separate and isolated cultures, but within their meeting and intermixture" (p. 108). Our location in downtown Atlanta allows GSU to draw students from the historically multicultural local population as well as from around the world, enriching

students' learning through a wide range of perspectives and identities represented. For example, one group of students that included men and women with backgrounds from Georgia, Jamaica, and Sub-Saharan Africa examined stories of Anansi the Spider that travelled with the Diaspora and evolved in new contexts. Another woman from Hungary led her group of mostly local students to investigate the Romani culture and was able to bring in handicrafts and musical instruments she had acquired in her home country. In composing music for their puppetry arts project, students also have an advantage of exploring and utilizing the School of Music's impressive collection of world instruments (Figure 3).

The Puppetry Arts Project

In the sections that follow, we will describe each phase of the puppetry arts project undertaken by students in our course. These productions integrate content and processes from across the curriculum, expose participants to global knowledges, and demonstrate strategies for performance-based assessment through the Arts.

Cultural Research Presentation

As soon as students identify a population or language group to focus upon, they begin researching specific topics—gathering information and examples of arts, crafts, music, dance, and folk tales. They then investigate the relationship of these cultural products to the environment, economy, history, beliefs, practices, and current circumstances of this population. Group members divide information gathering amongst themselves; one might find two or three traditional folk tales or stories; another music examples; and others focus on general information

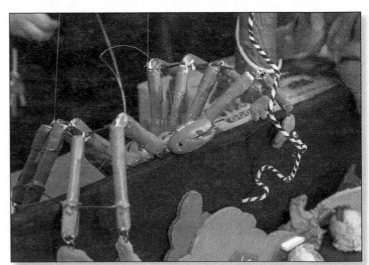

Figure 4. This elaborate Anansi the Spider puppet was constructed from wire, hanger tubes, and model magic.

about the history, location, status, lifestyles, beliefs, and resources of their targeted cultural population.

In music class, students explore various forms and techniques of music making, singing folk songs, moving to music from various styles and traditions, offering their own examples, and improvising and creating using the School of Music's extensive instrument collection. They also analyze video examples of performing musicians working with local elementary school children using instruments from around the world.

By our fourth or fifth class meeting, after gathering and sharing what they have learned within their own groups, our ECE students are asked to create a presentation to share with their classmates so that others might learn more about these distinct peoples. Using software such as PowerPoint or Prezi, each group shares an informative overview of the population they have researched. They include maps, demographic information, images of artwork, and video and audio clips. Students may bring in costumes, artifacts, instruments, or other items of material culture. They impart information about political status and current struggles as well as successful contemporary adaptive strategies, such as catering to tourists through staged dance performances or selling artifacts and artisanry.

Through this sharing process, students begin to see commonalities among nondominant cultures and better appreciate how some human populations fail and some succeed in their efforts to preserve and transmit their unique knowledges, while adapting to demands of late-modern capitalism. Our students discover concepts such as cultural hybridization, idea diffusion, colonization, Diaspora, appropriation, authenticity, and so forth on their own through this part of the project.

Introduction to Puppetry

Before visiting the Center for Puppetry Arts, students are asked to consider how environmental degradation affects human and animal populations. To explore the interdependence of humans and animals within specific cultures, each class member brings in images and information about an endangered species from the ecological settings where their chosen populations live. Students then make paper puppets representing their endangered species and write a short script to perform from the animal's perspective. From these brief performances, students begin to recognize the fragility of some environments and also begin to see how puppetry can be useful in performance-based assessment. This introduction to

simple puppet making provides a foundation for the field trip that they take after these performances, while integrating science content into their coursework

Puppetry Arts Production

After their field trip to the Center for Puppetry Arts, students officially begin production of their own puppet shows, based upon what they have learned through the semester so far and the storyboards they developed from their folk tales. They are graded individually and as a part of the group, understanding that they will organize themselves utilizing the strengths of each member. We have found that our classes contain a surprisingly wide array of well-developed skills and talents. By exercising their negotiating skills, they are preparing themselves for the type of cooperation they will need as part of a grade-level team. The remaining weeks of the semester find students engaged in the many different problem-solving challenges of staging an eight to ten minute production, including the following aspects.

Storytelling. Because the project is based on storytelling, language arts become a significant component of preparation for the puppet shows. Before students depart the Center for Puppetry Arts, we distribute storyboard worksheets and have them brainstorm their stories and consider the number of scene changes needed, visual elements, sound effects, and where music might be inserted. Before the next class, they sketch out rough ideas of sequence of scenes and narration to share with group members, negotiating the shape of the tale they wish to present. They must decide what to tell, what to show, what to eliminate, and how to use music, lighting, and movement to create an appropriate mood.

Original music creation and performance. Students are led through a number of creative processes in music class, introduced by videos of musicians working with children through GSU's "Sound Learning" program. Projects include singing folk songs from their chosen culture, either phonetically, in translation, or with text freely adapted. They create and perform original instrumental compositions that reflect mood, motion, attitude, and environment. Instruments available to them include drums from various continents, Orff instruments, toy instruments, shakers, tambourines, cymbals, bells, electronic keyboards, music software, piano, autoharps, guitars, and their own personal instruments. They also create original songs using their own lyrics built around popular formats, such as rap, blues, pop, or jazz. Each group records and saves these compositions for final

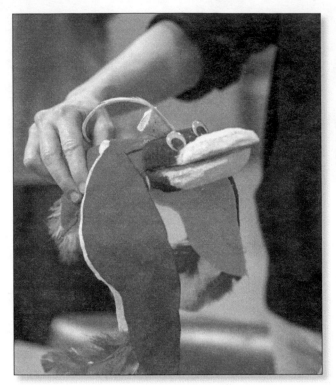

Figure 5. This bird in a tale from the Xavante culture featured carved foam, felt, feathers, paint, and googly eyes.

Figure 6. For another story featuring Anansi the Spider, students constructed this tree and spider web from foam core board, twisted kraft paper, and starched yarn.

editing on their own laptop computers using high-quality digital sound recorders supplied by Stevens.

Soundtrack development and recording. After students record their scripts, music, and sound effects, they assemble soundtracks for their stories from these recorded elements to be played during their final performances. Students learn to use soundtrack software programs Audacity and GarageBand, digital pulse code modulation recorders, video cameras, and basic video editing software. Some groups incorporate technologies in ingenious ways, including live video, black lights, rear projections, iPhones, and tablet computers. During the audio editing, students utilize math and technology for timing, audio alignment, digital effects, and musical transposition.

Puppet show design and construction. The design of each puppet depends upon its function within the story, whether it has a big speaking part, needs to move freely, fly, or gesture. Many simple puppet patterns are available in books or online, but most students wind up creating their own designs using available materials. Backdrops and props are designed and produced utilizing visual art techniques learned in class (Figures 5 and 6). One group constructed a cardboard volcano that spewed

barbecue corn-puffs as lava, effectively mimicking the violent explosion of a real volcano, while another transformed the puppet stage into a windmill with functional blades six feet across turning slowly throughout the production.

Lighting and choreography. Students also consider the use of movement and lighting to enhance their narratives. Some select shadow puppetry, others use a black light and fluorescent paint for dramatic effect. Some have mixed shadow puppets and three-dimensional puppetry to tell a story within a story, as a dream or flashback. Scrolling backdrops depict long journeys, while life-size, live-hands puppets contrasted with smaller characters emphasize the persona of a god or shaman. These design decisions function to enhance the effectiveness of the storytelling (Figures 7 and 8).

Rehearsal and final performance. Intensely active days leading to the final performance reveal students' increasing sense of purpose and creative focus as they put finishing touches on their productions. There always seems to be too much to do and not enough time to do it; students begin to recognize the quality of what they have done and continue to brainstorm ways to make it even better. We see our ECE majors confidently going beyond their perceived limitations, and taking delight in the admiration of other class members when they share their work and sing their songs. We find that they are teaching each other about things they have learned to care about, especially cultural traditions of lesser-known populations.

During dress rehearsal, students take turns viewing and evaluating their work from the front of the stage, either live or through a video camera's viewfinder. While we encourage students to practice for a *live* final performance, some choose to record their shows ahead of time and present an edited video instead. On performance day, students invite friends, family, and other instructors to enjoy the fruits of their labors. All performances are videotaped, edited to DVD, and shared with students to become part of their portfolios. In these numerous samples[1] can be seen the hard work, cultural research, aesthetic decision-making, and performance-based assessment potential of this project.

Evaluation. The final puppetry project is performance-based assessment in action. ECE students get first-hand experience on how this type of assessment is intrinsically motivating and garners extrinsic validation, demonstrating what they have learned. After the performance, students are asked to reflect upon questions about

Figure 8. The use of blacklight and fluorescent paint for dramatic effect was inspired by a production at the Center for Puppetry Arts.

the dynamics within their group, their own learning experiences, and how to apply this to future teaching contexts. These evaluations help us—the visual arts and music instructors—determine what was successful and what changes we might make in this course in the future.

Reflections and Implications

As the primary instructors for this course, we are pleased that what had previously been perceived as a relatively unimportant part of the ECE curriculum has become popular among our students and respected among our colleagues. The students experience immersion in creative problem solving that is consolidated, shared, and validated in their final presentations. During this process, students learn about arts integration and become personally attuned to the commonalities and variations between cultural groups and their means of expressing worldviews and identities. Students experience myriad ways that people around the globe have used puppetry and storytelling to communicate human experience.

Our hands-on approach means that lessons learned will not soon be forgotten. Students may buy a djembe or log drum for their future classrooms because they loved playing it in class. They may set up a puppet theater because they learned that puppetry enhances their own capacities to express new understandings, so they know it can work for their students, too. They've discovered the absorption of creative work, how it improves the atmosphere in a classroom, and how they want to share their learning with their loved ones Those enrolled in our course tell us afterwards about buying new sketchbooks, enrolling in extra arts coursework, or other new activities they never

Figure 7. Some students choose to utilize shadow puppets to tell their stories.

Chapter 2: Port of Entry: Puppetry! An Interdisciplinary Arts Experience | Davenport and Stevens

21

Figure 9. This Welsh story featured rod puppets and a functional drawbridge.

Figure 10. A colorful backdrop and foreground created a lush forest for a crowd of finger puppets to interact with a rod puppet maiden in this Purepecha tale.

thought they would pursue. Many have told us of new interest in learning about indigenous populations and endangered languages. They have discovered a treasure of songs, artworks, and stories outside of their own local experiences.

Including puppetry arts in coursework for Early Childhood Education majors has proven an effective way to engage students in inquiry into people around the world. They learn the power of the Arts as personal communication, pedagogical strategy, and assessment tool. As Wheeler (1999) suggested, "the rewards are there for those students and teachers who become involved in a sophisticated multi-media project which challenges participants by its long view of life on this planet" (p. 24) (Figures 9 and 10). We encourage others to utilize puppetry arts to explore the world with their students.

AUTHOR NOTE

The authors wish to thank Kevin Hsieh, Mariama Ross, Melody Milbrandt, Kirby Meng, Yuri Strom, Kristina Hobby, Carol Mohor, Amy Sery, Michelle Mercier De Shon, Adriana Janse van Rensburg, Alan Louis, and Aretta Baumgartner for their contributions to the development and teaching of this course.

REFERENCES

Asher, R. (2009). Radical puppets and the language of art. *Art Education, 62*(3), 6–12.

Bodmann, M., & DeArment, C. (1997). *Making shadow characters.* Arleta, CA: Bali and Beyond.

Fenech, M. (2003). City museums and park museums. *Art Education, 56*(1), 46–51.

Goldberg, M. (2011). *Arts integration: Teaching subject matter through the arts in multicultural settings* (4th ed.). New York, NY: Allyn & Bacon.

Open University (Producer), & Sachs, A. (Director). (2003). *Windows on the mind: Children's drawings* [DVD video]. Princeton, NJ: Films for the Humanities and Sciences.

Smith, M. (2009). Puppetry as community arts practice. *Journal of Arts and Communities, 1*(1), 69–78.

Wax, M. (1993). How culture misdirects multiculturalism. *Anthropology and Education Quarterly, 24*(2), 99–115.

Wheeler, D. (1999). Sod blocks, lodge poles, and cornerstones: On teaching cultural history and structure through puppetry arts. *Art Education, 52*(3), 19–24.

ENDNOTE

1 Examples of student work are available at www.youtube.com/user/2300PuppetShows

CHAPTER 3

Using Artifacts to Promote Cultural Awareness in Cyprus Primary Schools

FOTINI LARKOU
Cyprus Ministry of Education and Culture

As societies become increasingly diverse in the sense of their cultural contexts, the necessity of changing educational orientations and aims becomes imperative. Teachers should help schools lay a foundation on which all learners can build a global perspective and gain understanding and respect for themselves and others. Education should seek to eliminate racial, ethnic, cultural, and gender stereotypes and resolve or ameliorate problems associated with racism and prejudice (McJilton, 2002). Also, education should prepare students for living in the world, and teach them how to get along with classmates from diverse groups and develop a deep appreciation for others.

Cultural diversity is widely considered to be central to the vitality of a national culture and a distinctive feature in many countries throughout the world. In the last few decades, in order to address students' cultural differences, many countries have made multicultural and intercultural education a high priority for their educational systems. Education for cultural diversity means promoting respect for and understanding of different cultural traditions and practices, through promoting a sense of mutuality and cultural sensitivity. Art education has a lot to contribute in this direction.

This chapter presents development of an art curriculum model and unit resulting from a larger research project that investigated the potential of an artifact-based pedagogy to promote cultural and global understanding in Cypriot Primary Schools. The general aim of this research was to design, implement, and evaluate a curriculum model and unit embedded in common aims for human rights education and art education that would support classroom teachers. A new Art Model for Increasing Cultural Awareness (AMICA) was developed for this purpose, which as its name suggests, aims to eliminate hostilities and misunderstandings among people around the world and bring them closer together.

Art Education Theories and Human Rights Education

Many scholars have argued that art education is an appropriate curriculum subject to promote cultural understanding and global awareness (Ballengee Morris, 2004; Blacking, 1986; McFee, 1991; McFee & Degge, 1977). Their views provided a conceptual framework for art education in that they maintained that learning about art and culture together can open the door to increased understanding and cultural sensitivity. On the other hand, the concept of human rights education can encourage teachers to use different means and tools to support and inspire students' artworks (Anderson, 2000; Carter, 2004; Krain & Nurse, 2004; Lefler, 1999; Sheesley, 2000; Stomfay-Stitz & Hinitz, 1996; Stout, 1999; Virshup, 1993).

By studying works of art from different cultures around the world, students can become familiar with the values and beliefs systems shared by specific cultural groups (Sheesley, 2000). By extension, students' learning experiences can be initiated by exploring their own cultures (Tillman, 2001), as well as studying works of art from other cultures. According to Nyman (2002), primary teachers are in a good position to promote students' understanding and awareness of other cultures through art. Education through art can indirectly effect social change when students gain awareness of and appreciation for cultures other than their own.

The curriculum model combines art and human rights education and is based on Räsänen's (1997) argument that it is crucial to connect the realities of artworks, artists, and viewers, not only to make learning more meaningful, but also to help learners see artifacts from different points of view. But the model went beyond this point by adopting both an historical and a cross-cultural point of view. The ultimate goal of human rights education is to legitimize another's point of view so that positive changes of attitude can weaken prejudice, and more positive ways of relating to the other side can be understood (Harris, 2004; Salomon, 2004).

Cultural understanding is conceived of as the skills, attitudes, and knowledge that young people need to practice in order to be able to see and understand another's point of view. It is important to start by teaching the human

For Further Consideration

As a class exercise, arrange students into several small groups. Provide each group with an artifact or image(s) of an artifact with which they are likely to be unfamiliar. Provide only basic clues about the artifact, such as the type of information one might find on a legend placard in a museum. Using the Inquiry/Questioning Strategy provided below, assign each group a task of deciphering the possible purpose(s) and meaning(s) of the artifact within the cultural context of its creation. Afterward, direct students to share their findings with other groups of students and invite discussions about or challenges to the appropriateness of their interpretations.

1. Students can discover facts about an artifact (viewer's point of view):
   • Write a brief description of this artifact that would give a clear picture of it to someone who has never seen it.

2. Students can discover facts about life there and then (from a cultural and historical perspective):
   • Why was the artifact made? What were the sociocultural and economic conditions that demanded its making?
   • How was the artifact used? How else could it been used? Can you draw it being used (functional context)?

3. Students can investigate the development through time and the transmission of the artifact in contemporary life and in their daily lives:
   • How did this type of object develop through time?
   • How was the artwork influenced by earlier artworks? Did it influence later artworks (narrative or storytelling)?
   • If a maker a hundred years ago would create and/or use the same artifact, how might he/she do so differently?

4. Students can speculate on what an artwork meant to the maker (from the creator's perspective—social and cultural ideas):
   • Was the artifact of great or little value to the maker? What details imply this?

5. Students can investigate relationships among artifacts from different cultures (synthesizing):
   • Does the artifact look like other artifacts from different cultures (style)?
   • Do people from different cultures respond to similar artifacts in the same way?
   • What does this artifact tell you about the person or people who created it?

rights values of cultural understanding with this in mind to help young people fully accept and respect the premise of human dignity. The concept of a material culture was helpful in justifying the use of an artifact-based inquiry approach as a means of developing cultural understanding.

The Art Curriculum Model

In this chapter, I present how I developed an art curriculum model with strategies for linking art and human rights education that arose from my concern about cultural conflict within Cypriot society.[1] As each strand of theory had specific implications for practice, it was challenging to try to find a way to incorporate them into the Cypriot primary curriculum, where there is little tradition of teaching about Others, especially those considered enemies. Reviewing the literature enabled me to gain a better understanding of what was needed in this regard and how to develop a curriculum model for primary teachers.

According to the National Advisory Committee on Creative and Cultural Education (1999), one aim of education is "to help students find their future and understand their pasts" (p. 23). A decision was made to include comparison of past and present artifacts with the same function from different cultures. I decided to adopt a functionalist perspective to teaching art heritage and used an artifact-based inquiry approach as a means of promoting cultural understanding, rather than base learning on more traditional methods stemming from art history and criticism. I wanted students to be actively engaged in investigating meaning, function, and value of selected artifacts. I agree with Kader (2003) that everyday artifacts provide the best means of studying the diverse interactions that exist between human beings and things, and studying them is more meaningful when they are examined under the scope of their cultural, sociological, and historical dimensions and functions. I therefore used an inquiry-based questioning strategy for art lessons to study *containers* from different cultures, together with two cooperative learning strategies to promote cultural understanding in Cypriot students aged 11 years. I also encouraged group interaction through use of a variety of cooperative learning strategies (Mosley & Sonnet, 2003). The inquiry-based questioning strategy set out to develop students' understandings of artifacts from different points of view (Figure 1). It required them to:

1. Respond to an artifact at a personal level (students' points of view) by looking and talking about it.

2. Learn about the cultural context of the artifact (cultural point of view), discussing and sharing ideas in groups.

3. Learn about the maker and the background of the artifact (maker's point of view), working with partners to discover how the artifact was made, for whom, and why.

4. Study the development of the artifact over time (group work) to find out how it was used (style, materials, function), developed, or changed, and why (historical point of view).

5. Compare the same artifact in different cultures (group work), finding similarities that reinforce the fact that people all around the world have common values and needs, and also differences that give the special character to each culture (cross-cultural point of view).

Completing all five steps when artifacts are studied is important, and learning occurs over a series of lessons. The difference between the strategy for studying artworks developed for this model and others I studied in the literature is that students have to consider all five viewpoints while participating in cooperative learning activities. The students constructed understanding through questioning, listening, reading, writing, and visual investigations. The inquiry/questioning strategy in particular was facilitated by analyzing artifacts, playing games, reading work sheets in groups, taking notes, and engaging in dialogues with classmates and/or the teacher in talking circles and groups. All the strategies adopted for the model share a common denominator of engaging students in active participatory learning.

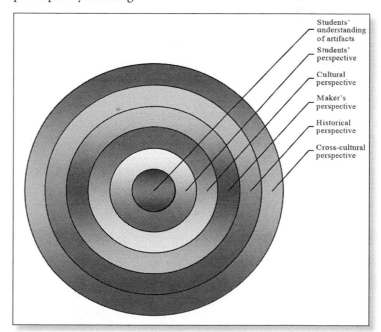

Figure 1. Inquiry/questioning strategy on students' understanding of artifacts.

The following labels appear in the figure:
- Students' understanding of artifacts
- Students' perspective
- Cultural perspective
- Maker's perspective
- Historical perspective
- Cross-cultural perspective

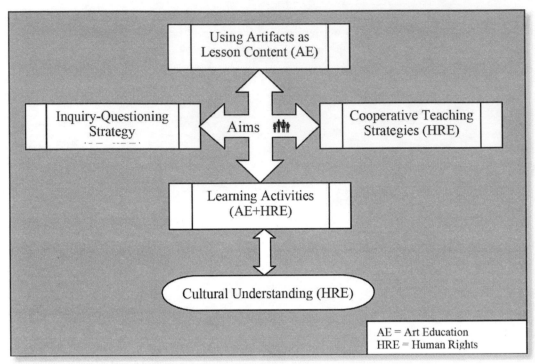

Figure 2. Art Model for Increasing Cultural Awareness (AMICA).

For the curriculum model it was necessary to select questions and activities that would stimulate learners' critical thinking, as well as extend their knowledge and develop inquiry skills. Teachers need to pose questions about the artifacts that challenge students' views and facilitate closer observation. Determining the historical, social, physical, or cultural setting of an artifact necessitates finding information about how it was made, how it was used, its development through time, design and decoration, meaning, significance, cultural values, and the context in which the artifact was created. The questions were not intended to be an end in themselves, but a means to challenge critical thinking. Taking into account all of the above, I noted that this inquiry/questioning strategy could promote cooperation and discussion. It was adopted as a main teaching and learning strategy. All the different components of the AMICA are presented in Figure 2.

Developing a Curriculum Unit

A modified action research model was developed (adapted from Elliott, 1991), aiming to enhance cultural understanding. The process of developing the model consisted of four cycles. Following the development of the conceptual framework and model, the aim of Cycle One was to develop a theoretical model and identify teachers'

needs. Cycle Two consisted of classroom-based action, and used a teacher and student questionnaire to collect feedback on the model. The main aim of Cycle Three was to create the curriculum unit. Decisions were made about the cultures (Cyprus, Greece, Egypt, and Turkey) and artifacts (water jugs for carrying, storing, and serving water) on which this curriculum model development would concentrate (Figures 3–5). Formative evaluation of the curriculum unit and resources by teachers and me was ongoing throughout the design process. This led to revisions and a final summative evaluation of the curriculum in Cycle Four, after the final product had been tested over a period of three months by two art teachers in their schools. The model I crafted (adapted from Rowntree, 1974) for implementing the curriculum model involved five phases: (1) setting the aim of the research, (2) determining teachers' needs, (3) designing the artifact-based inquiry curriculum, (4) evaluating the curriculum, and (5) improving the curriculum (Figure 6).

I then engaged in planning the draft curriculum unit and preparing materials for distribution to teachers. Water jugs for carrying, storing, and serving water were selected as curriculum content. Specifically, a Cypriot clay water jug (*kouza*) and clay water jugs from neighboring countries of Greece (*stamna*), Egypt (*koula*), and Turkey (*testi*),

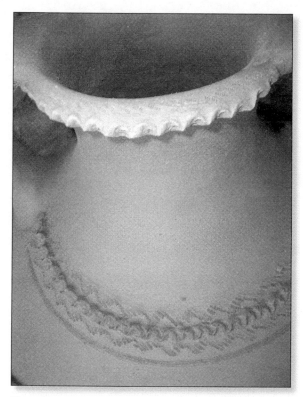

Figure 3. Detail of decoration. *Photo by the author.*

Figure 4. Kouza making. *Photo by the author.*

Figure 5. Kouza storage. *Photo by the author.*

made and used in the same time periods (19th, 20th, and 21st centuries), would be the focus. Having researched the cultural context of Cypriot, Greek, and Turkish water jugs, I proceeded to formulate learning outcomes and design and develop the curriculum unit. The curriculum unit included instructions for ten lessons and also suggested two additional follow-up lesson plans to be implemented at a later date.

It was important to consider students' prior knowledge, experience, skills, interests, and values in the formation of teaching and learning activities. Also, cooperation with teachers was a key factor to test and evaluate the curriculum unit and model. The five criteria used to select these cultural artifacts were developed from the findings of Cycle Two as well as from the literature review and document analysis. These criteria are as follows:

1. Students' interests, preferences for artifacts, and developmental stages;

2. Demography of students' cultural backgrounds in Cyprus;

3. Availability of background information for artifacts, both visual and verbal;

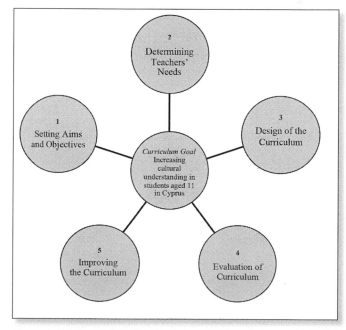

Figure 6. Educational Technology/Systems Model (Adapted from Rowntree, 1974).

4. The function of the artifacts (containers should be used for carrying, storing, and pouring or serving water); and

5. The potential of the artifacts to raise issues of stereotypes and prejudices in discussion.

Curriculum design, implementation, and evaluation were at the core of this curriculum model development. I considered the strategies, possible aims, content, methods, specific teaching strategies, resources, and evaluation methods for preparing an artifact-based curriculum to promote cultural understanding and increase cultural sensitivity. The completed curriculum unit included the lesson plans, an introduction, teachers' guidelines, and information about the water jugs, while the educational resources included images, a CD, and worksheets for students. Lesson One is an example of the first of ten lessons in the curriculum unit, translated into English. The same lesson in Greek, created by a professional designer, is presented in Figure 7.

Lesson One

This first lesson of the unit introduces students to the main teaching and learning strategies of the curriculum unit. Students are to be engaged in activities in a talking circle. Active listening and discussion are the main strategies used in the curriculum unit.

A. Lesson preparation

Before the lesson, ask students to bring a *favorite object* to school from home they would like to show classmates. Students should be advised to bring a 'safe' object from home, such as something that is not sharp or fragile.

1. **Materials**
   a) *For practical artwork*
      - drawing materials (e.g., pencils crayons, soft pencils, oil pastels)
      - sketchbooks
   b) *For group work*
      - students' sketchbooks
      - students' worksheets
      - pieces of paper
      - drawing/writing materials

2. **Equipment**
   - Required: CD player, pillows, artifacts
   - Optional: digital camera, computer, projector

3. **Objectives**
   a) *Cultural learning*
      Students will:
      - understand that artifacts (favorite objects) are integral to daily life.
      - recognize that their own viewing experience of an artifact may be different from that of their classmate who owns it and for whom it has a special meaning.

   b) *Inquiry and collaborative learning skills*
      Students will:
      - share stories about an artifact that is special to them working in a circle.
      - practice working together with others on different activities.
      - practice observation and describe artifacts.

B. Lesson Activities

1. **Talking circle** (12 minutes)

Students are sitting in a talking circle. All of them are given an opportunity to talk about their special object, without any strict directions by the teacher. In their circle, students show their favorite artifacts in turn and share the story of their objects. Other students listen carefully, and learn why the object is important to classmates.

2. **Word wheels activity** (10 minutes)

Teachers direct students to stand in a word wheel composed of an inner and outer circle. Each student holds his/her favorite object and asks questions about students' objects in the other circle. Students in the inner circle ask questions of those in the outer circle. After a minute the teacher gives the signal so that the outer circle rotates and then they change roles.

3. **Group work** (8 minutes)

Students are organized into groups and the teacher gives each group a list of questions to study artifacts. They are encouraged to select one of their classmates' artifacts and ask questions so as to learn more about it and why it is special for him or her.

After that the teacher asks each child to write a two line description of it on a piece of paper in such a way that it is not obvious to which one it refers. In this way, students of each group give different descriptions for the same object. The teacher explains that afterwards they will have to read out loud some of these descriptions by playing a guessing game.

The teacher asks the students to bring the artifact of each group to the front desk while he or she collects, mixes the descriptions (5–10) and then reads some of them out loud. Students try to fit the descriptions to the artifacts through a whole class discussion.

4. **Artmaking** (8 minutes)

Students are sitting in a talking circle. The teacher places one student's favorite artifact in the middle of a talking circle so that each student can see it from a different point of view. Students draw it in their sketchbooks. After they finish they compare their drawings and discuss how and why they are different or similar. They also talk about the actual artifact and how it relates to people and everyday life.

If the school has digital cameras the object could be photographed from different viewpoints by a group of students. When their classmates present their drawings, they could project them on the computer for further discussion. This activity presupposes preparation and relevant Information and Communications Technology resources.

C. Assessment of Students' Learning

1. **Musical chairs game** (11 minutes) (activity on a volunteer basis)

The teacher, with the help of students, arranges some chairs in a circle, facing away from the center. The number of chairs should be half the number of students so that the same number of students are sitting down and standing.

The teacher asks students who would like to borrow artifacts for this activity. She or he explains that they should treat the artifacts with respect and be very careful so that they do not damage them. They put an artifact on each chair.

The teacher explains the rules of the game and gives an agreed signal or puts on music to start students walking around the chairs. As soon as the teacher gives the signal or stops the music, students have to try and sit on the chairs. The rest have to ask one of the students sitting, about the artifact s/he holds. The students' questions and answers indicate if the lessons' objectives were achieved.

2. **Ongoing Evaluation**

The teacher could assess students by observing them working in groups so that he could gain insights into students' capabilities to cooperate and practice active listening and discussion throughout the different activities. She or he also could assess skills that are successful in the talking circle.

D. Follow up activities—Future learning

Students could collect and display a range of everyday objects that can be used to carry, store, and serve liquids. They could research such artifacts at home, school, in magazines or books, or in the neighborhood. Students who have digital cameras at home could take photos of the same objects (e.g., their mother's favorite artifact) from different viewpoints. They could print them and make a collection of artifacts for in class use. A teacher may ask students to think about a situation where people have different points of view. She or he encourages discussion asking why this is the case or offers examples.

Figure 7. Lesson One professionally designed in Greek.

The Lesson in Practice

This introductory lesson was intended to help teachers gain a general idea about the curriculum, its aims, objectives, a rationale, suggestions for how to use it, explanations of the lessons, and strategies to be used. The lesson also includes playful activities that encourage students to formulate questions that help them to become more critical and inquiring, so as to start seeing artifacts from multiple perspectives.

When all ten lessons had been designed, I put the whole curriculum unit into practice in my own classroom. Subsequently I made revisions to the lessons based on my observations of their strengths and weaknesses, as well as student feedback. Formative evaluation questions considered before and after the intervention were:

- What are the information needs, prior experiences, beliefs, and values of the learners relative to the topic of instruction?

- What changes in thinking or performance do I want to occur? How will I know if these changes have occurred? How can I provide opportunities for learners to examine issues that may stimulate changes in their thinking or performance?

- How do learners respond the lessons and materials?

The two art teachers who participated also gave me feedback in informal phone conversations and face-to-face interviews, and then I revised the lesson plans again. The different stages of the design and development of the curriculum unit culminated in a final implementation and summative evaluation of both the unit and model. For the purposes of this chapter, I focused on conclusions about students' responses to the choice of artifacts in Lesson One and identified the strengths and weaknesses of the model as I had translated it into practice. I also determined its potential for increasing learners' cultural sensitivity.

Conclusion

This teaching and learning experience revealed that using artifacts under the umbrella of Art Education and Human Rights could increase cultural understanding. Although the majority of the students were initially prejudiced against Turkish culture, the choice of artifacts from countries that neighbor Cyprus was effective because it made them aware that they had things in common with their "enemy." Another finding from this research was that Cypriot primary school students operated at different levels of ethnocentrism. Learners' views about cultural difference varied from total denial of its existence to minimizing its importance. Thus, for the Cypriot educational context, this experience heightened both teachers' and students' cultural awareness and thereby constituted a first step towards achieving the aim of cultural understanding. According to Bennett (1993), this is the first step toward cultural sensitivity and respect. There was evidence that AMICA does contribute to developing cultural awareness.

Following the implementation of the curriculum unit, the students participating in the study viewed the cultural artifacts in a different light. They noted that people can understand more about other people through studying artifacts. Through studying the water jugs from Turkey, they noticed similarities to those of Crete and Cyprus and realized that the people from these cultures shared common traditions. Also, they stressed that these art lessons made them think about how art has an ability to make different cultures appear similar. Bennett (1993) claims that when people are in this ethnocentric stage, the strategy to facilitate development revolves around avoiding premature discussion of significant cultural differences. I conclude that the Curriculum Model does in fact challenge students to move from the stage of ethnocentrism to cultural awareness.

Use of everyday artifacts carrying personal and affective values encouraged students to actively participate in their own learning. The students exhibited a high level of enjoyment when engaging in activities that involved personal artifacts. Furthermore, they expressed various emotional associations toward these objects. During group discussions at an interpersonal level, they also actively demonstrated an involvement and interest in the artifacts selected by their peers, showing empathy and cultural

sensitivity. This supports Marshall's (2002) argument that artifacts invite children to explore something that is familiar to them within their everyday environment.

Participant teachers acknowledged the educational potential of using artifacts to promote cultural understanding in their classrooms. They claimed that students had a chance to see that different cultures have common needs and create similar artifacts. This in turn provided an opportunity for them to compare objects from different cultures and to learn to respect other cultures. However students' preferences, especially in the case of the Cypriot and the Turkish water jugs, were based on affective rather than aesthetic grounds. In both cases they neglected to refer to the visual characteristics of the artifact or its aesthetic value, and their feelings about its country of origin dominated their responses. This finding suggests that when students are emotionally involved in the study of an artifact, without prolonged exposure, they tend to see it from a singular, ethnocentric point of view.

Thus it is clear the use of artifacts alone in an art lesson does not guarantee a successful lesson, or even promote cultural sensitivity. Placing artifacts in their cultural contexts without including prejudice reduction activities can reinforce cultural misunderstandings or mistrust (Bennett, 1993). The Turkish water jug (*testi*) represented a culture that Greek-Cypriot students exhibited a distinct prejudice against, due to historical and political incidents of Turkish invasion and occupation. The curriculum model utilized in this study set out to change students' perspectives over an extended period of time about artifacts to which they had negative reactions. It is anticipated that eventually ethnocentric perspectives of artifacts can be changed, and cultural denial can be replaced by cultural awareness and understanding, but this will take time.

Using AMICA generated evidence that cooperative learning strategies (talking circle, active listening, and discussion) foster cooperation and respect for the feelings of others. This finding is supported by Krol, Sleegers, Veenman, and Voeten (2008), who claim that cooperative learning strategies strengthen active learning and promote students' cognitive and social development. A conclusion is that a material culture approach (Bolin & Blandy, 2003) to investigating artifacts using the proposed model has potential to increase cultural understanding and sensitivity, although this can only be a long-term aim. AMICA therefore has potential to increase students/learners cultural awareness, which is a first step in developing cultural sensitivity.

REFERENCES

Anderson, T. (2000). The Guernica children's peace mural project. *The International Journal of Art and Design Education, 19*(2), 141–151.

Ballengee Morris, C. (2004). Telling many stories. *International Journal of Arts Education, 2*(2), 98–113.

Bennett, J. M. (1993). Cultural marginality: Identity issues in intercultural training. In R. M. Paige (Ed.), *Education for the intercultural experience* (pp. 109–135). Yarmouth, ME: Intercultural Press.

Blacking, J. (1986). *Culture and the Arts.* Paper presented at the University of London Institute [unpublished]. London, England: National Association for Education in the Arts.

Bolin, E. P., & Blandy, D. (2003). Beyond visual culture: Seven statements of support for material culture studies in art education. *Studies in Art Education, 44*(3), 246–263.

Carter, C. C. (2004). Whither social studies? In pockets of peace at school. *Journal of Peace Education, 1*(1), 77–88.

Elliott, J. (1991). *Action research for educational change.* Philadelphia, PA: Open University Press.

Harris, M. I. (2004). Peace education theory. *Journal of Peace Education, 1*(1), 5–20.

Kader, T. (2003). Material culture studies and art education: Connecting artifacts with making art. *Art Education: The Journal of National Art Education Association, 56*(5), 19–23.

Krain, M., & Nurse, A. M. (2004). Teaching human rights through service learning. *Journal of Human Rights Quarterly, 26*(1), 189–207.

Krol, K., Sleegers, P., Veenman, S., & Voeten, M. (2008). Creating cooperative classrooms: Effects of a two-year staff development program. *Educational Studies, 34*(4), 343–360.

Lefler, L. (1999). Listen to my picture: Art as a survival tool for immigrant and refugee students. *Journal of Art Education, 52*(4), 12–17.

Marshall, J. (2002). Exploring culture and identity through artifacts: Three art lessons derived from contemporary art practice. In Y. Gaudelius & P. Spiers (Eds.), *Contemporary issues in art education* (pp. 279–290). Upper Saddle River, NJ: Prentice Hall.

McFee, J. K. (1991). *Art and culture: Change and the cultural dimensions of art education.* Unpublished paper, University of Oregon, Eugene.

McFee, J. K., & Degge, M. R. (1977). *Art, culture, and environment: A catalyst for teaching.* Dubuque, IA: Kendall/Hunt.

McJilton, T. (2002). Creating world peace: One classroom at a time. *Journal of Young Children, 57*(6), 90–94.

Mosley, J., & Sonnet, H. (2003). *101 games for social skills.* Cambridge, MA: LDA.

National Advisory Committee on Creative and Cultural Education. (1999). *All our futures: creativity, culture and education.* Sudbury, England: DfEE.

Nyman, L. A. (2002). Cultural content, identity and program development: Approaches to art education for elementary educators. In Y. Gaudelius & P. Speirs (Eds.), *Contemporary issues in art education* (pp. 61–69). Upper Saddle River: NJ: Prentice Hall.

Räsänen, M. (1997). *Building bridges, experiential art understanding: A work of art as a means of understanding and constructing self.* Helsinki, Finland: University of Art and Design Helsinki.

Rowntree, D. (1974). *Educational technology in curriculum development.* New York, NY: Harper & Row.

Salomon, G. (2004). Comment: What is peace education? *Journal of Peace Education, 1*(1), 123–124.

Sheesley, M. F. (2000). *The effect of a selected multicultural art education strategy on third-grade student attitudes toward diverse cultures.* Unpublished PhD thesis. The Florida State University, Tallahassee.

Stomfay-Stitz, A., & Hinitz, B. F. (1996). Integration/infusion of peace education into early childhood education programs. *International Journal of Early Childhood, 28*(2), 29–36.

Stout, C. J. (1999). The art of empathy: Teaching students to care. *Journal of Art Education. 52*(2), 21–34.

Tillman, D. G. (2001). Educating for a culture of peace in refugee camps. *Journal of Childhood Education, 77*(6), 375–378.

Virshup, E. (1993). *California art therapy trends.* Chicago, IL: Magnolia Street.

ENDNOTE

[1] Cypriot education needs to deal with a significant cultural issue stemming from the Turkish invasion and occupation: namely cultural conflict. In 1974, Turkey invaded Cyprus and occupied 36% of its territory. It was the first time in the island's long history that the communities of Cyprus were separated socially, politically, economically, and culturally by force. At this time, one third of the Greek-Cypriots (200,000 people) became displaced from their homes and properties and fled to the southern government-controlled section of the country, and 45,000 Turkish-Cypriots fled to the northern section. The ceasefire line runs right across the island and cuts through the heart of the capital, Nicosia (*Lefkosia*), dividing the city. Since 1964, a UN peacekeeping force has been stationed on the island, supervising the buffer zone and maintaining the ceasefire.

CHAPTER 4

Exploring Ritual Through Art

ANGELA M. LA PORTE
University of Arkansas

Art inspired by ritual can present secondary and postsecondary students with a vehicle to create meaning from their significant life experiences. Whether through ceremony, habit, or custom, rituals can take many forms, such as meal preparation for a special occasion, daily obsessions with technology, or other significant routines. Rituals are embedded in everyday life and offer a gateway into personal stories that have global, interdisciplinary, and cross-cultural significance. Through interdisciplinary inquiry, reflection, interpretation, and artmaking, students can better understand ritual as a natural part of human experience that can nurture cross-cultural sensitivity and acceptance of others.

Ritual has long been an integral part of art throughout the world and has been central to human cultural experiences. Since prehistoric times, rituals have been represented in art, from the mystical and religious to the secular, changing with culture over time and reflecting its aspects (Brown, 1980; Dissanayake, 1988; Durkheim, 1912). Yet, its defining properties have provoked controversy. According to Whitaker (1980), ritual "must be symbolic, repetitive, stereotypical, and a complexly patterned event" (p. 316). It can represent "our patterns of behavior which we have inherited and practice and pass on to our descendants" (Brown, 2005, p. 127). However, there is no universal understanding of the term *ritual*, and some non-Western cultures lack a comparable word (Bell, 1997). For the purpose of structuring a theme for ritual within an art curriculum, I follow a flexible and generalized definition based on Grimes (1990). Ritual can be defined as a religious or secular act; performed repetitively or reactivated by a person or group; and involving a conscious or unconscious act using the body and/or the senses, sound, language, and/or material culture.

Several religious rituals that have flourished for centuries are in decline, while others have become more secular expressions (Bastien & Bromley, 1980) and reflect inventions and objects related to time, place, and culture. These new forms and their predecessors imbue everyday life with a sense of comfort and predictability in a world fraught with fear and instability. Observe how many people compulsively check their Facebook or text messages. An art curriculum investigating rituals encourages cross-cultural sensitivity through studying the works of local, regional, and global artists from diverse ethnic and cultural backgrounds. It is a motivational, meaningful, and thought-provoking topic for encouraging student artmaking through a variety of intercultural perspectives.

Over the past 50 years, ritual has become a prominent theme among artists cross-culturally, often rooted in ceremonies and traditions. Perhaps this resurrected interest is a response to humankind's need for stability, ancestral connections, and a safe, comfortable, predictable environment in a world where change is threatening. Art often reflects its societal roots, and many artists apply ritual themes in their work. For example, Romare Bearden produced a collage series, *Prevalence of Ritual*, inspired by memories associated with his African American heritage. Carmen Lomas Garza shared her Mexican American culture in the paintings

Birthday Barbecue and *Empanadas* (Garza, 1996). Artists have often used ritual as a format for a mix between tradition and social or political commentary rich with metaphor and juxtaposition, such as Santa Barraza's altar installation at the University of Arkansas Fine Arts Gallery, recognizing women who died from dehydration crossing the Mexican border into the United States. A social constructivist, Lee Mingwei, created *The Letter Writing Project*,[1] part of The Museum of Modern Art 2009 exhibition: Eat, Sleep, and Pray: Everyday Rituals and Contemporary Art.[2] His installation encouraged viewers to write letters that would communicate unexpressed emotions to absent friends and family. The MoMA PS1 Gallery 2008 exhibition—NeoHooDoo: Art for a Forgotten Faith[3]—referred to the theme of ritual as an artistic process and religious practice related to an underlying human need to rediscover spirituality. The same year, an international exhibition—Reinventing Ritual: Contemporary Art and Design for Jewish Life—debuted at The Jewish Museum in New York, expressing a reinterpretation of traditional Jewish rituals (Belasco, Eisen, Lasky, Ruttenberg, & Rubin, 2009). Also in New York, ritual was the theme of the annual Public and Performance Art Festival, Art in Odd Places 2011,[4] where artists from around the world transformed old rituals and created new expressive forms such as commentaries inspired by culture and world politics. Artists' interpretations of ritual offer a cross-cultural and cross-disciplinary view of art with rich motivational possibilities for developing a contemporary art education curriculum.

Ritual as a Theme for an Art Education Curriculum

Ritual is a theme with an *enduring idea*, one that connects to "human concerns that have been of significance over time in multiple cultures and contexts" (Stewart & Walker, 2005, p. 26). This chapter will introduce an art education unit—Exploring Ritual Through Art—to broaden students' understandings of art as global, cross-cultural, and interdisciplinary, motivating a personal reflection of ritual and inspiring meaningful artmaking.

In recent decades, art educators have utilized material culture, visual culture, and popular culture to evoke deep, meaningful understandings of our global world and the complexity of the objects and experiences within it. These approaches to art education are easily illustrated through examination of ritual and objects associated with it. For example, Carpenter (2003) shared his study of a barbershop, a ritual site within his community, as a place with which students can easily connect. "By starting with the familiar, students can better understand the unfamiliar" (p. 16). Stokrocki (2001) led teenagers in the aesthetic investigation of their local shopping mall, which was considered a ritual site. Through open-ended questioning, she encouraged students to reflect about the aesthetic experience of the space as well as the objects and people within it, and to come to an educated awareness of the manipulative power of shopping malls. Years later, Stokrocki (2009) implemented dance as a theme for art curriculum in an Arizona lower-income, inner-city school, where most students responded positively to question prompts about dancing and created drawings based

For Further Consideration

1. How would you define ritual?
2. Make a list of rituals you engage in on a personal level, community level, national level, and worldwide level. Into what other categories might rituals fall?
3. How have artists incorporated ritual into their art throughout history? How has that representation changed over time? Why?
4. Why might ritual be an important art education curriculum theme?
5. How might themes of ritual call forth differing responses based on one's cultural experiences? Give specific examples.

upon their personal experiences, primarily about their school dance ritual. Brisco (2006) engaged high school students in depicting their morning rituals through assemblage art. At the postsecondary level, Amdur (1999) had university students identify rituals they inherited from family members that led them to become more aware of their histories and encouraged creative breakthroughs in their artwork. In addition, "time or life passages such as losing a first tooth, riding without training wheels" are significant rituals that are authenticated through art (Gradle, 2006, p. 13). Approaching art education through study of ritual connects directly to students' lives and offers an interdisciplinary and global understanding of our shared world. Whether students examine their own or others' rituals, they gain contextual knowledge about them through history, social studies, and so forth, culminating in an appreciation for similarities and differences among cultures in our world.

Unit Objectives

The following unit objectives that focus on the theme of ritual are appropriate for teaching secondary and postsecondary students in various educational settings.

Students will:

- Understand multiple and open-ended definitions of ritual.
- Understand that ritual is a common practice of humans throughout history and the world.
- Understand that ritual can be a unique personal or shared experience.
- Learn how artists from around the world express ritual in their art.
- Improve their understanding of personal history, culture, values, and beliefs about ritual in their daily lives and in the lives of others.
- Understand how to communicate various ideas about their own rituals through artmaking.
- Gain acceptance for the differences and similarities in the history, practices, values, and beliefs of others.

Students can acknowledge the cultural roots of their own identities and learn to accept the differences of others. Preservice teachers, in particular, can become more accepting of the growing cultural diversity of their future students, as Liggett and Finley (2009) suggest is important to be included in successful teacher education programs.

Phases of the Ritual Unit

This unit includes six adaptable phases. First, the instructor leads a collective discussion to define the word *ritual* and identify examples of meaningful rituals. One way to begin this discussion is to have students read Miner's (1956) article, "Body Ritual Among the Nacirema," a humorous, anthropological, objectified view of American culture's fascination with the body. I ask students:

1. What is Miner's role in the investigation of body ritual?

2. How does he define *body ritual*?

3. How does his 1956 interpretation of body ritual compare with Americans' and other countries body rituals today?

4. What has influenced body ritual since this article by Miner was published?

To expand upon the definition of ritual, I often have students break into groups and ask each to define ritual (noting certain characteristics), to list some common rituals that people practice, and to develop categories from their lists. They soon begin to understand that rituals lack specific boundaries. Then, I ask them to consider how some aspects are cross-cultural or unique, and how and why they have changed over time. For example, students associated ritual with several terms: routine, purpose, comfort, unconscious, habitual/good and bad, taught/learned, and valued/meaningful. They soon discovered through their long lists of rituals[5] that some share certain characteristics, but that each one is unique based on the context of time, culture, place, and other factors. Students decided that groups or individuals might perform rituals, and they could be religious and/or secular acts.

Next, students are asked to compare and contrast how and why artists from around the globe[6] portray ritual in their art, to amplify their understandings of and/or experiences with similar forms of ritual. In addition to some of the artists mentioned earlier in this chapter, I share my own commemorative artwork, *Mother, Mary*, which is loaded with cultural objects of ritual with an emphasis on the juxtaposition of my mother's canning jar at the center of an altar that contains randomly cut remnants of diet caffeine free Coke cans (Figure 1). I ask students:

1. What objects of ritual can you identify?

2. What are the historical and cultural connections to these objects (canning jars, braided garlic, etc.)?

3. What format did I use to place these objects and why?

4. What meaning does the juxtaposition of these objects portray?

Figure 1. Mother, Mary: *Sculptural installation by Angela M. La Porte.*

Many students are able to identify the small pieces of diet caffeine free Coke cans, a radiation mask, the MRI scans of the brain, and so forth. I explain the molecular configuration on the center jar: that aspartame changes into formaldehyde when consumed. We discuss what formaldehyde is (a carcinogen, preservative) and collectively interpret the work. We examine other artworks mentioned earlier concerning subject matter, historical and cultural contexts, as well as media choices and decisions, attempting to understand what each artist wished to portray in his or her work.

Then, students write about a personal meaningful ritual experience, a detailed description of the ritual identifying how certain senses, objects, and/or bodies are involved in the experience. They include the ritual's social, cultural, and historical significance, how the ritual has changed over time, how specific changes have affected culture, and how changes in culture have affected the ritual. I ask students to write how the ritual might be similar or different when performed by other people around the world and why this is important to consider.

Prior to creating their art, the students reflect on their interdisciplinary investigations of the history and cultural connections to their chosen ritual. Then, they decide how to transform their ritual through artmaking so that it communicates a personally meaningful message. The result could be a direct visual representation of history, a social or political commentary, and/or a new ritual that might reflect a recent or revised cultural practice. Next, students write a proposal to describe how and why they want to transform their ritual into an art product, including three preliminary thumbnails or storyboard sketches for a formative assessment. Formative assessments include research and analysis of the ritual, sharing ideas with other students, and defending decisions about the format, materials, and organization of the final artwork. The instructor can suggest possible formats and material options as applicable. Students can work independently or in small groups and come to an agreement with peers through sharing and debating in-process ideas. Some students might want to focus on a particular object of importance from their ritual, as represented in the work of Alexis Canter in the Jewish Museum exhibition, "Reinterpreting Ritual." She takes a wishbone, a memento from her Jewish family's traditional chicken dinner, casts it in 14K gold from an actual wishbone, and places it on a gold jewelry chain. Others might choose to portray their ritual theme in a more traditional art form.

A Unit on Ritual in a High School Setting

According to the high school art teacher who taught my unit on ritual, her students varied in their artwork choices, research, and representations. This was evident when they reflected on their teenage ritual experiences including cheerleading, texting on their cell phones, a la Quinceañera fiesta,[7] making art, and applying facial make-up. Their art took the form of artist books, mixed media assemblages, drawings, and paintings. Students realized that everyone practiced both similar and distinctly different rituals. Some chose direct representations of rituals in the form of a book or collage and reflected on the cultural significance of their rituals. Others discovered deep meanings and insights. One teenager represented her daily application of facial make-up (Figure 2). At the end of the unit, she reflected:

> To be beautiful… that's what every girl wants. In our society, cosmetics play a huge part in most women's daily routine. By doing my project on this ritual, my whole perspective of make-up has changed … Women do not need make-up to be beautiful. Our society has pushed even young girls to feel they need to layer their faces in necessity. Hopefully, others will realize their true beauty. (B. Babb, personal communication, February 10, 2012)

The examination of meaningful rituals offered an opportunity for sharing and contemplation as well as media choices and challenges.

Figure 2. Make-up: *Collage by high school student Bailey Babb.*

A Unit on Ritual in a University Setting

My university art education students represented meaningful rituals through installation, photography, mixed media, drawing, and painting. Many provoked interesting discussions using or reconstructing material culture in their art. For example, a female drummer in a band built a three-dimensional drum to represent her ritual of drumming in a rock band (Figure 3). She researched drumming as a gender specific ritual and how it has changed over time. She chose to portray a drum constructed of cardboard, transparent paper heads, and photos of herself playing on a drum set with flowers visible inside the drum. A class discussion about the interpretation of her artwork brought up gender issues surrounding the cross-cultural history of drumming. It led students to question the roles of drumming and the challenges still faced by females as musicians in popular bands.

Figure 3. Drumming: *Sculpture by preservice teacher Anna Wingfield.*

Throughout the process, students at both high school and university levels broadened their knowledge of cultural practices and traditions. They learned how art could reflect our everyday lives and uncover complex and meaningful revelations about human practices.

Forms of Assessment for High School and University Contexts

Assessment should be formative and summative and relate to unit objectives and applied curriculum frameworks. Criteria for assessment can be established by a teacher or discussed and negotiated with students near the beginning of a unit. For example, preservice teachers in my university class agreed that their research, thumbnail sketches, class participation, and collaboration were important forms of formative assessments. They also decided that their artwork should be evaluated on summative assessment criteria: craftsmanship and use of media and aesthetic choices that complemented a topic that portrayed a ritual. Each student reviewed his or her own work and completed evaluations on the work of two other randomly selected students.

Prior to summative assessments, students developed questions for peer presentation and discussion of their artworks. One student, inspired by Carmen Lomas Garza's painting *Birthday Barbecue*, chose a birthday ritual as her topic (Figure 4). Some of the discussion questions posed by students were:

1. What is your first impression of this work?
2. What do you see as the subject of this image?
3. Why are different types of candles used in the art?
4. Why do you think the candles are in the position they are in?
5. What type of meaning does the placement of candles have?
6. Why is there an absence of a cake?
7. How does the lighting affect the work?

These questions also led the students to contemplate how birthdays change in significance as we age and how this varies in other cultures. The emphasis of candles in her work sparked conversation among students about cultural experiences with aging and birthdays. They contemplated the missing cake as being the least significant, since students related aging with birthday candles. Many agreed that the first birthday is the most significant with only a single candle. As the candles increase in number, the enthusiasm continues. At some point, the birthday candles diminish and often disappear. The event becomes

Figure 4. Birthdays: *Mixed media by preservice teacher, Courtney Kruger.*

less celebratory and more intimate, with close friends and family. Many students associated this fading of candles with ageism in the US, noting that age is more respected in other parts of the world in which rituals are less commercialized. Some students interpreted the arrangement of candles as a circle of life moving from the right to left and back to the right. The candlelight offered contemplative atmosphere that many associated with their own birthday experiences.

In the high school, assessment criteria reflected state frameworks with a focus on research, craftsmanship, and media choices/application. Formative assessments included research involved in studying relevant artists and a sketchbook for planning to depict ritual practices. Summative evaluation involved self and peer reviews of student artwork. The final assessment included communication of a ritual (media choices relative to the concept), craftsmanship (technique and use of materials), and perception (formal design). Students wrote self-evaluations of their work and one peer evaluation based on the same rubric. Regardless of the type of formative or summative assessment used, it should relate to student level, unit objectives, and selected curriculum frameworks.

Outcome

The overall goal of this unit was for students to understand that rituals are cross-cultural and global, and a natural part of meaningful human experiences that can be better understood through interdisciplinary investigation. According to the high school art teacher who taught the unit on ritual, her students learned about different rituals and were motivated to make art due to the broad range of personal and global connections they could make on this topic (see Figures 2 and 4). One student initially thought ritual was "a tribal thing, but now I realize that rituals are everywhere" (personal communication, February 1, 2012). The university preservice teachers discovered

many interesting cross-cultural connections and uniqueness as well as historical references connected to their topics about ritual. For example, one student attended movies regularly and he researched the historical origin of movie theatres and found similarities in worldwide movie-going rituals. Popcorn, soda, and candy were commonly associated with watching films in the US while other countries consumed their own favorite foods. Overall, he found advances in technology and current cultural practices and beliefs were now influencing movie theatre experiences around the world.

Based on student reflections and comments from global, interdisciplinary, and cross-cultural research; student artmaking; and discussions by all student groups, many grew more conscious of and knowledgeable about their own rituals, the rituals of others, and their similarities

Figure 5. la Quinceañera: *(fifteenth birthday, marking a transition for young girls to womanhood). Collage by high school student Gasela Navarette.*

and contrasts. Some students gained cross-cultural and interdisciplinary knowledge, as well as social and political awareness, through sharing information and research on celebrations. Examples included texting on a cell phone, drinking tea, voting, going to school, cheerleading, pumpkin carving, watching movies, and eating lunch at school. Many students tapped into the history of birthday celebrations and the similarities and differences between a sweet sixteen birthday in the US, la Quinceañera in Latin America (Figure 5), and the all-ages tradition of lighting candles on a birthday cake. One student investigated the worldwide trend of texting and cell phone usage and found that it moved people away from acknowledging and appreciating their natural environment, as well as causing an increase in traffic accidents.

Conclusion and Implications

Exploring ritual through art offers many opportunities for student engagement and multicultural education. Since ritualized behavior is ingrained in everyday life in so many ways, possibilities for art education are endless. Whether introducing the topic as a way to uncover the stories of formal ceremonial practices or examining meaningful rituals that emerge from secular culture, students can gain insight into what it means to be human and how we create meaning. As creatures of habit, and particularly in times of instability and fear, many people seek belongingness, comfort, security, and predictability in ritual behavior. Students can gain an awareness of how artists and students from diverse backgrounds interpret ritual, and learn empathy and cultural understanding by drawing comparisons between ritual behaviors and illuminating differences.

There are numerous approaches to using ritual as a theme for an art education curriculum. One can challenge students to define ritual as it relates to their life experiences, and to look for inspiration from the many artists around the world who have transformed rituals into art. Teachers can introduce specific themes that are relevant to students' individual interests. Examples abound in school or community life, and as celebrations or special occasions. Media forms can be chosen depending on student knowledge and skills. Novice artists can transform rituals into art products using a specific medium, simplified into a still life drawing of a ritual object, a print, sculpture, or painting, where the student develops specific skills associated with a medium. For advanced students, with basic knowledge in a variety of media, choices and applications can be more subjective.

Through ritual themes, art educators can develop curricula units that explore and respect the common humanity of all cultures and peoples. Artists of diverse cultural heritage provide abundant examples to guide student research, reflection, and artmaking. Students come to view their own, often unconscious, behaviors as manifestations of a human condition, which cultivates open-mindedness and a broad cultural understanding. Overall, the purpose of this unit is to expand students' concepts of art, embracing cross-cultural and global concerns; to encourage their use of interdisciplinary research methods that foster the understanding of personally meaningful rituals; and to inspire creative self-expression.

REFERENCES

Amdur, M. (1999). Rituals that rewrite one's rules. *Art Journal, 58*(1), 90–91.

Bastien, J. W., & Bromley, D. G. (1980). Metaphor in the rituals of restorative and transformative groups. In R. B. Brown (Ed.), *Rituals and ceremonies in popular culture* (pp. 48–60). Bowling Green, OH: Bowling Green University Press.

Belasco, D., Eisen, A. M., Lasky, J., Ruttenberg, D., & Rubin, T. (2009). *Reinventing ritual: Contemporary art and design for Jewish life* [exhibition catalog, 13 September 2009–10 May 2010]. New York, NY: Jewish Museum.

Bell, C. M. (1997). *Ritual: Perspectives and dimensions.* New York, NY: Oxford University Press.

Brisco, N. D. (2006). Rituals of the morning. *School Arts, 105*(5), 30.

Brown, R. B. (1980). Ritual one. In R. B. Brown (Ed.), *Rituals and ceremonies in popular culture* (pp. 1–18). Bowling Green, OH: Bowling Green University Press.

Brown, R. B. (Ed.). (2005). *Profiles of popular culture: A reader.* Madison: University of Wisconsin Press.

Carpenter, B. S., II. (2003). Never a dull moment: Pat's barbershop as education environment, hypertext, and place. *Journal of Cultural Research in Art Education, 21*, 5–18.

Dissanayake, E. (1988). *What is art for?* Seattle: University of Washington Press.

Durkheim, E. (1912). *Les formes élémentaires de la vie religieuse* [The elementary forms of religious life]. Paris, France: Alcan.

Garza, C. L. (1996). *In my family.* San Francisco, CA: Children's Book Press.

Gradle, S. (2006). Developing artistry in teaching: Ritual art and human concerns. *Art Education, 59*(2), 12–19.

Grimes, R. L. (1990). *Ritual criticism: Case studies in its practice, essays on its theory.* Columbia: University of South Carolina Press.

Liggett, T., & Finley, S. (2009). Upsetting the apple cart: Issues of diversity in preservice teacher education. *Multicultural Education, 16*(4), 33–39.

Miner, H. (1956). Body ritual among the Nacirema. *American Anthropologist, 58*(3), 503–507.

Stewart, M. G., & Walker, S. R. (2005). *Rethinking curriculum in art.* Worcester, MA: Davis.

Stokrocki, M. (2001). Go to the mall: Adolescents' aesthetic values. *Art Education, 54*(2), 18–23.

Stokrocki, M. (2009). Preadolescents reflect on their drawings of dance: Students' voices in art learning. *Art Education, 62*(4), 7–12.

Whitaker III, W. W. (1980). The contemporary American funeral ritual. In R. B. Browne (Ed.), *Rituals and ceremonies in popular culture* (pp. 316–325). Bowling Green, OH: Bowling Green University Press.

ENDNOTES

1   www.leemingwei.com/projects.php

2   www.moma.org/explore/multimedia/audios/156/1668

3   http://momaps1.org/exhibitions/view/205

4   www.artinoddplaces.org
For art examples from the 2011 Art in Odd Places Festival, see:

http://hyperallergic.com/37466/art-in-odd-places-2011-1/

http://culture.wnyc.org/articles/features/2011/oct/04/art-odd-places-festival-invades-14th-street/

www.kickstarter.com/projects/aiop/help-art-in-odd-places-2011-festival-publish-a-cat

5   Examples might include brushing teeth, eating breakfast, watching television, family gatherings, marriage, religious services, and so forth.

6   Examples of artists connecting with ritual are: Janine Antoni, Santa Barraza, Romare Bearden, Nick Cave, Judy Chicago, Mel Chin, Carmen Lomas Garza, Mike Kelley, Dominique Mazeaud, Lee Mingwei, Shirin Neshat, Otis Polalenema, and Mierle Laderman Ukeles.

7   The celebration of a girl's fifteenth birthday in communities of people from Latin America and in other places.

CHAPTER 5

Learning and Teaching About Traditional Ghanaian Art Forms:
Developing Global Perspectives Using Digital Media in Art Education

LAURIE ELDRIDGE

Ira A. Murphy Elementary School, Peoria Unified School District, Arizona

Part One: Thinking About Ghana and Its Traditional Art Forms

Do people hunt for their food over there? Do they, like, eat lions and things?
(Question from a 7th-grade student)

In June of 2010 I was notified by the National Art Education Foundation that I had received a Mary McMullen Grant to fund the writing of a curriculum, *Global Citizenship and Digital Media in Art Education: A Curriculum Model.*[1] The two major objectives of the curriculum were: (1) to develop an art education curriculum model that focused on developing art resources with global perspectives through use of new media, and (2) to develop middle school students' skills and understanding about new media at the same time as they begin to develop their identities as members of a global digital citizenship group. Understanding commonalities shared by all people and appreciating differences between and within cultures (Zimmerman, 2001–2002) was the emphasis of the global education program I wanted to put into action.

I made a commitment to extend my own education about diversity, and in doing so found a way to consult with people and visit their cultural settings in ways to which I previously would not have had access (Andrus, 2001). This decision involved my traveling to the West African country of Ghana, where I would stay with my friend Mariama Ross, who taught art education courses at the University of Kwame Nkruma in Kumasi. Related to my grant, she invited me to visit her at her home in Kumasi, Ghana, where I could experience art education programs and benefit from her local connections and deep knowledge of indigenous Ghanaian arts. With the assistance of the Mary McMullen grant, I hoped to be able to widen the worlds of the economically challenged, primarily Hispanic students in the Title I[2] school in the American southwest, where I teach art. The majority of my students are of Mexican descent, and in their daily lives they must transcend the cultural borders of mainstream American life. This can sometimes lead to stereotypical and sometimes racist attitudes among all the students. I wanted to help them transcend their cultural borders by creating a space of interaction with people from another cultural group (Bastos, 2006).

As a tribal member of the Cherokee Nation of Oklahoma, I wanted to travel to Ghana as an indigenous scholar and educator, not as a simple tourist. Tourism can be seen as a way of travelling nostalgically through the past. Frequently tourists can be seen as promoting or maintaining beliefs about an exotic Other, racism, or cultural hierarchy (Ballengee Morris & Sanders, 2009). As an educator, I did not want to reinforce racist or classicist stereotypes that my students might have of indigenous thought and material culture, such that only its novelty or exoticism would be considered worthwhile (Ballengee Morris & Sanders, 2009).

Ross (2004) has written about the neo-colonialism of the education system and problems of imposing a British system onto traditional Ghanaian society and thought. That sort of critique was not the intent of the development of my curriculum model. I was concerned with the representation/misrepresentation of The Other in my curriculum. I did not want to essentialize, romanticize, or fictionalize the Ghanaian artists who would share their crafts with me. I also did not want to perpetuate any stereotypes that my students held about Africans or about Africa itself. Stereotypes are reinforced through school, movies, and cultural media, and it is important to assist students in broadening their frames of cultural reference in order to advance their own senses of self and the world (Carpenter, 1999).

Focus of the Curriculum

I desired to focus on some of the indigenous arts of Ghana, not because I saw them as the only authentic works of art produced there, but because tradition is fundamental to any social environment (Picton, 1999). There was a time when Ghanaian artifacts gathered by anthropologists and others were considered timeless and

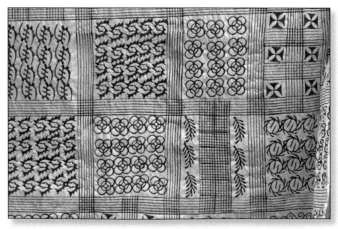

Figure 1. Traditional adinkra cloth. Photo by Laurie A. Eldridge.

unspoiled by the arrival of missionaries, educational institutions, or industrialization. Changes to timeless crafts were not seen as processes of negotiating identity and change (Picton, 1999). I did not want my interest in traditional crafts to be a form of neo-primitivism, I wanted to present to my students a notion that there are artists thinking through their own cultural inheritances and presenting interpretations of their relevance to present contexts.

Part Two: Being in Ghana and Learning About Its Traditional Art Forms

African art is characterized by multiplicity of meanings and intellectual complexity (Blier, 2001). The vast majority of Ghanaian arts use *adinkra* symbols that draw imagery from or are named after plants, animals, objects, and human experiences. Often associated with a proverb, folktale, boast, insult, riddle, or other verbal form that extends the meaning of a given subject, it is this visual-verbal nexus of Ghanaian art that is one of the defining features of adinkra (Ross, 1998). For example, a symbol of a crocodile stands for adaptability, since the crocodile lives in water yet breathes air. Ghanaian arts include a repertoire of several thousand adinkra visual motifs, from abstract symbols to representational scenes and objects, and each motif is associated with one or more verbal forms (Cole, 2001).

Adinkra

I became fascinated with adinkra cloths, which are large pieces of cotton fabric stamped and comb-lined[3] by men (Kelly, 1997). Adinkra probably originated as mourning clothes, with hand woven strips of cloth sewn together to form one large cloth. Warp and weft are dyed brown, brick red, or black; the darkness of the color indicates the closeness of the mourner to the deceased. Most adinkra are stamped in squares that are divided by combed lines (Figure 1). Patterns are stamped with carved calabash stamps and combs, using dye made by women who boil a certain tree bark with iron-bearing rock or slag. When reduced to a tar-like consistency suitable for printing, the dye produces stamped motifs that have a desired sheen to them. White and many other colors of adinkra, called *Sunday* or *fancy* adinkra, can be worn for most festive occasions or even daily, but only dark clothes are worn for mourning (Cole, 2001; Kelly, 1997).

Adinkra is composed of over 500 different motifs that are associated with parables, proverbs, and sayings. Some have fallen out of use, but over 200 are popularly used

For Further Consideration

1. Eldridge describes how her students—who are members of minority cultural groups within the United States—were engaged in explorations of the artistic expressions of a distant, unfamiliar people. In what ways and to what extent did the approach she used to instruct Ghanaian adinkra to her students differ from the heroes-and-holidays approach described by Banks (1986)?

2. Eldridge shares her own cultural background with her students at the same time that she engages them in inquiry about a Ghanaian cultural expression. How did she incorporate her own background experiences as a Native American and experiences from her immersion into the Ghanaian community into the art instruction of her students? What role did the students' cultural backgrounds play in the teaching/learning experience?

3. Eldridge describes how her students grappled with ethical concerns. For example, Eldridge's students were concerned that peers from a less prosperous nation might experience feelings of jealousy if they perceived the American students as living privileged lives. Consider and discuss how this issue was handled by Eldridge. What other ways might these kinds of questions about differences in worldviews and everyday experiences be addressed?

4. Do you think it is necessary for an art teacher to become physically immersed in a different culture or have had first-hand experiences interacting with artists of another culture in order to be qualified to teach to or about the art and artists of that culture? Why or why not? What other forms might immersion in a culture take?

5. How, and to what extent, did this curriculum unit transcend "tourist" art education?

6. In what other ways, given the equipment available, could this art educator have integrated digital media into her classes to support sensitive teaching about diverse populations? What current technologies are you aware of that might facilitate greater authenticity in teaching and learning about unfamiliar cultures?

References

Banks, J. A. (1986). Multicultural education: Development, paradigms and goals. In J. A. Banks and J. Lynch (Eds.), *Multicultural education in western societies* (pp. 2–28). New York, NY: Praeger.

today, many with their original meanings. Ghanaian indigenous and contemporary artists also create new symbols with contemporary connotations (Kelly, 1997; Cole, 2001).[4]

My Experience With Adinkra

While in Ghana I saw the sign, "Op. Yaw Boakye, Adinkra Printing, Demonstrations, Make Your Own Cloth," and was deeply, yet quietly, excited to be in a place where I would have an opportunity to see contemporary craftsmen creating cloth printed with adinkra symbols. Peter Boakye, a tall, robust young man with dreadlocks, who looked to be in his thirties and who was to be my teacher for the afternoon, met Rali Debra (my graduate student guide) and me at the front of the craft village. Peter Boakye spoke excellent English, but I had to listen very closely through his Ghanaian accent to follow the deep intonation of his voice.

First Peter Boakye led Rali Debra and me back to the area where there were several large cast iron pots over a long fire, centered between one-story buildings. Chickens meandered across the red earth. A kid could be heard bleating for its mother, roosters crowed, and the hum of the World Cup soccer game was emanating from a small radio. It was hot already, and I began to sweat profusely, due to the heat from the fire.

Peter Boakye carefully explained the process for rendering badie tree[5] bark into *adinkra duro*, the colorant used to stamp color onto the fabric. One step in the process was to pound the bark into shreds with a large mortar and pestle that looked like the kind used to make *fufu* (pounded cassava roots), and by my Cherokee ancestors to pound corn into flour. He encouraged me to try pounding the approximately four-foot-long pestle into a mortar that looked like it had been carved from a tree trunk. When I grasped the mortar and began pounding,

Figure 2. The author using adinkra stamps with the help of Peter Boakye. Photo from the collection of Laurie A. Eldridge.

I felt as though I had stepped into a different world, the world of craftspeople whose traditions go back generations into antiquity. I experienced a profound respect for Peter Boakye, the craftswomen who were tending the boiling bark on the fires, and their ancestors who had taught them the knowledge and skills required for making adinkra.

Next, Peter Boakye allowed me to select from several adinkra stamps made from calabash gourds, so that I could print my own fabric. A deep, quiet excitement resurfaced and I felt as though I would like to use each stamp, but settled on three. I then selected a long yellow cloth that had been hand woven on a single heddle loom on the premises. As I carefully pressed each stamp in turn onto the cloth, the heat seemed to disappear, my lightheadedness vanished, and I became immersed in the process of creating a message with adinkra. Rali Debra remarked on how carefully I was working. Peter Boayke seemed impressed with the care I was using to create my stamped fabric, and gave me tips to improve my printing (Figure 2). Although I do not know what aspects of adinkra printing might have been kept secret from an outsider, I was grateful for his willingness to share aspects of his knowledge, cultural heritage, and daily life with someone foreign to his culture.

Comparison With Cherokee Customs

I am a member of the Cherokee Nation of Oklahoma. I did not grow up in a traditional Native American community, but spent summers with aunts who were traditionalists—in that they participated in stomp dances, powwows, and the practices of the Native American Church. I could not help but compare my Native American background with Ghanaian art and culture. During the short time (two and a half weeks) that I was in Ghana, I found several similarities between Ghanaian and Cherokee people, both of which are of tribal cultures.

I had an interesting conversation with Rali Debra one afternoon, in which we discussed how alike Ghanaian traditions were as compared to Native American traditions, with regard to respect for ancestors and older people. In Ghana, Native Americans are called "red Indians," a term I was willing to accept for the short time I was in Ghana, but with knowledge of how damaging the term has been for Native peoples in America. I explained to her that I was a red Indian and I had noticed that she had been very deferential to me as both a person who was older than she and as a person who held an advanced degree; for example, she was very careful to carry my bags of purchases if she felt they looked too heavy for me.

Rali Debra, in turn, described how older people in Ghana are taken care of as part of the family and treated with respect by non-family members and society in general. People will give older people a good seat in the *tro-tros* (minibuses used for local transportation), and lift their packages for them in the market so they can carry them on their heads, if there is no one to carry things for them. I mentioned how Native American elders are often treated with similar respect.

I said that I noticed that I often saw elderly people on Sundays, wearing adinkra as if going to a funeral. Rali Debra explained the importance of funerals in Ghanaian life, and that funerals were often held on Sunday. Going to funerals is considered a duty for all, but especially for those who were close to the deceased or are family members. One can discern the relationship of the funeral participants to the deceased by the color of the adinkra cloth they are wearing. Brick red means that the deceased was very close. I would sometimes see the deep red of mourning surrounding an elaborate coffin, which was shaped to suggest the deceased's employment, favorite possession, or pastime. Coffins could be in the shape of a fish, a Mercedes Benz, or any number of other shapes that reflected the interests of the deceased.

Although funerals are of importance to my Native people in northeastern Oklahoma as a time for family, friends, and community members to mourn, there are many differences in our funerary observances as compared with Ghanaian observances. But the important aspect of this discussion was that Rali Debra was acknowledging and commending how our similarities are enacted in our complex, diverse world.

Part Three: Teaching About Ghana and Ghanaian Traditional Arts

I began teaching about the traditional arts of Ghana to middle school students in five art classes by focusing on adinkra. As I taught the unit, I answered many questions such as: "Are all people in Africa black?" "Do they hunt for their food?" "What kinds of clothes do people in Africa wear?" Students wanted to know if I had a good time, if I learned a lot, if I would go back. I found that through my answers I was able to help them understand that Africa was a continent and that Ghana was a country in Africa. I was able to paint a picture of life in modern Ghana where people watch TV, love soccer, drive cars, and wear Western clothing; yet they also don traditional fabrics, and chickens, goats and cows roam throughout the city. Many of my students who were from Mexico said it sounded a lot like Mexico to them. I answered that in some ways it was, but in other ways not. There were no fast food restaurants, people communicated mostly by cell phone, and there were few bicycles in Ghana. Also I told them about how I found similarities to my own people, the Cherokee, and differences as well.

As I begin teaching about adinkra to my 6th- and 7th-grade students, I felt a sense of joy in being able to share with them some of the artifacts, perceptions, and experiences I had encountered in Ghana. I placed my photo album on my desk so students could flip through it. I also created a bulletin board with artifacts and pictures from Ghana, and organized my videos so they could see some of what I had experienced. I was determined not to teach from an aspect of cultural tourism, so as I described adinkra to them, I emphasized that this was a contemporary art form that Ghanaian artists used in many ways, but I was only showing them some of the traditional uses of adinkra. During the first class period, I had shared with students the adinkra cloth that I had purchased, the cloth that I had made with Peter Boayke, stamps that I had purchased, and other artifacts, such as a wood carving and a calabash water dipper decorated with adinkra symbols used in contemporary artmaking.

When I explained that I wanted the students to create their own adinkra, and not just copy symbols that were used for centuries, I was initially confronted with an "Aw, come on, let us copy" attitude by students who had difficulty thinking conceptually, and with a "Can I write my own proverb?" attitude by students who were more fluent in conceptual thinking. I was gently leading students through a discovery of printmaking processes at the same time. They defined proverbs and idioms, and completed

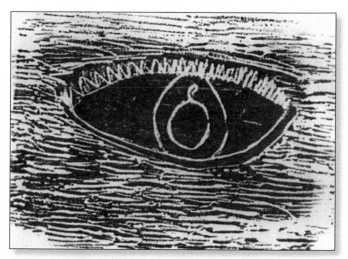

Figure 3. Apple of My Eye (2011) by Serah. Collection of Laurie A. Eldridge.

a fill-in-a-blank worksheet of common proverbs that we had discussed in class. I found this necessary to get them to think about proverbs with which they were familiar, as well as less familiar. They then began designing their own original symbol of a proverb or saying that would later be transferred to Styrofoam for making a printing plate.

We began the second class by reading together and filling out a short answer worksheet of essential questions about adinkra (e.g., who what, where, when, and why). Then I showed the students my original drawn design, my completed printing plate, and a series of four prints that I had made. Some students were astounded that all the prints looked alike. I explained that was the point of printmaking, that an artist could make multiple images of the same picture.

We started making the Styrofoam printing plates, and the focus of the students shifted to the process of making the plates. I had difficulty convincing them of the need to draw large, which is a perennial problem that I attribute to the general low self-esteem of these preadolescent, primarily economically challenged students, and an observation that concurs with a similar finding by Coles (2003). I knew lack of drawing large would affect the quality of their prints, but I figured that the experience of printing, which was novel to them, would outweigh the quality of the product they produced. Although they struggled with their designs, they enjoyed engraving lines with pencils into the Styrofoam (Figures 3–6).

Attempts to Incorporate New Media

Another component of the curriculum was to incorporate new media skills and new media literacy by having students document their responses to the two visiting artists

Figure 4. *A Broken Heart (2011) by Jessica. Collection of Laurie A. Eldridge.*

Figure 5. *Peace (2011) by Maricela. Collection of Laurie A. Eldridge.*

my school because all available computer lab time is used for conducting programs that focus on reading and math.

I had attended a class offered by my school district on how to set up a classroom website. I learned that we only had a certain amount of space we could use on the school district's portal. I found I only had room to load two Photostory projects—a kind of slide presentation of still photos—that I made of my experiences in Ghana so that I could share them with students. There was not additional room to load videos or Photostory projects of visiting artists made by students. Also, my understanding of the class was that students from Ghana and students from my classes would be able to communicate back and forth using a wiki and e-mail. The reality was that the school district only allowed students to communicate with others located on the school district's intranet, and students were not allowed access to the Internet via e-mail or wiki sites.

So to get around the problem, I asked my students to develop questions for students who attended Joy Standard School, a school in Kumasi with which Mariama Ross worked closely. I e-mailed the questions to her; she then shared them with students at Joy Standard. She e-mailed me the Joy Standard students' replies, which I then shared

who came to our school that year. They used a digital camera and a digital video camera, both purchased with grant funds, to demonstrate how art and culture related to the students' local communities could interact with the art and communities from another place in the world (Zimmerman, 2001–2002). I had planned for my students to communicate with students in Ghana, and build a *wiki* together. A wiki is a shared document that can be edited and added to by different wiki members. This is where we started to run into problems. Every school in my district is wired with high speed Internet, but access to the Internet is extremely limited because the district—for safety reasons—does not want students to interact with individuals or groups outside the district's intranet. Art teachers can face greater obstacles than most teachers in their efforts to integrate technology into their curricula (Gregory, 2009). As an art teacher, my classes are not included in the cyclical use of the two computer labs in

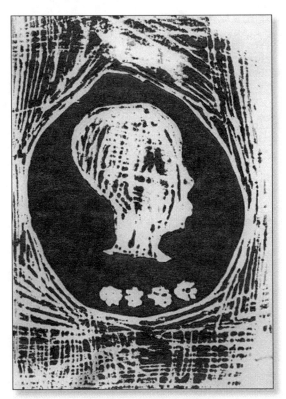

Figure 6. *A Penny for Your Thoughts (2011) by Victoria. Collection of Laurie A. Eldridge.*

with my students. Although this method was clumsy and not as elegant as having students e-mail one another directly, my students did begin to think critically about the use of new media. I asked my students to write short statements about what life was like for them in the United States or draw a picture of something from their daily lives. Then they were asked to write questions for the Ghanaian students to answer.

Students' Ethical Reactions

Several students who were writing statements were concerned that they did not want the Ghanaian students to feel jealous of their lives in the US. I emphasized to all students that life in Ghana was different, not better or worse than life in the US. I asked the students to think about how they phrased their statements and questions, and they worked together collaboratively to develop phrasing that was neutral and not reactionary or stereotyped. All students worked in small groups to develop and select questions to send to Ghana. As a large group, we identified the questions that were repeated and selected those questions that seemed to be on almost everyone's minds. These questions included things like: "What are your favorite foods?" "What ceremonies do you participate in?" "What is it like to live away from your parents?" (Joy Standard is a boarding school.) Questions that were unique, yet insightful, were also selected, such as: "How are women treated in your society?"

My students learned from the Ghanaian students that other people besides those coming from Mexico had to learn English as a second language, that they celebrated different holidays from the US and Mexico, and that they were proud of students who earned good grades. My students also garnered from the responses that the Ghanaian students loved their families and their country.

My students did begin to develop more intercultural competencies as they interacted with students from cultures not their own, both in their classroom and via new media. In one instance, my students became more aware of a peer who was born in Nigeria. They respectfully asked him questions about how he came to America and what life was like in Africa. This young man grew visibly more confident as the curriculum progressed and as the students and I treated him as our resident expert on Africa. I found that he, two other students who were born in Africa, and African American students who were in my middle school art classes welcomed this attention paid to their family origins. My African American students were ignorant of the role that West Africa had

played in American slavery, and one student would turn in my photo album again and again to the pictures of the Cape Coast slave castle after we had discussed the issue of slavery in the US.

My students also learned to work together in a more cooperative manner as they shared responsibility for documenting artists who visited our school. With only one video camera and one still camera, students had to be patient with one another, take turns, and be responsible for equipment and the segment they were documenting.

Part Four: Conclusions

I found that much of what I learned from this experience upholds findings of other scholars concerned with art students becoming culturally literate in a digitally interconnected world. My students had many questions about the artwork created by the Ghanaian artists and their art worlds but they did not once question the Ghanaian artists' abilities, authority, or intelligence due to the color of their skin (Carpenter, 1999).

My students developed their cultural sensitivity as they came to terms with content that conflicted with their initial perceptions of Africa; they began to understand why people from cultures other than their own expressed similar and different beliefs than they did (Carpenter, 1999; Zimmerman, 2001–2002). They found personal meaning in their learning about Ghanaian art by developing their own adinkra symbols derived from their life experiences, rather than merely imitating already existing adinkra symbols (Andrus, 2001).

I learned that, in an increasingly interconnected world, art teachers need to be concerned with content, social context, and development of cultural identity of their students (Davenport, 2000). Art educators have crucial roles to play in promoting tolerance and understanding of diversity of peoples from a variety of cultures and settings around the world (Zimmerman, 2001–2002). They should encourage their students to study about cultures other than their own and view themselves simultaneously as citizens of multicultural societies and as people living in an interconnected world (Zimmerman, 2001–2002). This kind of interculturalism provided my students with the tools to explore cultures and to know about, interact with, and appreciate similarities and differences of others and their customs (Stokrocki, 1999). I believe that I found a way for my students to begin to look beyond the narrow confines of their lives and see themselves as citizens of the world.

REFERENCES

Andrus, L. (2001). The culturally competent art educator. *Art Education, 54*(4), 14–19.

Ballengee Morris, C. B., & Sanders, J. H., III. (2009). Culture, identity, presentation: The economic policies of heritage tourism. *International Journal of Education through Art, 5*(2&3), 129–142.

Bastos, F. M. C. (2006). Border-crossing dialogues: Engaging art education students in cultural research. *Art Education, 59*(4), 20–24.

Blier, S. (2001). Africa, art and history: An introduction. In M. B. Visona, R. Cole & H. M. Harris (Eds.), *A history of art in Africa* (pp. 14–23). New York, NY: Harry N. Abrams.

Carpenter, B. S., II. (1999). Thought on Black art and stereotypes: Visualizing racism. *Journal of Multicultural and Cross-cultural Research in Art Education, 17*, 103–115.

Cole, H. M. (2001). Akan worlds. In M. B. Visona, R. Cole & H. M. Harris (Eds.), *A history of art in Africa* (pp. 194–227). New York, NY: Harry N. Abrams.

Coles, R. (2003). *Children of crisis.* Boston, MA: Back Bay Books.

Davenport, M. (2000). Culture and education: Polishing the lens. *Studies in Art Education, 41*(4), 361–375.

Gregory, D. C. (2009). Boxes with fires: Wisely integrating learning technologies into the art classroom. *Art Education, 62*(3), 47–54.

Kelly, J. (Ed.). (1997). *Adinkra: The cloth that speaks.* Washington, DC: National Museum of African Art.

Picton, J. (1999). Tradition and the 20th century. In N. Fall & J. Pivin (Eds.), *An anthology of African art: The twentieth century* (pp. 329–333). New York, NY: Distributed Art.

Ross, D. H. (1998). Asante: Kingdom of cloth. In D. H. Ross (Ed.), *Wrapped in pride: Ghanaian kente and African American identity* (pp. 31–38). Los Angeles, CA: UCLA Fowler Museum of Cultural History.

Ross, M. (2004). Art at the crossroads: The contested position of indigenous arts in Ghana's post-colonial education system. *Studies in Art Education, 45*(2), 117–134.

Stokrocki, M. (1999). Response to Hernandez' article. *Journal of Multicultural and Cross-cultural Research in Art Education, 17*, 32–34.

Zimmerman, E. (2001-2002). Intercultural art education offers a means to promote tolerance and understanding. *Journal of Cultural Research in Art Education, 19 & 20*, 68–80.

ENDNOTES

[1] The author wishes to thank Mary Stokrocki for her comments on an earlier draft of this paper, and Mariama Ross for her generous hospitality. This project was supported by a grant from the National Art Education Foundation.

[2] Title I schools have over 50% of students receiving free or reduced meals.

[3] Lines are made by combs.

[4] Examples of *adinkra* symbols, with graphics that are free for non-profit, educational use, can be found at www.adinkra.org

[5] The badie or Bridelia Ferrungia tree is indigenous to Africa.

CHAPTER 6

Becoming Empathic Storytellers:
A Curriculum for Developing Cultural Sensitivity

JONATHAN SILVERMAN
Saint Michael's College

> Learning about the other by being the other requires the use of all aspects of memory, the memory of body, mind, and heart, as well as the words. (Smith, 1993, p. xxvii)

Fires in the Mirror, a play by Anna Deveare Smith (1993), portrays a racially provoked incident in Brooklyn, New York City, through 26 characters, all with different perspectives and all performed by one person. This piece inspired me to think how critical it is for each of us to understand one another's viewpoint in order to enrich our own identities within a multicultural and global world. It occurred to me that individual identities are shaped and sustained not only by a collection of aesthetic, ethical, and cultural influences, but also by fear of the unknown, and an unwillingness to look beyond one's own prism. I began to wonder how I might adapt Smith's collage of voices in an educational context where students would use their imaginations, artistic skills, and storytelling to have opportunities to meaningfully experience cultural sensitivity and global understanding.

In this chapter I explore the importance of metaphorically stepping into another's shoes as a catalyst for practicing empathy, storytelling, and aesthetic sensibility. I describe how a curriculum focused on artistically representing stories of others can enhance perception, social responsibility, and global awareness. Many educators speak to how the arts offer a literacy that transcends cultural gaps and empowers students by giving them voice. Shin and Willis (2010) believe that students develop respect and understanding for other cultures when they share stories and are involved with other cultural norms. For Greene (2005), engaging in another's story leads to dialogue where students "come authentically 'face to face'" (p. 79). Similarly, Meban (2009) describes the value of an inter-subjective process where aesthetics make possible sensitive communication and awareness of positionality—the values adopted by a person within a specific social context.

To extend perspectives and values, educators need to create an environment where, as Hiltunen (2008) advocates, students are "able to meet each other and express different points of view" (p. 108). A curriculum built on storytelling enriches perception and empathy and promotes authentic relationships (Osinsky, 2007; Pellish, 2012). For Buschkühle (2010), the first step in expanding cultural worlds is to bridge the boundaries between school and home, and encourage shared vulnerability. He encourages developing a curriculum where sequencing of skills and emotions corresponds with increased perception and imagination. The exchange of positions encourages a movement of consciousness and sensitivity to cultural differences

(Greene, 2005; Hiltunen, 2008; Peralta, 2010) and leads to acquiring habits of mind, such as creativity, empathy, divergent problem solving, communication, and collaboration, that transcend a local experience and extend it to a global perspective (Eisner, 2002; Taylor, 2011).

Description of the Process

As an educator who teaches required courses in both art and elementary licensure programs in higher education, I strive to raise both the cultural and aesthetic awareness of prospective and current teachers. In three courses I teach, Aesthetic Perspectives; Heroes, Art, and Social Justice; and Art, History, and Social Studies, I ask students to think about one of the following: influences on their sense of beauty, a personal hero (not a family member), or what was occurring in their families at specific times in history. My intent in this first lesson, which I label "Cultural Narratives," is for students to revisit their cultural identities formed from such influences as beliefs, rituals, media, religion, neighborhoods, and interactions with others.

Then, each student exchanges his or her story with someone from class they do not know and whose cultural background and perspectives may be very different. I provide guiding questions to help them interview one another, gain access to the other's story, and extract as much detail and emotion as possible. From their field notes and imaginations, students create a narrative of their partner's story using a range of media including

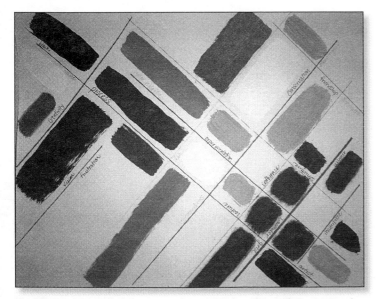

Figure 1. Adele, Visual Poem, acrylics and colored pencils (artist Katelyn Zeigler, photographer Jonathan Silverman). This cultural narrative illustrates a partner's path to artistic, cultural, and social transformation influenced by a relationship with a mentor.

watercolor, paint, sculpture, visual poems, digital montage, and performance (see Figure 1). These interpretations of their partners' cultural narratives are presented during the second and third weeks of class.

This chapter is based on the courses I taught from 2008 through 2012. My sources are reflective papers students submitted as part of the course curriculum, a questionnaire administered to current and former students, in-depth conversations during class critiques, synthesis of end of semester journals, and my own observational journals. I was interested in learning about the students' discoveries through the progressive parts of the lesson that were based on choosing a story to tell, telling that story to a classmate who the person did not know, representing the story of another classmate artistically, witnessing one's own story as told by a partner, and participating actively in the sharing and critiquing of all the stories from class members. In the questionnaire, I requested reactions to how students' experiences influenced their participation in lessons I taught later in the semester. I note that I participated in these cultural narratives as a way of expanding my practice of cultural sensitivity, sharing others' vulnerability and risk, and creating an inclusive and participatory learning environment.

Four recurring themes emerged that cultivate cultural sensitivity through storytelling: awakening the process of creating art; breaking molds to cross cultural boundaries; searching for truth and authenticity; and creating community. Identifying these themes helped me articulate characteristics that may enhance global awareness and, in the future, influence my choices when designing curriculum. Although I primarily focus here on reflections from cultural narratives, I include perceptions on how this lesson initiated a semester-long curriculum in which conceptual and practical skills were developed for increasing global sensitivity. In the following discussion, I identify all students by pseudonyms and I use the pronoun "we" when referring to all class members including myself.

Awakening the Process of Creating Art

At its best, story provides us with ways to see ourselves, ways to affirm our struggles to overcome adversities, ways to reach out to others and forge relationships. (Lester, 2004, p. 49)

Cultural narratives invited students to use their imaginations, compassion, and aesthetic acuity to tell another's story. The idea of portraying another's story was daunting and perplexing; it was not as easy as telling one's own story. We relied on our partner's descriptions and our own experiences as a way to understand context, piece together the puzzle of another's story, and make it our own. We deliberated about how to represent another's cultural identity through images that included people, scenarios, sensory experience, and emotions outside our memory banks. Elementary classroom teacher Rita reflected:

> I imagine any storyteller first has to get to know their characters, whether they're fictional or real, and develop a kind of relationship with them. I needed a physical picture in my head of each person, character traits that summed them up as individuals, and in relation to one another.[1]

Many of us felt intimidated by such a personal process, wanting to be respectful and not make any assumptions or do anything offensive. We all faced a question that author Julius Lester (2004) asks: "How willing am I to exchange my story for someone else's?" (p. 76).

The many media of storytelling chosen for cultural narratives mirrored the diversity of stories being told. As Highwater (1994) reminds us, borrowing stories and the diversity of ways to tell stories open up new visual realities. Many in class referred to an instinct to steer away from typical solutions and explore new possibilities for communicating intent. Robert, a high school media arts teacher, reflected that previously he "never thought about creating a visual poem." A few mentioned how becoming a third party, a conversant, between a partner and the character of a partner's story, helped their art interpretations. Others assumed the role of another's character in order to imagine how to tell the story. We carefully chose

a medium that would uphold the power, tenderness, and sincerity of what we heard. Barbara, an English teacher, felt liberated when she found a flexibility and openness she had been searching for when she created a series of small paintings.

"The mythic dimension of art is its capacity to wrench us away from ourselves" (Highwater, 1994, p. 13). The intersections between stories, creative habits, and composition expanded the students' perceptions. Students engaged actively in processes of creating artwork when they extended their abilities to use their imaginations, critically responded to what they saw and heard, and took risks while facing ambiguity. Robert noted, "Each of us comes in with preconceived notions of color, shapes, and composition." By challenging our artistic preconceptions about creating art, we discovered new ways to meaningfully connect to another's culture, analyze social situations, and communicate openly and sensitively with others.

Art has the language to portray something that otherwise may be inexplicable. Jenna, a community arts educator, remarked: "When you cannot find the words to explain a personal experience or connection, it is the aesthetic experience that allows you to process your innermost feelings and express them in an effective manner." Our cultural narratives became what Bourriaud describes as the "in between" (p. 235, quoted in Illeris, 2005), the means to initiate relational aesthetics that lead to a social construction of communication among a variety of narratives. A shared responsibility for each other's story fos-

For Further Consideration

1. Who are our heroes today and what are their characteristics? What instructional strategies in the arts will help K-12 students meaningfully encounter the dispositions that reflect the best of humanity in a global society?

2. How do we learn the stories of others?
   - How might our discoveries from the stories of others teach us about our self in relation to the world?
   - How might the perspectives of others raise awareness of global issues and cultural sensitivity?
   - How can we be storytellers in visual art?

3. How might the process of telling another's story through art enrich creativity and inquiry?

4. How might art educators foster a caring and thoughtful arts community that nurtures risk taking and authenticity both in making and critiquing artwork?

tered commitment, compassion, and a sense of obligation and honor. After being absorbed by our partner's story we wanted to artistically capture the essence and passion of what the other person experienced and felt.

"Art is about the story. It is not about the facts. And to tell the story, to paint or write it or dance it or compose it, an artist must grasp its mythic dimensions: its subtle shape and its 'virtual meaning'" (Highwater, 1994, p. 12). We used metaphor to bridge contextual, global, and cultural differences to convey a story's accessibility and timeliness. Jenna's deliberate use of crayons illustrated a medium that children "use regularly without fear and the melting of the wax as the increased vulnerability and self-consciousness we feel as we get older" (Figure 2). She also talked about how the melting of colors reflected today's blurred boundaries of cultures. Jacqueline, an arts administrator, fondly recalled her partner's use of a paper collage maze as a metaphor to depict her hero, a middle school student with resiliency and optimism despite severe hardship. "My partner did not pry for depth to these stories, but simply created a piece of art that perfectly depicted my [own] mentee's current reality and a hopeful reality to come." Jacqueline continues to use this metaphor when working with her own student mentee, "navigating the maze with her, widening the walls of hope, and entering a new space of opportunity."

Figure 2. Jacqueline, Faith amidst crayon, *crayons and melted wax (artist Catherine Welch, photographer Jonathan Silverman). The crayons in this cultural narrative are a metaphor for A Wrinkle in Time by Madeleine L'Engle, which inspired a partner's imagination, care for others, and cultural and global understanding. The fingerpainted "faith" represents how connected this partner is to her religion.*

Our artistic choices and use of metaphors brought to life emotions experienced by others and helped initiate a space for authentic interaction.

Breaking Molds to Cross-Cultural and Global Boundaries

Identity is not a question of awareness of the status quo, but a dynamic idea of a person who is constantly subject to a diversity of influences and is thus constantly changing. (Buschkühle, 2010, p. 310)

Many students acknowledged that their understanding of another's story and their ability to retell this story required a change in perspective. Justine, a prospective art teacher, suggested we "broke a mold we may have had in our heads of what society tells us is acceptable. Breaking down these stigmas is one simple way cultural sensitivity is growing and being facilitated." Due to the responsibility of artistically interpreting another's story, each of us had to acknowledge and respect values and customs that might be very different from our own.

The intimacy of being inside another's story helped us practice empathy; we recognized the multidimensionality of an individual and welcomed acceptance despite differences. Consistent with Spehler and Slattery (1999), who see imagination as moving students beyond inhibiting personal boundaries, our cultural narratives asked viewers to peer into another's space and culture and envision social issues from a different lens. Students reflected on how they had to speculate about unfamiliar experiences and emotions from those suffering from Alzheimer's, victims of racial slurs, or immigrants moving from one country to another with a different set of social values. As Abowitz (2007) submits, our aesthetic perceptions became intuitive and ethical as we experienced the social and cultural context of others. By noticing differences and similarities between cultural paradigms and then bringing this awareness into our artistic storytelling, we moved beyond our own provincial boundaries to expand self-knowledge and instill a foundation for global awareness. We became aware of what Adele, a museum educator, suggested is a "small degree of separation between myself and a complete stranger." Rita reminded us that we all have personal values that may not be apparent when meeting and that artmaking can offer literacy that sensitively moves us from one province of knowledge to another. The exchange of stories about immigrants for Jessica, a prospective elementary teacher, helped her distinguish as well as make connections between tailors who arrived from Italy and tailors from China. She gained new insights on gender roles, working habits, materials, fashion, and challenges of assimilation.

Rosa, a prospective art teacher, had a slightly different viewpoint. She confessed how difficult it was to overcome her bias in portraying an immigrant arriving in the United States from Mexico. "I can't help but approach this issue with my baggage of what is going on about Mexico with all the press on drugs, kidnapping, overpopulation, and political corruption." However, she went on to challenge her perception: "This is not a political issue but a human one. I don't think we lend ourselves to any of the dignity of the Mexican culture. Immigrants can feel a strong sense of ambivalence with their choices" (Figure 3).

It seems as if our cultural narratives promoted a transparency that opened doors for the sensitivity needed to both represent the story of others as well as receive our own stories conveyed by our partners.

Figure 3. Rosa, Immigrants journey to the United States, *mixed media collage (artist Kristen Watson, photographer Jonathan Silverman). This is a close up of a cultural narrative collage depicting cultural associations and mixed emotions of an immigrant's passage from Mexico to the United States.*

Searching for Truth and Authenticity

I am a type A artist who believes that everything done must be done well. I felt that my voice must do justice to these others' voices. (Rosa, a prospective art teacher)

Through our cultural narratives we engaged in a multi-layered aesthetic experience; we perceived images being told to us, discerned what and how to artistically represent stories, and found a sense of truthfulness in our communication. Repeatedly students wanted to "get it right." Justine "was afraid of getting something wrong.

This project was a partnership of ideas and expression and I wanted to hold up my end of the bargain." She felt it was her job to be honest and respectful. Knowing that others in the class would be viewing the cultural narratives was intimidating. What others thought mattered to her. Creating co-constructed cultural narratives empowered each of us to care about the perspectives of another, a critical attribute for cultural sensitivity and global understanding.

By assuming the responsibility of "holding" another's story, we wrestled with accuracy and truth. Repeatedly students talked about the multiple levels of trust. One remarked:

> There was trust to share my hero narrative with [Joan]. I trusted [Joan] to accurately portray the strong feelings I have about my hero, and [Joan] trusted me to do the same. We had mutual awareness of how we not only portrayed our heroes but also how others interpret [Sandy].

We listened to a short synopsis of another's life and then had to fill in any gaps. Many of us struggled with how to connect with other people's consciousness, do justice to other voices, and subsequently represent our partner's story accurately without making any inaccurate global generalizations about others' lifestyles. Rita spoke for many of us in confessing she "was hesitant to make any assumptions or do anything offensive." The challenge was to put aside any narrow, preconceived notions based on our own reference points. All of us sought not to fail our partner. The crossing of cultures breeds uncertainty; we felt both confusion and responsibility in our search for cultural truthfulness. Some researched the cultural context in which a story was being told. Jessica, born after John Lennon was murdered, needed to research how he could be perceived as a father figure. Rita had to envision what it was like to be a Korean American raised in Vermont.

We assumed the role of researchers as our task was to be active in "constructing of knowledge through creative exploration and interpretation" (Marshall & D'Adamo, 2011, p. 14). Rosa described her empathic goal "to represent with clarity and respect the context, character, values, and emotional connection conveyed to me." To tell the story we had to move beyond bias, ignorance, and resistance; open ourselves up to research unfamiliar cultural experiences both locally and globally; and delicately bring in our own artistic and cultural context.

The wide range of styles, materials, and compositions in which narratives were being communicated sparked our aesthetic sensibilities. Barbara thought: "The way my story was represented was completely different than what I could have imagined. It was refreshing to see the essence of the character represented in a new imaginative way despite its slight inaccuracy." A few students wrote later that there were shortcomings in their stories as told by their partners that had to do with generational or cultural gaps. Nonetheless, they still appreciated how the artistic renderings captured their stories' essence. Rosa had a different experience. She confessed her artistic bias when viewing a colleague's interpretation:

> My indifference to the piece had to do with my own art baggage—the implication underlying art education is that we as artists will be judged by our mastery of the classical disciplines and that falling short of mastery means that nothing else we produce is as valuable or worth viewing or experiencing.

To alleviate the fear of "rightness" and initiate meaningful conversations about the process and work, I introduced the Critical Response Process (CRP), developed by choreographer Liz Lerman (Lerman & Borstel, 2003). CRP brought authenticity and structure to our communications about our cultural narratives. The process begins with statements of meaning by those responders participating in the critique process. This is followed by the artist asking responders for specific feedback. Then, responders ask the artist questions phrased in a neutral tone with the intent of learning from the artist. Finally, with permission from the artist, responders can offer opinions. By promoting honesty, relevance, and community engagement, the CRP shifted our focus from the particulars of one story to issues that pertain to the human condition and resonate across cultures and countries. We developed a safe place in which to recognize our own biases and misrepresentations, and empowered our sensitivity to honor creative risk taking and storytelling (Buschkühle, 2010).

Creating Community

> I believe the entire class got to know each other in a deeper way through cultural narratives. Not only did it establish trust right from the start, but it helped me feel more open to discussions and activities from a much earlier point in the semester. (George, a high school art teacher)

Cultural narratives immediately attended to the diversity of each class member. The exchange of stories transformed focus from my own individual story to stories from our community. Sandy commented: "The risks we took in telling the story of another encouraged risk-taking in our communication with each other." Students consistently

noted how this lesson forged closer and more comfortable relationships among classmates. As Highwater (1994) suggests: "art is easily grasped as an endowment of the community rather than the property of an individual" (pp. 60-61). The sincerity of empathizing with another and the vulnerability to create and share artistically proved to be, as Robert commented, "a great way for students to learn more about each other, recognize the differences in their unique histories, and also see that they have more in common than they may think." Justine's depiction of her partner's kindergarten teacher included nine small canvases depicting the activities that occur in a kindergarten class. Her baking of 12 individually designed cupcakes representing a classroom of students with different ethnicities, rituals, and values sparked Jenna to comment, "we are all cupcakes in a pan" (Figure 4). Through cultural storytelling we built trust and shared risks. We witnessed our transition from the stereotypic depiction of diversity to a more inclusive and global temperament built on openness and understanding.

Figure 4. Barbara, Imagination and diversity in Kindergarten, acrylic and cupcakes (artist Emily Cseh, photographer Jonathan Silverman). *This student painted a story of an inspiring kindergarten teacher. The small canvases represent various activities, while the cupcakes represent the diversity of students. "We are all cupcakes in a pan," one student commented.*

Stories of heroes, whether a musician singing songs of protest in Europe or Asia, an immigrant brave enough to illegally cross to the US, a beloved children's author writing about a peaceful world, an African American baseball player surrounded by racism, or a child with disability, inspired us with a spectrum of humanity across cultures, global boundaries, and time. Several students remarked how crucial it is to create learning environments where students connect one story to another and develop a sensitivity to make a stand for what they believe in.

Initially, I wondered if I was asking too much too early in my courses. However, several students shared how this project broke habits of communication and immediately led to outside-the-box thinking, interdisciplinary learning, and cross-cultural and global understanding. Students recalled how the intimacy and care for another's story by creating an artistic representation distinguished this exercise from other, more predictable educational experiences as we created a new social dynamic built on trust and sincerity.

Cultural narratives helped establish a strong sense of community early in the semester. This was critical for subsequent curriculum activities focused on empathy, artistic exploration, and global perspective. For example, through museum visits and visual culture critiques that followed the cultural narratives, students transferred their investigation of Other into their viewing of and artistic response to images that offered different perspectives on social norms, space, culture, media, and artistic elements. In addition to attending museum exhibitions, students were assigned to experience a visual culture unfamiliar to them. By synthesizing their art experiences from visiting such places as a Vietnamese street festival, a Vermont Refugee Resettlement Program, a local diner, an Asian grocery store, and a 75-year-old machine repair shop, the students were able to reflect personally on their experiences and broaden their perspectives of other worlds.

Cultural and global narratives provided a foundation for the culminating lesson in my classes, an arts-based community project. Recent projects include bookmaking with children living in a homeless shelter, artistically interpreting seniors' stories of home, and a Claymation video about how to become conscientious consumers in a global society. Cultivating characteristics such as empathy, perception, sensitivity, and imagination through cultural and global narratives and other lessons described above enriched the students' participation and experiences in these arts-based community projects.

Conclusion

What would the world would be like if everyone just listened to one person's story every day? (Rosa, a prospective art teacher)

Joan's cultural narrative and personal reflection speaks to Rosa's belief that by listening to a story we might assume responsibility to coexist in a global world. She first shared how she could have easily printed photos, a medium she works in regularly, to illustrate how the movie *Invisible Children* (Russell, Bailey, & Poole, 2004), about child soldiers in Uganda, influenced her partner. "However, I wanted to get across the filmmakers 'privilege white boy' [sic] qualities and how they managed not to be typical and could make a difference." Joan role-played for us the naïve and precocious adolescent her partner described first sitting in a school assembly, "forced" to watch *Invisible Children*, which she perceived to be another boring film. Then she animated how awakened she was by the film's content. In her follow up discussion on *Invisible Children* Joan reflected, "Uganda is not someone else's worry!"

When we create opportunities to foster the dispositions that lead to the everyday practice of cultural sensitivity, we break boundaries of provincialism and silence and awaken a consciousness of global responsibility (Abowitz, 2007; Greene, 2005; Illeris, 2005). Cultural Narratives is one example of how art educators can initiate a curriculum where students become empathic storytellers and practice the sensitivity to live honestly and openly in a global society.

REFERENCES

Abowitz, K. K. (2007). Moral perception through aesthetics: Engaging imaginations in educational ethics. *Journal of Teacher Education, 58*(4), 287–298.

Buschkühle, C.-P. (2010). Freedom and dignity: Identity through creation. *International Journal of Education through Art, 6*(3), 309–326.

Eisner, E. (2002). *The arts and the creation of mind*. New Haven, CT: Yale University Press.

Greene, M. (2005). Teaching in a moment of crisis: The spaces of imagination. *New Educator, 1*(2), 77–80.

Highwater, J. (1994). *The language of vision: Mediations on myth and metaphor*. New York, NY: Grove Press.

Hiltunen, M. (2008). Community-based art education in the north: A space for agency. In G. Coutts & T. Jokela (Eds.), *Art, community, and environment: Educational perspectives* (pp. 91–112). Bristol, England: Intellect.

Illeris, H. (2005). Young people and contemporary art. *International Journal of Art and Design, 24*(3), 231–242.

Lerman, L., & Borstel, J. (2003). *The critical response process*. Washington, DC: Liz Lerman Dance Exchange.

Lester, J. (2004). *On writing for children & other people*. New York, NY: Penguin.

Marshall, J., & D'Adamo, K. (2011). Art practice as research in the classroom: A new paradigm in art education. *Art Education, 64*(5), 12–18.

Meban, M. (2009). The aesthetic as a process of dialogical interaction: A case of collective art praxis. *Art Education, 62*(6), 33–38.

Osinsky, M. (2007). There's more to heroes than he-man. In W. Au, B. Bigelow & S. Karp (Eds.), *Rethinking our classrooms* (Vol. 1) (pp. 84–85). Milwaukee, WI: Rethinking Schools.

Pellish, J. (2012). Past, present, and future: Stories of identity in an elementary art room. *Art Education, 65*(1), 19–24.

Peralta, A. (2010). The art of storytelling: The co-construction of cultural knowledge. *Art Education, 63*(2), 25–30.

Russell, J., Bailey B., & Poole, L. (Directors). (2004). *Invisible children* [Documentary film]. Retrieved from http://topdocumentaryfilms.com/invisible-children

Shin, R., & Willis, S. (2010). An intercultural learning of similarities and differences of rituals and customs of two cultures. *International Journal of Education through Art, 6*(3), 361–380.

Smith, A. D. (1993). *Fires in the mirror*. New York, NY: Anchor Books.

Spehler, R. M., & Slattery, P. (1999). Voices of imagination: The artist as prophet in the process of social change. *International Journal of Leadership in Education, 2*(1), 1–12.

Taylor, B. (2011). The skills connection between the arts and 21st-century learning. *Education Week, 30*(19), 22, 26.

ENDNOTE

[1] All teacher and student quotations in this chapter are personal communications from classes I taught from 2008 to 2012.

CHAPTER 7

Looking, Creating, and Making It Public:
Strategies for a Globalized Approach to Arts Education

MARIT DEWHURST
City College of New York

JEN SONG
New Museum of Contemporary Art, New York

The visual, material, and information cultures in which we live are complicated, intertwined, and ever evolving. Media coverage of violent conflict fills our television channels; race, class, and gender inequalities are debated on various blogs and social media platforms; partisan politics are the name of the game in many governmental spheres; and intranational migration of people and ideas is constant. To empower students to be thoughtfully engaged citizens within this complexity requires an approach to education that transforms conventional classrooms into spaces for critical thinking and action. Art is often a site for investigating and expressing multiple ways of being that open new avenues for understanding ourselves and our communities. While many educators recognize the importance of providing students with tools to navigate identity, power, and agency in an increasingly interdependent society, they need concrete pedagogical strategies to successfully facilitate such learning.

A Global Perspective Through Contemporary Art

Throughout history, the arts have been deployed across cultures as spaces for social critique, community mobilization, and cultural resistance (Reed, 2005). Serving as cultural critics, artists often draw viewers' attention to the overlapping nature of our world and the unnamed inequities that exist in society. Uniting art with current social concerns, such artists use skills and dispositions they learn through the arts to investigate, critique, and take action against the conditions of inequality and injustice that touch their lives (Cleveland, 1992; Desai & Chalmers, 2007; O'Brien & Little, 1990). As today's artists continue this tradition, nowhere are the intricacies of intersecting identities, power relationships, and social oppression made more visible, or more public, than through contemporary art practices (New Museum, 2010) that can nurture a deeper awareness of global sensitivity amongst both students and educators.

Our desire to teach the skills necessary to collaborate across socially constructed identity barriers, analyze how systems of power influence our daily lives, think creatively about the interdependent nature of the world, and contribute to the creation of a more just and equal society is rooted in an explicitly global view of education. The following strategies for teaching with contemporary art through this global perspective are composed of three layers. First, it is imperative that the *content* of any art lesson draws on artists, artwork, art histories, and art analyses from many vantage points—particularly those often left out of conventional narratives. In addition to inclusion of artists from African, Asian, South American, and Native American contexts, we must also infuse our lessons with viewpoints that represent various race, class, gender, sexual orientation, and ability groups. Second, the *themes* we wrap our lessons around must directly confront the complicated, provocative, layered, and challenging issues of contemporary life. We must not back away from teaching about complex ideas such as migration, the distribution of resources, human rights, homelands, faith, and cultural differences. Third, our *pedagogy* must reflect ways we want our students to engage in the world beyond our classrooms. This global approach to art education moves beyond simply including artists from diverse backgrounds to preparing students to be thoughtful and creative actors within a complex and interdependent world.

Looking to Museum Education

In recent years, many museums have developed multifaceted programs that connect everyday experience, social critique, and creative expression with classroom learning (Cahan & Kocur, 1996). Inspired by the participatory and critical nature of learning in such spaces, we draw on museum education practices emphasizing object-based, experiential, and inquiry-based learning, museum education practices that can provide both in-school and out-of-school educators with practical tools to navigate global awareness through contemporary art. Rooted in close observation of works of art and artistic processes, these tools enable learners to develop critical analytic skills, experiment with creative expression, and consider the public nature of art today. In the sections that follow, we outline three strategies, with examples from our own teaching practices, for engaging in a globally aware and critical approach to learning that can be adapted for a variety of settings.

Beginning with exercises for looking at works of art, we highlight several *questioning strategies* that explore issues of global identity and cultural understanding while promoting critical thinking and evidential reasoning. In analyzing how contemporary artists create works of art,

we suggest ways to facilitate *open-ended artmaking* with students. Finally, we introduce how the act of *taking art to the public domain* can enable young people to see art as a tool for participating and transforming the world around them.

Strategy 1: Inquiry-Based Questioning

Many an educator would agree that questioning is a powerful process of both learning and teaching that can empower students as learners, and prepare them to actively engage in the world. While there are many ways to incorporate questioning strategies in the classroom, few are as empowering or able to promote expansive thinking as those provided by inquiry-based teaching. Driven by the use of open-ended questions, in inquiry-based teaching, "there's no one right answer, since the purpose is to elicit students' thoughts, and then help them examine their thinking" (Schmidt, 2004, p. 93). This approach can encourage students to engage in the kind of flexible thinking, consideration of others' perspectives, analysis of social and cultural constructs, and imaginative problem-solving required to develop the ability to participate in a more global society.

Suggestions for Implementation

The following suggestions for generating questions offer educators useful techniques for application in any arts learning setting.

Create an environment for discussion. Invite students to share their responses to artworks. Encourage them to listen and respond to each other's observations. Stress that students' own comments are welcomed and that right or wrong interpretations are not expected. Set aside time for conversations to unfold, so unexpected directions can be explored. Continue to foster a culture of dialogue by making discussion about works of art a part of regular classroom practice.

Use language that encourages and invites student-directed discussion and interpretation. Avoid convergent questions that shut down dialogue or imply a right or wrong answer (i.e., "Is the artist making a political statement?"). Craft empowering questions that encourage students to use critical thinking to speculate, connect, and deduce about an artwork (i.e., "What do you think the artist might have intended here?"). Avoid assumptions about knowledge or experience that could discourage students from engaging (i.e., "What do you notice about the painting's composition?" might alienate students who are unfamiliar with technical vocabulary and lack previous knowledge). Tap into students' prior knowledge and opinions (i.e., "What have we learned about conflict in Lebanon that might help us understand this artist's message?").

Vary questions for dialogue to create multiple points of entry. Draw on a range of question types to invite different types of responses for all types of learners. Begin with questions about observations that can be answered by anyone without any prior knowledge (i.e., "What do you notice about the color red?"). Introduce questions that encourage interpretation (i.e., "What might the use of red symbolize? Do you think it is the same for all cultures?") and imaginative thinking (i.e., "What do you imagine these figures might say to one another?"). Encourage debate and inquiry as you challenge students to ask questions of each other and challenge their own and their peers' interpretations in a thoughtful and productive manner.

Scaffold questions to drive growth in understanding of objects and concepts over time.
Sequence questions to begin with observational, more apparent questions that lay the groundwork for more complex interpretative questions. Increasingly incorporate relevant information into the conversation in accessible bite-size chunks as a way to scaffold understanding of the object over time. Employ questions that encourage students to synthesize what has been said and to build on that knowledge. Encourage students to reflect on their own interpretations to discern information about their own responses (i.e., "So far, we've explored what we think the figure's dress reveals about his personality; are there any other visual elements in the painting that complement or counter our interpretation?").

Guide students toward self to world connections. Relate questions to personal experience by making connections to local information, contemporary issues impacting students, developmentally relevant experiences, and specific knowledge about students' interests. Reflect on the issues of cultural relativity rooted in students' own experiences (i.e., "What forums allow us to express our opinions about current events? What does this artist do to convey his dissatisfaction with local politics?"). Deploy theme-based questions to draw connections between personal experience and concepts and themes embedded in artwork addressing global concerns (i.e., "What overlapping *communities* do we belong to? What does this artist include in her work to convey a sense of *community*, and at the same time, challenge it?").

Focus object. *Obama Skirt Project* (2009) by Aisha Cousins (see Figure 1)

Relevant information. An African American performance artist who lives in Brooklyn, New York City, Aisha Cousins often addresses ideas of beauty, black culture, and social change in her D.I.Y. (Do-It-Yourself) public art projects. Inspired by the election of Barack Obama, Cousins engaged in a performance art piece in which she collected fabric from Sub-Saharan Africa printed with Obama's image to design dresses that she wore for a full year. After the first year of this project, Cousins has continued to recruit additional "Obama Skirters" to participate in her performance art.

1. Begin with simple observational questions about Aisha Cousins' *Obama Skirt Project*: What's going on in this work? What do you notice?

2. As students describe the images, encourage them to provide evidential reasoning as their interpretation evolves: What does the artist include in her work that conveys a sense of identity? What is similar or different between the images?

3. Incorporate information to drive the conversation along: Aisha Cousins wore dresses made from African fabrics printed with Barack Obama's image every day for 1 year beginning on July 19, 2009. Made in Nigeria, Ghana, Mali, South Africa, and Tanzania, the fabrics were converted into dresses by designers living in Cousins' neighborhood, many of whom were African immigrants. The tradition of wearing black presidents on clothing, a common African practice, began in the

Figure 1. From Here I Saw What Happened and I Could Not Understand (a.k.a. The Obama Skirt Project), *Aisha Cousins. Courtesy of the artist.*

1960s as African countries gained independence and began electing black leaders into office.

4. Ask follow-up questions and move students toward interpretation: What message do you think Cousins might be expressing through her choice of clothing? How does Cousins draw on the cultural practices of one nation and integrate them into her own lifestyle and culture? What impact might Cousins' dress have on viewers, initially and over time?

5. Encourage students to use their imaginations: What questions would you ask the artist if you could have a conversation with her? If you could choose a public figure to wear on your clothes every day for 1 year, who would it be and why? What other cultural practices do you know of that celebrate public figures? Which of those practices would you adapt for use in your own life and how?

6. Have students make connections to their own personal experiences: How does our dress or style of dress define our identity? What role does dress play in determining social identity or culture? How do images of public figures circulate in our lives? What messages are sent about these public figures and how?

7. Draw connections between cultures: How does dress relate to individual, local, national, or other kinds of identity? What dress customs do you know of that exist in other countries? What are similarities and differences in these customs? What would happen if you adopted those dress customs from another culture in your own life, immediately or over time? What customs or methods do we have to celebrate or show our support of public figures?

8. Facilitate a final synthesis and reflection: What surprised you most about Cousins' project? How do you think people responded to Cousins and her outfits?

9. Encourage further investigation into an artist's work or practice: Cousins' artistic practice includes performance projects that cut across cultures to draw on ritual and custom and explore issues of identity formation, gender stereotypes, and nation-building. Examine other projects by Cousins and identify unifying themes in her work.

Strategy 2: Open-Ended Artmaking

In analyzing how contemporary artists create works of art, we explore ways to facilitate open-ended artmaking with students that encourages critical analysis and a sense of agency. Open-ended artmaking empowers students to pursue their own artistic inquiry by allowing them to take ownership of as many creative decisions as possible. As Douglas and Jaquith (2009) write, "choice-based art education provides for the development of artistic behaviors by enabling students to discover what it means to be an artist through the *authentic* creation of

For Further Consideration

1. What strategies might educators use to engage young people in social critique or cultural resistance through analysis of contemporary art?

   - What types of questions might be asked?
   - How might students test their interpretations for accuracy?
   - How can artmaking be understood and enacted as social critique?
   - How do contemporary artists address current social issues in their artwork?
   - How does the use of contemporary art in the classroom create opportunities for youth empowerment?
   - How are others engaged in social critique through art?

2. What local artists or cultural resources might educators bring into the classroom to encourage discussions of identity, power, or agency?

   - What unfamiliar (foreign or invisible) cultural groups might be brought into these discussions? How might they be invited to participate in these discussions?
   - How might these discussions relate to or open students to ways of being in a global world?

artwork" (p. 3). Departing from conventional approaches to arts education wherein the teacher sets out a specific step-by-step process to making a preconceived work of art, this open-ended view of artmaking encourages students to creatively identify and solve their own projects—a much-needed skill in a world in which there are no cookie cutter solutions to our complex challenges. This encourages students to think critically about materials and artistic processes as they make decisions about their own artwork—another shift that allows them to develop an ability to see how different choices have different outcomes based on an original vision.

If we combine these open-ended or choice-based approaches to making art with a focus on real life global issues, we create spaces for learning that encourage young people to analyze and make sense of the world around them. When that investigation relates to generative concerns in their own lives—be it environmental sustainability, body image, educational inequality, family relationships, or even the economies of fashion––young people can engage in a similar critical artistic inquiry as found in global art practices today. If we want to create opportunities for learning that are intriguing and challenging for our students, we must root those lessons in their own lives and let them take ownership of their own artistic inquiry.

Suggestions for Implementation

To develop an open-ended artmaking project, educators must be willing and able to relinquish some control over the development of students' artworks. While this ability will vary based on the context in which the art takes place (e.g., after-school or museum settings tend to allow for greater freedom of expression), the following suggestions offer some guidelines on how to approach open-ended artmaking.

Identify a generative idea or theme to guide artwork. To provide some focus and cohesion for students, it is useful to offer a general theme or idea around which to base their artwork (e.g., transformation, contradictory identities, balance, provocation, humor, etc.). These themes should evoke many ideas and allow space for multiple interpretations. Based on the theme, educators can identify learning goals that encourage students to examine how these themes impact their lives.

Show multiple examples of how diverse artists have created work around the same theme. To inspire students to think broadly about how they can create artwork around a given theme, use examples from artists that show diversity of materials, opinions, or messages expressed; global cultural contexts; and historical perspectives. These artist examples should be chosen specifically to expand and challenge students' perceptions about the range of possible forms their own artmaking can take.

Provide an assortment of materials and artistic techniques from which students can choose. Offer short demonstrations about a select number of techniques and allow students to choose their own working materials. Once students have chosen their materials, provide more in-depth instruction on the uses of these materials. Encourage students to experiment with one material and then try to create a similar image with a different material so they learn to critique the advantages of each material.

Emphasize process and encourage revision. Discuss the importance of process with students as an important and unpredictable part of making art. Share stories about experimentation and how artists turn mistakes into new ways of working in the arts. Provide opportunities to revise work through regular critiques—both individually and collaboratively. Use conversations about revision to help students solidify the ideas they want to convey in their art by reflecting on how audiences in other cultures around the world might interpret their work.

Sample Activity

Focus object. *La Femme libérée américaine dans les années 70 (Liberated American Woman in the 1970s)* by Samuel Fosso (see Figure 2)

Relevant information. Born in Camaroon, Fosso moved from Nigeria to Biangui in the Central African Republic to escape the Biafran war in 1972. There, Fosso apprenticed to a photographer and opened his own portrait studio at the age of 13. Not wanting to waste leftover camera film, Fosso began a self-portraiture practice that involves elaborate tableaus featuring the artist in real and imagined positions, and merges identity politics with an eclectic range of sociopolitical and cultural references.

1. Using the questioning strategies described in this chapter, guide students through a discussion about the ways in which Fosso performs, questions, and challenges identity in his work. Draw attention to different cultural conventions and uses of photography, the impact of posed studio photography versus candid family documentation, and the concept of truth and

Figure 2. La Femme libérée américaine dans les années 70 (Liberated American Woman in the 1970s), *Samuel Fosso. Courtesy of the artist and Jack Shainman Gallery, New York.*

Figure 3. Le Chef (qui a vendu l'Afrique aux colons), *Samuel Fosso. Courtesy of the artist and Jack Shainman Gallery, New York.*

fiction in photographic practices. Discuss why an artist might draw on photographic traditions outside of his or her own cultural experience and how the artistic decisions artists make can convey additional meaning through their work.

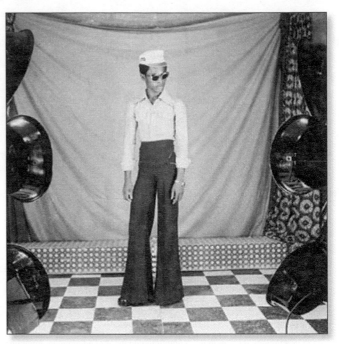

Figure 4. Autoportrait des anneés 70, *Samuel Fosso. Courtesy of the artist and Jack Shainman Gallery, New York.*

2. Have students identify aspects of identity that they wish to draw attention to, question, provoke, or analyze. Consider facilitating a freewrite assignment to encourage deeper thinking about the concept of identity.

3. Have students investigate the cultural role of photography in their own lives. When are photographs taken? By whom and for what purpose? How do we prepare for photographs? What do they typically seek to emphasize? As an additional option, have students research the history of photography in another context as a comparison.

4. Demonstrate various techniques drawn from different traditions of photography to create and manipulate images: for example, painted backdrops similar to West African traditions, or costumes of the early American West.

5. Allow students to choose the most appropriate photographic tools needed to construct three different self-portraits that question, highlight, or perform a specific aspect of identity.

6. Upon completion, lead students through a guided conversation about their work: What photographic tools did they choose and what messages are conveyed through those tools? How does their own culture's use of photography impact their decisions? What other

cultural conventions of photography might they draw on and how would that impact their work? What aspects of identity did they focus on and why? What identity markers did they choose and why?

Strategy 3: Making Art Public

Finally, we introduce how the act of bringing art to the public domain can empower young people to see art as a tool for participating in and transforming the world around them. When we create spaces for young people to share their art with a wider audience, we not only validate the importance of their work, we also provide avenues for others to truly listen to youth perspectives. Opening such spaces is a tool to nurture dialogue about complex social issues across barriers of difference, thus modeling how we want students to engage in the wider world. In recent years, contemporary artists have increasingly found ways to make their work more accessible to a larger public audience through street art, performance art, interventionist practices, and relational aesthetics, a move that has opened up important discourses about the role of art in creating social change (Quinn, Ploof, & Hochtritt, 2012).

When art enters the public sphere it invites engagement. This engagement creates a space where both students and audience members can learn from each other; learning expands to include both creators and viewers. This shift is significant in that it opens up the possibility for wider social change. As Dewhurst (2010) writes,

> Art that is created to challenge or change injustices must be allowed to leave the confines of the room in which it was made in order to reach the intended impacts of the artist. This step can open up avenues for students and educators to be sensitive to criticism and censorship, whereas to lock it up is to prevent the work from actually influencing inequality and therefore really becoming activist art. (p. 12)

Drawing on contemporary global art practices, the move to bring art to the public sphere shows students how their work can have a lasting impact beyond the classroom. In addition to honoring the voices and perspectives of young artists, public art exhibitions or interventions give audiences a chance to better understand, communicate with, and potentially collaborate with young people as they re-envision the world around them.

Suggestions for Implementation

Identify an audience early on in the artmaking process. Encourage students to identify a specific audience for their artwork based on the theme and ideas they would like to convey. Have students interview family,

friends, and community members to determine the best audience for their work. Use this imagined audience to guide conversations about revision (for example, lead role plays where students act as audience members).

Prepare the audience and the artists. Research the history, cultures, and perspectives of the intended audience. Work with local community organizations to find a relevant site to share student work—ideally for a wide public audience. Discuss possible surprises and expectations that both students and audience members might have. Prepare an orientation for audience members (either written or verbal) that introduces the context for student work (i.e., program hand-out, exhibition text, online statement, artist statement, etc.). Consider the possibility of hosting an informal talk-back or panel to accompany the exhibition or performance of student work.

Share widely. Take advantage of many online venues to share artwork beyond immediate community limits. Ensure you have student and parental/guardian permission prior to posting images online, and credit students appropriately. Using social media platforms to share images of student work can allow for additional public interaction with artwork when local, national, and international audiences can leave comments or post responses.

Document responses for further reflection. Discuss with students possible ways to document their own and audiences' responses to making their work public. This may take the form of video, photography, or simply leaving comment boxes or Post-it notes available for feedback. At the completion of the project, these documentation sources can be used to analyze and reflect on the artwork, perhaps opening up ideas for further artmaking or activism in global contexts in their local communities and beyond.

Sample Activity

Focus object. *Brinco* (2006) by Judi Werthein

Relevant information. For *Brinco*—meaning "jump" in Spanish—Werthein, an Argentinean-born, New York City-based artist, created border-crossing sneakers to help illegal immigrants cross from Mexico into the United States. Accessorized with useful items such as a compass, medicine, and a map of popular border crossing points and decorated with protection symbols, the shoes were both sold as art objects and distributed to potential illegal immigrants for free.

1. Using the questioning strategies described in this chapter, guide students through a discussion of Werthein's *Brinco*. Ask students to report to each other on recent legislation involving restrictions on immigration to the United States. Focus on the ways in which the artist intervenes in the public through her work. Encourage students to reflect on how the world's political and social borders are constructed, and bring to light any recent shifts and their associated conflicts. Examine the concept of borders, including personal, local, national, and global borders. Identify the borders—real, perceived, constructed, abstract, and physical—in students' lives. Engage students in a debate that advocates for or against Werthein's project.

2. Create a collaborative definition of public intervention art through a discussion of the roles of the artist, the artwork, and the audience. Include a discussion of the nature of such art (i.e., "What makes it art? Where is the art? How might definitions of public or intervention art shift based on the culture in which it takes place?").

3. Examine closely the borders that they experience in their own lives. Conduct research about one (or more) of these borders. Consider asking who created the border, what its history, characteristics, strengths, and weakness are, and if and how this border has been transgressed.

4. Create an object or intervention that draws attention to, crosses, or dismantles this border. Strategize where it must be displayed and who must see it in order to impact the border.

5. Write a brief contextual statement for the intended audience, describing the work.

6. If the works cannot be publicly performed or displayed, consider online platforms so that they can be viewed in a variety of contexts.

Conclusion

Contemporary art offers educators a practical medium through which we can empower learners to creatively grapple with complex ideas about our world. As museum educators we offer several useful pedagogical strategies that encourage learners to consider multiple perspectives, articulate their own views, and participate in public dialogues that can shape their understanding and ability to be thoughtful agents of change in society. Guided investigations of artworks by Aisha Cousins, Samuel Fosso, Judith Werthein, and many other contemporary

artists can provide learners with unique perspectives on inequality, cultural awareness, and social activism.[1] Tapping into these powerful sites of contemporary cultural expression can empower students to both analyze the social structures and events around them, and also begin to imagine and create new ways of being in this increasingly globalized world in which we live.

REFERENCES

Cahan, S., & Kocur, Z. (Eds.). (1996). *Contemporary art and multicultural education*. New York, NY: New Museum of Contemporary Art, Routledge.

Cleveland, W. (1992). *Art in other places: Artists at work in America's community and social institutions*. Westport, CT: Praeger.

Desai, D., & Chalmers, G. (2007). Notes for a dialogue on art education in critical times. *Art Education, 60*(5), 6–12.

Dewhurst, M. (2010). An inevitable question: Exploring the defining features of social justice art education. *Art Education, 63*(5), 6–14.

Douglas, K., & Jaquith, D. (2009). *Engaging learners through artmaking: Choice-based art education in the classroom*. New York, NY: Teacher's College Press.

New Museum. (2010). *Rethinking contemporary art and multicultural education*. New York, NY: Routledge.

O'Brien, M., & Little, C. (1990). *Reimaging America: The arts of social change*. Philadelphia, PA: New Society.

Quinn, T., Ploof, J., & Hochtritt, L. (2012). *Art and social justice education: Culture as commons*. New York, NY: Routledge.

Reed, T. V. (2005). *The art of protest: Culture and activism from the civil rights movement to the streets of Seattle*. Minneapolis: University of Minnesota Press.

Schmidt, L. (2004). *Classroom confidential: The 12 secrets of great teachers*. Portsmouth, NH: Heinemann.

ENDNOTE

[1] Cousins, Fosso, and Werthein reflect a small margin of international artists suitable as entry points for discussing issues of cultural sensitivity in the global world. Other artists—like Hasan Elahi, Cao Fei, Carlos Garaoica, Emily Jacir, Wangechi Mutu, Rivane Neunschwander, and Walid Raad, to name a few—deal with complex issues related to social, political, and global identity formation. To research contemporary artists dealing with global themes, educators might turn to online web resources, artist databases, and local museum exhibitions.

CHAPTER 8

The Story of Doris:
Cultural Sensitivity in Action

PAMELA STEPHENS
Northern Arizona University

In this chapter I report how I followed an at-risk Navajo student as she successfully navigated the complexities of a post-secondary art education program and, in the process, became a role model of cultural sensitivity for her peers. Here is the story of Doris.[1]

The impact of social and cultural differences for this young woman—typical for many American Indian students—posed significant challenges, ranging from limited classroom participation to constrained interactions with peers and instructors. These challenges, which Doris slowly overcame, I discovered to be mostly related to what Apthorp, Kinner, and Enríquez-Olmos (2005) refer to as "cultural duality, learning to live in two or more worlds" (p. 3).

A positive shift occurred at about the midpoint in Doris's academic career when she was classified as a junior. This shift, it seems, came about in large part as interpersonal behaviors between Doris and her non-Navajo peers strengthened. An unexpected richness unfolded as group members explored artworks from diverse cultures around the world and began to understand and compassionately value each other's traditions and beliefs. From a tenuous start with expected failure, Doris stepped forward to become a student for others to emulate.

As with any educational environment, Doris's ultimate success relied upon a variety of contextual factors. One such factor was a sense of shared community. Another factor was a climate of cultural exchange without fear of prejudice, reprisal, or derision. Kofi Annan, former Secretary-General of the United Nations, succinctly described global benefits of such an environment when he stated, "we can thrive in our own tradition, even as we learn from others, and come to respect their teachings" (2001, para. 27).

Opening to a Wider Vision

In reflecting upon Annan's statement, the larger question for educators is: How do we embed these ideas to guide our students toward this global ideal? How do we instill in our students awareness and unbiased attitudes toward those worldwide who are unlike them? How do we go beyond stereotypes that popular culture would have us believe? Doris's story shows one clear path toward cultural sensitivity, a path that ultimately led to her personal success while awakening her peers to be more thoughtful toward individuals whose heritages and belief systems flow counter to the majority—not only in their own classroom, but globally as well.

To begin this important journey toward cultural sensitivity, I first set forth what cultural sensitivity means to me. In *Building Cultural Bridges* (Stafford, Bowman, Ewing, Hanna, & Lopez-DeFede, 1997), the phrase is defined as being aware that cultural differences and similarities exist and have an effect on values, learning, and behaviors. As the authors point out, being aware is only a part of the equation. Cultural sensitivity suggests an environment with a focus on curiosity and respect that investigates shared and diverse interests, encourages thoughtful listening, and venerates reciprocal compassion.

Figure 1. Southwest Landscape. *Photograph courtesy of Libby Cluett.*

Context: A Sharp Contrast in Place

Doris was born in Colorado, where she lived until she was about 15. Desiring to know more about her Navajo roots, Doris moved to the Navajo Nation, a semi-autonomous territory governed by Native American councils. Occupying a portion of Arizona, New Mexico, and Utah, the Navajo Nation covers some 27,000 square miles and is roughly equal to the combined size of Massachusetts, Connecticut, and Rhode Island. The Navajo Nation (also known as the Navajo Reservation or simply the Reservation) boasts the largest federally recognized tribe in the United States (Kehoe, 2005). The economy of the Navajo Nation traditionally relies upon sheep and cattle ranching, wool production, weaving, silversmithing, and manufacture of crafts. Coal mining and wind farming also contribute to the economy. Because advancement opportunities are somewhat limited for many Reservation residents, relocation is often required. Moving away from the largely rural atmosphere of the Reservation to a city setting then becomes a balancing act of honoring tradition, beliefs, and heritage while at the same time assimilating as a minority into an unfamiliar urban environment. It should be noted that rural-to-urban migration is not isolated to the US. Most apparent is the recent influx of Chinese citizens moving from poor villages and farms into flourishing industrialized cities such as Beijing and Guangzhou. Personal sacrifice, adaptability, and perseverance are part and parcel of financial advancement for Chinese who move from the countryside into municipalities (Loyalka, 2012). The distinct differences between quiet, bucolic settings and noisy, crowded cities in China are parallel to rural and urban environs in the US (Figures 1 and 2). Such is the case in Northern Arizona.

In close proximity to the southwest border of the Navajo Nation is Flagstaff, Arizona. Although the city is physically near the Reservation, it has been said that the two places are philosophically as unlike as distant foreign countries. Significant underlying factors leading to an

Figure 2. Flagstaff. *Photograph courtesy of Matt Kirkpatrick.*

alien feeling are the difference in noise levels and methods of communication. The pastoral atmosphere of the Reservation is generally quiet and "talking is kept to a minimum" (Morales, 2007). Without sounds such as constant conversation, heavy traffic, or background music in shopping malls, life on the Navajo Nation stands in sharp contrast to noisy life in town.

Positioned at the base of Humphreys Peak—the highest natural point in Arizona and one of four sacred mountains for the Navajo—Flagstaff is home to a large population of Native Americans. Demographic data from 2010 indicates the population of Flagstaff as 65,870 individuals (United States Census Bureau, 2010). Of that population, 73.4% identify as Anglo and 11.7% identify as Native American. The U.S. Census does not specify tribal affiliation; however, the nearby proximity of the Navajo Nation and the Hopi Reservation suggests that the majority of those individuals identifying as Native American in Flagstaff are from one of these two tribes. This same demographic data shows that Flagstaff has more than twice the overall percentage of individuals who identify as Native American than any other city in Arizona, further suggesting that the city holds a certain allure for financial and personal advancement outside of the Reservation. Besides wage-paying jobs, Flagstaff offers a four-year state university. It is in the latter environment where Doris met her success and shared it with others.

Background: Understanding Doris

Not unlike their counterparts from around the world, a variety of factors can influence whether Navajo students pursue secondary and post-secondary education. One such factor is the Navajo philosophy known as Blessingway. Dykeman (2004) points out that Blessingway "regards change as a fundamental aspect of tradition" (p. 1) and reflects an adaptability of the Navajo culture to environmental change related to mobility. Another significant factor at play is the Navajo tradition of parents allowing children to self-determine their adult paths. Navajo children often are left to decide whether they will attend school and complete a K-12 or post-secondary education (Frankland, Turnbull, Wehmeyer, & Blackmountain, 2004). These two factors (among others) colored Doris's decision to leave the familiar surroundings of the Reservation to embark upon what she eventually decided would be her educational path.

As a high school student, Doris had the option of attending classes at a traditional secondary campus or a boarding school (both located on the Reservation). Based upon stories she had heard about Reservation boarding schools, Doris decided upon the traditional campus. The traditional campus proved a challenge. Doris became rebellious. As a result of continued insubordination, Doris was labeled as an at-risk student. During her senior year, Doris returned to Colorado where she enrolled in an alternative high school. Not long after enrolling in the alternative high school, Doris discovered the root of her academic and behavioral problems likely stemmed from a mild learning disorder that manifested in poor reading comprehension. It was during this time that the art classroom quickly became an academic safe harbor for Doris; it was a place where she could explore her interests and discover success. When the art teacher suggested that she consider becoming an art educator, Doris's immediate reaction was that she had no desire to deal with unruly teenagers such as herself. Although she wanted to pursue a post-secondary career in art, teaching was not the first option Doris entertained.

Through diligence and hard work, Doris managed to graduate from high school a semester early; however, circumstances following graduation prevented Doris from immediately entering a university program. Instead, she found herself needing to work to help support her mother. It was during the years following high school graduation that Doris came to realize the wisdom of her art teacher's suggestion. Working in a retail store where she frequently was required to educate customers about products being sold, Doris began to realize that she had some innate teaching skills. After some heartfelt soul searching, Doris decided to combine her love of art with her teaching inclinations; she decided to become an art teacher. Determined to make a positive difference in the lives of Navajo students, Doris enrolled as an art education major with the intent of eventually returning to the Reservation to teach (a goal that she has since reached). Of utmost importance to Doris was making a positive difference in the lives of Navajo students. It was this sort of empathy that soon carried over into the preservice art education classroom.

Doris entered the art education program four years after receiving her high school diploma. As such, she was a few years older than most beginning students. She came into the classroom ever so quietly that first day, a consequence of cultural conditioning that values solitude. There was nothing overtly remarkable about Doris as she began her art education studies, nothing that set her apart from the other slightly nervous students embarking on their careers as art educators. During subsequent semesters, however, Doris's peers grew in self-confidence and became more outspoken as they frequently engaged in debate or questioned each other and me, their art education instructor. Meanwhile, Doris maintained her quiet, respectful, and introspective manner while occasionally offering a well-measured comment or sly joke accompanied by a broad smile. Doris, along with her classmates,[2] was growing in self-confidence and knowledge, but she expressed that self-confidence and knowledge in a different way than her colleagues. The impact of her story would soon unfold.

The Turning Point

The Global Learning Subcommittee of the Task Force on Global Education at Northern Arizona University suggests that curriculum is the most direct and profound method by which values can be embodied in programmatic activities related to important issues such as cultural diversity and global engagement (Northern Arizona University Faculty Senate, 2010). While diversity covers ideas such as mutual respect and valuing of differences, global engagement involves civic contributions that individuals make toward a common domestic or international good. In essence, global engagement encourages individuals to question how they see, connect to, and interact with others worldwide. One way to foster global engagement with students is through meaningful curricula that value curiosity about others, provide opportunities for discovery, and contribute to development of partnerships. It was through an art education curriculum developed by Doris that she and her classmates were able to connect in a deep and significant way. In fact, this was the turning point for Doris that elevated her from a former at-risk position to excelling.

It was one of those days that teachers hope to experience: a day when students have an all-important moment of shared cognition—an awakening, if you will. At the heart of the awakening was Doris. The signature assignment for the course in which Doris was enrolled was development and presentation of an art-based unit of study. Doris chose for her unit of study a selection of paintings created by a well-known and highly acclaimed contemporary Navajo artist, Shonto Begay. The content of Begay's

paintings (O'Hern, 2011) is a rich source of information that non-Navajo viewers likely find unfamiliar. With this visual armament, Doris led a low-key charge that at once informed her audience about misunderstandings related to her Navajo heritage while guiding the group to consider the folly of looking solely through the lens of their own social or ethnic backgrounds to interpret artwork created by artists from other cultures and places, whether local, national, or global.

Projected onto the interactive digital white board was a painting of a group of young Navajo gathered outdoors. Doris began her lesson by urging her classmates to describe what was seen in the painting, *Since Night's Victory* (see O'Hern, 2011, p. 55), then to search for evidence to determine what each clue could possibly mean. Looking at the painting through their individual filters, students discovered the obvious: shoes, yucca stems, nighttime, and what appeared to be some sort of game in progress. Doris listened attentively without comment to each response. Of no surprise, the responses were tempered by each student's own somewhat skewed understanding of Navajo traditions and beliefs. Basing their responses upon personal experiences and preconceived

For Further Consideration

1. If you are an in-service teacher, consider who your students are in terms of their cultural backgrounds; if you are a preservice student in a teacher education program, consider the cultural backgrounds of your peers.
   - Where are they from and where do they live now? What is their cultural background and how does that compare to the backgrounds of others in the (past or present) geographic community?
   - How will you find out?

2. What does this information tell you about your students (or your peers) and how they might learn?
   - What are the dangers in assuming students will learn in a way that reflects what you discover or know to be true of their cultural backgrounds? How will you counter assumptions with knowledge?

3. How will you use this knowledge to design an environment that supports the learning of all your students?
   - Can one environment support students who approach learning from differing perspectives and/or have diverse learning needs?
   - Describe features of the learning environment that would be adaptable or applicable to those who approach learning differently.
   - Is the design practical? (Can it be done given the restrictions and constraints of teaching?)

4. Why do you think your design will work well?
   - How will you know it is (or is not) successful?
   - How might you modify the design of your teaching environment if it does not work for all students?

ideas, the students' interpretations were far afield from what the painting actually depicted.

At this point Doris interjected vital information to guide her peers to deeper understanding. Games in Navajo culture, she explained, are sometimes more related to ceremonies than play time and, as such, communicate principles, beliefs, and traditions from one Navajo generation to the next. It should be noted that games as methods of instruction are not unique to the Navajo culture. A variety of games used as teaching tools exist throughout the world. For example, on the first night of each New Year Romania children make "bridges" from small tree branches to symbolize connections between the old and new in an effort to dream about destiny. Oral storytelling, Doris added, also is a part of the Navajo tradition. Like storytelling from India and the African continent, the rich custom keeps alive important cultural narratives that might otherwise be lost. Begay's paintings, like oral storytelling, are a way of recording and sharing ideas about the contemporary Navajo way of life.

Doris then went on to explain that shown in *Since Night's Victory* is *Keshjee'*—also known as the shoe game ("Navajo Stories of Gaming," 2008). A betting game played only in winter when the animals are asleep, *Keshjee'* pits two teams against each other. Objects required for this ceremonial game include a ball created from a yucca root, a cedar branch, yucca stems, and four shoes. The ball is hidden inside one shoe and then all the shoes are buried in sand. Teams take turns betting in which shoe the ball is hidden. When a shoe is chosen it is struck with the cedar branch. Far from being simply a game, *Keshjee'* ceremoniously retells how the cycles of day and night came to be and how natural order cannot be altered. The game itself encourages life lessons of teamwork, loyalty, and fair play.

Following Doris's presentation, noticeable changes occurred in Doris and her peers. Doris, although still respectfully quiet in class, participated more than before. Although they sometimes needed prompting, her classmates began to be more thoughtful about accepting at face value artwork produced by artists from various global cultures; instead, they tended to look deeper and question their own interpretations (Figure 3). The students often engaged in lively conversations with one another and me. During some classes, cultural taboos were discussed. During other classes, disparate backgrounds of the students (Caucasian, Latino, Jordanian, Hawaiian, and Navajo) and their respective countries

of origin (US, Mexico, and Jordan) were freely compared. These changes in student behaviors can easily be attributed to a globally and culturally sensitive learning environment, where unbiased and non-prejudicial questioning led to better understanding and acceptance of differences. Of perhaps greater importance is that some of these art education students are now educators who bring this sense of cultural sensitivity and caring to an exponential number of young children in both domestic and international schools.[3] The majority of Doris's classmates currently teach in the US, some along the Arizona-Mexico border. Others have joined international faculties as far away as Qatar and China. I see these newly minted art educators as open-minded, global citizens who recognize and hold in high esteem the interconnectedness of humanity.

Figure 3. A preservice student learns to look for contextual clues. Photograph courtesy of the author.

Lessons Learned

Reflecting upon the time that Doris and her peers moved through the art education program, three important factors that contributed to the environment of cultural sensitivity come to mind: awareness, attitude, and knowledge. The following provides a summation of these factors and suggests ways to incorporate them into any classroom context.

Cultural awareness implies identifying personal biases. It is an important first step—sometimes the most difficult first step—toward achieving a culturally sensitive teaching and learning environment. Becoming culturally aware is often difficult simply because we are each programmed from birth by our own surroundings. As such, we have a tendency to accept our way as the only way or as the best way. This sort of inward thinking can be dangerous in that it tends to disregard beliefs and traditions of those unlike ourselves—beliefs and traditions that are certainly as valid as our own. Doris underscored this concept by allowing her non-Navajo classmates to interpret artwork from their own vantage points before she offered details to assist with understanding her background. To become culturally aware requires introspection of personal beliefs as well as a tenacity to question what those beliefs are and how those beliefs inform our outlook toward others.

Attitude is a conscious act or disposition revealed through actions. A culturally sensitive attitude will manifest in a sense of balanced objectivity, tolerance, and impartiality toward others. When cultural differences arise, questions should be asked if there are issues that are not understood. Be respectfully curious as commonalities and differences are sought. Encourage sharing without fear of ridicule. Discourage antiquated terms, wholesale categorizations of entire groups, or stereotyping. As in the case of Doris, her classmates presumed to understand Navajo cultural practices based upon their own perspectives, which had been mostly learned from pop culture. This one-sided and naïve interpretation, while not intentionally biased, can create a distorted and unrealistic outcome. Nigerian author Chimamanda Adichie (2009), who appeared on a TED video, refers to this as "the danger of the single story." Overcoming a single story about cultures from the US and other countries requires enlightening personal perspectives. Such viewpoints are best attained by seeking knowledge and understanding about people whose beliefs are somewhat similar or wholly different from one's own (Figure 4).

Knowledge suggests familiarity with facts. Without knowledge we only assume. Assumptions are oftentimes counter-productive and incorrect. Take time to become acquainted with an area's different populations. Start with local, regional, national, and global data banks. Dig in to discover demographics that can provide a snapshot of people in a selected place. While quantitative data about a population cannot provide in-depth understanding of individuals, it can offer a general overview. Ask how knowing this sort of information can lead to a better understanding of the belief systems and common behaviors of groups that might be unfamiliar or foreign. Demographics in Northern Arizona point to a likelihood of Navajo students such as Doris enrolling in an art education program. Simply expecting the probability of American Indian students enrolling in art

Figure 4. Doris exchanges interpretive ideas with a classmate while visiting the Philip C. Curtis Gallery at the Phoenix Art Museum. *Photograph courtesy of the author.*

education courses suggests a need to prepare a learning environment to meet their academic needs. Although it is illogical to expect an educator to completely understand all cultural nuances of a place, especially those places with highly diverse populations, seeking knowledge of a variety of people from different backgrounds and their associated traditions can build trust among a learning community. As an art educator, it is important to learn about people from countries around the world and how traditions of these people are the same or different from those generally highlighted in art education programs. Knowledge helps to create a classroom environment that celebrates commonalities and differences in our global society.

Conclusion

Doris's story is one of cultural sensitivity in action. Not only did a classroom structured upon global and cultural sensitivity help Doris to find her own voice and academic success, students who moved through the post-secondary program with Doris have been forever changed. These students are now teachers who are better equipped to deal with culturally diverse 21st-century classrooms than if they had not been in the program; they are art educators willing to listen and learn without preconceived prejudices of other cultures. As contemporary educators, these individuals connect with one another and with artists and artworks through social media and other electronic technologies. These are educators aware of global diversity in its many forms.

It may safely be concluded from Doris's story that factors both subtle and obvious contribute to a globally sensitive classroom atmosphere. Teachers are the most important factor in implementation of culturally sensitive classrooms. For this reason, educators should thoughtfully model what they expect students to emulate. Show interest and be willing to learn about the traditions and beliefs of other cultures around the world. Be flexible and open-minded when culturally based issues arise. Be tolerant. Keep lines of communication, both real and virtual, open. Demonstrate tolerance, caring, empathy, and lack of prejudice.

In his 1854 book, *Walden*, Henry David Thoreau penned, "Could a greater miracle take place than for us to look through each other's eyes for an instant?" (p. 11). Perhaps this concise observation should be a directive to educators who seek to establish a culturally sensitive classroom in a global world.

REFERENCES

Adichie, C. (2009, July). *Chimamanda Adichie: The danger of a single story* [Video file]. Retrieved from www.ted.com/talks/chimamanda_adichie_the_danger_of_a_single_story

Annan, K. (2001, December 10). *Nobel lecture.* Retrieved from www.nobelprize.org/nobel_prizes/peace/laureates/2001/annan-lecture.html

Apthorp, H, Kinner, F., & Enríquez-Olmos, M. (2005). *A teacher's tool for reflective practice: Racial and cultural differences in American Indian students' classrooms.* Retrieved from www.mcrel.org/~/media/Files/McREL/Homepage/Products/01_99/prod35_teach_tool.ashx

Dykeman, D. (2004, October). *Shifting for success in the Southwest: Early Navajo culture change, A.D. 1500–1800.* Paper presented at the meeting of the Arizona Archaeological Council, Phoenix, AZ.

Frankland, H., Turnbull, A., Wehmeyer, M., & Blackmountain, L. (2004). An exploration of the self-determination construct and disability as it relates to the Diné (Navajo) culture. *Education and Training in Developmental Disabilities, 39*(3), 191–205.

Kehoe, A. B. (2005). *North American Indians: A comprehensive account.* (3rd ed.). Upper Saddle River, NJ: Prentice-Hall.

Loyalka, M. (2012). *Eating bitterness: Stories from the front line of China's urban migration.* Berkeley: University of California Press.

Morales, L. (2007). *A Navajo student feels the tug of home.* Retrieved from www.npr.org/templates/story/story.php?storyId=6845552

Navajo stories of gaming. (2008, November 16). *The Arizona Republic.* Retrieved from www.azcentral.com/arizonarepublic/news/articles/2008/11/16/20081116navajocasino-legend1117.html

Northern Arizona University Faculty Senate. (2010). *Recommendations of the global learning subcommittee of the task force on global education.* Retrieved from http://globallearning.nau.edu/files/global_learning_legislation.pdf

O'Hern, J. (2011, December). The inn at the end of the trail. *Western Art Collector, 52,* 50-55. Retrieved from www.lafondasantafe.com/about/art-of-la-fonda

Stafford, J., Bowman, R., Ewing, T, Hanna, J., & Lopez-De Fede, A. (1997). *Building cultural bridges.* Bloomington, IN: National Educational Service.

Thoreau, H. (1854). *Walden.* Retrieved from www.eldritchpress.org/walden5.pdf

United States Census Bureau. (2010). *State and county quick facts.* Retrieved from http://quickfacts.census.gov/qfd/states/04/0423620.html

ENDNOTES

1. Doris is the actual name of the student in this chapter. She fully cooperated in the writing of the chapter and has given her permission for her name to be used.

2. A total of 31 students were enrolled in this undergraduate, preservice art education class. All were full-time art education students between the ages of 18 and 26. Of these, 24 students were female (78%) and seven were male (22%). Ethnic make-up of the class included 22 Caucasian students (71%); six Latino students (19%); and also one international student (Jordanian), one Hawaiian-Pacific Island student, and one Navajo student (10%).

3. Education students at Northern Arizona University (NAU) have the option of completing an internship abroad through the Department of Defense Dependent Schools (DoDDS). Experience with the DoDDS program often leads to teaching positions in schools outside the US. Students from the NAU art education program have been hired in Asia, the Middle East, and Europe.

CHAPTER 9

Changing Perceptions About Stereotypes of Art Images Through Investigations of Views About Native American Art

JENNIFER STOOPES-MOKAMBA
Mandaree Public School, Fort Berthold Indian Reservation

Much has been written about the importance of a culturally pluralistic approach to education. In the last 30 years this approach has fallen into a wide array of applications, from thoughtful, in-depth inclusion of under-represented cultures to the repetitive copying of culturally specific objects. How a culturally pluralistic education is translated into the art classroom often can be very different from its educational intentions. Within an art classroom, several difficulties can arise. A lesson with a global focus is sometimes presented as a form of cultural tourism, with certain elements plucked out of context from the complex history of a culture and used as exemplars to be carefully copied by students. These lessons often are simplified, because presenting an in-depth history behind an artwork being examined cannot be accomplished within the limited timeframe in which most art lessons take place; therefore the lesson misses significant religious, historical, and cultural references related to the artwork itself. The result is a project that is afloat in a sea of lessons without containing any real or authentic meaning.

Secondly, an art educator may have limited resources or access to resources. With funding issues being forever a concern in an art classroom, a teacher may feel pressure to follow lessons that are familiar to him or her that have no additional costs. Resources also may not be available about the in-depth study of the richness of a specific culture or cultures, with projects that reflect complex ideas related to that culture. Too often lesson plans that are readily available for little or no expense may be superficial and will sometimes reflect a cultural tourism approach.

Lastly an educator is limited by his or her own experiences and knowledge. It is not possible to have a deep knowledge about every culture. Many art teachers have often taken only one class, if any at all, on the art of a culture different from their own. Almeida (1996), when discussing an anti-bias curriculum about Native Americans, stated:

At best, educators may have heard a lecture on developing instructional materials about Native Americans as part of an education workshop, or they may have briefly researched Native Americans as part of an anthropology course… the result is limited and often inaccurate knowledge on the part of the teachers concerning Native Americans and Alaska Natives. This compromised experience then gets handed down to the next generation. (p. 2)

Stereotyping is present within societal institutions and perpetuated by a majority culture. These perceptions are present in movies, television, children's books, newspapers, sports, and so forth, all part of our daily interaction with a dominant culture. Simply put, our view of another culture usually is based not on first-hand information, but on what we see, what we read, conversations with our families and friends, and perhaps one interaction that has reinforced our often stereotyped view of another cultural group.

Such limited viewpoints are present not only in lesson plans related to Native Americans and Alaska Natives, but can also be found in lesson plans developed globally around other cultures such as those found in Latin America and Africa. Lessons about African cultures often are presented around masks from the Benin culture (Nigeria) or Kente cloth from the Ashanti culture (Ghana). Almeida (1996) refers to this as a "dead and buried approach… lessons tend to present information in the past tense" (p. 2). While presenting materials as exemplars of work created by a culture in the past may have a place in the art classroom, this approach does not allow for students to gain a greater understanding and appreciation of a living culture. Ultimately, a greater understanding of any culture should foster a high level of positive interaction between people from different countries and cultures.

Knowing Other Cultures

In reality, no one can truly *know* another's culture. When viewing what we perceive as someone else's culture, our personal perspectives always influence our interpretations. This is true for an art educator as much as it is for a history teacher. Art is generally viewed through the lens of Western art history: that is, art created from a Eurocentric perspective is considered "high" or "fine" art, while art from non-Western cultures has traditionally been viewed as "craft" or "primitive" art. By examining their assumptions about art and acknowledging their own biases and perspectives, art teachers can begin to present thoughtful examinations of art created by those from national and international backgrounds that differ

from their own. By considering use of language and images in particular environments and through media, a richer and deeper understanding of others' perspectives can be attained. This understanding may make some educators uncomfortable or uncertain about their own body of knowledge. A process of self-discovery can be uncomfortable, but such a process can produce lesson plans in which depth of understanding is encouraged and thoughtful choosing of specific artifacts as exemplars is accomplished.

Authenticity

Authenticity of an artifact is in itself a biased concept. The viewer determines the notion of authenticity. That is, the concept of authenticity is biased by its very function; it suggests that from a Western perspective an artifact is found to be an accurate representation of a specific culture. Knowing this, it is still important to use artifacts as exemplars that are authentic as determined by the cultural group being studied. Is this even possible given the Eurocentric perspective of Western art education? If, for example, in contemporary Western art, images with high contrast often are considered to be aesthetically pleasing, it stands to reason that those of similar cultural backgrounds will determine that high contrast is aesthetically pleasing when present in a non-Western culture being studied. An art educator can be aware of this dilemma and be thoughtful in choosing images that the culture being studied have considered to be authentic, rather than those outside the culture. Alfred Young Man (2010) from the Department of Indian Fine Arts at First Nations University of Canada has written:

In the area of studio art, non-Native students are bewildered to learn that there is something called Indian fine art. Canadian and American students are regularly taught biased attitudes about Indians from high school onward, taught that there is no such thing as Indian art, more particularly that nothing from the Native perspective is thought to exist by that name. By the time university students enroll in first year Indian art history and studio courses, their knowledge and practical experience and behaviour must be completely reevaluated and the student reeducated about the true nature of the Native artistic experience, creativity and expression, if they are to learn how to judge and justify its authenticity, integrity and value. (para. 22)

An additional way in which an authentic exemplar can be viewed is through the use of contemporary artwork. Using contemporary art sometimes can allow for information about the work directly from the artist, where intention, meaning, and personal history can be understood, rather then relying only on an outsider's interpretation. Art—whether it is two-dimensional or three, abstract, or realistic—can be aggregated with information about the context in which it was created, along with personal information from the artist. This view of authenticity allows a student to understand an artist's role as creator and his or her own role as the viewer. It allows the students in an art class to discuss authenticity from a viewer's position, rather than as a fixed truth imparted by someone outside of the culture where the artifact was produced. Students can then compare artists' statements about their own artwork with those of art critics and discuss authenticity, which explanations resonate with them, and why.

Using contemporary art also encourages a teacher and students to understand an artist's intentions from a personal perspective. This approach ensures that students see people from another culture as individuals living complex lives in communities both similar to and different from their own; doing this can help eliminate a "dead and buried" (Almeida, 1996, p. 2) approach. "The relevance of contemporary art to multicultural education cannot be overstated… In this new art, issues of *how* and *what* constitutes difference have been given a new weight and gravity" (Cahan & Kocur, 1996, p. xxii).

Zimmerman (1990) also has suggested, "Art should be studied in a context in which people are linked through their communities and nations with people in other communities and nations throughout the world" (p. 1). A global perspective can be introduced into the classroom through lessons that demonstrate relationships between artworks around the world. Students can then examine issues of equality, western values, and historical contexts through a global lens.

Authenticity is significant to the curriculum that I will present in the lessons in this chapter. I will use contemporary Native American art as an instance of how understanding other cultures can lead to a more culturally sensitive view with respect to similarities and differences of human experiences within and across diverse cultural groups. Historically Native art has been seen as either an example of primitive art, objects with a utilitarian pur-

For Further Consideration

A component of a strong art education program is the study of art history. Yet, examining a national or cultural group from a historical perspective might only leave students with an impression that people from that culture are locked in the past.

Working in small groups, select a national or cultural group that is frequently taught from a historical rather than contemporary point of view (for example, Greek, Egyptian, or diverse Native American or African cultures). Consider what historic motifs or ideas about this group are frequently applied as stereotypes of its contemporary peoples.

1. Find three examples of contemporary art from the selected culture that honor or recall ancient traditions, while also describing cultural life in the 21st century.
   - Analyze the contemporary artworks from technical and conceptual perspectives. Interpret the meaning of each artwork.
   - Look up the artists' statements about these works.
   - Do the statements challenge, support, or extend the groups' interpretation of the artworks? If they challenge or extend the groups' interpretation, discuss what the group may have missed or misunderstood during the analysis phase of the activity that resulted in such an inaccurate or incomplete interpretation.

2. Brainstorm a curriculum unit or teaching strategy that might inform students about the historic traditions of the selected group, while also engaging understanding of contemporary (21st century) life in this national or cultural context.

3. Share findings with others in the class. Engage discussions about the intended and (possibly unexpected) outcomes of the proposed unit or teaching strategy.

pose, or an artifact studied for its ethnographic interest. Contemporary Native artists span the art/craft spectrum, with artists choosing to define their own work. Native American artists have expressed concerns about the way in which Western art continues to be used as a lens through which all art is viewed. Rushing (1999) suggests,

> The terms in which Native art can be discussed continue to be determined by the concerns of non-Native people, even when they involve an expiatory working out of old guilt... The imposition of the dichotomous categories of the traditional and contemporary are a prime example of this control. (p. 105)

Work of Edward S. Curtis

The work of photographer Edward S. Curtis (1868–1952) of the American west is an example of this perspective. Curtis had not trained as an anthropologist and only took up photography as a hobby. It was during his travels to the American West that he found a passion for photographing American Indians. He was very much an individual of his time. Grouping all Native tribes together, his perspective of Native people was to view them as one vanishing group. His point of view was colored by Western views of America as an unoccupied land, ready to be settled by Europeans anxious to remake their personal histories within a "new land." It would not have occurred to settlers of the West that in reality they were displacing large groups of people who already occupied this land for a long period of time and had their own cultural histories.

Our views of the past are colored by our definitions. "History is not neutral. That is, it is not an objective retelling of past events. Rather, histories are written from particular perspectives informed by specific assumptions that are philosophical in nature" (Malott, Waukau, & Waukau-Villagomez, 2009, p. 9). Certainly Curtis did a tremendous amount to document his personal perspective of Native Americans at a particular moment in history. His wax recordings and written accounts of languages and customs make up a significant portion of his legacy.

Because Curtis would manipulate a scene (remove artifacts with Western influences) and have his subjects change into traditional clothing when he wanted a certain image (he would sometimes provide the clothing), his work has been discounted within certain fields. However it would be a mistake to view his subjects only as hapless victims. As an outside viewer, it may be difficult to see that there was an exchange between Curtis and his subjects that benefitted both parties. Documentation supports the notion that the subjects were paid for putting on clothing and posing, therefore earning an income. It has been thought that some of the Native community at the time found photography a remarkable invention and took great pride in showing an image of themselves to family members (Sandweiss, 2001).

Many Native Americans viewed—and continue to view—Curtis with ambivalence. Artist Larry McNeil (Tlingit/Nisga's Nations) has said, "I've always considered that Curtis was trying to make genocide into something poetic in his series of photographs of Indians" (cited in Devon, 2006, p. 51).

> By emphatically not representing either his own contemporary present or that of his subjects, and paradoxically using a modern medium to construct a romantic past, Curtis created distorted images that established the myth that the Indian vanished at the turn-of-the-century. (Hauser, cited in Devon, 2006, p. 51)

This difficulty with Curtis' motivations among Native American artists and critics has led to Curtis being used as a source of material within Native American artwork. Larry McNeil (Tlingit/Nisga's Nations) appropriates Curtis's work into his own, "by creating images of Curtis's Indians as feisty and contentious individuals who challenge Curtis to reconsider his portrayal of Native people as stoic and heroic" (cited in Devon, 2006 p. 51). Tom Jones (Ho-Chunk Nation) is a photographer who assumes:

> A responsibility to portray the Native American experience and the contributions to the history of the United States of Native peoples, who have largely been without a voice in the documentation of this history... Typically, photographs of the Native American Indian was [sic] taken by outsiders. We have generally been represented with beads and feathers. (Jones, cited in Devon, 2006, p. 76)

Lessons: Creating a Visual Image of a Stereotype

As an art educator I was struck by the comments I heard from my high school students about Native Americans that seemed to demonstrate a lack of understanding and a belief that Native culture was "dead and buried" (Almeida, 1996, p. 2). I questioned whether I was doing enough to give students an educational experience in which their world was expanded to include all people. Having taught art in elementary school with an African centered focus, I was familiar with using culturally specific art exemplars from African countries in classrooms of predominately African American students. There I included traditional masks from sub-Saharan and West Africa into lessons about African American artists from the Harlem Renaissance.

At the high school level, my goals were to challenge students to understand how stereotypes are both visually affirmed and dissented. Through this process, I wanted to see if it was possible to change my students' negative perceptions about Native Americans. The class consisted of 34 students in a visual studies class. This class is a basic general art class and was made up of predominately 9th graders, as well as some students from the upper grades. The student body consisted largely of working class families and presented a diverse racial and ethnic blend. A third of the students were of European descent, approximately a third were of African descent, and the remaining students drew from diverse backgrounds. Essential questions and the production of two works of art were used over a 13-day period to challenge students to examine stereotypes they held about racial and ethnic groups.

Lesson 1: Examining Stereotypes and Creating a Visual Image of a Stereotype

In the first lesson, we looked at photographs by Edward S. Curtis. I used his work since Curtis has been criticized for his manipulation of scenes and Native Americans within these scenes. Discussion focused on whether Curtis perpetuated stereotypes of Native Americans and if so, whether or not these stereotypes still exist. Class discussions included considerations of the historical context of Curtis's work (early part of the 1900s) and mainstream public perceptions about Native Americans during that era. The term ethnography and definitions of culture were explored. Students were encouraged to consider whether his photographs may have colored perceptions about Native Americans for future generations. Resources were available in the room for further study, but students were not required to research Curtis on their own. Students were encouraged to try to look at his photographs from a Native American perspective. Discussion took place about the effect Curtis's photographs may have had on Native Americans who have not vanished. Student responses were thoughtful and they were able to incorporate history into their responses.

The class then watched the YouTube video *Smiling Indians*[1] by the Native American group the 1491s. The opening scene to this video is dedicated to the memory of Curtis. Watching this YouTube video motivated students to ask questions about the subject matter, and their responses demonstrated a willingness to look beyond their initial assumptions about Native Americans. For example, students stated, "I didn't know Indians had dark brown hair," or "They all looked different. I thought all Indians looked the same."[2] One student noted, "I

didn't know they wore regular clothes." The students then worked in teams to create a visual stereotype about a topic of their own choosing. While this stereotype did not have to relate directly to the perceptions about Native Americans, the class discussion would circle back to the images we had viewed at the introduction of the lesson.

The process for coming up with a stereotype to produce as an artwork consisted of generating ideas through the use of word webs or brain dumps in which they related all they knew about a topic under discussion. Students worked in groups of two or three, and each group had to produce three thumbnail sketches of their ideas. After gaining approval for their final image, the groups would begin to work. Students were free to use colored pencils, graphite, photography, or collage as their medium of choice. They could not use typeface or words in this first stage of the project. I wanted them to have to use visual images to demonstrate a stereotype, without relying on the written word to tell the viewer what they should be seeing.

Some of the stereotypes were very personal, such as "Black girls don't have long hair," or "all Asians are nerds" (Figure 1). Some were specific to particular students, such as the two athletes who drew a male student using steroids in an empty locker room. What was particularly interesting about all of the stereotypes illustrated in this initial lesson was the dialogue that occurred during

Figure 1. "All Asians are nerds" was the stereotype illustrated.

critiques. Students tossed around ideas about each stereotype and were prepared to offer opinions that looked at more than one side of a topic under consideration. Critiquing was respectful, and every group was anxious to present their work.

Lesson 2: Creating a Visual Image That Represents the Inaccuracy of a Stereotype

The second lesson used the artwork of Richard Ray Whitman (Yuchi) and Thomas Ryan Red Corn (Osage), as well as non-native artist Keith Haring, as exemplars of work that drew attention to the inaccuracy of stereotypes. The work of Australian artist Gordon Bennett (Aboriginal/European) had been considered for part of the lesson plan, but ultimately was presented with the work of Frank Big Bear (Ojibwa) in a separate lesson. While both of these artists examine stereotypes in unique ways, they also have a theme of "home land" within their work.

For this lesson I assigned partners, and the pairs were to create an image in which they protested or pointed out the inaccuracy of a stereotype. This time they could use typeface in the artwork. Some of the topics chosen were "not all Muslims are terrorists," "not all jocks are bullies," and challenges of notions such as "girls are not good at math" (Figure 2), "vegetarians are skinny," or "Black couples are ugly." The "not all Muslims are terrorists" poster showed an individual dressed in traditional garments, smiling, with words that described the person in the picture. These words included "peaceful" and "happy." The "vegetarians are skinny" poster showed a large man in a very small boat eating a carrot. The humor in the image was evident in the contrast between the sizes of objects as well as in the details such as the fishing hat, the PETA (People for the Ethical Treatment of Animals) sign flowing off of the boat, and the greens coming off of the carrot. I was unfamiliar with some of these stereotypes, but the teens in this class came up with the individual topics of interracial relationships, myths about differences in hair types, ethnicities, and gender identity as it relates to academics. The topics were not limited to local teen worries, but reflected a diverse student body and world-wide concerns of teenagers. Again, the critiques were remarkable examples of students really understanding their personal positions and learning from the positions of other students. During this second lesson critique, thought provoking responses invited discussions about what is true and what is opinion, how stereotypes evolve, and what an artist can do to dispel stereotypes

Figure 2. The inaccuracy of the stereotype "Girls are not good at math" was illustrated in part two of the project.

within his or her own work. Students were engaged in their team projects as well as with what other classmates were encountering. Exciting discussions and debate were the norm. During a discussion, I would refer students back to the work of Curtis and Richard Ray Whitman in order to understand how their student work related to the topic of stereotypes and what commonalities their work might have with contemporary artists.

Part of the lesson procedure was to have students respond to an essential question that was written on the board. A thoughtful, complete response was expected in each student's sketchbook. Sketchbooks are part of the state standards and, as such, are checked, and students are given a sketchbook participation grade every 4 to 5 weeks during a semester. Sketchbooks are also used for thumbnail sketches, word webs, and demonstrating art techniques, and as a place to answer a daily essential question, which centers on the lesson presented. Some of the answers to essential questions during this 13-day period consisted of one word, while others were complete sentence responses.

Initially students were asked to write down ten stereotypes about Native Americans. The top five stereotypes cited by students were:

1. wears feathers
2. serious/never smile
3. all hunt
4. live in tents/tipis
5. all ride horses

What was of particular interest was the similarity of the lists between what the students had initially thought about Native Americans and what they now perceived as stereotypes. Nevertheless none of the students mentioned how their first ideas had in fact been aligned with what they now recognized as being cultural stereotypes about Native Americans.

The final essential question I posed was, "Has your opinion changed about any of the groups listed? African Americans, Native Americans, Asians, or Latinos." Responses included: "I've realized that stereotypes about these groups aren't necessarily true," "My views has [sic] changed about Native Americans because of the things people [students in the class] say," "Don't be quick to judge someone because of what their appearance is," "Stereotypes have been around as long as people," and "My views have not changed since this project. I have never liked assuming something about a person. However I have noticed the views of other people, whether it be gender or race, stereotypes are everywhere and about everything," "African Americans: not all are ghetto [sic], Native Americans: that they are not all nature/hunter/gatherer people, Asain [sic] not all are smart, and Latino's: not all are Mexican." A final response:

> Examining stereotypes changed my point of view about my own stereotypes a lot. I no longer judge people so much. Stereotypes most of the time are not nice. People who are not nice are ugly and mean. I do not like most stereotypes at all.

In addition, the essential question that was asked—"How has examining stereotypes changed your point of view about your own stereotypes?"—elicited some thoughtful responses. These included:

> I've seen a lot of stereotypes lately and I've now seen these stereotypes affect people. People shouldn't be stereotyped because most of the time these stereotypes are wrong. I don't like being stereotyped so I shouldn't be putting people into stereotypes. [They] can be hurtful and can be taken the wrong so society should do away with stereotypes,

and,

> It has made me open up my eyes and not judge at first sight. It has made me want to fight against stereotypes too. It also makes me want to change some of my ways.

Conclusion

The art classroom is ideal for the type of global experience I described, because making art and understanding art can be both universal and individual. As an example, Young Man (2010) suggests, and anecdotal stories confirm, "Canadian and American students are regularly taught biased attitudes about Indians from high school onward" (para. 22). This bias can be challenged by the art teacher who "takes an opportunity to facilitate informed dialogue and civilized interaction among students, or encourage further exploration of political events occurring in a student's or artist's everyday lives" (Lai, 2012, p. 21). Certainly more studies are needed to examine the role art can play in changing perceptions about racial and ethnic groups, both nationally and internationally. However, an art teacher has an opportunity to change the way young people think about the larger world. The ability to think outside of your own cultural construct expands the world for students and opens lifelong opportunities for positive interactions.

Examining works by artists from other countries may invite explorations of the similarities and differences of experiences addressed by artists from many countries and cultures. Pairing the works of Gordon Bennett (Australia) with those of Frank Bigbear (Ojibwa), and Brazilian Artist Nele Azevedo when studying Andy Goldsworthy (Scottish) and Jiang Pengyl (China), later enhanced the lessons in which I focused on contemporary Native American artists by introducing concepts that further encouraged students to consider the world as a source of complex relationships between people, within a culture and across cultures, while at the same time further examining their own personal values and perspectives. Using global exemplars is an important way to extend beyond national boundaries. Knowing an artist as a person rather than as a culture or a history increases chances that these students' future interactions will be enhanced, and stereotypic views of others will be eradicated.

REFERENCES

Almeida, D. (1996). Countering prejudice against American Indians and Alaska Natives through antibias curriculum and instruction. *ERIC digest*. Charleston, WV: ERIC Clearinghouse on Rural Education and Small Schools. (ED400146). Retrieved from www.eric.ed.gov/PDFS/ED400146.pdf

Cahan, S., & Kocur, Z. (Eds.). (1996). *Contemporary art and multicultural education*. New York, NY: Routledge.

Devon, M. (Ed.). (2006). *Migrations: New directions in Native American art*. Albuquerque: University of New Mexico Press.

Lai, A. (2012). Culturally responsive art education in a global era. *Art Education, 65*(5), 18–23.

Malott. C., Waukau, L., & Waukau-Villagomez, L. (2009). *Teaching Native America across the curriculum*. New York, NY: Peter Lang.

Rushing, J., III. (Ed.). (1999). *Native American art in the twentieth century*. New York, NY: Routledge.

Sandwiess, M. (2001). Picturing Indians: Curtis in context. In E. S. Curtis (Ed.), *Photographs of the Plains Indians* (pp. 13–39). Lincoln: University of Nebraska Foundation.

Young Man, A. (2010). Racism & the politics of Indian art study. *CAUT Bulletin, 57*(6). Retrieved from www.cautbulletin.ca/en_article.asp?articleid=3086

Zimmerman, E. (1990). Teaching art from a global perspective. *ERIC Digest*. Bloomington, IN: ERIC Clearinghouse for Social Studies/Social Science Education, Adjunct ERIC Clearinghouse for Art Education. (ED329490). Retrieved from www.ericdigests.org/pre-9219/global.htm

ENDNOTES

[1] www.youtube.com/watch?v=ga98brEf1AU

[2] Student quotes throughout this chapter were taken from sketchbook responses and discussions that occurred during the project, which took place in in the fall of 2011 at a school in Georgia.

Knowing and Honoring Self in Local and Global Communities

SECTION TWO:
KNOWING AND HONORING SELF IN LOCAL AND GLOBAL COMMUNITIES

Introduction

STEVE WILLIS

This section is divided into chapters that present strategies, insights, and resources for developing understandings about Self and Others within and beyond the local community. Authors describe specific circumstances within unique communities. As these are discussed by art educators working within the various communities, the authors' narratives focus on how personal valuing within communities develops foundational experiences which facilitate vision beyond localized cultures.

Shifting focus from how we see the world or how others see us to how we *see the world together* requires an awakening of empathy; empathetic instincts are brought to consciousness through attention to resonant thoughts and feelings of others. Authors of this section grapple with empathy as that respectful consideration of Self and Others which evolves through acts of conscious, intentional mindfulness. In doing so, they conclude that identifying and experiencing components of consciousness in oneself are necessary prerequisites to recognizing and appreciating the complex consciousness of others. As students explore how answers to universally experienced questions about life are deeply rooted in cultural experience, they begin to understand why answering these questions has led us to differing conclusions. By carefully attending to, or conscious and intentional mindfulness of, the experiences of Self and Others, we can decode cultural differences, experience empathy, and construct sustainable cross-cultural relationships.

In the first chapter of this section, Jocelyn Salaz challenges the tendency in dominant society and art education to measure the authenticity or value of Hispanic and Native American art and artists against the past, or teach about their traditions through mere copying of forms. She searches her own childhood experiences to find an alternative way of teaching students to recognize Native cultures as living, in a vibrant present tense. She describes designing and implementing a teaching/learning experience in "All Dressed Up: A Cultural and Personal Exploration of Clothing." By inviting students to use recycled materials to create collage clothing for paper dolls, she guides her students to become cognizant of how cultural traditions; economic, social, and environmental circumstances; and availability of materials influence dress. They also become aware of how local and global economic conditions and consumerists' demands might affect people and natural resources in distant regions of the world.

In her chapter, "Culture Interlopers and Multiculturalism-Phobics: Theoretical Approaches to Art Teaching in a Global World," Joni Boyd Acuff reflects upon her experiences as an outsider to the cultural lives of others. Working with lesbian, gay, bisexual, transgender, and questioning (LGBTQ) youth in weekly artmaking workshops centered on topics of social justice, Acuff found that critical race theory and art education pedagogies were tools that could be put to use in establishing rapport with youth who are different from herself.

Within this empathetic space, she and her students experienced self-acceptance and supported one another in a collaboratively constructed, caring community.

The adage, "We do not see things as they are. We see them as we are," is applicable if we rely upon our own identities and cultures as mirrors that guide our perceptions of others. Seeing the lives of others as through a window, rather than a mirror, requires a readjustment of focus. By journaling her own travels through an unfamiliar Mexican landscape, Courtney Weida, an art educator from the United States, explores issues of cultural representation. In "Glimpses of Guanajuato: Encounters and Expressions of Borders in Art Education," she retraces her journey of seeing, reflecting, inquiring, and exchanging, as she grew increasingly sensitive to representations of culture. In doing so, she presents a model whereby art teachers might reflect thoughtfully upon their own lives and locales in relation to their students' differing life experiences.

Likewise, Kathryn Coleman and Susan Coleman explore issues of cultural representation. In "Suburb as Site: Creating a Global Collaborative Art Environment in Secondary Art and Photography Classes," they describe how their students engaged in reflective considerations of their personal space in local and globalized contexts. The program they designed for secondary-level photography students, who were living in a suburban area of Australia, required the students to critically explore what living in this space meant for them. As students visually recorded and reflected upon the physical and human environment of a suburb, they also examined how artists in other parts of the world viewed ideas of suburbia, and they dialogued with peer photography students who lived in a suburban area within the United States. The students' explorations and collaborations, which were facilitated by interactive communication technologies, brought new understandings of how a global concept might be experienced in uniquely local ways.

Experiencing culture through total immersion is realistically impractical for the majority of students. Nevertheless, in virtual spaces, not only can students communicate interactively with one another, but they also may view broadened landscapes of aesthetic artifacts and resources. Kristin G. Congdon and Doug Blandy consider how resources for teaching globally sensitive art education might be accessible to students worldwide. In "It's About Them, It's About Us: Using ChinaVine as an Educational Tool," they describe an Internet site that permits interactive communication and encourages students to explore, question knowledge content, recognize continuous change, work collaboratively, and experience learning in a global context.

Mary Erickson, Laurie Eldridge, and Marissa Vidrio found resources in a local museum that could be used to inform teachers and students of the rich cultural diversity of their geographic region. In "Using an Art Center's Online Curriculum to Teach Elementary Students About Cultural Identity," they describe culturally sensitive features of an art educational program employed by Tempe Center for the Arts (TCA). These features include: developing a place-based, welcoming mission; providing a broad inquiry scaffold to structure, direct, guide, and encourage independent inquiry; and articulating broad, cross-cultural themes in life that lead to broad themes in art. Through suggested pedagogical strategies and engagement with images and artifacts made available by museums and galleries around the world, students become informed about diverse cultural expressions of everyday life.

A concern of art educators and other adults regarding the globalizing influences of mass media and Internet access is that peoples of the world may lose the diversities of cultural expression that present a fascinating montage of world cultures. In the last three chapters of this section, authors address this concern by describing how peoples in differing regions of the world contribute variety to global art worlds by attending to that which is unique within their nations or geographic regions.

Glen Coutts and Timo Jokela describe programs that were designed to engage students and adults in new understandings of the uniqueness of their personal and communally shared experiences through artmaking in "Art, Community and Context: Educational Perspectives." They describe how artists, art teachers, students, and members of communities in Scotland, Lapland, and Russia worked together—within their respective communities—in ways that contributed to harmonious social interactions, strengthened cultural identity, and integrated community.

An international group of researchers—Estefania Sanz Lobo, Pablo Romero González, Atsushi Sumi, Li-Hsun Peng, and Hyeri Ahn—discuss children's drawings from four countries in "Youth Culture Expressed in Teenagers' Drawings From Spain, Japan, Taiwan, and South Korea." The authors evaluated drawings for visual codes and themes that reveal global influence mixed with local cultural effects. Their findings suggest that art educators can: set scenarios within which both local and global cultural heritages may be known and appreciated, encourage a critical distance from the culture of globalized consumption, and recognize the expression of ideas and agency of young people as cultural creators.

Finally, Fatih Benzer and Olcay Kırışoğlu bring us to awareness that peoples of a nation may be torn between practical needs to compete for a place of power in the globalized world and instinctive desires to honor, value, and give voice to their unique national identities. In "Living on a Bridge: The Effects of Cultural Policy on Art Education in Turkey," the authors consider how differing cultural, political and educational policies have been tried and tested by modern-day citizens of Anatolia (the culturally attributed name of Turkey), which has been as a cradle for many cultures from 10,000 BCE to the present era. In their examinations, they give voice to young Turkish artists and art educators who hope their uniquely Anatolian aesthetic, which has evolved from a convergence of complex historic experiences and artistic traditions, may not be obscured or obfuscated by globalizing influences. The authors conclude that by knowing and appreciating one's unique cultural circumstances, young artists may evolve empowered visions that contribute textural variety to the global art world.

CHAPTER 10

All Dressed Up:
A Cultural and Personal Exploration of Clothing

JOCELYN SALAZ
Rio Rancho Public Schools, New Mexico

I once viewed an art lesson during which tinwork was presented to elementary students as a traditional Hispanic craft that has been practiced in New Mexico since the late 19th century. Students learned that artists converted tin from canned food into decorative frames and niches for devotional images that were displayed in homes. After viewing images of tinwork, students were given premade designs to punch onto precut pieces of tin. While it was obvious students enjoyed the opportunity to make a lot of noise with nails and hammers, I wondered what understanding of aesthetic or artistic practices students would take away from this experience.

I teach in rural New Mexico to a population of students who are children of Hispanic and Native American parents. There is a need for alternative aesthetic sensibilities for students of these cultural backgrounds. This need arises from the tendency in the dominant society, and in art education, to measure the authenticity and value of Hispanic and Native American art and artists against the past or teach about their traditions through mere copying of traditional forms in curriculum, as illustrated in the anecdote above. Chicana and Indigenous perspectives and approaches to artmaking have influenced me as an artist and a teacher. Utilizing these perspectives and approaches as a basis for curriculum, instead of copying or dictating art forms and materials, can broaden children's understanding of people from communities around the world, specifically through a unit study of clothing I created for 4th-grade students. During the unit "All Dressed Up!" students investigate ideas they have about identity, while using everyday and recycled materials to create collage clothing for paper dolls.

Local Culture and Multicultural Art Education

Peter Smith (1999) calls attention to the absence of literature about the history of art education in the United States' Southwest, despite New Mexico's active art scene. He notes with irony that little or no attention is paid to Native American or Hispanic arts, and the "conceptual foundations in these cultures for doing, using or thinking about the arts" (p. 115), by the developers of Discipline-Based Art Education at the Getty Center for Education in the Arts, even given the center's close proximity to these cultures in the Southwest. Art educators interested in exploring historic and contemporary artistic and educational practices, and conceptual foundations of Native American and Hispanic art in the Southwest, must look beyond resources within the discipline of art education. Locating resources is crucial to rectifying the lack of attention given to Native American and Hispanic arts and issues in New Mexico art education, as it affects how teachers envision teaching art to the local populations.

Common multicultural approaches I have experienced, both as an art student and as an art educator observing other art teachers, echo what Desai (2005) described as teachers presenting the art objects of Other cultures within cultural, historical, social, and political contexts, followed by studio projects that redirect the lesson from understanding the experiences of people in other cultures to translating understanding into their own personal experiences. These studio projects, created in the style of the culture in question, reveal the assumption that "art forms are located in one culture—the culture of origin" (Desai, 2005, p. 293), and expose a danger that non-Western cultures be reduced to constructed ideas of essential characteristics. Desai critiqued multicultural art education's concern with providing accurate and authentic representations of the art of racially and ethnically marginalized groups in the United States and around the world by challenging notions of *authentic* and *accurate* as politically constructed, universal claims made to control images and maintain domination across social class, race, sexuality, and gender lines (Desai, 2000).

An examination of how the notion of authenticity has played out historically and contemporarily among Native American and Hispanic artists, patrons, critics, and educators is necessary for what Desai (2000) advocated as the need for multiculturalism to address the complex relationship between subjectivity and power in relation to culture, with an awareness of the political nature of how teachers choose to describe and represent another culture in art classes. Hutchinson (2001) exposed how discussions of Native American artwork have been and continue to be framed by notions of tradition and authenticity, pointing out how early historians of Native American art privileged artistic traditions untainted by Western influences, deeming hybrid forms as inauthentic, assimilationist, or degenerate. She highlighted debates surrounding the point when Native American art became modern, emphasizing that distinctions were made depending on the work's audience (Native or non-Native), whether Western preferences in media were used to produce the objects, and/or the utilization of modernist idioms. In addressing works by contemporary Native American artists, Charlotte Townsend-Gault (1992) asserted that the terms *tradition* and *authenticity*, used to describe the degree to which cultural practices and artistic products of Native Americans compare to mythologized pasts, relegated Native Americans to a place outside of the present.

Laurie Beth Kalb (1992) explored similar notions of authenticity in terms of New Mexican Hispanic identity and artistic production. She described how *Santos*, a type of religious imagery that arose in the second half of the 18th century, came to represent northern New Mexico Hispanic culture to the general public as the result of early 20th-century Anglo[1] interest. These objects, removed from their original contexts in churches, chapels, and homes, were admired more for their age, beauty, authenticity, and generalized spirituality than their previous functional and religious value within the cultures that produced them. She argued that the formation of the Spanish Market[2] in the 1920s by outside preservationist groups that wanted to display and sell crafts made by Hispanos was a commercialized endeavor, in which participation of artists hinged more on their willingness to replicate subjects, styles, and techniques practiced 200 years previously, in order to fulfill outside patrons' expectations of authenticity, than on the cultural concerns of the people who made them (Kalb, 1992).[3]

In light of these underlying issues surrounding Native American and Hispanic art in New Mexico, how can I, as a responsible art educator, respond to and re-present local art and aesthetic sensibilities? How can I, as an art educator, challenge these notions of authenticity surrounding the art created by the diverse groups whose children comprise my school population? How can art curriculum offer students opportunities to create art in ways that acknowledge cultural traditions and their own visual culture, but also address contemporary concerns, through different media, materials, subject matter, and formats that are pertinent and relevant to their experiences in the 21st century? Gude (2000) encouraged teachers to choose art issues that are foundational for specific teaching settings. An examination of artistic strategies utilized by historic and contemporary artists and communities can provide a strong foundation for the creation of culturally sensitive multicultural art curriculum.

Play and Clothing in Curriculum

A quality curriculum must be rooted in the life experiences and interests of the teacher and students, and also in their experiences of artmaking (Gude, 2011). "All Dressed Up!" draws from my own childhood experiences of utilizing play as an important artistic and meaning-making strategy. Reflecting on my childhood, as I often do as an elementary teacher, I recall how much I enjoyed creating and playing with paper dolls, fabricating interchangeable clothing and accessories made from scraps of paper, fabric, tape, and recycled household items. I investigated ideas about identity, family, relationships, future aspirations, and important events during play with paper dolls and took great pride in the work of my hands. The process was playful but intense; stories were performed through conversation, song, and narration inspired by real-life events or fantasy, interrupted by long artmaking sessions when the need for new clothing and accessories arose.

Making and playing with paper dolls, typically associated with female children, can be thought of as a practice that functions within the sensibility described in *Domesticana: The Sensibility of Chicana Rasquachismo* by Amalia Mesa-Bains (2003). Domesticana, characterized as a feminist aesthetic of survival, is influenced by people from working-class backgrounds, who made use of everyday materials in order to make the most from the least. It acknowledges meanings rooted in popular culture and practices. Some Chicana artists play with traditional imagery and cultural materials in the making of home altars and displays of family mementos that embody survival, self, and cultural affirmation (Mesa-Bains, 2003).

My intention for using clothing as a point of exploration for students is to investigate clothing as a form of visual culture that has the ability to operate in the public, a space characterized by Appadurai and Beckenridge as "an arena where other types, forms and domains of culture are encountering, interrogating, and contesting each other" (quoted in Desai, 2000, p. 123). By making students aware of how clothing operates in terms of revealing or concealing identity—protecting or transforming its wearers—children learn to interpret, question, and assert themselves using this form of visual culture. Historic and contemporary Native American artists like Angel DeCora, Hulleah Tsinhnahjinnie, and James Luna have utilized examinations of clothing, as these relate to identity politics and challenge stereotyped notions of the authentic Indian.

In *Modern Native American Art: Angel DeCora's Transcultural Aesthetics* (Hutchinson, 2001), transculturation is defined as a concept that "describes the painful impact of colonialism on indigenous culture as more than the simple replacement of traditional beliefs with European ones." It is rather an "uprooting of old cultural forms and the creation of new ones that reflect marginalized peoples' relations to mainstream culture" (p. 740). Western notions of authenticity may lead people to assume that DeCora, a Ho-Chunk artist, whose images closely resemble European American imagery of the period, was assimilated into mainstream American culture. Therefore her work often is not recognized as that of a Native American artist. However, DeCora's use of traditional Native American

For Further Consideration

1. Reflect upon how a cultural group that composes your (or a specific) school's population is represented in dominant discourses. Research artistic traditions and contemporary artists from within that cultural group.
   - How might research about the aesthetic sensibilities of these artists impact how you might design a curriculum unit for these students without merely perpetuating dominant discourses?
2. Identify materials you gravitate toward in your own artmaking.
   - What are the histories of these materials?
   - What types of aesthetic sensibilities do these materials propagate?
   - How can you explore the properties, abilities, and cultural implications of these materials with students in a curriculum?
3. How do people manipulate mass-produced items to express collective or individual identity?
   - How can students explore identity through examining mass-produced items they own?
   - How can students explore identity through the process of making art?
4. How can recognition of our individual identities, in relation to the materials and processes of artmaking, help us make connections to, open dialogues with, and come to mutual appreciation of people in global contexts?
   - What activities might be initiated to bring about these dialogic exchanges and (possibly) collaboration?

and European American artistic idioms and her consideration of dress as an important form of identity reveal her transcultural position. DeCora expressed her struggle between her desire to attend school and the awareness that this meant she would be forbidden to wear her tribal clothing by the government-run school policies meant to "civilize" and "Americanize" Native people (Hoxie, 1984). Her concern with tribal specificity of clothing in her paintings was a response to peers' complaints about the tendency of non-Indian artists to produce generalized, inaccurate representations of Native Americans. In doing so, she reveals the importance of clothing in tribally mixed boarding schools, as a way of reinforcing and expanding tribal identity (Hutchinson, 2001).

In the work of contemporary Seminole/Muskogee/Diné artist Hulleah Tsinhnahjinnie, hybridity, expressed in dress, serves as a theoretical model for understanding Native American identities today. Hybridity acknowledges the absence of purity among human cultures due to transculturation (Fowler, 2007). In *Portraits Against Amnesia*, photographs of members of Tsinhnahjinnie's family are intermixed with photographs of American Indian people purchased from eBay. These images are valued by Tsinhnahjinnie for their hybridization as Indians in European-American dress. In purchasing, collecting, and elevating the status of these photographs in her own work, she challenges collectors' aggressive bidding for photos of American Indians in "authentic" tribal dress, and confronts the construction of Indians as disconnected from modern life. Tsinhnahjinnie's intentional use of hybridity in her photographs is read as a refusal to Europeanize or Indianize her subjects, but to create an alternative (Fowler, 2007) that I believe contests binary and essentialist definitions of identity.

Clothing Unit: "All Dressed Up!"

"All Dressed Up!" began with the observation and discussion of carefully selected images, followed by sessions of brainstorming around questions that guided students to gain a more comprehensive understanding of clothing. During the creation of their paper dolls, students observed a partner who modeled for them. Students drew and colored one outfit of clothing and collaged more items of clothing that could be attached with Velcro to their paper dolls. I provided scrap pieces of fabric, patterned paper, buttons, ribbons, tissue paper, and leather and upholstery scraps purchased by our school or donated by local community members and businesses. Some students brought their own materials from home.

Discussions about clothing began with consideration of the concepts of form (which defines what clothing looks like) and function (in terms of how clothing reveals or conceals identity, provides protection, or transforms a person). To help students understand the extent to which form or function can dominate or work harmoniously together in a piece of clothing, they examined common clothing forms such as uniforms that identify their wearers as professionals or individuals of a team. Next I showed photographs of costumes students have worn during school plays, Mexican folk or contemporary Hispanic and Diné dances performed as part of the school's multilingual (i.e., English, Spanish, and Diné) program.[4] Discussing costumes and tribal dress children have worn themselves helped them to recognize, from their personal experiences, when and why people wear costumes or tribal dress, and how clothing can transform a person and evoke emotions or change behavior in both wearer and viewer.

Inherent in the idea and platform of multiculturalism is how teachers represent a culture other than their own (Desai, 2000). I selected clothing from the Kwakwaka'wakw and Naskapi Innu to expose my 4th graders to Native American tribes that are rarely mentioned in mainstream narratives. I contextualized how physical and natural processes of the land impact the visual and material culture of the people. In re-presenting the Kwakwaka'wakw button robe, I discussed the development of crest imagery, its significance in terms of familial and cultural history, and the wearing of the robe during potlatch ceremonies.[5] In contextualizing the Naskapi Innu summer hunting coat, I related Subarctic spiritual beliefs and necessities in light of the harsh climate, and how this affected the creation of clothing. As students viewed the Innu (Naskapi) hunter's summer coat, I described the Innu belief that animals preferred to be killed by hunters wearing coats with specific designs. I explained how the time and effort an artist puts into painting designs on the caribou-skin coat were signs of respect to the animal spirits that, in turn, gave themselves to people to provide food, clothing, and shelter. The ritual painting of the coat helped to keep the animals' abilities in the coat, gave its wearer confidence, and helped them to communicate with animals (Berlo & Phillips, 1998). Presenting this coat countered what Berlo and Phillips identify as a Western tendency to separate utilitarian from artistic concerns. It encouraged students to consider the reciprocal relationship between function and form in all clothing. This also provided an opportunity to acknowledge hybridity by revealing how the fitted cut and flared skirt of the coat were influenced by French clothing traded with Native peoples (1998). Children saw how contact between cultures from different parts of the globe led to new forms of art that continued to address the practical and aesthetic needs of their makers.

Basing the creation of paper dolls and clothing on students' own experiences and desires helped them to avoid thinking about their work as the creation of an authentic representation of a cultural group. I asked students to share examples of special clothing they have worn, and describe those occasions that required the wearing of such clothing. Students shared activities they enjoy and what they wear when they do those activities. I asked children to consider the type of clothing they might design if they were clothing designers. Students created a list composed of examples of clothing that reveal or hide identity, protect or transform. What types of clothing show power? How does clothing reveal personal interests? Students discussed what they like to wear, and how they feel when they wear different types of clothing. Brainstorming about how clothing can transform a person and the creation of more than one set of clothing helped students to understand how multiple aspects of their identities can be expressed with different types of clothing.

Outcomes

Students asserted that in order to relay their ideas about clothing successfully, details such as colors, patterns, words, logos, hats, and badges should be included to show how clothing reveals, disguises, or transforms identity. Many students made clothing identifying themselves as part of or with specific sports teams or cheerleading groups, while others focused on participation in these activities. Students' ideas for clothing changed as a result of the materials available for the project, and students responded enthusiastically and creatively with the materials: fur trim for stylish shirts, stripe-patterned paper for neck ties, strips of cloth in different colors for trimmings, tissue paper for tutus and ruffles, sheer fabrics as scarves, and decorative buttons serving as pendants (Figures 1 and 2). One student in particular cited many specific events, like National Dance Institute (NDI) and ballet performances, for which clothing could be worn and commented on how different materials (i.e., leather) inspired her creations (old Western-style dress). Her process was very playful and involved personal experiences as well as her wishes for the future (Figure 3).

Through discussion and the artistic process, students recognized the importance of clothing during special

Figure 1. A 4th-grade student created an outfit based on her participation in soccer and another based on play with materials.

Figure 2. This 4th-grade student embellished her clothing with buttons, fur trim, and dog-print fabric.

occasions. A boy recalled wearing a tuxedo for his grandfather's funeral, a girl described the big, white dress with flowers and ruffles she wore for her first communion, and another boy related how his traditional[6] Diné dress, composed of brown pants and a red and turquoise belt and headband, was worn to show respect and honor to couples during wedding ceremonies. Students related how costumes worn during plays could disguise someone, reveal the identity of a character, and awaken the imagination of people in the audience. One boy explained that

Figure 3. Paper doll with a variety of clothing by a 4th-grader at Cuba Elementary School.

Figure 4. Football Super Hero *by a 4th-grader at Cuba Elementary School.*

blending in with trees in his camouflage clothing during hunting made him feel "sneaky and lucky!" (C. Cavazos, personal communication, February 15, 2012).

Students acknowledged that being made to dress in certain clothing can make them feel self-conscious or embarrassed, and voiced that they preferred to wear casual and comfortable clothing. Talking about the uniform dress code at our school allowed students to reflect on issues of agency in determining dress. When asked why students think they must wear school uniforms, words like rules, responsible, and appropriate dominate

their responses, revealing how clothing relates with ideas of social control. They acknowledged that uniforms prevent students from wearing clothes that depict violence that can be used to scare or threaten other children, and some students even like that uniforms are comfortable and easy to match. Other students argued that it is very dull to wear the same thing over and over again.

Students heavily associated transformation with superheroes, and imagination played a crucial role in articulating these ideas in their artwork. During preliminary figure-drawing studies, one student was meticulous with the details on his football uniform, including a chain with his name hanging from his neck and wings spread out behind him. The student explained he was like a superhero; the wings helped him to fly and he was able to throw the football very far (Figure 4). For his paper doll, he selected a basketball pose that was later changed to depict a Mexican soccer player, which linked him to his country of origin. He created a black leather suit over a white satin shirt with a striped paper necktie and sunglasses (Figure 5), and related these features to articulations of wealth and power that are projected by business suits, medals, badges, and gold jewelry.

Figure 5. Paper doll with soccer uniform and dress suit by a 4th-grader at Cuba Elementary School.

Clothing and the Global Economy

Classroom discussion skirted around issues surrounding mass-produced clothing. For example, some Diné students elaborated on the variety of materials that comprise costumes worn during dances, including commercial velveteen and sateen fabric for shirts and dresses, and belts woven from sheep's wool, a product of small family farms. Recognition of a link between locally grown and globally marketed materials used for dress brought up more important questions and issues for students to consider. Where does our clothing come from? Who makes our clothing? Any discussion of clothing must address human rights issues in the global garment industry. Students might compare a living wage that allows for basic needs such as food, clean water, shelter, education, health care, and transportation with the minimum wages that garment workers are paid in many developing countries. Students can examine the economies of countries that produce clothing and the economies of consumer nations like the United States, and note the disparity between them. The stories of individual garment workers can reveal the working conditions as well as health and safety risks that endanger the lives and well-being of garment workers. In light of the transnationality of art and global economy, Desai (2005) advocated instructional approaches that examine the relationship between local and global in order to develop critical global citizenship amongst our students.

Artist Pepón Osorio provides additional questions for considering the impact of the global economy on clothing. He engages concerns about the market economy and how consumers define themselves by objects they own and produce, through the material transformation of commodity objects in his own work. He asks, "What does this manufactured object that deals with my identity have to say to me? What does it mean when I bring it home?" (quoted in González, 2008, p. 173). These are important questions for students to consider when they contemplate how mass-produced clothing can express their interests and individuality.

How can students transform objects from commercial products into personalized expressions of culture and values? Extensions to this clothing curriculum can include the deconstruction of students' own apparel to reveal the messages and values these items and the wearing of them promotes. How do these messages align or clash with students' own values? How might they reinforce conflicts or contribute to social injustice? Students can identify social justice issues that are important to them; create text and logos that communicate their opinions, attitudes and beliefs about these issues; and transfer them onto t-shirts using traditional or non-traditional transfer techniques. This allows students to carry a message on their bodies with text and image, but also through the materials and the artistic process of personalizing their own apparel.

Conclusion and Implications for Art Education

"All Dressed Up!" is a culturally sensitive unit of study that utilizes Chicana and Native American aesthetic sensibilities and approaches to explore multiple facets of identity using clothing. Students are asked to consider the form and function of many types of clothing and to examine their own experiences, ideas, and attitudes toward clothing to inspire the creation of collage clothing made from recycled, everyday materials. The focus on issues of cultural identity and clothing reveals problematic links between local and global markets and makers, and provides opportunities for students to consider clothing within broader contexts of multiple cultural identities, social justice issues, and ecological concerns.

While there may be a place for introducing students to historic artistic traditions of diverse local and global cultures, young students also need to understand that authentic cultural expressions are complex and exist in a present tense. Units of study—like "All Dressed Up!"—that focus on artifacts of students' everyday lives, and require them to situate artmaking in local and global contexts, may help students gain an understanding of artistic cultural practices in ways that mere imitation of traditional art forms or processes cannot. Exploring how the artistic practices we employ and artifacts we use in our everyday lives describe and define who we are in the local present honors the complexity of cultural experience.

REFERENCES

Berlo, J., & Phillips, R. (1998). *Native North American art.* New York, NY: Oxford University Press.

Desai, D. (2000). Imaging difference: The politics of representation in multicultural art education. *Studies in Art Education, 41*(2), 114–129.

Desai, D. (2005). Places to go: Challenges to multicultural art education in a global economy. *Studies in Art Education, 46*(4), 293–308.

Fowler, C. (2007). Hybridity as a strategy for self-determination in contemporary American Indian art. *Social Justice, 34*(1), 63–79.

González, J. (2008). *Subject to display: Reframing race in contemporary installation art.* Cambridge, MA: The MIT Press.

Gude, O. (2000). Investigating the culture of curriculum. In D. Fehr, K. Fehr & K. Keifer-Boyd (Eds.), *Real world readings in art education: Things your professor never told you* (pp. 75–81). New York, NY: Falmer Press.

Gude, O. (2011). Rubric for a quality art curriculum. Retrieved from http://uic.edu/classes/ad/ad382/sites/AEA/AEA_02/AAEA02a.html

Hoxie, F. (1984). *A final promise: The campaign to assimilate the Indians, 1880–1920.* Lincoln: University of Nebraska.

Hutchinson, E. (2001). Modern Native American art: Angel DeCora's transcultural aesthetics. *The Art Bulletin, 83*(4), 740–756.

Kalb, L. B. (1992). *Consuming devotions: The negotiation of tradition in contemporary New Mexico Santos* (Unpublished doctoral thesis). University of Pennsylvania, Philadelphia, PA.

Mesa-Bains, A. (2003). Domesticana: The sensibility of chicana rasquachismo. In G.A. Arredondo, A. Hurtado, N. Klahn, O. Nájera-Ramírez & P. Zavella (Eds.), *Chicana feminisms: A critical reader* (pp. 298–315). Durham, NC: Duke University Press.

Rhetts, P., & Awalt, B. (2011). *Contemporary Hispanic market: 25 years.* Los Ranchos, NM: LPD Press.

Smith, P. (1999). The Unexplored: Art education historians' failure to consider the southwest. *Studies in Art Education, 40*(2), 114–127.

Townsend-Gault, C. (1992). Ritualizing ritual's rituals. *Art Journal, 51*(3), 51–58.

ENDNOTES

1. *Anglo* is the term utilized to describe White Americans in New Mexican ethnic discourse that celebrates New Mexico's population as tricultural.

2. The Spanish Market is an annual event held in Santa Fe, New Mexico.

3. The Contemporary Hispanic Market, held contemporaneously and adjacent to the Spanish Market, was formed in 1986 by Hispanic artists who wanted the opportunity to display their work and meet with buyers and collectors, without restrictions on subject matter, materials, and techniques (see Rhetts & Awalt, 2011).

4. Our bilingual program consists of a program for maintaining student's home language (Spanish or Diné), and an enrichment program for a smaller percentage of students that are not English Language Learners (ELL). Furthermore, Diné students attend Diné bilingual classes and Hispanic students attend separate Spanish bilingual classes.

5. Information about the Kwakwaka'wakw button robe and Innu summer hunting coat was taken from Berlo and Phillips' (1998) *Native North American Art.* Strengths of this book as a reference are its blending of historical and more recent forms of art, and acknowledgment of North America's colonial history and its effects on the artistic practices of the Native North American tribes discussed in the book.

6. My Diné students use the word *traditional* to describe Diné clothing worn during dancing or ceremonies.

CHAPTER 11

Cultural Interlopers and Multiculturalism-Phobics:
Theoretical Approaches to Art Teaching in a Global World

JONI BOYD ACUFF
The Ohio State University

There I was, an overly enthusiastic researcher standing before five less-than-enthusiastic teenaged research participants in a 6-by-8-foot, non-air-conditioned room at the Kaleidoscope Youth Center (KYC).[1] With looks of apprehension, the lesbian, gay, bisexual, transgender, and questioning (LGBTQ) youth waited to hear what I—an outsider to their group as a heterosexual, Black woman—had to say about art that would make them *want* to stay in this claustrophobic sweatbox for 60 minutes each week. Years ago, had our situations been reversed, I might have had a similar query. Fortunately, my years of research work, which intertwine critical race theory and art education, provided me with pedagogical tools to attempt to guide and engage this group of youth. For 4 months, the youth at KYC voluntarily participated in Kaleidoscope He(Arts)[2] weekly artmaking workshops centered on social justice topics. What emerged from that squared petri dish of a classroom were thought-provoking artworks and more socially and culturally conscious—albeit sweaty—teens who did not mind being taught by a "Catholic."[3]

Students sometimes identify teachers as interlopers in their cultural milieu. I experienced this labeling firsthand as a heterosexual in KYC. This disconnect can be the result of difference in age, culture, ethnicity, gender, sexual orientation, religion, or other socially constructed identity signifiers. In addition, there can be tensions between teachers and students because of the teacher-student dichotomy. When this relationship is hierarchical in favor of teachers, it can be oppressive to students. Therefore, it is pivotal to identify best practices that deconstruct such damaging barriers in order for effective learning to occur fluidly. Two theoretical tools I found helpful for effectively teaching students from any culture and background include: (1) a multicultural and social reconstructionist approach to education, and (2) participatory action research (PAR).

Implementing multicultural education is central to teaching in a global world (Banks, 2009). In the United States and other countries, growth in international migration has resulted in a demographic divide of students in the classroom; this affects both teaching and learning (Banks, 2009). Multicultural education has a national, even global, context (Banks, 2009). According to Banks, "Multicultural education shares characteristics across nations, but it is always reflective of the national cultural and political context in which it is embedded" (p. 2). However, while there are variances in each context, the primary goals of multicultural education are consistent—to help students "acquire the attitudes, knowledge, and skills needed for productive employment in a highly technological and global society, participate effectively in the political system, and take action to increase equity in society" (p. 3). Therefore, it is crucial that teachers utilize teaching approaches that have such universal goals. Sleeter and Grant's (2007) multicultural and social reconstructionist approach[4] to education is multidimensional in this way. Sleeter and Grant (1994) explain that this approach deals

> directly… with oppression and social structural inequality based on race, social class, gender, and disability… The approach prepares future citizens to reconstruct society so that it better serves the interests of all groups of people and especially those who are of color, poor, female, gay and/or disabled. (pp. 209-210)

Teachers admittedly avoid teaching about cultural differences because of fear of misrepresenting other cultures (Gall, 2008). Part of this stems from educators simply misinterpreting a basic goal of teaching about cultural difference (Gay, 1995)—the interrogation of power and privilege (May & Sleeter, 2010). A multicultural and social reconstructionist approach can help bring this objective back to the forefront of culturally sensitive art education. Furthermore, a multicultural and social reconstructionist approach is ideal when considering education in a global context. Global education requires educators to think about cultural interdependence, and to view the "whole picture" of education (Case, 1993). Case explains, "Promoting the perceptual dimension involves nurturing perspectives that are empathetic, free of stereotypes, not predicated on naïve or simplistic assumptions and not colored by prejudicial sentiments" (p. 318). A multicultural and reconstructionist approach supports these global educational goals because it suggests various ways of viewing the world, as well as prompts questions regarding power relations, like stereotypes and culture (and knowledge) subjugation.

Pairing a multicultural and social reconstructionist approach with PAR aids in cultural sensitivity in the classroom. Facets of PAR, such as collaboration and using local knowledge as expert knowledge (Stringer, 2007), generate opportunities for cross-cultural learning that satisfies needs of a heterogeneous group of people. The youth demographics at KYC were dynamic; participants were Black, White, Native American, Latina, Mexican, mixed race, Christians, atheists, Jews, heterosexual, homosexual, transgendered, male, and female; and ranged in age from 12 to 20 years old. The tenets of PAR facilitated thoughtful interactions with these students, allowing me to address the needs of this specific population.

Critical Race Theory: A Lens for Constructing Global Sensitivity

Ladson-Billings (1999) writes:

> Critical race theory begins with the notion that racism is "normal, not aberrant, in American society" (Delgado, 1999, p. xiv), and, because it is so enmeshed in the fabric of our social order, it appears both normal and natural to people in this culture. (p. 213)

Those working toward social justice attempt to unmask and expose racism and other oppressions in their various permutations (Ladson-Billings, 1999). A key principle of critical race theory is that "people's narratives and stories are important in truly understanding their experiences and how those experiences may represent confirmation and counterknowledge of the way society works" (Ladson-Billings, 1999, p. 219). It is crucial for educators to closely recognize students' plural realities and culturally diverse life experiences (Chalmers, 2002; Gall, 2008); multiple narratives told by a diverse group of students are necessary to support a dialogic process to aid in the negotiation of ideologies.

The multicultural and social reconstructionist approach and PAR have foundational groundings in critical race theory. Primarily, they purposefully integrate alternative voices of authority (Gunew & Rizvi, 1994, as cited in Chalmers, 2002; hooks, 1994), which is a central goal of critical race theory (Ladson-Billings, 1999). A multicultural and social reconstructionist approach suggests critical questioning and democracy in the classroom, components embedded within critical race theory. PAR is in line with critical race theory, as it similarly desires to give voice to silenced narratives by recognizing local knowledge as a truth. PAR esteems collaboration towards collective goals, which mimics critical race theory's tenet of interest convergence. These collaborative initiatives increase ally support and facilitate new coalitions looking to attain joint goals (Ladson-Billings & Tate, 1995). The promise of a critical race theory framework is its ability to "be deployed as a theoretical tool for uncovering many types of inequity and social injustice—not just racial inequity and injustice" (Ladson-Billings, 2004, p. 61). This "uncovering" encourages a critique of many traditional approaches to [art] education. A multicultural and social reconstructionist approach and PAR provide methods for teachers to reconsider ways to be sensitive to students' needs, value their voices, show compassion to respective identities, and develop empathy and respect for varying cultural perspectives. In the following sections, I describe how I utilized the two approaches during a research journey, teaching in a learning space wherein I was a perceived as a cultural interloper.

Solution 1: A Multicultural and Social Reconstruction Approach in Art Education

A multicultural and social reconstructionist approach is theoretically situated in a social justice framework; it claims to lead students into thinking critically about equity, human decency, social responsibility, systemic oppression, and hierarchal power structures (Sleeter & Grant, 2007). This approach differs from traditional multiculturalism that simply add "cultural" content to hegemonic curriculum without questioning, analyzing, and acting against systemic issues or the status quo. These contributions or *additive* (Banks & Banks, 1989) types of approaches cause many teachers to avoid teaching in a culturally sensitive way for fear of misrepresentation. I suggest that the two primary tenets of the multicultural and social reconstructionist approach, critical questioning and democracy, help transcend such trepidation.

Critical Questioning

Sleeter and Grant's (2007) multicultural and social reconstructionist approach embraces Freire's development of critical questioning amongst groups who have learned to accept the status quo and succumb to powerlessness. Freire recognized institutional and structural oppression, including media impact like newspapers, textbooks, films, and even libraries, in the maintenance of power by the dominant class. For this reason, Freire asserted that empowerment begins with the questioning of everyday living conditions and refusing to simply accept ideas as "truths" (Freire, 1970). To practically apply Freire's theoretical ideas, Sleeter and Grant (2007) suggested creating lessons specifically around critical inquiry, with emphasis on questions such as, "Is it true?... Who says so? Who benefits most when people believe it is true? How are we taught to accept that it is true? What alternative ways of looking at the problem can we see?" (p. 260).

At KYC, I used similar probing questions that required students to explain, clarify, or verify assumptions and beliefs (Thoms, 2011). This resulted in students better identifying underlying, systemic problems. For example, the students chose immigration as a social justice topic to cover in the workshops. We reviewed and discussed the Arizona Immigration Law SB 1070,[5] as well as political cartoons that made commentary on the issue. This engagement initiated questioning of governmental and ideological systems. Students asked questions such as: "Isn't this unconstitutional?", "The police have no authority in this area," "They cannot ask for immigration papers, can they?", "What does 'looking illegal' look like?" and "Who defines what looking illegal looks like?" (Anonymous students, personal communication, August 16, 2010). This dialogue was integral in the development of critical consciousness (Adams, 1997).

For Further Consideration

1. How might cultural knowledge become subjugated in the art classroom, and how might a teacher's pedagogical or instructional methods disrupt these hierarchical positions?

2. Reflect on a past classroom project that was not specifically attentive to varying cultural perspectives. Consider the components of PAR and the multicultural and social reconstructionist approach, and reflect on how these frameworks might alter that project to ensure diverse cultural voices are present.

   • In what ways would the revised project differ, physically and contextually?

   • How would assessment of the project evolve?

3. How does (or might) your facilitation and support of educational equity, accessibility, and goals of global education in the art classroom assist students in gaining personal agency of their own learning?

Figure 1. Collage. Stop It! *Student work addressing homophobia.*

After the discussion, the students created their own political cartoon about any issue they wanted. Their ideas varied, but each student's artwork was a commentary on power. This kind of critical questioning can be facilitated in any classroom, regardless of the background or identity differences of the teacher or students. Such a process not only promotes cultural sensitivity to those who are Other, it can expose systemic and institutional issues that support oppression, which consequently requires empathy.

Critical questioning is a practical skill students can use in their daily lives (Sleeter & Grant, 2007). While the Arizona law was not culturally specific to the students, they were able to apply the skill of critical questioning to other artmaking workshops that were more personal. For example, critical questioning was employed during an individual collage project in which each student chose a social justice topic that was significant to them. The students collaged a canvas using magazine text and imagery. This project resulted in notable conclusions about media content. While sorting through the magazines, the students recognized a steady trend in the (mis)representations of gay men. They discussed the over-sexualization of gay men in media and how this representation contributes to stereotypes about the gay community. The students realized how media reinforces stereotypes about certain groups. We discussed how homosexual identity was constructed semiotically. The students identified language, text, and media as hegemonic tools that help

the dominant group to maintain power (Freire, 1970; Sleeter & Grant, 2007). This project initiated the question, "How are we taught to accept that it is true?" (Sleeter & Grant, 2007, p. 260). To counter the magazines' messages, one student created a collage that juxtaposed some of the over-sexualized images of gay men with images of men that were perceived heterosexuals (Figure 1). The student aimed to portray the diversity of the gay male. This project was evidence that critical questioning helps us reject stereotypes of one another, and those we have accepted of ourselves (Collins, 2002). By simply engaging students in personalized inquiries, I effectively orchestrated an invaluable artmaking project for students who blatantly identified me as someone from the outside. I did not have to assume an expert position on homosexuality to engage them in a meaningful multicultural project that directly related to their lives as homosexual youth.

Democracy

Leuthold (2011) confirms, "The contact, conflict, negotiation, and conciliation between members of different cultures and races is a central global theme of the last fifty years" (p. xi). Moreover, the impact of globalization on education is a critical point for investigation (Zajda, Davies, & Majhanovich, 2008). Specifically, educational equity is an explicit concern of those from varying cultural groups, as group status and privilege tends to affect educational accessibility and resources. Banks (2009) writes, "In nations around the world, some languages have higher status than others, and students from language minority groups frequently experience alienation, low academic achievement, high dropout rates, and identity problems in schools" (p. 3). Because of this, I see democracy, with emphasis on equity (Davies, 2008), as a significant practice to introduce in the classroom. The ideas imbedded in the concept of democracy enable students to recognize and respect global perspectives surrounding varying issues, as well as "break into practices which continue injustice" (Davies, 2008, p. 19). Davies (2008) calls this direct form of democracy *interruptive democracy*, which "uses the notions of dialogue, encounter and challenge in order to promote positive conflict in education institutions" (p. 19). Democracy focuses on the possibility of change.

A democratic classroom is one wherein students respect divergent cultural and linguistic differences, and challenge what has been traditionally designated as "normal." For art teachers specifically, it is imperative that we acknowledge the complexity of cross-cultural relationships because cultural ideologies are sometimes inherent in a culture's art and artistic expressions (Leuthold, 2011). Students must be aware and open to cultural perspectives different from their own; teaching and practicing democracy in the classroom can support this goal. Democracy teaches students and teachers to listen to alternative points of view, especially those who have often been silenced.

Democracy promotes negotiation and multiple authorities (Creighton, 1916; Sleeter & Grant, 2007). This atmosphere can be constructed by encouraging students to contribute to the curriculum agenda. For example, during the first artmaking workshop at KYC, the students and I collaboratively developed a list of social justice issues to address in the art curriculum. Everyone proposed issues and commented on others' ideas. Through discussion, the students helped one another communicate the significance of particular issues. While the students listed about ten topics, through compromise, the students settled on five issues. This process came with slight confrontation, but in the end, the students saw the choices as fair, as everyone connected with the chosen topics, although in different ways. These democratic skills that the KYC students embraced can be transferred to the larger global context.

Creating a democratic space in KYC transcended the weekly workshops. For a mural project, I offered *all* of the KYC youth an opportunity to develop and vote on the mural's overall concept and location. This process communicated to the students that their voice is critical in deciding on what happens in their community space. Consequently, the students became more invested in the artmaking. While only four students actually voted on the mural concept, design, and location, approximately fifteen students ended up participating in its creation (Figure 2). Interest peaked as participating students described to non-participating students that the project was student initiated, planned, and executed. The mural became a talking point during student-led tours at the center. They used the mural to discuss the mission of KYC and the overall journey into learning about issues related to coming out and identity (Zermeno, personal communication, January 29, 2011). In this case, practicing democracy resulted in student agency and increased feelings of self-validity.

Critical questioning and democracy provide criticality to multiculturalism (Sleeter & Grant, 2007). These tenets can help teachers re-conceptualize their teaching and guide them to facilitate engaging, mindful dialogues with students who see their teachers as cultural interlopers. They also help students address transnational, interconnected topics such as human rights, peace, and security, all of which are the focus of a global, culturally sensitive

Figure 2. Mural. Student driven collaborative project addressing gay equality.

educational framework (Kniep, 1985). As teachers in a diverse world, we are often positioned in a learning space where many of our learners differ from us culturally and ethnically; this requires us to choose educational approaches that consider such facts.

Solution 2: Participatory Action Research (PAR)

Art education scholars Stuhr, Ballengee Morris, and Daniel (2008); Garber (2004); Gude (2007); Hicks (1994); Hutzel (2007); Knight (2006); and Zimmerman (1990) have researched how to create culturally sensitive learning experiences. However, suggestions given by these scholars are not often applied (hooks, 1994; Ladson-Billings, 1999) in art classrooms. This could be out of simple lack of knowledge (Gall, 2008). PAR helps with these issues, as it relieves the teacher of the role of classroom expert.

PAR is a method of inquiry that focuses on collaboration and the creation of change on a local level (Stringer, 2007). PAR strategies are informed by "Freire's development of counterhegemonic approaches to knowledge construction within oppressed communities" (McIntyre, 2008, p. 3). The fluidity of the PAR process can be described as spirals of iterative, self-reflective cycles of plan, act, observe, and reflect (Kemmis & McTaggart, 2000). PAR thrives on collaboration and group dynamics in research and teaching. It supports stakeholders developing their own solutions to their problems and situations (Stringer, 2007). PAR works to dissolve the hierarchy existent within traditional research/classroom relationships: researcher over participant or teacher over student. As a result, research/curriculum is context specific.

At KYC, curriculum development was collaborative. During the first week of Kaleidoscope He(ARTS), the students compiled a list of social justice issues they wanted the curriculum to address. Then, I developed art projects to support student exploration of the topics. While student input concerning specific artmaking projects would have been ideal, I had some predetermined goals that were specific to my dissertation research, one being to teach students how to manipulate very specific media. Under different circumstances, like an unlimited budget and no accountability for a dissertation, I would have preferred that the students make decisions about the media they learned in the workshops. These logistical matters influenced the amount of student input as it related to media choice. Still, the students played a significant role in making other choices related to curriculum development, specifically workshop foci.

Each workshop began with a discussion around one of the social justice issues chosen by the students, and the latter half of the workshop was dedicated to artmaking. Using the students' inquiries as points of exploration initiated deeper learning (Freire, 1970; Stringer, 2007). In addition, the students' role in curriculum development altered their comprehension about the teacher-student dichotomy. Initially, the students seemed apprehensive about asserting their power during curriculum planning. However, the students eventually realized that I perceived them as experts, as their ideas remained at forefront of the artmaking workshops. The students at KYC transitioned from listener and observer to active contributor and discussant (Perumal, 2008). Once the students realized they had the power to control their learning, their outlook on the workshops evolved positively. Student participation increased from five participants during the first workshop to 11 participants by the end of 4 months.

PAR works toward shifting the power over knowledge ownership. Participatory action researchers see stakeholders' local knowledge as vital. Research is often built around this local expertise (Torre, 2009). Similarly, in a classroom where a teacher uses PAR, curriculum is built closely around students' knowledge. When individuals help guide their own learning, knowledge becomes sustainable (Freire, 1970). The process of PAR assists in working toward this goal by supporting the aspiration to de-stabilize naturalized power hierarchies, especially the teacher over student dichotomy (Torre, 2009). With students in the role of expert, they can communicate what is important to them and their culture; teachers no longer

have to assume how culture is relevant to their students' learning and knowledge creation.

PAR requires a relinquishing of power (Stringer, 2007) and it recommends that teachers be responsive and open to the needs of stakeholders. So, while students chose curriculum topics on the first day, the topics were negotiable. For instance, bullying was not a topic established during the first workshop session. However, about 4 weeks into the Kaleidoscope He(ARTS) program, there was an increase in reports of suicides of LGBTQ teens by various news sources.

The KYC director introduced anti-bullying films and implemented new bullying support programs. To react to the immediacy of this issue in the lives of the LGBTQ youth, the students and I engaged in an art workshop in which they developed anti-bullying messages and logos; then I taught the students how to silk-screen and transfer their images onto paper and t-shirts (Figures 3–5). Some students even wore their t-shirts to a KYC anti-bullying event. In this case, the act of creating art provided opportunities for increasing personal awareness and expanding knowledge about social justice. Additionally it incited action (wearing the t-shirts to an anti-bullying event),

Figure 3. Silkscreen. Bullying: See It, Solve It, Stop It.

Figure 4. Silkscreen. Laugh Now, Cry Later.

Figure 5. Silkscreen. No Bullying.

which supports PAR's goal for marginalized groups to critically examine their own realities, and consequently make efforts to improve and change their own conditions (McIntyre, 2008).

Ultimately, I cannot assert that PAR made me any less of an outsider to the students at KYC. But it is not important to be an insider to be a successful educator. PAR methods guided me in facilitating an atmosphere of respect. Students freely articulated their personal beliefs and worldviews, while simultaneously being cognizant and sensitive to the interpretations and perspectives of others. My support of such compromise and reciprocity did not require me to understand the various complexities of LGBTQ culture. I recognized the desire and need for students to create knowledge through a personal, cultural lens. All the while, my objective to teach various art methods was not disrupted. PAR initiated this collaborative teaching and learning transaction by countering the traditional teacher-learner dichotomy and recognizing alternative ways of knowing. As a result, ultimately, the students' definition of me as a "Catholic" was irrelevant to the overall experience.

Conclusion

There has been a push for global education to be institutionalized and implemented in the daily practices of teachers (Case, 1993). While this goal has yet to come to fruition, educators can at least adopt strategies that demonstrate they are mindful of cultural sensitivity. I claim that a multicultural and social reconstructionist approach and PAR are effective in this way, as they each support the study of human values and characteristics (e.g., equality, justice, and liberty) that transcend simple group identity, a critical objective when teaching in a global world (Kniep, 1985). These two strategies can help teachers navigate through the complexity of culture and difference, as well as inform the creation of global citizens. While there is no explicit solution that alleviates fear of teaching in a diverse, global context, these two theoretical approaches can help teachers make closer connections to students' lives, regardless of difference. They initiate the reevaluation of and change in teaching, curriculum development, and student involvement in learning (Mesa-Bains, 1996). Using them, I was able to *hear* the needs of my students and *respond* with meaningful, relevant art content. A multicultural and social reconstructionist approach and PAR generated opportunities for learning that did not rely on my knowing everything about a specific culture. Multiple student voices orchestrated the learning and knowledge-making experience. This resulted in a curriculum that met the demands of varying learners.

Lee (2009) writes, "The role of culture in learning is complex and fundamental" (p. 246). As teachers in a global world, "our work in education should be informed by theories that account for the variation in pathways for learning across cultural communities" (Lee, 2009, p. 246). A multicultural and social reconstructionist approach and PAR can guide teaching, as well as promote respect and empathy in students. Learning skills like critical questioning, democracy, and respecting alternative narratives often results in caring and openness to difference (Sleeter & Grant, 2007). This not only affects the immediate classroom, but also affects how students consider and react to the ideas and beliefs of others all over the world.

REFERENCES

Adams, M. (1997). Pedagogical frameworks for social justice education. In M. Adams, L. A. Bell & P. Griffin (Eds.), *Teaching for diversity and social justice* (pp. 30–43). New York, NY: Routledge.

Banks, J. A. (Ed.). (2009). *The Routledge international companion to multicultural education.* New York, NY: Routledge.

Banks, J. A., & Banks, C. A. (Eds.). (1989). *Multicultural education: Issues and perspectives.* Boston, MA: Allyn and Bacon.

Case, R. (1993). Key elements of a global perspective. *Social Education, 57*(6), 318–325.

Chalmers, G. (2002). Celebrating pluralism six years later: Visual transculture/s, education, and critical multiculturalism. *Studies in Art Education, 43*(4), 293–306.

Collins, P. H. (2002). Defining black feminist thought. In P. Essed & D. T. Goldberg (Eds.), *Race critical theories* (pp. 152–175). Malden, MA: Blackwell.

Creighton, J. E. (1916). Review of the book *Democracy and education,* by J. Dewey. *The Philosophical Review, 25*(5), 735–741.

Davies, L. (2008). Interruptive democracy in education. In J. Zajda, L. Davies & S. Majhanovich (Eds.), *Comparative and global pedagogies: Equity, access and democracy in education* (pp. 15–31). New York, NY: Springer.

Delgado, R. (1999). *Critical race theory* (2nd ed.). Philadelphia, PA: Temple University Press.

Freire, P. (1970). *Pedagogy of the oppressed.* New York, NY: Continuum.

Gall, D. (2008). Navigating a way through plurality and social responsibility. *International Journal of Art & Design Education, 27*(1), 19–26.

Garber, E. (2004). Social justice and art education. *Visual Arts Research, 30*(2), 4–22.

Gay, G. (1995). Bridging multicultural theory and practice. *Multicultural Education, 3*(1), 4–9.

Gude, O. (2007). Principles of possibility: Consideration for a 21st century art & culture curriculum. *Art Education, 60*(1), 6–17.

Hicks, L. E. (1994). Social reconstruction and community. *Studies in Art Education, 35*(3), 149–156.

hooks, b. (1994). *Teaching to transgress: Education as a practice of freedom.* New York, NY: Routledge.

Hutzel, K. (2007). Reconstructing a community, reclaiming a playground: A participatory action research study. *Studies in Art Education, 48*(3), 299–315.

Kaleidoscope Youth Center. (2009). *About us.* Retrieved from www.kycohio.org/about-us.html

Kemmis, S., & McTaggart, R. (2000). Participatory action research. In N. K. Denzin & Y. S. Lincoln (Eds.), *Handbook of qualitative research* (2nd ed., pp. 567–605). Thousand Oaks, CA: Sage.

Kniep, W. M. (1985). Defining global education by its content. *Social Education, 50*(6), 437–446.

Knight, W. B. (2006). Using contemporary art to challenge cultural values, beliefs, and assumptions. *Art Education, 59*(4), 39–45.

Ladson-Billings, G. (1999). Preparing teachers for diverse student populations: A critical race theory perspective. *Review of Research in Education, 24*(1), 211–247.

Ladson-Billings, G. J. (2004). New directions in multicultural education: Complexities, boundaries, and critical race theory. In J. Banks & C. Banks (Eds.), *Handbook of research on multicultural education* (2nd ed.) (pp. 50–65). San Francisco, CA: Jossey-Bass.

Ladson-Billings, G., & Tate, W. (1995). Toward a critical race theory of education. *Teachers College Record, 97*(1), 47–68.

Lee, C. (2009). Cultural influences on learning. In J. A. Banks (Ed.), *The Routledge international companion to multicultural education* (pp. 239–251). New York, NY: Routledge.

Leuthold, S. (2011). *Cross-cultural issues in art: Frames for understanding.* New York, NY: Routledge.

May, S., & Sleeter, C. E. (2010). *Critical multiculturalism: Theory and praxis.* New York, NY: Routledge.

McIntyre, A. (2008). *Participatory action research.* Thousand Oaks, CA: Sage.

Mesa-Bains, A. (1996). Teaching students the way they learn. In S. Cahan & Z. Kocur (Eds.), *Contemporary art and multicultural education* (pp. 31–38). New York, NY: Routledge.

Perumal, J. (2008). Student resistance and teacher authority: The demands and dynamics of collaborative learning. *Journal of Curriculum Studies, 40*(3), 381–398.

Sleeter, C. E., & Grant, C. A. (1994). *Making choices for multicultural education: Five approaches to race, class, and gender.* New York, NY: Merrill.

Sleeter, C. E., & Grant, C. A. (2007). *Turning on learning: Five approaches for multicultural teaching plans for race, class, gender, and disability.* New York, NY: Merrill.

Stringer, E. (2007). *Action research.* Thousand Oaks, CA: Sage.

Stuhr, P., Ballengee Morris, C., & Daniel, V. (2008). Social justice through curriculum: Investigating issues of diversity. In R. Mason & T. Eca (Eds.), *International dialogues about visual culture, education and art* (pp. 85–93). Chicago, IL: Intellect Books.

Thoms, K. (2011). Critical thinking requires critical questioning. *The Professional & Organizational Development Network in Higher Education: Essays on teaching excellence.* Retrieved from http://teaching.uchicago.edu/oldsite/pod/98-99/Thoms.htm

Torre, M. (2009). Participatory action research and critical race theory: Fueling spaces for *Nos-otras* to research. *The Urban Review, 41*(1), 106–120.

Zajda, J., Davies, L., & Majhanovich, S. (Eds.). (2008). *Comparative and global pedagogies: Equity, access and democracy in education.* New York, NY: Springer.

Zimmerman, E. (1990). *Teaching art from a global perspective.* Bloomington IN: Adjunct ERIC Clearinghouse for Art Education, ERIC Clearinghouse for Social Studies/Social Science Education. Retrieved from www.ericdigests.org/pre-9219/global.htm

ENDNOTES

[1] Kaleidoscope Youth Center is a community organization with the mission "to work in partnership with young people [ages 12–20] in [Columbus] Ohio to create safe and empowering environments for lesbian, gay, bisexual, transgender and questioning youth through advocacy, education and support" (Kaleidoscope Youth Center, 2009, para. 2).

[2] He(Arts) is a play on words, emphasizing the word "Art" embedded in the word "heart"—a vital organ in the body.

[3] I was called a "Catholic" by a youth participant during one of the artmaking workshops. I learned that "Catholic" is a slang term used for a person who does not identify as LGBTQ.

[4] A multicultural and social reconstructionist approach is one of five approaches to multicultural education specified by Christine Sleeter and Carl Grant, two forerunners in multicultural education. Introduced in the late 1980s, this approach is considered to be the most effective of the five that they presented, as it comprehensively attends to power and social justice in and out of the classroom, an overarching goal of multicultural education in general.

[5] A component of this law allows law enforcement officers to ask for and verify the immigration papers of any person or persons who are perceived to be an illegal immigrant in the United States. For more details and provisions of the law, visit www.ncsl.org/research/immigration/analysis-of-arizonas-immigration-law.aspx

CHAPTER 12

Glimpses of Guanajuato:
Encounters and Expressions of Borders in Art Education

COURTNEY WEIDA
Adelphi University

I find that I am envisioning language barriers as a layer of ice between people: beautiful, mysterious, softening sound, invisible in some lights, and yet still a boundary. How are our many borders beautiful and terrible? (June 2009 travel journal,[1] first night in Mexico)

For art teachers to explore issues of cultural representations and sensitivities in their own classrooms and other teaching spaces, and to relate theory to practice, they must reflect thoughtfully upon their own lives, living places, and contexts in relationships to their students. I have had the opportunity to teach several university-level courses in art, art education, and art history around compelling issues of gender and culture. As a female, I feel somewhat comfortable exploring particular questions and representations of gender because I am familiar with these works, on personal and professional levels. But as a person with uncertain but likely Caucasian heritage, I am less at ease investigating several cultural traditions and issues. I have often been fortunate to teach art not only to college students, but also to adolescents. I looked for connections between multicultural art history college courses in Latin American art and my younger, predominantly Latino students. My undergraduate students and I utilized Brenda Jo Bright and Liza Blakewell's (1995) *Looking High and Low: Art and Cultural Identity* and Lucy Lippard's (1990) *Mixed Blessings: Art in a Multicultural America*, which thoughtfully address some of the challenges of relating and researching from many different artistic and cultural perspectives. Bright and Blakewell (1995) argue that art is created across various evaluative, social, cultural, and geographical boundaries, and that art historical analysis should consider these forces within aesthetic production and critique.

With such an approach, teachers can meaningfully explore the artistic and national boundaries between two countries, the United States and Mexico (something I endeavored to do when teaching art to middle school students). More recently, as an art education professor in the Northeastern US, I was given the opportunity to cross national boundaries and visit Guanajuato, Mexico (Figure 1). I compared my literature-based experiences of Mexican art with art lectures and events in museums, galleries, studios, and schools. Since that time, I reflected upon my visit and incorporated images, ideas, and questions from these rich experiences into my creative processes as a K-12 teaching artist and teacher educator. This chapter explores my glimpses of Guanajuato, Mexico, in the context of subsequent teaching experiences in Garden City, New York, with preservice art teachers.

Figure 1. The author in Guanajuato, Mexico.

Figure 2. Guanajuato: view from above.

Garden City to Guanajuato: Glimpses

I would emphasize *glimpses* as the operative term here—not only for obvious alliterative purposes, but also because I want to be upfront about my own healthy anxiety surrounding issues of authenticity and authority as an author and educator. Desai (2000) reminds us that accuracy in representations of culture may often be impossible, so I will provide some glimpses and related questions that I hope art educators will find useful. While this chapter will not argue that sprinkle and stir[2] approaches

to art education across cultural borders are appropriate as an end, it will seek to explore how art teachers might draw from diverse works of art and cultural contexts as outsiders, with growing but limited knowledge. In other words, I hope to see and write beyond the level of tourists' postcards.

Perhaps it should go without saying that I loved the beautiful blue-green hummingbirds, relished fresh guacamole, and was dazzled by the rainbow of houses in Mexico (Figure 2). However, I do want to acknowledge the allure of a somewhat tourist-like, consumerist emphasis to exoticize culture by limiting observations to this superficial category. As La Pocha Nostra (2011), an artist group including Guillermo Gómez-Peña specifies, art and cultural expression within particular contexts also "furthers dialogue by creating various pathways, trajectories, and unsuspected intersections which are mostly discovered/

For Further Consideration

Weida describes an immersive journey through an unfamiliar landscape that altered her thinking about culturally sensitive teaching practices. Think back on a trip to another part of the country or world that introduced you to unfamiliar scenery and people, and/or new artistic practices and aesthetics.

1. To what extent did the encounter with the unfamiliar affect your understanding of The Other? What effect, if any, did this have on your artistic practices?

2. Would you describe your experiences as of a tourist-like nature or as profoundly transformative? Explain.

3. What strategies did Weida employ that assisted her in making connections to or with the unfamiliar?

4. Based on your own experiences, what additional strategies or extended strategies would you recommend as initiating students inquiry and deepening awareness/understanding of other national or cultural artistic practices and expressions?

learned through the body and later circulated through language and actions" (para. 16). Through juxtapositions of my travel journals with research in art and art education pertaining to Mexico, and with related learning explorations of culture and identity by my students, I will present some pathways and possibilities in pedagogy.

Mexico and Mexican Artists in North American Art Education

Maybe because I had often been charged with teaching courses in multicultural art history in the Americas, I was especially pleased to be so close to actual Latin American art in museums and churches. I smiled with fellow travelers at the signs outside a church that read "Te llama al corazon, no al celular" (I call the heart, not the cell). (June 2009 travel journal, tour of Guanajuato churches during day 2)

Perhaps as the above quote suggests, lesson planning (like art) should speak to and from our hearts (Figure 3). Before I traveled to Mexico, I conducted a survey of some recent art educational resources from the US that explored Mexican artists and art forms. My own K-12 art experiences as a student in the 1980s and 1990s had barely touched on any Latin American artworks, and I was curious about shifts and continuities in contemporary art curricula. Alabama museum educator Sartorus (2006) created an interesting art history lesson plan addressing Mexico and Modernism in painting. Although they contain some evocative images and ideas, such lessons can pose challenges for educators in that indigenous people are nameless and somewhat generalized, while European artists are referenced by name and with biographical context. Further, the art historical content of Sartorus' (2006) lesson includes quotes from Marsden Hartley's writing that Mexico devitalized him, making his depiction of Mexico limited and perhaps inappropriate if isolated from other experiences of the locale. While this lesson includes interesting examples of nature's influence on painting, it does not serve to change what Garber (1995) refers to as the Eurocentric narrative of education, in which the canon of often White, often male artists is reaffirmed, while people of color are omitted.

Yarborough and Reynolds (1996) proposed teaching about Mexican art in a more developed dialogue between original, indigenous art and creatively inspired processes and contexts of students. The curriculum introduces brightly-painted folk-art wood carvings of animals, mermaids and other fantastic creatures from the valley of Oaxaca (pronounced Wa-HAH-ka), in Mexico, that have become popular in the US in recent years. Including

Figure 3. Sign outside a church in Guanajuato.

information about makers, families, and cultures, the lesson encouraged students not to reproduce mythical characters from another tradition, but rather to imagine creatures of their own that might live in the noisy air ducts of their own schools (or in another local context where monsters could lurk). This quality of respect for both local and distant culture contrasts with Klemenson's (1985) *Art Education* article, which suggests that students studying crafts of Mexico for one semester in an East Islip High School were able to "capture the essence of Mexico" (p. 21). Although this is an admirable goal, such an exaggeration can gloss over the complexities of a vast diversity of Mexican cultures and their art forms. Further, I have found that part of the challenge and possibility of teaching across cultures is the incompleteness of any single lesson or unit of instruction. Simone Bourque, an elementary art teacher, actually traveled to Mexico and subsequently integrated explorations of skeleton iconography within her teaching (2010). Using focused information about *Dia de los Muertos* celebrations in Mexico, Bourque invited her own students to depict their own dancing skeletons at parties. This lesson impressed me with its balance of nuanced cultural imagery and content that is relatable to many North American young people, such as celebrations or parties, ultimately inviting students to create inspired but not blindly derivative works.

Mexico and Various Aesthetics of Death

I saw an exquisite spider last night under the "luna caliente" (hot moon) and then I drew a tall, elegant woman with a skull (calvaria) for her face. I love the way colors, textures, and symbols begin to creep into my dreams and thoughts, and yet I do not want to appropriate selfishly, simplistically, or inappropriately. (June 2009 travel journal, day 3 in the hotel, El Meson de los Poetas)

One of the interesting phrases I heard frequently from Mexican artists and Mexican art historians in various incarnations during my travels there was that "Mexicans carry their deaths with them." In pondering different manifestations of this idea, I think of the images of Dia de los Muertos that flooded my childhood consciousness of Mexico. I can recall how enchanting this was for me, and yet I want to go beyond caricatures, if not to see authentic images, then to at least begin to distinguish between parodies, representations, and layered complexities. We can begin to envision Mexican concepts of death not as a composite pink sugar candy skull to be consumed but as culturally, religiously, metaphorically situated concepts. Exploring contemporary Mexican art through discussions with Mexican university professors, their art students, and museum docents I encountered in my trip deepened my interest in concepts of border crossing, of identity, and representation in art. If one creates art outside of Mexico, or about issues that may or may not seem Mexican, various experiences of un-identity and alienation can result. As has been noted by Barbosa (2001) in an invited lecture about Mexican and Brazilian art, for culturally colonized countries, artists' international recognition generally translated to success at home, as was the case with folks like Héctor Márquez and Frida Kahlo. At the same time, it is odd and perhaps disconcerting to gain recognition as a representative of a place one has left.

When I was in the Museo del Pueblo, I saw exhibits that seemed to be inspired by the *Frida* film (Green, Hayek, Polstein, & Taymar, 2002) and Julie Taymar's use of a visual effect of actual objects and actors fading into reproductions of her paintings. In the Museo del Pueblo, objects dangle in front of the background of the paintings to highlight the objects and their arrangements. Specifically, cardboard reproductions of items from *My Dress Hangs There* (1933) underscore the juxtaposition of Kalho's traditional Zapotec clothing with a range of U.S. luxuries and atrocities including the toilet, smoke stacks, and government buildings, surrounded by flames. Although Guanajuato is the birthplace of Frida Kahlo's husband, Diego Rivera, the other professors and I saw as much art, literature, and tourist items about her as about him. The growing popularity of Frida seems to lead to a diversity of reconfigurations, representations, and interpretations of her work that can both continue and defy tokenism. The most unusual and surprisingly interesting of these representations of Kahlo I encountered in Guanajuato was a book about her bathroom, *El Bano de Frida Kahlo* (Bella-

tin & Iterbide, 2008), which includes somewhat hagiographic images and descriptions of this room of smocks, body casts, and some of her writings and paintings hung/scrawled there. However, the book also includes a fictional text that imagines what sort of work Frida would create if she were alive today. To me, this is the sort of imagining through art objects that may be of use as a framework for students to make meaningful sense of biography and art history in light of contemporary life.

Frida perhaps remains important for educators not only because she was an incredible surrealist painter, but also because her representations of deep fragmentations of culture, sexuality, and the body resonate today. Bartra (2003) adds, "women and folk art share a common fate in Latin America and the Caribbean: though ubiquitous, both are almost as invisible as they are disrespected by those that study this region" (p. 2). This absence and neglect serves as a call to us as educators to locate a variety of artists who address curricular themes of human experience. For example, Mexican-Spanish Remedios Varo (1908–1963) also has a great deal to offer in politics as well as art, with stunning paintings of androgynous figures and paintings with feminist themes. Leonor Fini (1908–1996) was an Argentine artist who balanced writing novels and working in fashion with surrealist painting. Fini eschewed marriage and lived with up to 23 cats at a time, and she was known also as an unapologetic painter of women. Leonora Carrington (1917–2011), a British-born surrealist who lived in Mexico and drew artistic influence from folklore and mythology, should also be mentioned among Latin American women surrealists, a realm usually discussed with examples limited to Salvador Dalí and René Magritte. I often invite my students to play games like "But can you name two?" which asks them to go beyond tokenism and Eurocentism, or "Instead of Picasso, try _____!" to help them give their own students visions and versions of art that allow meaningful participation from Latin American women and others from outside the canon of their own art historical educations.

Colonialism, Cultural Borrowing, and Conversation

University of Guanajuato Professor Benjamín Valdivia speaks of seeing Mexico with strange eyes. Is that what my eyes are? What do I see and fail to notice? (June 2009 travel journal, day 4)

Even as I note tendencies to celebrate difference in culture, I would like to point out ways in which Mexican culture can surprise and contradict well-meaning tendencies to assume conquest and view only difference and victim-ization. In the Museo Iconográfico del Quijote, my fellow professors and I were surprised by the nature of cross-cultural exchanges through art. There were unexpected identifications and representations across cultures, all related to the story of Don Quixote. The museum director spoke of Don Quixote de La Mancha as the first truly human character of a novel, making the book a sort of universal work of literature. The other professors in my tour group were quite confused that Mexican identity would be so strongly linked to a Spanish character. However, the collection of visual art representing Cervantes, Don Quixote, Sancho Panza, windmills, the book itself as an object, and several other aspects of the book originally belonged to Eulalio F. Rodrígues (1920-2009), who was born in Spain but considered Mexico his home. Museum founder Rodríguez first read the book during his internment as a soldier in the Spanish Civil war. After being warmly welcomed to Mexico with other Spanish exiles, Rodríguez was moved to create this museum, which he donated to the people of Mexico in 1987. He came to be described as publicist, author, academic, Cervantistas, and sponsor of Latin American culture. His collection included nearly every artistic media, many styles, and artists from several nations and cultures. Their arrangement and curatorial contexts add new dimensions to a well-known tale. In this way art itself offers richness and complexity to history, literature, nationalism, and cross-cultural conversations. Further, I discovered that one really has to see the art and the museum in this fascinating context to begin to understand its nuances. This museum visit reinforces the power of cultural context through experience. When I returned to the US, I often remembered this moment and it inspired me to ask my students to compare their own encounters with literature and images to those experiences they had in schools and museums, to expand the frames and lenses of their thinking.

Gazes and Voices: Seeing and Hearing Cultural Diversity in Art

> To me it's of little importance
> that you paint only a woman
> playing the violin against a backdrop of stars
> or a European landscape copied from an old calendar.
> What does leave me speechless is your voice
> your voice speaking the same shade as your hair.
> (June 2009 travel journal, excerpt from verbal poetry reading
> of Benjamín Valdivia, day 5)

My encounters in Mexico were often multisensory and evocative experiences of touching, hearing, and seeing Mexican art richly, as is described in Guanajuato

University Professor Valdivia's poem. Listening to the voices of students and professors at the university and visiting local restaurants and museums with them during these conversations provided a sort of synesthesia. I also encountered connections to my field that I might not have experienced otherwise. For example, over drinks I learned that poet and philosopher Valdivia also writes children's books that probe the experiences of disability and isolation in the US. He dramatized the situation of exclusion as a cage in playgrounds that divide children by difference, where everyone begins to realize nuances of their own difference, and enter into conversations with one another that defy categories and boundaries. This too inspired my continued interest in cultural contexts of art education, including visions of U.S. education from Latin American educators and artists. For example, I worked with preservice educators in a Harlem summer program where we invited children to compare and contrast illustrations accompanying folk tales from many cultures around a common topic, such as Cinderella.

Valdivia and his colleagues also located a great deal of powerfully cross-cultural themes and conversations in and about Mexican art that I now enjoy sharing with my own art education students. For example, Gabriel Orozco's Venice Biennale piece, *Empty Shoebox* (1993), can help us question what art is and can be in a way not entirely unlike Marcel Duchamp's *Fountain* (1917). Orozco's work could be seen as a commentary on production of shoes, a criticism of the function of the box itself, a reaction against art, or an homage to other conceptual artworks. Valdivia reminded us that Orozco once compared the art of photography to a shoebox, so that the artist places objects in a box for keeping and contemplation. To see one's entire art form as a sort of container for ideas is a fascinating way to begin a new art project with students. Orozco is also featured on Art21's website[3] for teachers, providing several resources tailored to teaching.

In addition, we talked about Héctor Zamora, who creates social interventions that are based upon deep research into the history of a particular site as well as the collective memory of local cultures. However, his works are not directly anthropological or documentary, but rather take the form of photo collages that represent fictional festivals like his *Enjambre de dirigibles* from 2009. Instead of depicting static culture, this art shows an awareness of the construction of culture and artifacts, noting an artist's own criticality as maker and interpreter of multiple meanings. We cannot assume that all art is a direct reflection and function of culture, and works like

Zamora's call attention to how culture and its rituals can be constructed, imagined, revised, and reframed. This is a wonderful example of an activity that students could explore, investigating ways in which rituals and festivals are researched, constructed, performed, and revised.

Glancing Back at Guanajuato in Garden City: Concluding Comments

Before I left Mexico, I bought a therapist shrine for my therapist mother: a tiny box filled with a very Freudian-esque couch, a skeletal patient, and a skeletal doctor; beautiful pottery for my apartment, and a mermaid (la sirena) for a friend, as well as art books for my students. What else will I bring from Mexico? What kind of "boxes" can we create and illuminate to think about all these images and ideas? (June 2009 travel journal, day 8 in San Miguel)

Reflecting back on my short time in Mexico, I like to think of it as an experience that begins to frame questions and ideas about certain cultural exchanges through and about art. While it is beyond the scope of this chapter (or any single volume) to fully theorize Mexican art and identity in the different global spaces of art education, I draw from this provocative experience to suggest points of departure for thinking about how preservice art teachers and teaching artists can make the acts of cultural visitation and exchange part of one's teaching portfolio process and daily practice. These diverse practices can include compassion toward an Other, however variously defined (self, student, spectator, one's religion, sexuality, etc.). Upon my return, my deepened interest in Mexican art as part of art education included explorations of women's altars, from researching Kay Turner's (1999) *Beautiful Necessity: The Art of Women's Altars* and related sources on the topic, to collaborative community altars at my university celebrating Dia de los Muertos (Figure 4). I have

Figure 4. Collaborative Dia de los Muertos altar at Adelphi University, November 1, 2009.

also been inspired by my colleagues in Mexico and their forms of arts-based research for study-abroad students to explore new ways of seeing, processing, expressing, and knowing, in order to cultivate students' awareness of difference in a way that does not blanket/highlight everything in US/Other terms (Rodríguez, 2006).

Some of the questions I ask my New York students to continue through digital conversations with the students of some of my colleagues in Mexico include:

1. How is each person always somehow Other? Can you reflect upon those aspects of self that are different/Other in the local community and in the classroom?

2. How does this Otherness affect looking at art, teaching about art, and looking at students looking at art?

3. How can you make room for this Otherness through your roles as artist, teacher, spectator/critic, or community member?

4. How might the art object itself somehow facilitate, mediate, contain, or transform these processes?

The discussions and artistic responses of my students during their research, teaching, and artmaking further the dialogues that began in Mexico. Some students in my art education courses began to question teachers' roles in studying and discussing indigenous and localized art forms, emailing art teachers in other countries to survey and rethink various approaches. Others have reframed cultural issues through metaphor, looking at the art teacher as a sort of Other in school culture. One student wrote of the *coexistence* of art teachers and others within school communities, in terms of ways in which creativity can be a link or bridge between different subject matters. This comment resonated a sense of the art teacher as a sort of outsider or ambassador, perhaps parallel to other cultural workers. In addition, my students also addressed Otherness and culture through dis/ability culture, or through biographical representation. Two students found connections in their work around the common theme of portraiture. In looking at both her own work and that of a student in Mexico, one student commented that they both showed an interest in "capturing people during moments through their everyday lives" (C. Streeff, personal communication, December 1, 2011). (See Figure 5.) This was particularly intriguing because the New York students had been invited to explore their fieldwork and artmaking experiences through portraiture methodology, an ethnographic interviewing framework that compares the art of conversation to that of

Figure 5. Portrait by Casidhe Streeff, exhibited in 2012 Student Exhibition at Adelphi University in Garden City.

creating a portrait. Portraiture methodology, as described by Lawrence-Lightfoot and Davis (1997), encourages the researcher to describe and interpret the words of research participants in a parallel process to that of artistic portraiture, attempting to represent research participants in a way that aims to coincide with and extend some of their views and visions of themselves. Just as a painted portrait is likely to show some aspect of the sitter that is recognizable, research portraits may also introduce new and interesting aspects of him/her. Similarly, the students' portraits in prose and paint were often experienced as ways of "connecting."

There is no single way to connect or implement cross-cultural reflection in the teaching of art. After my trip to Mexico, my approaches to teaching shifted in many ways: not only to include more contemporary Mexican artists and histories in my teaching, but also to bring direct quotes, objects, and experiences from Mexico into conversations with preservice art teachers. In doing so, I wanted to highlight ways in which teachers can examine well-known Mexican artists like Kahlo in new lights; locate historical complexities of conquest and cultural borrowing within artistic identities; and thoughtfully explore the shifting roles of culture, documentation, and imagination within contemporary Latin American art. I hope that the various connections and juxtapositions of this chapter can begin to inspire teachers and students to move beyond tourism and consumption to explore practices of reflection and processes of artistic inquiry and exchange around national cultures and artistic expression.

REFERENCES

Barbosa, A. (2001). The esculeas de pintura al aire libre in Mexico: Freedom, form, and culture. *Studies in Art Education, 42*(4), 285–297.

Bartra, E. (2003). *Crafting gender.* Durham, NC: Duke University Press.

Bellatin, M., & Iterbide, G. (2008). *El Baño de Frida Kahlo; Demerol Sin Fecha De Caducidad* [*Frida Kahlo's bath; Demerol without expiration date*]. Mexico City, Mexico: Editorial RM.

Bourque, S. (2010). The skeleton's Halloween. *Art & Activities, 148*(2), 36–37.

Bright, B. J., & Blakewell, L. (1995). *Looking high and low: Art and cultural identity.* Tucson: University of Arizona Press.

Desai, D. (2000). Imaging difference: The politics of representation in multicultural art education. *Studies in Art Education, 41*(2), 114–129.

Garber, E. (1995). Teaching art in the context of culture: A study in the borderlands. *Studies in Art Education, 36*(4), 218–232.

Green, S., Hayek, S., & Polstein, J. (Producers), & Taymar, J. (Director). (2002). *Frida* [Motion picture]. United States: Ventanarosa, Miramax Films.

Kelmenson, L. (1985). A sense of Mexico. *Art Education, 28*(1), 21–22.

La Pocha Nostra. (2011). What is pocha? Retrieved from www.pochanostra.com/what

Lawrence-Lightfoot, S., & Davis, J. H. (1997). *The art and science of portraiture.* San Francisco, CA: Jossey-Bass.

Lippard, L. (1990). *Mixed blessings: Art in a multicultural America.* New York, NY: Pantheon.

Rodríguez, K. (2006). Experiences with poetry, pedagogy and participant observation: Writing with students in a study abroad program. *International Journal on Education and the Arts, 7*(1), 1–19.

Sartorius, T. (2006). Modernist in Mexico. *Arts & Activities, 139*(3), 30–32.

Yarborough, B., & Reynolds, N. (1996). Duct monsters: Elaboration on Oaxacan folk art. *Arts & Activities, 11*(8), 24–25.

ENDNOTES

[1] From June 1–8, 2009, I traveled to Guanajuato, Mexico, with a group of other professors. This chapter includes excerpts from an extensive travel journal I kept during this time.

[2] *Sprinkle and stir* approaches to art education are understood as tokenism, or including a few superficial references to women and people of color outside the Western canon (Garber, 1995).

[3] See www.pbs.org/art21/artists/gabriel-orozco

CHAPTER 13

Suburb as Site:
Creating a Global Collaborative Art Environment in Secondary Art and Photography Classes

KATHRYN COLEMAN
SUSAN COLEMAN
Liverpool Girls' High School, New South Wales, Australia

Suburb as Site was a program designed to engage secondary-level photography students in global spaces and community citizenship through cultural and structural frames,[1] as defined in the New South Wales, Australia Board of Studies Syllabus.[2] Students in the program explored uses of visual coding and semantic cues, considered how visual literacy skills could be applied to photographic artmaking activities, shared photographic ideas about life in their suburban community, and collaborated with students inter-nationally in creating art based on evolved understandings of suburbia. As a visual arts educator and teacher charged with developing a curriculum for photography students of our school, the Suburb as Site program conceptualized art practice as a narrative (Brown, Lysaght, & Westbrook, 2007) in which students' original ideas of a *suburb* as a *site* might be depicted. The project was taught as a multi-national collaboration between students from Liverpool in southwestern Sydney, Australia, and students in Denver, Colorado, United States of America. The goal of the project was to establish an authentic learning experience for students as an online community of photographers, similar to Instagram (http://instagram.com) and Hipstamatic (http://hipstamatic.com), which are social, online portfolio spaces inhabited by professional photographers. Through engagements with digital images of museum artifacts and artmaking, the cross-national exchange allowed students to discover and learn how images are socially valued and coded. Students also were able to hone their skills in literacy, language, culture, and geography through online collaborations.

In this chapter, we will present the concepts and the teaching and learning strategies employed as a result of Suburb as Site's theoretical underpinnings, as found in in the New South Wales (NSW) Visual Arts curriculum. We will also describe new technological and pedagogical strategies and learning opportunities that digital content, based on contemporary museum practices, provided students and their teachers. The original goals of the project were to situate visual arts education in a virtual global context and establish a collaborative artmaking experience between photography students in two geographically diverse school communities. The results, however, offered a number of unexpected learning outcomes and occasions to develop skills as members of a globalized art community through intercommunication, aesthetic and technical skill-development, and cross-national collaboration.

Suburb as Site

Suburb as Site was developed at Liverpool Girls' High School, a large, comprehensive, single-sex high school in southwestern Sydney, New South Wales, Australia. Liverpool Girls' enjoys a reputation as an inclusive high school that offers a high-quality academic curriculum that features a variety of learning opportunities for students. The school serves a large population of students from immigrant families who are from diverse cultural, social, and economic backgrounds. Eighty-six percent of the student body come with first-language backgrounds other than English. The major cultural groups represented in the school community are Middle Eastern, Eastern European, Pacific Islander, and South East Asian, as well as students from Vietnam and China. In the past few years there has also been an increase in refugee students from Iraq, Iran, and African countries including Guinea, Democratic Republic of Congo, and Sudan.

The visual arts faculty is successful in preparing students to achieve exiting exam scores at or above the statewide average. Subjects offered include Visual Arts, Photography, and Visual Design. Students are encouraged to participate in district and state programs such as gifted and talented art camps and art gallery and museum programs for selected students, and in 2010 the school was the recipient of an Australia Council funded grant for an Artist in Residence. We are two teachers from Liverpool Girls' High School, and in this chapter we will share and reflect on a curriculum project whereby our students participated in a cross-national online learning community focused by digital art.

The Suburb as Site project was designed as a collaborative effort, with two schools, two teachers, and two classes of students working together to develop skills and techniques as photographers. The theme of suburbia was selected because both schools are located in suburban areas of their respective cities. The partner school, Horizon High School, is located in Thornton, Colorado. It has a strong art program with extensive resources that are maintained by an active art faculty. The collaboration between the schools came about when chapter author Kathryn Coleman worked at Horizon High School through a Fulbright Teacher Scholarship and Exchange.

Colleague and friend Suzi Melly is the coordinating teacher at Horizon, as well as a practicing photographer and active member of the art community in Denver. Her artistic practices, experiences, and skills were important for the overall success of the project, as she led her students in the US on a journey of discovery with our students in Australia. Nevertheless, in this chapter, we will specifically focus on the learning outcomes, both expected and unexpected, of the Suburb as Site program from the perspectives of the Australian students and their teacher, Kathryn Coleman.

Photography and Collaboration

Suburb as Site was developed to foster a global engagement with photographic art and establish authentic, real world contexts in which students might develop skills of photography. Photographers often tell stories, present visual narratives of social environments, and comment on the world around them through their imagery. They capture images of life through their lenses and engage audiences by inviting them to explore these images. Thus, photographic work is by nature a collaborative interaction between a subject, photographer, and audience. Yet, in brick-and-mortar classrooms, our photography visual arts students often work in isolated spaces; the nature of darkroom work predicates independent work. Online, collaborative spaces that the Internet enables encourage shared art knowledge and practices, and social interactions of analysis and critique (Robbie & Zeeng, 2008).

Supportive learning and making practices were seen as particularly useful for photography students at Liverpool Girls' High School. These students have had a wide variety of life experiences. Many have seen trauma, experienced poverty, or suffered great economic stresses in their homelands. The move to Australia for some of these students has not been without anxiety. Some are new to the Australian way of life. They entered a new world as immigrants, without knowing the local language, and often alone as members of single families. In past teaching programs, their emotional and cultural issues were addressed by asking the students to visually present feelings, beliefs, and cultural representations about their home environments. Also, they were assigned, in art and photography classes, to develop images about the spaces and places where they live in their current community. This allowed teachers to address the New South Wales syllabus in their curriculum while students discovered things about their past and present communities through their artmaking.

For Further Consideration

Activity: Model the Suburb as Site Project

1. Practice
How do artists tell us about who they are? Where they live? What they do? Where they come from?

Investigate the genre of *suburbia*—or other geographic space that describes your living space—in photography by collecting images by local and international artists (or images by artists from very different cultures) that both live and work in the area where they practice. Use online museum and gallery sites through digitized collections to survey this subject. Share and present your findings in your digital portfolio.

2. Suburb as Site photo shoot
Who am I? Where do I live? What do I do? Where do I come from?

Produce a series of images that reflect your local community as site. Take introductory images of where you live, your building or house, letterbox, street, and local playground. Reflect on these images and title them. In your intentions and artist statement use your written reflections, research findings, stories about your geographic community, and thoughts from peers to construct a narrative about this space as site. Discuss and consider ideas about the term *site*, and share and present your images, ideas, and intentions in your digital portfolio.

3. Critical ideas
Using the Conceptual Framework (Artist, Artwork, Audience, and World) in Figure A, critically analyze the work of two artists of your choice.

Select two artists: one who lives and works in your local environment (community, city, state, country) and one international artist who lives and works in another space and/or environment unlike your own.

Explore the relationships between the artist as photographer, videographer, digital artist, filmmaker, and performance artist; their photographs and artworks; and the events, places, and spaces of their of the worlds, as well as the relevant audiences. These audiences are multi-level and interrelated, and include viewers, curators, authors, and others.

In your analysis, draw comparisons and conclusions to both artists' practices through the framework. What are the similarities and differences in their practices,

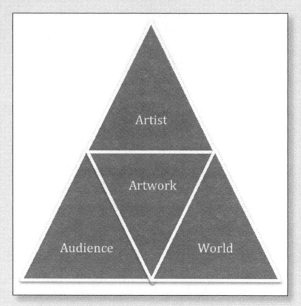

Figure A. Photographic and Digital Media Conceptual Framework, retrieved from www.boardofstudies.nsw.edu. au/syllabus_sc/pdf_doc/photo_dig_media_710_syl.pdf

photographs, topics, and genre in terms of the location of their practice?

4. Synthesis
Present your living space as site. Curate a series of photographic images (6-12) that reflect your self, family, friends, and neighbors through images of your suburb as a site of practice. Using the introductory images of where you live, your building or house, letter box, street, and local playground, and any other "iconic" and symbolic or specifically "local" images, to highlight where is it that you live—such as the local corner store, local fields, and significant environmental spaces, for example.

5. Evaluation
Create two pieces that reflect your practice and critical reflection.

Create two new images based on works selected from your practice and two images selected from your chosen artists from the critical study. Use "appropriation"[1] to reuse, repurpose, and recreate meaning from these site images to create two new images with new meaning, in order to make a new statement about your environment. Consider the frames (Subjective, Structural, Cultural, and Post-Modern) in Figure B to generate these two images.

continued on next page

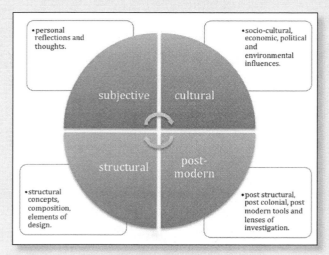

Figure B. The subjective, structural, cultural, and post-modern frames or lenses generate different understandings and ideas to provide a focus for different investigations about artist and self in practice. Make judgments about the value of these ideas or materials in your digital portfolio and curate the images in your presentation.

6. Critical Considerations and Extensions

What understanding of global cultural experiences does this exhibition reveal? What do audiences take away from the exhibition? If the exhibition were to be seen by audiences from the other (exchange) nation or culture, what differing impressions or messages might they take from it?

Consider asking exhibit audiences to leave comments in response to the viewing experience. Analyze these for understanding of audience reaction and responses to the work. If the exhibit is held in more than one country or site, compare the audience responses from site to site.

What new understanding of culture do these responses elicit?

Endnote

[1] Appropriation: When we use an image, sound, artwork, or idea which has been used before by another artist, we are appropriating, re-using and re-mixing the purpose and original intent to make a new comment. We often hope that the original source is still recognizable for the audience as it contains layered meanings and creates new ideas.

We extended a previously successful program, which involved an artist-in-residence working with students collaboratively through online microblogging[3] and in face-to-face encounters, by moving our collaborative explorations beyond the local community and our walled classroom. We invited a teacher and students from a school on the other side of the world to work with us as a combined art community. Suburb as Site introduced our students to new stories, images, and global perspectives beyond the cultural and geographic limitations of their past and present experiences.

Objectives and Assignments

Global citizens are aware of the wide diverse community and world that surrounds them; they act as responsible and respectful citizens (Oxfam, 1997). Global citizenship is an important aspect of learning and teaching in New South Wales (NSW) schools in Australia, particularly in the art classroom where we see how diverse world contexts influence artists economically, politically, socially, culturally, technologically, and environmentally. The aim

was to have students investigate artists and artworks that have been influenced by suburban themes and settings from digital museum repositories, then produce a series of personal images that present a clear narrative of their understandings of suburban life in Australia and the US. Strategies included communication between the students of the two schools through social media, and online museum experiences that were supported and facilitated at each stage by art teachers in both countries. Specific tasks asked of the students were:

- Develop a body of work from images based on the students' current home environment in the local suburban community: cultivate ideas for photo shoots and produce a series of 12 images.

- Create images as visual representations or narratives that explain visually how and where they live, and who else lives there. Use these images (i.e., a building or house, postal letter box, street view, etc.) to initiate discussions in edmodo.com4 about similarities or differences in everyday life.

- Use Photoshop or any personally preferred software or medium to develop an image in collaboration with a student from the school in the cooperating country. The finished image should integrate both of the suburbs in which the cooperating students live.

- Using reflective blogging techniques of online journaling, post weekly reflections about: (1) where we live, (2) how we live, and (3) who else lives here.

- Develop an online museum of images, from online worldwide collections of images, which demonstrates ideas of the suburbs as a site. Collaboratively curate these images as an exhibition.

Students were directed to consider typical "suburban" images suggested by the project planner Kathryn Coleman, because differences between these spaces in Australia and America were pronounced and visibly obvious. In Australia, for example, we post our letters and mail from a neighborhood post box located in the streets and not from our letterboxes, and our letterboxes do not have flags on the sides, as found in the US. Our train stations are the most used form of public transport and are in every city and suburb, whereas the car is the most commonly used form of transportation in Colo-

Figure 1. Screen shot of Edmodo homepage.

Figure 2. Screen shot from Suburb as Site website.

rado. Therefore, cultural artifacts selected for representation, reflection, and comment by peers cross-nationally included: (1) a letterbox, (2) the local garage (petrol station), (3) the corner store, (4) the train station, (5) a local children's park and, (6) a backyard clothesline. There were enough differences in how these objects and places were experienced to provide starters for discussions about suburbs as sites of representation of self in particular local contexts.

To integrate additional concepts of suburban spaces into the project, Kathryn designed the project Suburb as Site to incorporate links to online museum sites. This provided students from both schools with a selection of digitized art images of suburban life as points of reference for discussing and sharing their own personal life experiences.

Setting the Scene: Visual Arts Education in New South Wales

Curriculum guidelines for visual arts education in New South Wales (NSW) address contemporary and historical art content through practice, conceptual frameworks, and *frames*, which "give meaning and are the instrument for generating different understandings of the function of and relationships between artist-artwork-world-audience" (Board of Studies New South Wales, 2004, p. 12). Visual arts educators in NSW are obliged to teach a Postmodern and Humanist visual arts education that recognizes differing "positions may be taken about relationships among persons, art, and education and many of these positions are likely to be in conflict" (MacGregor, 1992, para. 1). Furthermore, values and beliefs about art are considered to be "constructed out of social interactions and indeed are designated 'art works' by those elements in society that sponsor them" (MacGregor, 1992, para. 1).

This Postmodern and Humanist pedagogical approach advocates that students engage in learning through study of artmaking, art criticism, and art history. Approaches to teaching art content may differ from school to school; however, curriculum guidelines require teaching of core hours and standardized assessable components, which are in school-based assessments and external exams in the Higher School Certificate (HSC).

New Technologies, New Pedagogies

Web 2.0 developments for teaching critical and historical studies in art education have been changed by

Figure 3 a and b. Student photographs from Liverpool.

spaces such as Art Project powered by Google (see www.googleartproject.com). This interactive virtual tour enables educators and students to see artworks up close, examine floor plans, and curatorially glimpse how works are displayed in major art galleries and museums around the world. Such tours are possible in Australian classrooms where digital cameras, projectors, and interactive whiteboards are standard features (Hunter & Beveridge, 2006). Many secondary students in NSW have net-books provided by the Federal Government, which supports schooling from Year 9 to Year 12. These made it possible for all of our students to participate in the Suburb as Site program. We designed an environment for students from differing cultural backgrounds to interact by utilizing blogs as collaborative writing tools. Blogs allow students to write reflectively about their learning experiences and can be found as free cloud spaces like Edmodo (edmodo.com), which was chosen as a blog and microblogging platform because it interacts with social spaces such as

Facebook. Edmodo is easily set up by teachers and used by students to replicate a learning system; it offers a survey or polling feature, online assignment submission, and a grade book.

Blogging, as a form of journaling, with its emphasis on writing, was an important tool for art students in this project, as it supports reflective, personal, and process-oriented thinking. Blogging also can provide peer support in a community of practice. Opportunities to personally reflect as well as receive feedback from peers and support from colleagues encourages self-direction. We found our students reflected on their learning in the blog formats more frequently and fluently than they had in the physical art journals they had been required to use in previous assignments. Furthermore, the students seemed to "gain a sense of empowerment and personal identity while learning how to interact with others online" (Oravec, 2002, p. 621). Microblogging, which differs from traditional blogging insofar as microblogs are briefer exchanges of communication, images, or videos, enabled participants to comment on and collaborate in their learning and share experiences based around a specific visual, video, or text-based item. Also, the microblogging tool, Edmodo, allowed teachers to control who was invited and who contributed to this virtual learning space.

Learning Tasks

The Suburb as Site project was designed to be an authentic "real-life" learning experience for students, insofar as it might hold real-world relevance for photography students in both the Liverpool and Denver sites. Learning tasks were sustained over a period of time and provided opportunities for examining the assigned topic from different perspectives. Learning tasks also provided opportunities for group collaboration and individual reflection and resulted in a group and individually valued end product (Herrington, Reeves, & Oliver, 2010).

The experience was structured to include three components: (1) Investigation of suburbs in Liverpool and Denver through critical examinations of images and media representations posted to each other in Edmodo (Figures 1 and 2); (2) online presentations of photographs taken of Liverpool and Denver suburbs by students, along with shared discussions of roles the subjects of the photographs played in the lives of students in each of these suburban spaces (Figures 3 and 4); and (3) a collaborative image where Denver and Liverpool students were paired to collaboratively create a digitally composited image that depicted both of their environments in one image (Figure 5).

Figure 4 a and b. Suburbia in Denver, Colorado: Student photographs.

Figure 5. Collaborative Digital Composite Suburb image (Liverpool student).

Students at both sites researched themes related to suburbia and narrative photography, then collected and collated the information they had gathered, including materials found on the Internet, and published these materials in an online repository as a shared resource and site of further learning. This learning activity required students to explicitly explore issues of suburbia through art as they related to each student's experiences. Additionally, students were required to conduct a media case study, by looking at their suburb through the eyes of media reporters and responding as photographers to images depicted in their stories. The media case studies, which were published in the blog, included histories of suburbia, media stereotyping representations of communities, folklore, and suburban myths. The media case study task asked students to consider how a photographer uses narrative to explore a theme.

Outcomes of Suburb as Site

This program, like all teaching programs in schools, had a number of unexpected outcomes. These included the nature of collaborations that resulted from discussions about cultural significance, cultural metaphors, and use of culturally laden language. Although both groups of students utilized the same museum sites for research and examination of artists' practices, and the same formative and summative assessment procedures were followed in both schools, interpretations of suburb expressed by students in southwestern Sydney and students in metropolitan Denver, Colorado, were worlds apart.

We had established the project to answer two important questions: How can we situate visual arts learning in a 21st-century digital and virtual environment? How can we establish collaborative artmaking within our school communities? Collaborations between Denver and Liverpool allowed students to openly address visibly apparent cultural differences, such as the wearing of hijabs by Muslim female students, and how this was experienced and perceived by others in the suburban community. Permission to openly address and discuss such differences and differing perceptions of one another's life experiences enabled students to develop cultural self-esteem and gain confidence in their interactions with one another.

The Australian students took on a personal responsibility in providing images of their social spaces, cars, and shopping malls, and exchanging information about school, school uniforms, the structure of the school day (such as bells ringing between classes), and how they selected subjects to study. American students filmed themselves in classes, published images from their homes, and reflected on who they were in these "suburbs as sites." For example, one student wrote about her feelings of security, and described her suburban neighborhood as a place where she could "explore and feel comfortable. If I need to clear my head, all I have to do is go for a walk down the street and take in my surroundings" (student personal communication, 2011). In response to a shared learning space, students who were from geographically, socially, culturally, and economically different circumstances and were from varied religious backgrounds were able to exchange information about experiences of their lives and images of the suburbs in which they lived. Our students were able to discover and learn from and about each other in different learning, social, and cultural environments. Experiences beyond the visual were shared, such as exchanges of information about favorite foods (Figure 6). Differences in language or accented speech also were examined from perspectives that had not previously considered, as was demonstrated in this exchange.

> American student: I love you guys' accents :)
>
> Australian student: we love your accent too.
>
> American student: we have accents? Weiiiird.
>
> Australian student: I guess we have accents to you guys.… Do you guys talk in our accent or is it just something we do?

Having endured many changes in their lives that may have affected their opportunities and abilities to learn, a number of Australian students lacked confidence in their academic and social skills. Some English as second language (ESL) students—who might have been disadvantaged by

Figure 6. Experiencing s'mores for the first time ever in Australia. "Yummy S'mores are awesome!…" "wow that looks better then the ones we make here."

linguistic barriers—and students who might have feared being marginalized due to cultural differences experienced being accepted as photographers, colleagues, and online friends in an environment where differences were subjects of exploration without preconceived negative assumptions. Thus, interaction with students from a different culture provided mutually meaningful learning experiences for students in each group (Ardichvili, Maurer, Li, Wentling, & Stuedemann, 2006).

Transformation

These transformational changes and outcomes were unintended; however, we knew anecdotally as art educators that when students can see themselves as active global citizens who make art and respond to art responsibly in a diverse community, they can see themselves as participants in the art world. Through participation in the program, each of the Liverpool students developed confidence in her ability to communicate ideas through photographic images; they were able to view photography as more than just a subject to be studied in school, but as a field that they could explore beyond schooling. Transformationally, the students were able to see a world outside of their school lives; the learning experience impacted their studies in visual arts and encouraged possibilities of future careers. Upon graduation, several students who engaged in the program have pursued careers in photography. This was a significant, life-directing experience for students who previously could have never seen the arts as a possibility for career and employment. Beyond the combined successes of image capturing and sharing, reflective writing, cross national exchanges, and collaborations—which encouraged students' sense of self-efficacy as photographers—exploring the theme of the Suburb as Site project resulted in a empowering understanding of self in community for the students in Liverpool.

Reflections

Our students in NSW schools were asked to act as reflective practitioners in subjective and objective reflection of their photographic practices and the practices of other participating artists. We used Edmodo, rather than personal art diaries, to open a social space for shared reflectivity. In this virtual global space, the art world was shrunk to enable students on both sides of the world to communicate, collaborate, and create together. Lighthearted conversations contributed to formation of trust and a sense of collegiality. As the groups discovered more about each other, they engaged in increasingly thoughtful communicative interactions including dialogue about their life experiences, artistic practices, and resulting images. Finally, they worked together on a work of art that required a collaboration of ideas, experiences, compositional skills, and technical skills.

Incorporating learning strategies such as the digital diary into the online learning space encouraged students to think as practising photographers and to reflect on their skills and capabilities, and also helped prepare more senior students for the world outside of school as digital citizens. Working as members of a cross-global community strengthened students' awareness of photography as a cross-disciplinary media and made it transferrable beyond school grounds and out into the art community. This might have been less possible in conventional face-to-face classroom experiences. The museums and galleries were brought to us, the students in another part of the world were brought into our classrooms, and ideas and processes of artmaking that were shared resulted in art products that revealed authentic understanding of one another's experiences and aesthetics. Students recognized that the role of a contemporary photographer is to tell stories, to conceptually invite an audience into an image, and to present a narrative. Technologies made this cross-national learning experience possible, and provided an arena within which diverse people could communicate, and consequently come to understand themselves and one another better.

ACKNOWLEDGMENTS

This program would not have had the success it had without the commitment, diligence, and professionalism of Suzi Melly at Horizon High school and her dedicated and passionate students. Melly uses Edmodo in all of her classes to regularly communicate with students. She posts assignments and announcements, conducts critiques, and awards badges in this user-friendly platform. Students feel comfortable with the interface and often end up being "resident experts," teaching other students (and Suzi) tips and tricks. Students in her Photography I class submit formative and summative digital projects. Edmodo allows Melly to view, grade, and give feedback to students in an immediate and meaningful way. Additionally, using Edmodo supports 21st-century technology skills that are part of the new Colorado Literacy Standards.

REFERENCES

Ardichvili, A., Maurer, M., Li, W., Wentling, T., & Stuedemann, R. (2006). Cultural influences on knowledge sharing through online communities of practice. *Journal of Knowledge Management, 10*(1), 95–107.

Board of Studies New South Wales (2000). *Photography, video, and digital imaging: Content endorsed course stage 6, syllabus.* Retrieved from www.boardofstudies.nsw.edu.au/syllabus_hsc/pdf_doc/photoviddig_cec_syl.pdf

Board of Studies New South Wales (2004). *Photographic and digital media: Years 7–10* [Syllabus]. Retrieved from www.boardofstudies.nsw.edu.au/syllabus_sc/pdf_doc/photo_dig_media_710_syl.pdf

Brown, I., Lysaght, P., & Westbrook, R. (2007). Analysing image and text: Voices of children. *Australian Visual Arts Education, 30*(2), 40–56.

Herrington, J., Reeves, T., & Oliver, R. (2010) *A guide to authentic e-learning.* New York, NY: Routledge.

Hunter, J., & Beveridge, S. (2006). *The ne(X)t generation.* Retrieved from www.eqa.edu.au/site/thenextgeneration.html

MacGregor, R. N. (1992). *Post-modernism, art educators, and art education.* Bloomington, IN: Adjunct ERIC Clearinghouse for Art Education. Retrieved from www.ericdigests.org/1992-2/art.htm

Oravec, J. (2002). Bookmarking the world: Weblog applications in education. *Journal of Adolescent & Adult Literacy, 45*(7), 616–621.

Oxfam. (1997). What is global citizenship? Retrieved from www.oxfam.org.uk/education/global-citizenship

Robbie, D., & Zeeng, L. (2008). Engaging student social networks to motivate learning: Capturing, analyzing and critiquing the visual image. *The International Journal of Learning, 15*(3), 153–160.

ENDNOTES

1   Frames "orientate investigations in making and in critical and historical studies and represent different philosophical views and frameworks of belief that affect interpretations of meaning and value" (Board of Studies New South Wales, 2000, p. 13).

2   See www.boardofstudies.nsw.edu.au/syllabus_sc/photo-digital-media.html

3   While a blog is an online site that serves as a personal or group journal that includes lengthy reflections, comments and responses, as well as links to other sites and resources, a microblog permits shorter comments and communications from and between individuals.

4   Edmodo is a microblog, a cloud-based learning management system that is managed by a teacher for a classroom environment where the group can learn together; the only participants are invited and have a code to enter the space.

CHAPTER 14

It's About Them, It's About Us:
Using ChinaVine as an Educational Tool

KRISTIN G. CONGDON
University of Central Florida
DOUG BLANDY
University of Oregon

Contemporary educators agree that the digital age has changed the ways in which we teach. Lawrence Summers (2012) claims it has done more than that: "It's [also] changed what we need to learn" (p. 26). In a limited fashion, educational organizations are still segregated into disciplinary content, and specific languages and research methodologies. According to Summers, our educational structures no longer reflect the ways in which people learn. He makes several suggestions, including that we learn how to: (1) process information as opposed to imparting it, (2) work more collaboratively, (3) utilize technology so that it can continuously change and question knowledge content, (4) engage students as active rather than passive learners, and (5) encourage global experiences. ChinaVine attempts to address all five of his suggestions, with an emphasis on global learning.

ChinaVine is an educational project dedicated to the documentation and interpretation of China's cultural heritage. It grows out of a partnership project initiated in 2007 between the University of Central Florida (UCF), the University of Oregon (UO), and Shandong University of Art and Design (SUAD). The project initially coalesced around the development of a website, ChinaVine.org. This initial effort was modeled on a UCF-based experimental website about Florida folk artists (www.folkvine.org) (Congdon, 2006). President Pan Lusheng of SUAD, Doug Blandy of UO, and Kristin Congdon of UCF all shared an interest in folk art; they saw an opportunity for an international collaboration associated with documenting and interpreting China's traditional culture, with the outcomes being made available on the Internet. Teams of scholars and students were set up at our three universities for this purpose. The teams worked together to engage in collaborative research and create content for the website. ChinaVine's connections quickly began to expand beyond the original three universities with the development of new partnerships.[1] ChinaVine's mission also broadened to incorporate material culture and contemporary art of all kinds.

Originally consisting of only a website, ChinaVine now takes full advantage of the Internet by including numerous social networking sites in the United States (US) and the People's Republic of China (PRC). While ChinaVine's original website was rich in content, it contained few possibilities for direct interaction between visitors and/or the scholars associated with ChinaVine. New strategies and goals were developed to take advantage of the interactive capabilities of the Internet. The UO's Interactive Media Group (IMG) began work redesigning the website with a new content management system that allows easier posting of content by scholars, as well as postings by youth and adults with an interest in China who have registered on the site. A sophisticated tagging and search structure is also available.

ChinaVine homepage.

In February 2012, after much pilot testing by educators and folklorists, the new website was launched. Using a customized version of WordPress MU, ChinaVine.org now permits ready access to content on the site as well as links to ChinaVine's supporting social media. This site now has the ability to allow interactive dialogue through text, audio, and visual materials. Two blog components of the site, VineOnline (http://aaablogs.uoregon.edu/vineonline) and EduVine (chinavine.org/eduvine), have been established to support the overall project and engage a variety of audiences in dialogue about China's art and culture.

A second, equally important, goal of the ChinaVine team is to establish a new kind of research methodology, one that is participatory and nonhierarchical (in comparison to traditional research teams), fluid and accessible in its communicative structure, and open to the expertise of scholars from many disciplinary areas of study. This research methodology is grounded in respecting the expertise and cultural perspectives of all ChinaVine participants. In keeping with this approach, the publicly available materials associated with ChinaVine are freely available for use for educational, non-commercial purposes under a Creative Commons license. The importance of Creative Commons to ChinaVine will be discussed more specifically later in this chapter.

In our chapter titled, "Developing China-Vine.org: Educating Inside and Outside the Site," in Robert Sweeny's anthology, *Inter/Actions/Inter/Sections: Art Education in a Digital Age*, we address ChinaVine's two goals by showing how one affects the other (Congdon & Blandy, 2010). In this chapter we discuss the importance of the free distribution of educational materials and how ChinaVine and its component parts can be used as an educational site; we also make recommendations on how teachers can use the website, along with its related social media, in the classroom. All aspects of our discussion are aimed at using our website as a teaching resource that assists individuals in learning about themselves and their own identity as they learn about others. Our approach focuses on teaching participants how to successfully live in our global world. In this effort, like Ruth Behar (2009), we acknowledge, "that identities and cultures are mixed, impure, and miscegenated in complex and ever changing ways" (p. 263). A recently received National Endowment for the Arts grant is supporting our educational efforts.

ChinaVine.org, Free Culture, Open Content, and Open Education

ChinaVine exists within the context of the "free culture movement," which takes its title from Lawrence Lessig's (2004) book of the same name. This movement advocates that creative works should be freely available for distribution and modification, and stands in opposition to many copyright laws that, because of their restrictiveness, are not conducive to creativity.

Copyright infringement versus an artist's right to public information is increasingly being debated (Ivey, 2008; Kennedy, 2012). ChinaVine takes an open content position, allowing participants access to almost all materials on the site, much like Alan Lomax's "global jukebox" that now has around 17,000 folk music tracks from around the world that can be streamed by the public. These tracks can also be incorporated into other music tracks, as Bruce Springsteen has done in his recent album *Wrecking Ball*, and the movie *O Brother, Where Art Thou* did in 2000 (Rohter, 2012, pp. C1 & C8). The recognition that social media can successfully build audiences today is so strong that novelist Paulo Coelho pirates his own work and "ignites conversations about his work by discussing it with fans while he is writing it" (Bosman, 2011, C1).

In the context of education, copyright encourages "high information costs, due to the nature of copyright subject matter, namely, non-tangible assets" (Liang, 2007, p. 13). This is particularly true in developing countries. Closely aligned with free culture is *open content*. While *open source* refers to the free use of software, open content refers to the free use of text, sound, and images.

Educators advocating for open content are associated with the Open Education Resources (OER) movement and are committed to educational materials being "offered freely and openly for educators, students, and self-learners to use and reuse for teaching, learning and research" (Hylén, 2007). OER is primarily associated with digital resources. Materials are typically issued under a license, such as Creative Commons, that stipulates how the materials can be used: original form, modified, remixed, and/or redistributed. The benefits of OER are that educational materials are created and distributed openly, allowing for vetting by the larger community using those materials. In this format materials can be applied in multiple ways, critiqued, and improved upon. Materials exist through multiple iterations rather than remaining stagnant and reified, akin to the ways individuals and cultures are continually changing in our global world. In such an environment, innovation in teaching and learning is likely to occur. In a time of dwindling resources for education, OER distributes costs over a large number of users. It also recognizes the fluidity of the cultural process.

According to an Educause (2010) position paper, the OER movement will lead to content that can be freely accessed online, allowing learners to create individualized courses of study. Additionally, more learners will have access to a wide and diverse range of content. In this regard, materials posted on ChinaVine include, but are not limited to, text, photographs, video, and audio.

Like many open education projects, ChinaVine is licensed through Creative Commons, which is dedicated to a culture of sharing (Creative Commons, 2012). Additionally, Creative Commons "develops, supports, and stewards legal and technical infrastructure that maximizes digital creativity, sharing, and innovation" (Creative Commons, 2012, para. 2). This is accomplished in a number of ways, including copyright licenses. ChinaVine materials are licensed under the Creative Commons Attribution-Non-commercial-ShareAlike 3.0 United States License (CC BY-NC-SA). To this end permission is granted to copy, distribute, and/or modify ChinaVine materials. This license allows others to appropriate the work on China-Vine for non-commercial purposes, as long as they credit ChinaVine and license any work created using ChinaVine materials in the same way.

Education, the Internet, and ChinaVine

So important to global learning is teaching students to become tech-savvy that Ron Tanner (2011) asks, "How can students have an impact on the world if we don't teach them to use the primary tool that makes such an impact possible" (p. B32), and Derek Bruff (2011) claims that his students' online exercises weren't just routine academic papers. Instead he describes them as "expressions of learning shared with the world" (p. B30).

ChinaVine is taking full advantage of the Internet as an educational environment. In total, ChinaVine consists of the website ChinaVine.org as well as a constellation

For Further Consideration

1. How does ChinaVine contextualize material culture for the purpose of interpreting China's cultural heritage?
2. What interpretive strategies are used by the scholars associated with ChinaVine to communicate China's cultural heritage to people outside of China?
3. How is ChinaVine contributing to critical debates over the roles of technology and media in education?
4. What strategies could be used in the classroom to assist students in critically engaging with, and contributing to, the materials available through ChinaVine?
5. How could you use ChinaVine to assist students in achieving the relevant skills for living in a global community?

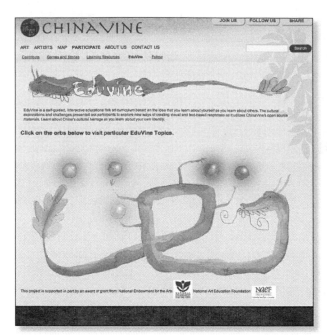

EduVine homepage.

VineOnline.

of social networking sites in the US and PRC including Facebook, Tumblr, Twitter, Soundcloud, vimeo, Flickr, Instagram, Weibo, and Toudou. Visitors to ChinaVine. org's homepage are invited to join, follow, and share. Also associated with ChinaVine are two interactive blogs, EduVine and VineOnline. The mission of EduVine is to engage English-speaking students in an online learning environment that asks them to explore their individual and cultural identities as they discover information about the diverse and complex lives of the Chinese.

VineOnline's mission is to pique interest in participating with ChinaVine by posting images and text associated with recent fieldwork, reporting on educational activities associated with ChinaVine, developing profiles of ChinaVine team members, and relaying important communications to the ChinaVine community. Visitors to VineOnline can comment on all posts in the blog stream. During the recent Chinese New Year, posts to VineOnline served as a way to send best wishes to the ChinaVine community, as well as illustrate the ways that some ChinaVine members celebrated the New Year. Another blog post focused on education majors from China doing a residency at the University of Oregon and being introduced to the educational capabilities of ChinaVine with the intention of using the site in their own teaching in China. Li Hongyun, a folk artist in Hennan Province, learned of ChinaVine through the Chinese version of Twitter, Sina Weibo. After participating with ChinaVine on Sina Weibo, her work was featured on

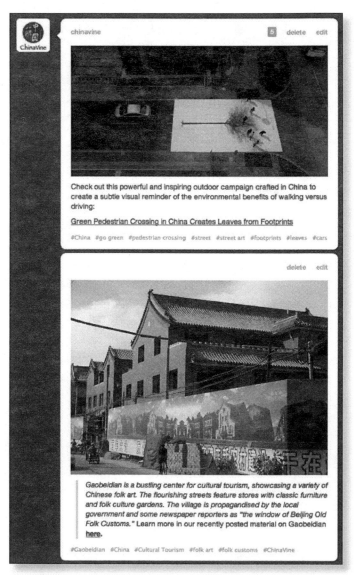

Tumblr post.

VineOnline. In the post, Hongyun shared her motivations behind crafting a South Henan Dui Xiu Nagamaki, an embroidered and painted cloth that incorporates colorful cottons, silks, and satins to depict local customs. Her piece contains approximately 1,396 characters celebrating the Chinese New Year in Huang Village.

Other possibilities for participating with ChinaVine include developing or responding to content for ChinaVine.org; posting images and sounds supporting the project to Flickr, vimeo, Soundcloud, and/or Todou; responding to ChinaVine content on these platforms, as well as Instagram; following and commenting on ChinaVine on Twitter, Tumblr, Weibo, and Facebook; and commenting on posts appearing on ChinaVine's blogs.[2]

Encountering The Other

In the 1960s and '70s, art educators began formulating ways that art could be used to help students understand cultural difference (Chalmers, 1974, 1978; McFee, 1966; McFee & Degge, 1977). Since that time the field of art education, in part by the hard work and high visibility of organizations such as the United States Society for Education Through Art (USSEA) and the International Society for Education Through Art (InSEA), has had a proliferation of publications promoting cultural understanding through the arts.

Likewise, numerous individuals have written about approaches to art and how the Internet is changing how we think and live. Some scholars and educators today view art institutions less as cultural containers and more as cultural interfaces, at the same time that artmaking, art history, art criticism, critical theory, and literary criticism are becoming more fluid (Osthoff, 2006). As disciplinary borders collapse, ideas about our identity and our home place are coming together. J. Di Stefano (2002) suggests that being at home "may have more to do with how people get along with each other—how they understand and are understood by others, as opposed to being in an actual space" (p. 38). Based on this perspective, he suggests that identities change with an ongoing narrative, "a narrative that provides a context within which… enactments of belonging may be positioned" (p. 38). Following Di Stefano's ideas, and recognizing that difference implies an interdependency that says, "I am like you," and "I am different," (Minh-Ha, 1991, p. 152), ChinaVine is developing a curriculum that allows students to talk about themselves while learning about Chinese culture.

For example, on the EduVine section of ChinaVine, participants will be asked specific questions about various Chinese practices and ways that these practices are the same and different from the folkloric practices of the participant. They can respond with image or text, and

EduVine lesson.

Instagram post as captured on followgram.me.
Rao San Ling Festival near Dali, Yunnan, PRC.

if they wish, they can utilize ChinaVine's content for their response. For example, a student might learn how someone makes noodles in a particular place in China and make a film on how they make noodles the same or different. They could design an insole[3] from their cultural belief system, by modifying the insole of a Chinese embroiderer.

Another visitor might manipulate a photo or film of a roof-raising in a rural Chinese village and place themselves in the image as if they were there to explain the shape and material of a roof on a dogtrot house in Florida. They might learn about the function of a Kitchen God[4] as they explore ways in which their culture protects their food and gives them good health. EduVine will not only teach participants about traditions and changes in Chinese folk culture, but it will ask them to reflect on how similar ideas are represented in their own culture.

ChinaVine aims to formulate a new kind of community, one that "is not defined by its agreement, but by its ability to accommodate difference" (Ott, 1994, p. 33). As it is impossible for us to understand everything about everybody in our diverse and complex world, we should therefore focus on learning about how to work within our differences. One way of doing this is to artistically and creatively exchange information with others on topics that play themselves out in similar and different ways. This way of working is far more active than simply learning facts about another culture. It utilizes technology to imagine a new community and world that develops citizens with relevant skills for living in a global community.

Recommendations for Teachers

The Internet is changing the way that people learn. Contributing to this change is the participatory culture that is inherent to the interactive qualities of the Internet. Participatory culture exists where people take an active role in shaping their reality. There is a close relationship between participatory culture and immersion in digital media and social networking through electronic forums. Jenkins and Bertozzi (2007) define participatory culture as

> one where there are relatively low barriers to artistic expression and civic engagement, where there is strong support for creating and sharing what one creates with others, and where there is some kind of informal mentorship whereby what is known by the most experienced is passed along to novices. (p. 174)

By joining, following, and sharing ChinaVine, students and teachers are a part of this participatory culture. The

national survey, "Speak Up 2009: Creating our Future: Students Speak Up about their Vision for 21st Century Schools," demonstrated that students are accessing a wide range of learning resources, tools, applications, outside experts, and each other to create personalized learning experiences (Project Tomorrow, 2010, p. 2). As Jenkins and Bertozzi (2007) recommend, teachers should take on the role of facilitators of participatory culture (p. 193). Project New Media Literacies (2012) advises teachers that the five characteristics of participatory learning are:

- Heightened motivation and new forms of engagement through meaningful play and experimentation

- An integrated learning system where connections between home, school, community, and world are enabled and encouraged

- Co-learning where educators and students pool their skills and knowledge and share in the tasks of teaching and learning

- Learning that feels relevant to students' identities and interests

- Opportunities for creating and solving problems using a variety of media, tools, and practices. (para. 1)

All of these characteristics have been highly influential to the design decisions that are now associated with ChinaVine.org and its supporting social media. Its interactively designed website affords a range of possibilities, only limited by the imaginations of those who engage with ChinaVine.

Teachers and students can use the material on ChinaVine.org as a source for teaching students about approaches to cultural interpretation using a variety of digital documentation techniques (text, images, and sound). Students studying this approach to interpretation could engage in transmedia interpretation about something associated with their own lives or communities that links with what they have discovered on ChinaVine. In turn, their interpretations can be posted to ChinaVine as a point of comparison.

Teachers and students engaged in the study of the PRC could compare and contrast what is being found in the popular press about PRC with what is appearing on the website and ChinaVine's social media. When participants amplify what they discover by responding to posts, they utilize critical thinking and encourage dialogue around issues of mutual concern. Through EduVine, students can engage in ethnographic fieldwork as they move through the site listening to music, learning about festivals,

ChineVine Twitter post.

and discovering ways of dressing and other traditional practices. As they learn about China's culture, they are asked to relate a particular tradition to their own cultural background. For example, students could be prompted to describe how a Chinese family sits around the dinner table and how that positioning communicates respect. They could then be asked to visually communicate how their family members position themselves when they share a meal and what that means in their household. To expand students' appreciation of what constitutes material culture, they could be asked to describe and document distinctive family foods. Again, this material could be used in posting on ChinaVine or as a source for responding to posts on ChinaVine's various interactive platforms.

Teachers and students engaging with participatory culture are positioned to also build *Personal Learning Networks* (PLNs). PLNs are defined as "deliberately formed networks of people and resources capable of guiding our independent learning goals and professional development needs" (Weisgerber & Butler, 2012, Slide 18). Emily Dobkin, a member of the UO ChinaVine team, has integrated the use of ChinaVine into the UO Jordan Schnitzer Museum of Art's Asia-focused curriculum for children and youth (Jordan Schnitzer Museum of Art, 2012). In connection with this effort, she worked with a teacher at McCornack Elementary School in Eugene, Oregon, to connect the classroom with the museum. Every teacher in the school has a "Wonder Page" in which they link relevant websites that pertain to what the students are learning in the classroom, so that they can further explore topics of interest during their free time or at home. ChinaVine is now a part of this teacher's "Wonder Page."

ChinaVine is specifically designed to support PLNs such as those being developed at McCornack Elementary School. Students and teachers participating with the project are able to experience and comment on scholarly content as well as public postings. Subscribing to the ChinaVine Twitter feed will provide information associated with the study of China and also connect students and teachers with others who are following ChinaVine on Twitter. They will be able to access the follower list and discover others interested in China's cultural heritage. Through the use of hash tags associated with specific topics, students and teachers will be able to access specific types of information. They will also be able to re-tweet and follow re-tweets to build and solidify their networks.

The blogs associated with ChinaVine also support PLNs. By accessing the blogs, students and teachers are able to discover others with similar interests and subscribe to RSS feeds. Through the use of Twitter, teachers and students can search out others who may be keeping blogs associated with topics of interest. In addition, students and teachers who add ChinaVine.org and the ChinaVine blogs to their chosen social bookmarking service (for example, delicious.com, digg.com, and diigo.com) will be able to see and communicate with others interested in the same bookmarks.

Many new kinds of teaching methodologies and ways of thinking about cultural participation can come from the interactions that take place through ChinaVine's social media. For example, we are looking into the possibility of establishing badges that can be earned to "certify skills and abilities" (Young, 2012, p. A1) much like there are in the Boy and Girl Scouts. Other kinds of teaching and learning methodologies will no doubt come from participants who imaginatively instruct us in new ways to think about ChinaVine's potential to bring diverse groups of people together.

As participants actively and artistically engage with others about how they live in our global world, they acknowledge the lives of others as they reinforce and elaborate on the ways in which they live their lives. Tradition bearers change as they encounter new cultural contexts; ChinaVine presents a forum for participants to formulate their own identities as they learn about what makes others themselves. Behar (2009) sees these kinds of cultural interchanges as messy and "lovingly entangled in the desire for human connection" (p. 251). In this entangled interchange where we experience getting to know ourselves as we learn about others, we utilize numerous disciplinary skills, moving from philosophy to anthropology and art to various other fields of study.

The process connects the disciplines in a like manner as it connects us to others. ChinaVine's potential to simultaneously teach us about ourselves as we learn about others seems extensive. In the process of exploring ChinaVine's resources, participants utilize technology as a way to artistically share knowledge and cultural ways of being, as they critically explore new ways of learning.

ChinaVine is just one project that art educators and their students can participate with, or look to, for the purpose of engaging with others committed to living within a global and multicultural context.[5] Projects such as these encourage teachers and students to use technology to engage with global issues to learn more about themselves, as they simultaneously engage with the larger international community in the exploration of common concerns. The degree of engagement ranges from exploring global concerns within the confines of the classroom to developing technologically enhanced formal and informal partnerships with teachers, students, and classrooms in other parts of the world.

REFERENCES

Behar, R. (2009). Folklore and the search for home. *Journal of American Folklore, 122*(485), 251–266.

Bosman, J. (2011, September 27). Best-selling author gives away his work. *The New York Times*, pp. C1, C2.

Bruff, D. (2011, November 11). A social network can be a learning network. *The Chronicle of Higher Education*, pp. B30–B31.

Chalmers, F. G. (1974). A cultural foundation for education in the arts. *Art Education, 27*(1), 20–25.

Chalmers, F. G. (1978). Teaching and studying art history: Some anthropological and sociological considerations. *Studies in Art Education, 20*(1), 18–25.

Congdon, K. G. (2006). Folkvine.org: Arts-based research on the web. *Studies in Art Education, 48*(1), 36–51.

Congdon, K. G., & Blandy, D. (2010). Developing ChinaVine. org: Educating inside and outside the site. In R. W. Sweeny (Ed.), *Inter/actions/inter/sections: Art education in a digital age* (pp. 72–79). Reston, VA: National Art Education Association.

Creative Commons. (2012). *Homepage.* Retrieved from http://creativecommons.org

Di Stefano, J. (2002). Moving images of home. *Art Journal, 61*(4), 38–51.

Educause. (2010). *7 things you should know about open educational resources.* Retrieved from http://net.educause.edu/ir/library/pdf/ELI7061.pdf

Hylén, J. (2007). *Giving knowledge for free: The emergence of open educational resources.* Paris, France: OECD. Retrieved from www.oecd.org/edu/ceri/38654317.pdf

Ivey, B. (2008). *Arts, Inc.: How greed and neglect have destroyed our cultural rights.* Berkeley, CA: University of Berkeley Press.

Jenkins, H., & Bertozzi, V. (2007). Art expression in the age of participatory culture. In S. J. Tepper & B. Ivey (Eds.), *Engaging art: The next great transformation of America's culture* (pp. 171–195). London, England: Routledge.

Jordan Schnitzer Museum of Art. (2012). *Teacher resource guide: Chinese art and culture outreach kit.* Retrieved from http://jsma.uoregon.edu/sites/jsma1.uoregon.edu/files/PDF/Chinese%20Outreach% 20Kit.pdf

Kennedy, R. (2012, January 1). Apropos appropriation. *The New York Times*, pp. AR1, AR8.

Lessig, L. (2004). *Free culture: How big media uses technology and the law to lock down culture and control creativity.* New York, NY: Penguin.

Liang, L. (2007). *Free/open source software: Open content.* New York, NY: United Nations Development Programme-Asia Pacific Development Information Programme.

McFee, J. K. (1966). Society, art and education. In E. L. Mattill (Ed.), *A seminar for research in art education* (pp. 122–140). University Park: Pennsylvania State University.

McFee, J. K., & Degge, R. M. (1977). *Art, culture and environment.* Dubuque, IA: Kendall/Hunt.

Minh-Ha, T. T. (1991). *When the room waxes red: Gender and cultural politics.* New York, NY: Routledge.

Osthoff, S. (2006). Elsewhere in contemporary art: Topologies of artists' works, writing, and archives. *Art Journal, 65*(4), 6–17.

Ott, G. (1994). The village of arts and humanities. *High Performance, 68, 17*(4), 32–33.

Project New Media Literacies. (2012). *PLAY! Framework: The 5 characteristics of participatory learning (CPLs).* Retrieved from https://playnml.wikispaces.com/PLAY!+Framework

Project Tomorrow. (2010). *Creating our future: Students speak up about their vision for 21st century learning.* Retrieved from www.tomorrow.org/speakup/pdfs/su09NationalFindingsStudents&Parents.pdf

Rohter, L. (2012, January 31). Folklorist's global jukebox goes digital. *The New York Times*, pp. C1, C8.

Summers, L. H. (2012, January 22). The 21st century education. *The New York Times, Education Life*, pp. 26–29.

Tanner, R. (2011, November 11). The myth of the tech-savvy student. *The Chronicle of Higher Education*, pp. B32–B34.

Weisgerber, C., & Butler, S. (2012). *Empowering students through personal learning networks built on social media platforms.* Retrieved from www.slideshare.net/corinnew/empowering-students-through-learning-networks?from=share_email

Young, J. R. (2012, January 13). 'Badges' earned online pose challenge to traditional college diplomas. *The Chronicle of Higher Education*, pp. A1, A4.

ENDNOTES

1 Five years after its beginning, ChinaVine consists of formal and informal connections with additional universities, such as Beijing Normal and the University of Maine; government entities, such as the Library of Congress in the United States (US) and the Center for Ethnic and Folk Literature and Art in the People's Republic of China (PRC); non-governmental organizations in PRC, such as the China Folk Literature and Art Association and the Beijing Folk Literature and Art Association; U.S. non-profits, such as South Arts and the International Research in Arts and Sustainability (IRASAS); and professional associations, such as the American Folklore Society and the Chinese Folklore Association.

2 ChinaVine consists of the following:
ChinaVine.org
chinavine.org/eduvine/
aaablogs.uoregon.edu/vineonline/
Blog.sina.com.cn/chinavine
Tudou.com/home/chinavine
t.sina.com/cn/chinavine
tumblr.com/blog/chinavine
Twitter: @chinavine
Facebook.com/chinavine
Vimeo.com/chinavine
Flickr.com/photos/vineonline
Soundcloud.com/chinavine
Instagram: chinavine

3 A traditional Chinese insole is an embroidered fabric insert placed on the inside of the shoe for comfort and good fortune.

4 In Chinese traditional culture, the Kitchen God is an important domestic god that protects the hearth and family.

5 Other examples include:

The Texas State Geography Field School-created interactive virtual environment in Second Life, within which instructors and students explore the isolated Hispanic village of El Cerrito in New Mexico (www.its.txstate.edu/departments/etc/researchanddevelopment/VirtualFieldSchool.html).

The Asia Society's "Partnership for Global Learning" educational initiative positions international education as core within curricula (http://asiasociety.org/education/partnership-global-learning/making-case/partnership-global-learning).

The Wing Luke Asian Museum, in Seattle, Washington, provides an ambitious curriculum, "Torn by War, Healing Through Hope," through its website (http://wingluke.org/teachers.htm), which prepares students to understand the history of the United States' conflicts with Viet Nam, Laos, and Cambodia. The primary means through which this is achieved is by focusing on art, literature, poetry, oral history, and community service. Integral to this curriculum is preparing students to do oral histories of immigrants, refugees, and veterans from the wars in Viet Nam, Laos, and Cambodia.

CHAPTER 15

Using an Art Center's Online Curriculum
to Teach Elementary Students About Cultural Identity

MARY ERICKSON
Arizona State University

LAURIE ELDRIDGE
Peoria Unified School District

MARISSA VIDRIO
Cartwright Elementary School District

The region around Phoenix, Arizona, is rich in diverse cultures and ethnicities. Every year, thousands of immigrants from Mexico and further south cross Arizona's long, desert border. A great many Arizonians are themselves newcomers from other regions of the US or immigrants drawn from across the globe to the region around Phoenix called the Valley of the Sun. The paths of many ancient, historical, and contemporary cultures have crossed this region of the Sonoran Desert where the Rio Salado (Salt River) and Gila River meet.

The rich cultural diversity of the region is reflected in the diversity of many of its arts institutions. The Valley of the Sun boasts several major art museums as well as several local community art venues, including the Tempe Center for the Arts (TCA). The TCA's challenge has been to make a place for itself within an already diverse regional art world.

In this chapter, we explain culturally sensitive features of the educational programs at the TCA. We identify underlying principles we believe can be useful to art teachers around the globe whose students are children of the mainstream cultures and of minority or immigrant cultures:

1. Develop a place-based, welcoming mission.

2. Provide a broad inquiry scaffold to structure directed, guided, and independent inquiry.

3. Articulate broad, cross-cultural themes in life that lead to broad themes in art.

4. Team with art teachers who are intimately familiar with and sensitive to the cultures served by their schools.

Additionally, we pose questions, separated in italics, to challenge readers to look for potential applications to their respective learning environments.

Place-Based, Welcoming Mission

Architect Barton Myers and Architekton, a local architecture and design firm, took inspiration from the physical and cultural environment in their design of the TCA. The exterior echoes the form of nearby Hayden Butte and encircling walls of ancient Southwestern architecture. The interior lobby is reminiscent of a plaza, while the public artworks integrated into the building evoke water, fire, earth, and sun. Perhaps the TCA's most important connection to its environment is its site on the shore of Tempe Town Lake. Desert dwellers, who pass the TCA while running or biking along the lakeside, find recreation and respite from the sun within its cool, colorful interior (Figures 1 and 2).

Consider: Every community has its own local character and concerns, which art centers and galleries are in a unique position to address. What's in your backyard?

Figure 1. Tempe Center for the Arts exterior. Photo by Tim Trumble.

Figure 2. Tempe Center for the Arts interior.

Broad Inquiry Strategy

To be truly welcoming, especially to novices, an exhibition needs more than a warm and inviting atmosphere. It needs to offer visitors support in making sense of what they find on view. The exhibition design and online curriculum of the Gallery at the TCA take a constructivist approach to providing such support. That is, its exhibition interface and educational programs are based on a notion that understanding cannot be delivered to visitors or students, but is constructed by them as they connect new ideas to their own prior experience. Art experts, such as art historians, practicing artists, and veteran art viewers, have a vast amount of organized prior art knowledge to draw upon as they view unfamiliar work. When they visit an exhibition, they dip into their long-term memories as they make sense of what they see. When beginners view artworks in an exhibition, they confront a great deal of stimulation all at once, which they must hold in their short-term memories because they do not have a structure already in place to help them organize and make sense of these phenomena (Kirschner, Sweller, & Clark, 2006).

The TCA uses four broad questions as a scaffold for docent training experiences, various gallery activities, and online lessons for each exhibition (Hmelo-Silver, Duncan, & Chinn, 2007). These are called Questor Questions after the curious bird, Questor, who is the Gallery's mascot for its inquiry approach (see Figure 3). At the TCA, docents greet visitors to the Gallery and conduct tours for groups of all ages. Guided by Questor Questions, they engage these museum audiences in conversation about works on exhibit.

Figure 3. Questor questions.

Questor and his questions are also a ubiquitous presence in gallery signage and online lesson plans, offering visitors and students starting points to explore artworks and other visual objects in the exhibitions. Online curriculum units include three lessons: (1) a pre-visit lesson with an illustrated PowerPoint that introduces the exhibition theme and key questions, which are versions of Questor Questions modified specifically for each exhibition; (2) a gallery lesson and worksheet that apply the theme and/or key questions to works in the exhibition; and (3) a post-visit artmaking lesson with PowerPoint showing students' step-by-step processes of making a personal artwork that focuses on the theme and/or key questions of a unit. Each lesson includes objectives, resources, activities, and assessment criteria. Additionally, online units include a PowerPoint of selected works from the exhibition, which serves not only as a preview, but also as a resource for teachers who wish to implement unit lessons but cannot visit the exhibition, or who wish to teach these lessons after the exhibition has closed.

Consider: Students can use broad questions to guide their inquiry about any artwork or cultural artifact. What inquiry directions would you choose?

Broad, Cross-Cultural Themes

Some visitors and students have not constructed understandings of art as particularly significant in their lives. The educational programs at the Gallery of the TCA address broad, cross-cultural themes articulated as Themes in Life that are familiar to people and cultures across the globe and throughout history. The Theme in Life is followed by the Theme in Art, which explains how art can play a significant role in dealing with experiences. For example, "It Only Looks Easy" is a unit developed in conjunction with an exhibition celebrating the achievements of cartoonist Chuck Jones, creator of Wile E. Coyote and the Roadrunner. It focuses on these themes:

- Theme in Life: We all learn every day.
- Theme in Art: Artists learn from teachers, from other artists, on their own, from family, and from the world around them.

"Cars and Guitars," an exhibition featuring customized cars and Fender guitars, inspired these themes:

- Theme in Life: Life is full of choices.
- Theme in Art: Artists create designs to influence us to choose (or like) one thing rather than another.

Consider: Broad, cross-cultural themes help students see connections between art and what is important in their lives. What themes could you develop to help students make connections?

Efforts to produce culturally sensitive curricula benefit from collaboration with teachers who are intimately familiar with and sensitive to diverse cultures (Chung, 2003; Eldridge, 2009a, 2009b; Erickson, 2000; Young, 2011). Erickson, a university professor of art education and the online curriculum developer for the Gallery at the TCA, teamed with art teachers Eldridge and Vidrio to develop lessons in conjunction with two recent exhibitions focused on culture. Eldridge and Vidrio taught the lessons to students at Ira A. Murphy and Bret R. Tarver Elementary Schools.

For Further Consideration

1. How might members of a culture select artworks differently to share privately or publically with others of their culture, compared to artworks they might choose to share with with people outside their culture?

2. How might the venue for exhibiting artworks raise concerns for members of the culture within which those artworks were created?

3. How might strategies described in this article apply to exploring cultural works from other peoples in global contexts?
   - What concerns would you have about explorations of unfamiliar cultural artifacts in the absence of explanations from those who created the works?
   - Would the use of the Questor approaches described in this chapter ameliorate those concerns?
   - Why or why not?

Culturally Sensitive Art Teacher Guidance: 3rd Grade

Ira A. Murphy Elementary is a small elementary school, which serves K-8 in the West Valley of the Phoenix metro area. The student body is primarily Hispanic with roots in Mexico. In this Title I[1] school, 81% of students receive free or reduced-fee breakfast and lunch.

The school is situated in one of the highest crime rate districts in the city. Children walk or ride their bikes to school, as the school serves about a square mile of residences and businesses. Nearby are a Goodwill (second-hand) store, a grocery, a gas station, some ethnic eateries, and other businesses. Within ten minutes' driving distance is a large metropolitan mall with a movie theater, upscale department stores, and restaurants. Many students have remarked that they have never shopped at the mall, or that they have been to the mall but never purchased anything there. On the other hand, all the students seem to know Goodwill and Wal-Mart. The assistant principal plays music every morning to encourage students to hurry to class and not be tardy. Salsa, samba, and other Latin American music are often played.

Within the school, students in grades 1-3 who are English Language Learners (ELL) are in a separate classroom from other students. This is in compliance with Arizona state law that requires ELL students to receive 4 hours of English instruction daily. They are integrated with the other students during recess, lunch, and special instruction, such as art.

Two groups of students in grade 3 received art instruction based on the downloadable lesson plans found on the TCA website that center on the exhibition "Outsiders Within." This exhibition, which is now no longer on physical display but survives in images on the museum's website,[2] focuses on the artworks of Native American and Latino/Latina artists who draw ideas from several cultures and art traditions.

Two overarching themes guide the unit:

- Theme in Life: We are all members of one or more cultures or groups.
- Theme in Art: Artists can get ideas from several cultures.

Three specific versions of Questor's broad questions guide the inquiry component of the unit:

- How do some artists use ideas from their cultures in their artworks (LEARN)?
- How do artists use line (LOOK)?
- What does the artwork mean (INTERPRET)?

There are three lessons, each with supporting resources, such as PowerPoint presentations that guide students in inquiry and artmaking, handouts for students to complete, and websites for students to visit with their teacher. The first lesson addresses "What is Culture?" the second asks "What Does it Mean?" and the third, "Creating Unity with Line," guides students through an artmaking activity.

Eldridge modified these lessons as she guided students through the unit. She began by introducing her 3rd-grade students to the concept of culture by showing them the digital presentation "What is Culture?" Students responded to the questions with enthusiasm, and Eldridge used herself as an example of someone who is a member of more than one cultural group by stating, "I am both American and a member of the Cherokee Nation. I also am a member of the art lovers group. We have our own special activities and words that we use, our own ideas that we think about."[3] In one group of predominately Mexican-American children, students chorused that they were both American and Mexican, with one student stating that he was Native American. In the second group of predominately European American children, some students recognized themselves as sports lovers or as animal lovers (an after-school group). Several identified themselves as artists. Two students in this latter group acknowledged themselves by their religious affiliation, two identified with their Native American tribal heritage, and several again identified themselves as Mexican and American.

Next, Eldridge passed out magazines so that students could search for images that represented their different cultural groups. The magazines included *Arizona Highways*, *Good Housekeeping*, other women's magazines, and car magazines. In the first group of students, several Mexican American students lamented the lack of images that were directly representative of their Mexican heritage. Students were encouraged instead to look for pictures of food, words, and images of other cultural groups to which they belonged.

Prior to introducing the artmaking lesson to the second group of 3rd graders, Eldridge purchased several magazines aimed at a Latina audience, and *O: The Oprah Magazine*, but unfortunately no sports magazines. Several students in the second group eagerly devoured the Spanish language magazines. Two African American girls were able to find images of women of color. However, some students were concerned about the lack of sports images in the magazines and one African American boy was disappointed at the lack of African American sports figures represented in the magazines.

One girl in the second group identified herself as Hopi and Navajo. Eldridge guided her toward *Arizona Highways* magazines. The student was very excited to find an image of a Hopi katsina[4] and images of Navajo elders (see Figure 4). One boy in the second group said in a disappointed voice, "There are probably no images of Yaquis." Eldridge replied that was probably true, but encouraged him to draw something to represent his Yaqui heritage. He decided to draw a Gila woodpecker feather, and then found some pictures of Sonoran desert animals in an *Arizona Highways* magazine. He asked if he could use them, as he and his Yaqui grandmother had often tried to identify different birds and animals when they had taken walks. Eldridge responded, "Of course."

In the second lesson, students watched a digital presentation from the TCA website that showed them how to make a collage. Students were encouraged to arrange the images they had carefully cut from the magazines into a composition that "looked finished, complete, unified." Then they were asked to add different types of lines to the collage to further unify their compositions. Some students drew lines that echoed the shapes in their collages (see Figures 5 and 6). Other students tried to express the fur of animals, or the speed of cars. Some students focused on creating different types of lines in their compositions. Students were able to express to their peers and teacher what kinds of lines they drew with adjectives such as "fast," "furry," and "wiggly." Eldridge felt the assignment had made apparent to her the lack of diversity in mainstream media, and the difficulty students had in

Figure 4. Collage by third-grade Hopi and Navajo girl.

Figures 5 and 6. Third graders' collages.

identifying more than one cultural group to which they belonged, although this could have been due to the young age of the students (8- and 9-year olds).

Consider: Culturally sensitive art instruction requires diverse resources. What resources do you have available?

Culturally Sensitive Art Teacher Guidance: 5th Grade

Bret R. Tarver Elementary serves 950 students in K-5. Tarver is a Title I school where 92% of the student body receives a free or reduced-fee lunch. Of the 950 students, 857 students are Hispanic and are predominantly bilingual. Tarver is an overflow school that serves townhouses, large apartment complexes, and a few single-family homes. Only a handful of students are from the immediate neighborhood. With the exception of approximately 150 students, most students are bussed to school. Overall, the school population is extremely transient.

Tarver Elementary is located in a defunct mall. It is a point of pride for members of the adjacent neighborhood that the school has brought back to life a once-dead commercial area. There is a junior high on the west side of the mall, a 6th-grade center, a family resource center, and Tarver Elementary on the east side of the mall, with a Wal-Mart in the center. The mall also houses a district warehouse and training center.

Perhaps because of the diversity of areas from which the school's students come, the unusual location of the school, and the transient population, Tarver has developed a strong culture within itself. Students wear uniforms to help them focus on learning and also to diminish the distinction between the "haves" and "have nots." All students receive ELL instruction under the assumption that even monolingual English speakers can improve their grammar and discourse with concentrated instruction. Students are tested for their English abilities and separated into classes based on their ability levels in English. In addition to uniform clothing and uniform ELL schooling, students listen to patriotic music in the morning before announcements.

All 5th-grade students at Tarver received art instruction based on the downloadable lesson plan that accompanied the TCA Gallery exhibition "Mixing It Up: Building an Identity." This exhibition is no longer on display, but exists on the TCA website.[5] The exhibition displays works by Mexican American artists who focus on issues of identity.

There are two overarching themes that guide the unit:

- Theme in Life: Every culture builds its identity from shared activities, beliefs, and values.
- Theme in Art: Artworks can help us understand the activities, beliefs, and values of our own and others' cultures.

Lessons approach the two themes through three specific versions of Questor's broad questions:

- Why do artists choose to use bright and muted colors in their work (LOOK)?
- Why do artists sometimes choose printmaking when they want to expose their ideas to more people (LOOK)?
- What activities, beliefs, and values from their own cultures do artists sometimes show in their art (LEARN)?

The first lesson invites students to ask "Who Am I?", the second explores themes and styles of artworks in the exhibit, and the third guides students in exploring their own identities through the use of bright and muted colors in printmaking.

Vidrio began the unit by having students examine Frank Ybarra's print, *Backyard Pachanga* (Figure 7). Students

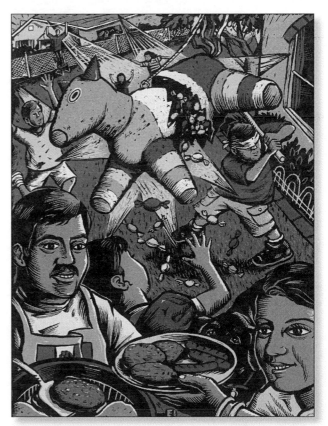

Figure 7. Frank Ybarra's Backyard Pachanga, *2003, serigraph.*

right away made the connection to Cinco de Mayo. They recognized things that were familiar to them such as the Mexican flag on the apron, a barking dog, and a piñata. Some students responded to the print by saying, "My parents are from Mexico." Other students picked up on the bright colors and that the man and family in Ybarra's print looked Hispanic.

Vidrio defined culture to her students as what groups of people know, believe, and do. To further explain the concept, Vidrio asked students to think about the culture at Tarver (i.e., wearing uniforms, walking quietly in straight lines, and focusing on education), and the 5th-grade culture (i.e., what objects they play with, such as Xboxes and Gameboys, or what music they listen to). Then she made a connection to the culture of sports (i.e., how some people are very much into many sports, some are interested in only a few, and others do not play or watch any).

Students also examined other images from the exhibition. Vidrio placed one image from the exhibition at each table where four students sat. She had the students discuss in their small groups, "What do you recognize?" and "What do you think the artist is trying to say?" The students were able to recognize the theme of coming from Mexico to the United States, and they recognized the figure of the Virgin of Guadalupe. They compared representations of the Virgin, and were able to recognize her as an iconic image from Mexico. They also recognized a picture of Elvis Presley as an iconic American image. Additionally, students were able to understand barbed wire as a barrier and recognized a green card, with some students saying, "My mom has one," or "My dad has one." Students understood that a green card was important because it allowed the possessor to stay in the US.

Vidrio then had each student choose three symbols that represented self or something about him/herself. She found that rather than selecting images from their family cultural backgrounds, students selected things they knew and liked such as pizza, ice cream, iPods, and Xboxes, which seemed indicative of their 5th-grade culture. Next, Vidrio asked her students to combine the selected three symbols to form a unified whole. In combining these elements, students melded the images so that the pizza became the cone for ice cream, and a religious image of a cross became the panes of a window. To integrate a language component, Vidrio had each student write about the artwork. Some of the comments were insightful and

Figure 8. Fifth grader's print of Magnifying Glass, Flute, and Taco.

Figure 9. Fifth grader's Lion Print.

thoughtful, and indicated understanding of self beyond the common 5th-grade culture. One student wrote "The taco represents my family who love to eat tacos, including me! The flute represents me. I play the flute. The magnifying glass represents my favorite subject. Science is cool!" (Figure 8).

Several images became more powerful with the written statements. A student who made a print that contained a lion wrote that every member of her family collected lions, which could be an example of a family culture (Figure 9). Vidrio feels that "sometimes we don't give 10-year olds credit for how thoughtful they can be." Another image that stood out was that of a mug with a

Figure 10. Fifth grader's edition of Hot Chocolate and Cookie-Saucer Print.

cookie for a saucer. This student created the print to represent how her father made her hot chocolate (Figure 10). Vidrio believes these are the kinds of moments that are remembered from childhood. She has strong memories as a child waking to the sounds of her father making tortillas in the early morning. He would give her a warm, buttered tortilla and send her back to bed.

Vidrio's students enjoyed learning about and experiencing the printmaking technique. Overall, the students were pleased with their results. The "Who Am I" unit not only provided students an opportunity to practice printmaking processes, but also opened them to learning about their peers and gave them insight into themselves. In retrospect, however, Vidrio feels this lesson pointed out the students' lack of knowledge about their own histories and cultures. "They don't know the richness of the cultures they come from," she said, "which is frustrating. I wish they knew more."

Consider: Students necessarily understand culture as they have experienced it. Even in schools where cultural traditions may be masked by uniforms and lost in the all-pervasive environment of popular images, food, and consumer goods, art can be an effective means to maintain connections to students' cultural inheritance. Are there people, places, or events in your community you might tap to enrich the cultural experience of your students?

Conclusions

Even though neither Eldridge nor Vidrio could take their students to the TCA, they were both able to modify and implement online lessons provided through the museum website to help their students use art to express their cultural identities. Four factors, identified as principles in the introduction to this chapter, contributed to their success. First, the TCA's place-based, welcoming mission drives its selection of exhibitions resulting in shows such as "Outsiders Within" and "Mixing It Up: Building An

Identity," which showcased the work of culturally diverse local and regional artists. Second, the broad inquiry scaffold underlying the TCA online curriculum provides an adaptable structure. On the one hand, it offers step-by-step PowerPoints to address key questions. On the other hand, teachers from different countries can use the key questions as focal points to modify and supplement lessons to best suit their own teaching situations. Third, the Theme in Life and Theme in Art that inspire each unit are so broad that teachers around the globe can use them to approach whichever artworks or other visual objects they judge to be most meaningful to their students. Finally, teachers who are intimately aware of diverse cultures are invaluable advisors and consultants in the development of culturally sensitive curricula.

We have focused on culturally sensitive uses of an online curriculum in schools that include many students who are members of the cultures whose art is showcased in exhibitions. Intimate cultural awareness is not only invaluable in the development of the curriculum, but also, ultimately, in the planning of the exhibitions upon which the curriculum is based. The voices of the cultures represented are paramount when teachers who are implementing the lessons and/or the students engaged in the activities are unfamiliar with the cultures presented. Representatives of cultural organizations played important roles in making both TCA exhibitions possible. A six-member curatorial team selected the artworks in the "Mixing It Up" exhibition, including the director and an associate of Arizona State University's Hispanic Research Center and the director of Advocates for Latino Arts and Culture. Staff observations reveal that the TCA audience is generally diverse and was especially so during the "Mixing It Up" exhibition and its artist-led workshop. Attendance was 5,559, of which 1,678 were children and teens. Only approximately 300 students participated in tours. Providing free online educational material is especially important in an era when funding for field trips is diminished.

Both exhibitions have long since closed. However, images of works from both "Outsiders Within" and "Mixing It Up," and educational resources developed in conjunction with those shows, are still available online for any teacher, parent, or other person who is seeking culturally sensitive curricula featuring Mexican American and Native American art. These TCA resources demonstrate how art museums and arts centers can fulfill an important part of their educational responsibilities, not only by serving those who are nearby and have the means to travel to exhibitions when they are open, but also to serve distant groups or groups with limited travel opportunities at any venue with an Internet connection.

Few countries are entirely monocultural. Using images from museum and art centers and asking students to think about themselves as multicultural persons may help students appreciate differences across and within groups.

REFERENCES

Chung, S. K. (2003). The challenge of presenting cultural artifacts in a museum setting. *Art Education, 56*(1), 13–18.

Eldridge, L. (2009a). Ruthe Blalock Jones: Native American artist and educator. *Visual Arts Research, 35*(2), 72–85.

Eldridge, L. (2009b). Teaching about Native American art: Issues for art educators. *Translations, 17*(2), 1–6.

Erickson, M. (2000). Crossing borders in search of self. *Art Education, 53*(2), 46-52.

Hmelo-Silver, C. E., Duncan, R. G., & Chinn, C. A. (2007). Scaffolding and achievement in problem-based and inquiry learning: A response to Kirschner, Sweller, & Clark (2006). *Educational Psychologist, 42*(2), 99–107. DOI: 10.1080/00461520701263368

Kirschner, P. A., Sweller, J., & Clark, R. E. (2006). Why minimum guidance during instruction does not work: An analysis of the failure on constructivist, discovery, problem-based, experiential, and inquiry-based teaching. *Educational Psychologist, 41*(2), 75–86.

Young, B. (Ed.). (2011). *Art, culture and ethnicity* (2nd ed.). Reston, VA: National Art Education Association.

ENDNOTES

[1] Title I is a federal program that provides funding for schools populated by children from economically impoverished neighborhoods.

[2] www.tempe.gov/index.aspx?page=861. Also see www.tempe.gov/modules/showdocument.aspx?documentid=8226

[3] All direct quotations from students and teachers in this chapter are from notes taken by Eldridge in the 3rd-grade class between August 1 and December 31, 2008, and by Vidrio in the 5th-grade class between October 1 and December 1, 2011.

[4] Dolls formed as representations of Katsinas, or spiritual messengers.

[5] See www.tempe.gov/modules/showdocument.aspx?documentid=8366

CHAPTER 16

Art, Community, and Context:
Educational Perspectives

GLEN COUTTS
TIMO JOKELA
University of Lapland

In this chapter we report on two community art projects, one in Finland and the other in Scotland. Our focus is on community-based arts practice in which artists and community groups work together to make art. This form of art education takes place at the intersection of art, education, and social work. The main benefit is not simply making art (for there are social purposes to the making), nor is it education in the traditional sense; perhaps it is a subtle blend of these components.

Terms such as "community-based art," "art in a social context," "art in the community," or "socially engaged art" have been around for a long time, and they have all been used to describe the activity that is our subject, but it is beyond the scope of this chapter to explore all the nuances of these terms. For the sake of consistency, we use the term *community art* to refer to projects that involve artists working with, and for, people in public.[1] Our title encapsulates the essence of our discussion; in discussing community art, we invite readers to consider the interdependence of art, community, and context. It was tempting to add a fourth word, culture, to our title, but, as seeking to understand, respect, and celebrate cultures is fundamental to community art practice, we felt it unnecessary to do so.

Using two projects by way of illustration, our discussion focuses on the educational potential of art in a community context and explores the three words comprising the first part of our title. First we address the notion of *art*; the physical outcome of each of the community projects is an art product, but in a sense the art is almost a byproduct of the process. The second issue we consider is the question of working with a *community*. The third issue we explore is that of *context*, which is fundamental to effective practice in community-based art. The famous dictum, "the context is half the work" (Tate Gallery, 2011, para. 9), coined by the Artist Placement Group (APG)[2] during the 1960s in the UK remains, we believe, a useful maxim. Artists and educators in this area must grapple with the complex and culturally sensitive notion of context from the outset.

In Europe, numerous community art initiatives have taken place since the latter part of the 20th century: for example, projects designed to promote education through art, artists in schools, artists in residence, and art-based urban or rural regeneration initiatives. Of the many possible variants of community art practice, we selected two examples that seem to us to delineate important features of the practice. For the purposes of this book, with its emphasis on culturally sensitive art education, we chose projects that promote cultural integration and social inclusion. In each project, the artists had to negotiate the processes and products of art with community groups, sometimes in very challenging circumstances: for example, with displaced peoples (asylum seekers and refugees[3] in Scotland), or in circumstances where sense of well being, cultural identity, and traditions were under threat (e.g., indigenous peoples in Finland, Sweden, and Russia) from cultural influences of a larger, surrounding, and encompassing mainstream society.

Because this handbook is aimed primarily at schools and art educators, we outline the community art activities and provide some references so that readers can learn more, but we do not offer lesson plans or units of work. Rather, we hope that by describing the projects, we will provide readers with some food for thought about community art and how it relates to culturally sensitive art education in the classroom. We invite art educators to consider if methods used in community art might be useful in their own classrooms, which are, after all, also communities, or what Kathleen Gallagher referred to as "communities of learning" (Gallagher, 1999, p. 93).

Art in Context

For an artist, personal vision and self-expression are an important purpose of artmaking, but the art produced by artists is always culturally bound and located in time, space, and place—or context. In this sense, an intuited or obvious human urge or need serves as a problem, which calls for an aesthetic solution; thus, problem solving is at the heart of making art.

Art educators also are supreme problem-solvers, but a major difference between artists and educators is one of context. When art is taught in K-12 settings, art educators must work within a curricular framework, a state,

and a school system; someone else sets the problem for educators. Is it possible that there could be some common ground where the worlds of community artist and educator might meet? What can one learn from the other? In our experience some of the most interesting work happens when art and education praxis converge; in other words, when art functions within a specific time, space, and place and for a specific purpose, this is what we mean by context. In community art, the notions of purpose, problem, and context are inextricably linked and exert a powerful influence on the artist and the outcomes of their work with communities.

At the core of community art practice lie the notions of participation, engagement, collaboration, and empowerment. A community artist is not an artist first and foremost; rather the artist acts as *facilitator* for a community group, bringing skills and experience to enable communities to arrive at solutions over which they have a sense of ownership. Essentially, to work in community art means taking a step back, handing over control, and allowing the artwork to emerge from the group. This is not an easy thing to do. Artists opting for this way of working must constantly refine and develop their skills, not just those required to create artwork, but also those necessary to understand different groups, cultures, and community issues. The artist must work in partnership with those who will have to live with the results of the process. Community artists need excellent communication, interpersonal, motivational, and organizational

For Further Consideration

1. The authors of this chapter believe that children suffer disconnects with both the local community and the larger global community when they do not experience the local community as being valued in the school community and do not see themselves represented in the global realm.

   - According to the authors, why is it important that as part of globally sensitive art education, the cultural identities of marginalized students be strengthened in the context of their communities?

   - Can you think of other reasons this might be important?

   - From your own experiences or observations, can you think of examples that support this argument?

2. According to the authors, why is it important that these types of initiatives be conducted by artist/teachers (rather than art teachers) and in the communities (rather than simply in schools)?

3. What practical problems might there be to enacting this model of pedagogy in contemporary community contexts? List and analyze these. How might the project be modified to address your local community situations?

skills. It is not an easy career option, and such a list of skills would not look out of place in an advertisement for an art educator.

Art produced by a community group must belong to the group and have its own integrity. The community artist's role may include acting as a catalyst for action, promoting group research, or some technical training (for example, in art techniques), but it is not to produce the art.

Community

What constitutes a community? When discussing art in a social context, questions inevitably arise about identity and cultural sensitivity; what are the implications for artists? We selected two examples of culturally sensitive community art engagements because they reflect what we consider to be good practice in community art and because of the nature of the communities involved. In the first example, the Glasgow project, Multi-story,[4] artists worked with asylum seekers and refugees—a group of people from different countries, cultures, and ethnic groups living in one area of the city. The second example, the project in Finland, included groups who live on the borders of three countries, where different cultures meet. The common factor is that both promoted inclusion and cultural understanding.

Project One: Multi-Story

More than 22,000 asylum seekers have been housed in Glasgow over the last decade or so, partly as a result of the last UK government's policy of dispersal, which sought to house asylum seekers throughout the UK. Glasgow has the highest number of asylum seekers in the UK; since 1999 it is estimated that 9,000 asylum seekers have been dispersed to Glasgow.[5] Multi-story is a community arts project that focuses on a pressing social issue in Glasgow and many other large cities: community integration. The project makes art, but the main aim is really community integration.

In 1962, Glasgow City Council developed the "Red Road Flats," six 31-story high blocks containing 720 flats (apartments), two 27-story blocks and one three-story block.[6] As people gradually moved from these tower blocks to other parts of the city, or elsewhere, the city was left with many empty flats. It made sense to offer these empty spaces to asylum seekers. Glasgow has a reputation as a friendly and welcoming city, but coming to live in a new country in a large city, and probably unable to speak the language, is a daunting prospect to say the least. As a result, many newcomers may suffer feelings of isolation

Before demolition. Photo credit: Iseult Timmermans/Multi-story project.

After first demolitions. Photo credit: Iseult Timmermans/ Multi-story project.

and social exclusion. The problem addressed by the project was: How do you start to feel at home, to belong, to be an integral part of the social fabric?

The clever title of this project, Multi-story, is a play on words: the idea of a tall building with several levels (or stories) meets the notion of people with many stories to tell. People with different histories and diverse backgrounds, and with many personal stories, are living together in these "multi-story" tower blocks. The project has been running for almost ten years and is led by the innovative Glasgow-based arts organization Street Level Photoworks,[7] which employed artists with a commitment to community art to work along with residents. Funding to support the work of this UK organization is drawn from a variety of sources, and significant funding comes from sources other than education or the arts funding agencies (for example the Scottish Refugee Council and the YMCA).[8] The longevity of Multi-story is testament to the skills of the artists and personnel of Street Level Photoworks as organizers and fundraisers.

One of the flats serves as a base and workshop area, and opportunities are provided to take part in creative activities such as traditional and contemporary artmaking. Artists work with participants in the project; residents use art to explore issues of integration and to celebrate cultural traditions or the changing dynamics of Glasgow's communities. Initially the artists singled out themes or issues, but increasingly the local participants took more of the initiative in making these decisions. Issues that emerged through mutual investigation and discussion were addressed using arts-infused[9] methods.

Over the years, Multi-story has resulted in projects focusing on documentary video, animation, storytelling, photography, traditional weaving, and craft as techniques to explore and communicate meaning. The Mothers of Purl, for example, had artists responding to community interests by working with women from Iran, Somalia, Turkey, Ivory Coast, Pakistan, Scotland, and other countries to create traditional crafts for exhibition and sale. "The group knits together making, sharing skills and stories from its diverse experiences" (Multi-story, 2008, para. 1). Thus, funding has tended to follow from work started by the artists and local people; projects provided some income for the community participants. Multi-story also has used photography, video, and animation as techniques to explore and communicate meaning.

Artists rather than art teachers led Multi-story, but we believe that art teachers could learn something from the way that the artists worked with local people (and artists could learn something from art teachers; see Table 1). In the project, displaced and marginalized children and adults were engaged in community integration through the processes of art, an example of culturally sensitive art education. The Multi-story model could be adapted or replicated in lessons by art teachers in other parts of the world; it is principally about using sensitive art practice as a tool to strengthen cultural identity and community integration.

Knit flower by Mothers of Purl. Photo credit: Iseult Timmermans/ Multi-story project.

Project Two: ArctiChildren

Turning now to the far north of Europe, the ArctiChildren 2006-2008: Cross-border Training Program for Promoting Psychosocial Well-Being Through School Education in the Barents Region was another example of community art. This multidisciplinary project was led by the University of Lapland. The art activities described here were from a "Culture and Identity" feature of the program, which was implemented by faculty and students of the university's Department of Art Education. The project took place in an area known as the Barents region (Northern Scandinavia and Northwest Russia) in three multiethnic villages in Sweden, Finland, and Russia—very much a border area where countries and cultures meet.

In recent years, the Department of Art Education (of the University of Lapland) has been developing community-based art education in schools to strengthen children's understanding of their own culture, ecological issues, and arts in the local context (Hiltunen, 2010; Jokela, 2008a, 2008b; Jokela & Huhmarniemi, 2008). A fundamental

Posters for the Young People's photography project. Photo credit: Iseult Timmermans/Multi-story project.

point of the ArctiChildren project was that more community involvement was needed in art education projects in northern multiethnic villages to support sensitive cultural understanding. The aim was to promote psychosocial well-being in schools by supporting cultural identity in collaboration with families and other sectors of social life in the villages. The art projects took place in the schoolyards of the villages. Planning and realization was made in collaboration with school teachers and students of the Department of Art Education and their university supervisor, whose artistic knowledge and experience of community and environmental art were utilized in the project. The goal was not to bring art to people, but to use art as a way of supporting understanding of the past and present, while imagining the future.

A key question in this project was preserving cultural diversity and the intrinsic nature of the visual arts in the North. For example, traditional Sami culture does not recognize visual arts, or even have art as a concept on its own. Art however, has a long tradition as craft; many see handicraft as the embodiment of Sami art and courses on traditional handicraft as adequate art education. On the other hand, by introducing the methods of contemporary arts, Sami artists have now broken the long period of having their culture depicted mainly by outsiders. Contemporary art has empowered artists to communicate their own lifeworld from within their culture. Veli-Pekka Lehtola (1997), Professor in Sami Studies, sees art "as

a representation, which not only describes the existing identity, but also continuously builds and generates it" (p. 23).

Northern forms of culture and cultural identities have emerged and grown in close relationship with nature. Therefore it was a natural choice to select environmental art and its wintry application—snow and ice art—as a tool for developing working methods in contemporary art to take place in northern communities—in this case, in schoolyards. Many teachers and researchers stated that Sami young people learn best by doing practical work outside the school building in natural surroundings (Hirvonen, 2004; Jannok Nutti, 2008). Working outdoors proved successful, and the methods used can be seen to be in harmony with the environmental relationship of the northern communities (Hiltunen 2005; Jokela 2007a, 2007b, 2008b).

Not only children, but also teachers, parents, and community members could help develop activities that build on local resources and histories. Community art positions local cultures and local contexts at the center of the work. This is particularly significant in rural contexts because the rich and unique cultural backgrounds of families living in such communities have tended to be neglected in curriculum development at a national level. The Barents Region not only includes the national territories of four countries, but it is also the traditional homeland of many indigenous ethnic groups. The

ArctiChildren project supported local identities and instigated art-based innovations in school, inspired by these diverse northern cultures, heritages, and unique environmental conditions.

Culture and Identity: Sevettijärvi, Jokkmokk, and Lovozero

Organized in several sections, the "Culture and Identity" section of the ArctiChildren project was carried out in school communities in three small villages, namely Sevettijärvi (Finland), Jokkmokk (Sweden), and Lovozero (Russia). The goal was to strengthen the cultural identity of the village school pupils through art, and so a community-based approach was adopted. The objective was to have the schools work in an outward-looking way, to make use of the potential of the schoolyard and to engage pupils in a dialogue about their cultural identity. Pupils, teachers, parents, and other members of the village community were invited to take part in planning and organizing the schoolyard workshops. Artistic work was used to provide the pupils with tools for creating social constructions of their own lifeworld.

The work started with the establishment of co-operative networks. The planning team for the ArctiChildren project consisted of two art education students, their artist/teacher supervisors (who were assigned to each of the schools), and also the teachers committed to this project. Joint planning work was based on a social-cultural analysis of the situations in villages. Members of the village community were involved in this knowledge production process and participated in the activities. At each school, an autumnal environmental art workshop took place using readily available material (willow), and a snow sculpture workshop made the best of the winter conditions. Parents were actively involved as facilitators in the workshops. Even though the methods used in the workshops were those of contemporary art, participants understood them as their own, since the natural materials were used in a way familiar to traditions in the culture.

Planning and implementation also served as training in the subject and different methods for all participants. Teaching materials in community-based art education, environmental art (Jokela, Hiltunen, Huhmarniemi, & Valkonen, 2006), and winter art (Huhmarniemi, Jokela, & Vuorjoki, 2003a, 2003b) were used to support planning and training.

Sevettijärvi. Photo credit Timo Jokela.

A shared feature of the villages and schools of Sevettijärvi, Jokkmokk, and Lovozero is the multiethnic background of the pupils and their close relationship with reindeer management, either through their parents, grandparents, or the wider village community. The pupils in Sevettijärvi were mostly Skolt Sami; pupils in Jokkmokk were Lulea Sami and Northern Sami. In Lovozero there are also Komi people and Russians in addition to Skolt Sami. During the workshop, ethnic differences were not highlighted or emphasized. The workshop content focused on village traditions and was approached through folk stories and beliefs relating to the environment. The richness and depth of these beliefs and environmental stories is a typical feature of Sami, and Northern cultures in general (Huuskonen, 2004). According to Jannok Nutti (2007), the Sami view on learning is based on Sami storytelling traditions. A special selection of animal myths and beliefs were chosen as inspiration for the workshops because children easily identify with those kinds of stories, thus bringing their own meanings into the work. In addition to the stories, reindeer husbandry and its cultural meaning for villages emerged as a theme in discussions with adults.

Although the planning was based on shared principles, the character of each school influenced the way the project became part of the school routine and what was actually done. Sevettijärvi School in Finland, Lapland, is the center of village activity. Administrators, faculty, and students of the school are actively involved in the village community, and its facilities are used for a variety of events; the school also has an approved status, which means that all village children attend it. The school serves as a center for reviving and renewing the entire Skolt

Sami culture, and the teachers seem to have understood the significance of project work in renewing the school and in supporting the cultural identity of the village.

Teachers, whose deep understanding and knowledge of the ways of the community have been formed through daily interactions with villagers and have accumulated during years lived in Sevettijärvi, have an essential role in developing collaboration with school, families, and other sectors of social life in the villages. It was easy to introduce planning in the form of a project to the school routine; teachers were enthusiastic and the development work was consistent. In winter the work was confined to the schoolyard, but extended to the wider landscape by the lake close to the school in autumn.

In Jokkmokk, Sweden, only some of the village children attend the Sami school, and so the school does not have the same kind of position as the village center as the school in Sevettijärvi. The administrators and faculty of the school set goals of increasing the visibility of the Sami cultural identity from the school community outwards in order to strengthen the whole school community. The self-contained but expansive and well-equipped school-yard offered a good starting point for working outdoors both in winter and autumn. The methods and starting points of environmental art and winter art were new and unfamiliar to the primary school teacher, who was accustomed to teaching a routine curriculum in a traditional way, but feedback was extremely positive from parents when pupils presented their artworks to the villagers.

Jokkmokk. Photo credit Timo Jokela.

Lovozero. Photo credit Timo Jokela.

The pupils of Lovozero Secondary School (Russia) were Sami, Komi people, and Russians. Due to some problems with communication, the workshop in Lovozero was not jointly planned; rather the project was more like an intervention, aimed at showing teachers what collaborative methods based on environmental art in schoolyards might look like. Compared with Sevettijärvi and Jokkmokk, the Lovozero schoolyard is a bare, open space equipped with just a few play structures. Working methods that are successful for improving a Finnish school community are not always applicable in another culture, and may lead to unexpected results; in the case of Lovozero, some of the unforeseen results were very positive. In the environmental art workshop, the marvelous willow reindeer made by teachers and pupils together were not left on the schoolyard but, quite surprisingly, distributed for the whole village community to enjoy. It was the pupils' idea to give two reindeer as a present to a lonely old man whose two valuable reindeer had recently been stolen. The willow reindeer had thus gained meanings specific to the Lovozero people; they had become shared symbols, place-specific community art that empowered its makers to act for the good of their own community.

Context

The notion of context is central to community art and also, we would suggest, to the practice of education. To grasp the overall situation and get a holistic view of circumstances and events is essential in community art. Over the past 30 years or so, particularly in the UK, Finland, and Australia, the idea of community art has gained currency and we have provided examples of what this can look like—while acknowledging that there are many different approaches and outcomes. These two projects—conducted in multiple sites, or contexts—illustrate just some of the ways that community artists have worked in a culturally sensitive manner. This field of study has great educational potential—either as practical "hands on" school art projects or as a critical and contextual inquiry that cuts across traditional school subjects, touching for example on art, literacy, history, geography, science, and citizenship.

As we have suggested, community art is not about self-expression; rather it seeks to make the most of arts-infused ways of working with groups. Around the world there is increasing interest in community art as a way of working in different contexts and cultures, from rural and remote areas to cities and towns. There are some differences however, between what might be called the "formal" (schools, colleges) and "informal" (out-of-school, community, local, voluntary) sectors. In Table 1, we have summarized what we see as some key differences between the formal and informal sectors, and we have labeled them Community Art and School Art, but both are about art education.

Table 1
Comparison of the key features of community and school art.

Community Art:	School Art:
Practitioners trained as artists/educators	Practitioners trained as educators
Locations vary	Locations fixed (i.e., school classrooms)
Focus is cross/multi-generational	Focus is on young people
Activities are issues/context driven	Activities are skills/techniques driven
Process emphasized	Outcome emphasized
Evaluated (sometimes)	Assessed (almost always)
Flexibility and freedom	Structure and stability
Participation voluntary: "opt in"	Participation compulsory: "opted in"
Funding insecure	Funding secure (reasonably!)
Initiative and creativity of participants	Initiative and creativity of teacher
Artist/facilitator model of delivery	Teacher/instructor model of delivery

Conclusions

In presenting these comparative scales, we are not suggesting one way is better than the other; we are saying that both have strengths, but we exploit the best of each. Of course there are overlaps between the informal and formal modes of working, and practice varies greatly according to context. What we are suggesting is that community art has potential to infuse art education practice in schools.

Art teachers might learn to work with local people as artists, in ways similar to those described in this chapter. Culturally sensitive art education might engage children and adults of marginalized groups in integration with the larger social context through processes of art. The models described are principally about using sensitive art practices as tools to strengthen cultural identity and community integration; as such, they may be adapted or replicated in lessons by art teachers in other parts of the world.

To conclude, as the distinctions between "education" and "art," between "artist," "maker," "teacher," and "facilitator," are becoming increasingly blurred, we believe there is scope for more research into the benefits of artists, educators, and communities working together; perhaps it is also time to reconsider how art educators are trained, and how we teach art in our schools.

REFERENCES

Gallagher, K. (1999). The drama curriculum: Process and outcomes. In C. Miller & J. Saxton (Eds.), *Drama and theatre in education: International conversations* (pp. 90–97). The Arts and Learning Special Interest Group of the American Education Research Association with the International Drama in Education Research Institute.

Hiltunen, M. (2005). The fire fox: Multisensory approach to art education in Lapland. *International Journal of Education through Art, 1*(2), 161–177.

Hiltunen, M. (2010). Slow activism: Art in progress in the North. In A. Linjakumpu & S. Wallenius-Korkalo (Eds.), *Progress or perish: Northern perspectives on social change* (pp. 119–138). Farnham, England: Ashgate.

Hirvonen, V. (2004). *Sámi culture and the school. Reflections by Sámi teachers and the realization of the Sámi school. An evaluation study of Reform 97.* Cálliid Lágádus, Norway: Karasjok.

Huhmarniemi, M., Jokela, T., & Vuorjoki, S. (Eds.). (2003a). *Talven taidetta: Puheenvuoroja talven kulttuurista, talvitaiteesta ja lumirakentamisesta* [Winter art: Statement on winter art and snow construction] (R. Foley, Trans.). Rovaniemi, Finland: Intellect.

Huhmarniemi, M., Jokela, T., & Vuorjoki, S. (Eds.). (2003b). *Talven taito: Puheenvuoroja talven kulttuurista, talvitaiteesta ja lumirakentamisesta* [Winter skills: A guidebook for snow and ice sculpting] (V. Välimaa-Hill, Trans.) Rovaniemi, Finland; Bristol, England: Intellect.

Huuskonen, M. (2004). *Stuorra-Jovnnan ladut: Tenonsaamelaisten ympäristökertomusten maailmat* [Stuorra-Jovnna's skiing tracks: Environmental narratives of the Sami of the Teno region]. Helsinki, Finland: Suomalaisen kirjallisuuden seura.

Jannok Nutti, Y. (2007). *Mathematical thinking within the Sámi culture: On the basis of the stories of Sámi handicrafters and reindeer herders* (Licentiate thesis). Department of Education, Luleå University of Technology, Luleå, Sweden.

Jannok Nutti, Y. (2008). Outdoor days as a pedagogical tool. In A. Ahonen, E. Alerby, O. Johansen, R. Rajala, I. Ryzhkova, E. Sohlman & H. Villanen (Eds.), *Crystals of schoolchildren's well-being: Cross-border training material for promoting psychosocial well-being through school education* (pp. 199–206). Rovaniemi, Finland: University of Lapland.

Jokela, T. (2007a). The lure of winter: Winter art as art, community and environment project studies. *LLinE, Lifelong Learning in Europe 12*(2), 90–101.

Jokela, T. (2007b). Winter art project. *The International Journal of Art and Design Education 26*(3), 238–250.

Jokela, T. (2008a). Collaborative project-based studies in art teacher education: An environmental perspective. In G. Coutts & T. Jokela (Eds.), *Art, community and environment: Educational perspectives* (pp. 217–240). Bristol, England: Intellect Books.

Jokela, T. (2008b). A wanderer in the landscape: Reflections on the relationship between art and the northern environment. In G. Coutts & T. Jokela (Eds.), *Art, community and environment: Educational perspectives* (pp. 3–27). Bristol, England: Intellect.

Jokela, T., Hiltunen, M., Huhmarniemi, M., & Valkonen, V. (2006). *Taide, yhteisö & ympäristö* [Art, community & environment]. Rovaniemi, Finland: Lapin yliopisto. Retrieved from http://ace.ulapland.fi/yty/english.html

Jokela, T., & Huhmarniemi, M. (2008). Environmental art and community art: Learning in northern places. In R. Mason & T. Eca (Eds.), *Intercultural dialogues in art education* (pp. 197–210). Bristol, England: Intellect Books.

Lehtola, V-P. (1997). *Rajamaan identiteetti: Lappilaisuuden rakentuminen 1920- ja 1930-luvun kirjallisuudessa* [Frontier identity: The settler's view of Lapland in the literature of the 1920s and 1930s.]. Helsinki, Finland: Suomalaisen kirjallisuuden seura.

Multi-story. (2008). *Mothers of purl.* Retrieved from www.multi-story.org/projects/mofpurl/mofpurl.html

Tate Gallery. (2011). *APG: Artist placement group.* Retrieved from www2.tate.org.uk/artistplacementgroup/chronology.htm

ENDNOTES

1   In the University of Lapland we refer to this field of work as "applied visual arts." See for example http://ace.ulapland.fi

2   To learn more about APG, please visit: www2.tate.org.uk/artistplacementgroup/

3   The UK Border agency has this to say about asylum seekers and refugees: Asylum is given under the 1951 United Nations Convention Relating to the Status of Refugees. To be recognized as a refugee, you must have left your country and be unable to go back because you have a well-founded fear of persecution because of your: race; religion; nationality; political opinion; or membership of a particular social group. See www.ukba. homeoffice.gov.uk/asylum/claimingasylum/whocanclaim

4   The Multi-story project was established in 2004 by Street Level Photoworks. Part of a community focused arts program, the staff included Iseult Timmermans (Coordinator and artist) and Lindsay Perth (one of the resident artists).

5   For more information see: www.scotlandagainstracism.com/onescotland/70.html

6   For more information about the Red Road Flats see: www.redroadflats.org.uk

7   For more information about Street Level Photoworks see: www.streetlevelphotoworks.org

8   Multi-story is a collaborative arts project based in the distinctive Red Road housing estate, North Glasgow. Established in 2004 by Street Level Photoworks in partnership with The Scottish Refugee Council and the YMCA, it supports the integration of asylum seekers and refugees through creative activity, celebrating the different cultural traditions coexisting within the changing community. www.redroadflats.org.uk/?page_id=454

9   By "arts-infused," we mean exploring issues and concepts through the processes of art, thus providing multiple ways of investigating and understanding (for example, using traditional arts or photography to communicate meaning).

CHAPTER 17

Youth Culture Expressed in Teenagers' Drawings
From Spain, Japan, Taiwan, and South Korea

ESTEFANIA SANZ LOBO
PABLO ROMERO GONZÁLEZ
Autonomous University of Madrid, Spain

ATSUSHI SUMI
University of Toyama, Japan

LI-HSUN PENG
National Yunlin University of Science and Technology, Taiwan

HYERI AHN
Kookmin University, South Korea

Current theories suggest that art education and visual culture are closely related to the development of cultural identities of youth (Freedman, 2003). Children and teenagers build their personalities and images of self and of the communities to which they belong or wish to belong as reflections of visual representations projected by mass media (Mirzoeff, 1999). In our globalized hyper visual[1] culture, the self-concepts of children and adolescents are influenced by globally disseminated visual representations (Freedman, 2003).

We are a group of five art educators from four countries—Spain, Japan, Taiwan, and Korea—who set out to explore how children and adolescents (ages 11–16) from our respective countries combine the aesthetics of globally disseminated visual representations with localized visual styles and traditions in their drawings. We began our inquiries with a conceptual framework that suggests global culture involves all those meanings, concepts, and productions developed by a hegemonic society which transverses several countries. Distribution of global culture is facilitated through and by mass media, especially in an iconic way.

Consumption plays an important role in a definition of globalization, whereby brands and advertising icons of multinational companies take on high relevance across all levels of society. The term *Kinderculture*, for example, refers to the way multinational industries commodify cultural objects as things to be consumed or possessed by children by disseminating a globalized ideal about how children are or should become acclimated to objects (Steinberg, 2011). As a result, children from different countries often share a common youth culture or imagery from global culture in terms of international brands, graphic narratives, sport clothes' logos, different video games, cartoons from Disney and Japanese comics, and animation films.

Recent developments in the cultural study of youth are focused on how young people, from early childhood to young adulthood, relate to mass media messages and consumerist society (Steinberg, Parmar, & Richard, 2006). Mass media is perceived as a tool for developing cultural connections with one another across disciplines and national, cultural, and socioeconomic barriers (Jenkins, 2006; Gauntlett, 2007), against a background of active, socially connected, visible, and public consumers. Youth culture also is seen as a construction sustained in commercial media, as a population of people living from childhood to adulthood in diverse circumstances are not a unified social group. From this perspective, young people often are called upon to consider themselves in terms of an imaginary unified youth culture community (Richards, 2011). Additionally, youth culture is seen as a transnational market ideology that is *glocalized*,[2] that is, both global and local in identity and consumption styles (Kjeldgaard & Askegaard, 2006).

We believe that older children's and teen's drawings are permeable to global culture, and show evidence of identities being changed by exposure to and interactions with people, ideas, and artifacts from global cultures. Yet, their images of global culture also may be adapted differently in local contexts (Sanz & Romero, 2011). We wondered about the extent to which local, cultural heritages survive and coexist along with icons of globalization. How is this coexistence reflected in the artworks of children and adolescents?

These questions motivated us to undertake research about cultural representations in the drawings of children and youth. We wondered about the elements depicted in drawings by children and teenagers from different cultural backgrounds, especially those related to global visual culture.[3] Our primary question was:

> How are children and teenagers building their identities in coexistence with global and local cultures?

> Related to this question were subquestions:

> 1. Is there a global youth culture that is shared by young people and teenagers from different parts of the world?

> 2. Are children and teenagers conscious about their own cultural identities and their cultural heritages?

Pictures From Distant Lands

In 2008 we collaborated on a project intended to explore and compare the effects of global visual culture on older children's and adolescents' drawings. The study has gone through several stages. We began gathering data in the form of drawings made by children and teenagers based on suggested themes, examinations of art education textbooks, and interviews with teachers and students from schools in Madrid (Spain), Toyama and Okayama (Japan), and Taichung (Taiwan). Subsequently, we collected similar data in Benicarló (Spain) and Seoul (South Korea). Between 2008 and 2012 we collected more than 1,500 drawings (based on specific themes) created by children and teenagers (aged between 11 and 16) living in culturally diverse countries. The researchers selected both private and public schools in their respective countries as sites of data collection. The teachers were informed about the research goals and agreed to participate in the study. In every school, complete classes were chosen according to students' ages: 11–13 years (early adolescents) and 14–16 years (middle teenagers). Students were not selected nor excluded based on their artistic skills. Drawings, collected in the schools during regular class hours, were assigned the following themes:

- *Me in My Favorite Place Doing What I Love to Do*. We expected these drawings might demonstrate visual global culture issues and consumerism related to hobbies and leisure activities.

- *Poetry Illustration*. Students were encouraged to illustrate a poem, chosen from among traditional local poets within the cultural context of each school.[4] We expected that these drawings might reveal aspects of these youths' local cultural heritages.

Analyzing Visual Data

Data analysis was carried out through a predominantly visual methodology. Use of visual data in research is becoming more widespread and valued in the academic field (Banks, 2001; Flick, 1998; Proser, 2008; Weber, 2008). Subjects' drawings as a source for research also have been widely used in social sciences and psychology (Diem-Wille, 2001). In order to keep this chapter to an appropriate length, we will emphasize only form analysis[5] of the drawings themselves, and not the teacher and student interviews.

In addition to the drawing collection, pictures from the schools' visual environments and examples of visual culture artifacts available in each country were collected in order to serve as a reference for our visual research. We took pictures of the schools and their architecture, the decorations of classrooms and how students and teachers use their space, school outfits both formal and casual, bags or pencil cases, and anything additional that might help us to understand certain visual references shown in the drawings of students in each cultural environment.

For the exploration of drawings about leisure, we used a visual content analysis that allowed us to identify thematic categories prevailing in the drawings of children and teenagers of our research (Sanz & Romero, 2009). An in-depth analysis of a limited number of drawings of each country[6] was also conducted. A sampling of these is presented in this chapter.

There was no requirement for students to write about the meanings of their works. Nevertheless, many of them wrote spontaneous explanations in their native languages, and a few (especially in South Korea and some in Taiwan) wrote explanations in English on the back or front of their papers. The explanations included gratuitous phrases as well as deep and interesting reflections. Among the latter comments were statements from South Korean and Taiwanese youth that reflected political tensions with North Korea and with mainland China, respectively. These students drew political satire images rather than the "Favorite Place" topic.

Our team was helped by teachers from the participating schools and by the schoolchildren as well, since they were interviewed to clarify meanings and small details in their drawings. This kind of collaboration was a valuable way for enlightening certain cultural topics depicted in the drawings. We used this collaboration in the triangulation of data analysis, comparing our interpretations of the drawings with those provided by teachers and young authors.

Depicting Life in a Global World: Outcomes

The proposal for drawing "Me at My Favorite Place, Doing What I Love to Do" allowed us to test the impact of global culture on the daily lives of teens. In all of the four cultural contexts of our research, the students defined their identity relative to global consumer entertainment, in combination with elements of their local culture.

For Further Consideration

1. In your opinion, is there a national style of visual representation (i.e., an aesthetic style) that could be identified as unique to your region or nation? If yes, do you think the style would be evident to foreigners as well as to your local (regional or national) compatriots?

2. Is there is a dominant aesthetic style which is spread and promoted (whether consciously or unconsciously) in art classrooms? If yes, is this disseminated or reinforced by the selection of canonical artists or styles that appear in textbooks or are displayed in classrooms?

3. Have you noticed a mixture of global culture and local cultural elements or influences in children's drawings in your class? If so, describe them.

4. Assuming the clothing styles of Japanese manga (which are depicted by teenagers in many parts of the world) demonstrate a back and forth exchange of Eastern and Western cultures, what other cross-cultural examples of visualization do you observe being enjoyed by youth in your school or community?

5. What kind of *glocalization* do you find in youth cultures of your country?
   • How it is reflected in visual products made by children and adolescents in your culture?
   • What does this suggest about these young peoples' understanding of the influences of global cultures in their lives?

6. Do you think that both the globalization trends and comic culture have influenced young children's drawings?
   • Do you think young people recognize non-local influences as "foreign"? Is recognition of distinctions between local/global phenomena important? Why or why not?
   • Is it important to discuss this with students?
   • If so, how would you approach such a discussion?

Visual Content Methodology

The scenes depicted in their drawings were coded into categories that related, firstly, to the use of spaces, and secondly, with the type of activity described. Spaces have been recognized as important for developing both personal and cultural identity (Spencer & Woolley, 2000). People usually feel attached to special spaces and sites that allow well-being and personal growth within an urban setting. In our research, we found that the spaces that children and young people felt attached to were shopping centers, theme-parks, and other "non-places" (Augé, 1992). These are new identity spaces where it is difficult to distinguish public from private; commercial spaces have become understood as private spaces for public use (Benach, 2000).

Passive leisure and consumer entertainment are shown in categories such as "shopping," "fast food leisure," and "playing with a game console." However, we highly value the active-leisure related categories, such as "free playing," "artistic and creative activities," "going to cultural events," and those that take place in interaction with others. We do believe that these categories of leisure facilitate growth as human beings in a creative way, because they promote use of complex thinking, invention, improvisation, and communication, among other acts involved in creativity (Sternberg, 1995). In addition, creative leisure activities work to consolidate cultural heritage such as sports and artistic and traditional cultural activities in each context. Another surprisingly strong category in all four countries was "sleeping in my room." Further investigation is needed to find out causes of the emergence of this category. Are we subjecting teenagers to so much pressure to get good grades, by having them participate in extracurricular training, tutoring, and structured learning, that their greatest desire is to rest? Could this be because their bedrooms are the only personal space within their homes that children can claim as their own?

Drawings made as illustrations of traditional poetry showed greater use of cultural tradition in both subject matter (landscapes, ancient architecture, local costumes, and local festivals or events) and styles (regarding form and procedure). This localized focus was in contrast to the previous set of drawings that permitted the children and adolescents to describe how they enjoyed their leisure time, and in which we found a great number of references to the global visual culture.

In-Depth Analysis

The in-depth analysis of visual images was based partly on analysis of visual discourse, and partly on cultural studies (Lister & Wells, 2001; Rose, 2001). It consisted of a cross-analysis, conducted simultaneously by at least two researchers. One researcher was placed in the position of expert of his/her own culture, and the other in a position of cultural estrangement so he or she could analyze a drawing from a globalized perspective. Some examples of interpretations based on this approach will be presented next.

Glocalization. In Taichung, Taiwan, in 2008 in a private junior high school, drawings were collected. The drawing topic was, "Me in My Favorite Place, Doing What I Like to Do." The artwork shown in Figure 1 is dominated by a comic style. There is a visible horizontal line in front of the composition. Above the horizontal line are placed the sun, moon, and star accompanying a six-hand Buddha, who is located in the center. The Buddha with six hands illustrates the almightiness of the deity. Below the horizon line are visual references to global popular culture. Attention is placed on the central subject of the composition, and the result is a complex and elaborate perspective and composition.

An interesting feature of this picture is the title of the painting, which is provided in an upper corner and refers to a dream universe. This dream has Eastern elements of the Buddha encountering Western global media, as exemplified by characters from Star Wars movies, computer

Figure 1. Drawing by a 15-year-old boy from Taiwan depicting leisure preferences: "Sleep on my bed, play in my dream."

games, downloaded cartoon clips, and signs from algebra. The reality of school's mathematic assignments may have triggered this youth's daydreamed fantasies of characters from global popular culture. The dream fantasies, however, are well controlled by a mighty Buddha under a harmonious sky with rays from the sun and a night view of a moon and star. The student-created Galactic Buddha, with a Buddhist symbol on his chest, raises light sabers in his six arms. In this case the protector Buddha acquires characteristics of global superhero, glocalized by local culture.

Globalization and familiar links. At a junior high school in Seoul, drawings were collected in 2010 with the drawing topic again being: "Me in My Favorite Place, Doing What I Like to Do" (Figure 2). A drawing created by a 14-year-old Korean student depicts him playing with a handheld video game console, Nintendo DS. He is alone at home, holding the portable device with both hands; his eyes are fixed on its flip-screen as if he is immersed in the game. This student's artwork shows one of the most popular recreational activities enjoyed by many Korean children and youth. Playing with Nintendo games is a prevalent phenomenon (Tobin, 2012, p. 128) among adolescents and young adults of all cultures, many of who have access to digital technologies. In 2010, *Business Week* placed Nintendo at the top of its World Best Company 2009 list. This drawing illustrates, on a personal level, how effectively the consumerist game industry has penetrated Korean youth culture.

In this youth's drawing, focus is on a large family picture on the wall of the living room. Due to the formal upright postures of the subjects (two generations of a family), who are shown in the photograph, the photo seems to have been taken in a commercial photography studio. During the last 2 or 3 decades, it has become customary to find at least one enlarged family photo in nearly every Korean middle-class home. This kind of family photograph is usually taken in celebration of special occasions, such as birthdays or wedding anniversaries. It is interesting to notice that the young boy has included this family picture in his drawing, while real people are not present around him. This might reflect the reality that family members are frequently absent in the lives of Korean children and adolescents, since parents are required to stay at their workplaces until late in the day and siblings may be involved in various academic or extracurricular activities after the regular school day ends. Therefore, the drawing demonstrates an aspect of global popular youth culture as an experience familiar to the sociocultural context and everyday lives of many Korean youth.

Spaces of attachment. From Toyama Elementary School in Japan, we see a 5th-year student's poetry illustration (Figure 3). The drawing incidentally also depicts the creator's favorite place. It describes a boy sitting on a bench on a sunny day in autumn. Lines were drawn by a lead pencil and spaces are decorated with color pencils. The boy is wearing a jacket that bears the logo NIKE (an American sports-clothing brand). Perhaps he likes the brand very much. There are two *kanji*[7] for "milk" written on the back of the bench upon which he is sitting. Perhaps the bench was provided by a milk company. There are also *kanji* for the name Tauchi, which may be the name of the milk company.

Figure 2. A drawing by a 14-year-old boy from South Korea shows him playing with a handheld video game in his living room.

Figure 3. Drawing by an 11-year-old boy in Japan illustrates a classical Japanese poem about the sudden arrival of fall.

The bench is set between deciduous trees. Changes in the four seasons are distinct in Japan, and Japanese people are made aware that autumn is deepening when they see leaves on the ground. The child depicts the colored falling leaves in a somewhat exaggerated manner, almost like water falling from a fountain.

When attention is drawn to the boy's facial expression, which is drawn in a *manga*[8] style, the shapes of the eyes are that of a person laughing, and he seems very relaxed. Maybe he is sitting there for the short moment between finishing school and going to cram school[9] on a warm autumn day. In Japan it is very important to get into a high school that has a reputation for having a high rate of students being accepted into college. Thus in addition to regular schooling, students as young as elementary school age may be enrolled in cram schools after regular school.

Between traditional and global styles. In 2009 in Madrid, at ESO (Compulsory Secondary Education) school, illustration drawings of a poem by Antonio Machado were collected. At a junior high school in Seoul (2010), drawings were collected of "Me in My Favorite Place, Doing What I Love to Do" (Figure 4). Comparing examples of pictures done in these two themes is interesting in terms of their similarities, despite the fact that a great distance separates the two groups of young artists. In the examples shown here, both artists use similar manga (Cohn, 2010) styles and conventions in their drawings.

The Spanish student (Figure 4) made a pencil drawing, using only expressive lines. Her character is depicted in a stylized sailor suit, which is a typical Japanese school uniform style, although in Spain students do not wear school uniforms such as the one depicted by her character. Besides the clothing, this student's depictions of hair, eyes, hands, body, and clothing are fully consistent with manga conventions belonging to the *shojo*[10] genre (Prough, 2010), and may make specific reference to the Sailor-Moon series[11] of manga and animé that is broadcast globally (Allison, 2000).

A student from Seoul (Figure 5) has used colored markers to provide a self-portrait with contour lines filled in with flat color. This procedure and style is similar to some Western comic or cartoon illustrations (McCloud, 1994) as well as various manga styles (e.g., The Simpsons[12] cartoons and Doraemon[13] animé). The simplification of the face's shape and the way the gesture or hair is presented also is done in manga style that has become a style of visual expression that is shared by young people from many regions of the world, as distant from one another as Spain and South Korea.

Discussion

After this data analysis, the first research question can be addressed. Children and teenagers are creating an aesthetic that integrates local and global sensibilities. Their artworks may suggest that they are able to develop personally relevant images that dissolve borders between global consumerism culture and their local heritages accordingly. Thus, there is evidence of *cultural creation* (Jenkins, 2003), insofar as they demonstrate flexibility in

Figure 4. A drawing by a 15-year-old Spanish girl illustrates the poem entitled Recuerdo Infantil, from Machado.

Figure 5. A drawing by a 12-year-old girl shows her listening to music. Seoul, South Korea.

their ability to draw from both global and local expressive resources. As they illustrated national-specific, traditional poetry, the participants in this study indirectly introduced "remakes" of traditional styles and representations of local culture. At the same time, new visualizations often appeared in hybrid ways, with local features that clearly showed influences of visual global culture.

To answer our second research question, which inquired about the existence of a global youth culture shared by young people and teenagers from different parts of the world, we found evidence of this aspect when we focused on aspects of life regarding leisure habits.

Depicting Leisure and Youth Culture

Drawings about their "Favorite Place" allowed us to find strong links between art productions from adolescents in countries as far apart as those participating in this study. They shared similar visual codes and stereotypes, but their drawings also reflected the same universe of leisure in which consumption (technologies, brands, and shopping malls) is replacing inventive activities and outdoor explorations, or even personal relationships. But there also are some clever appropriations of commercial culture icons and critical references to current social or political events evidenced in drawings from students from their respective countries, which may suggest these young people spend a portion of their leisure time thinking critically about such events.

The leisure and afterschool habits of young people in Spain, Japan, South Korea, and Taiwan are reflected in the collected artworks. These seem to match descriptions made by other researchers (Dwyer, 2004; Dwyer & Ide, 2004; Yi & Wu, 2004). Dwyer and Ide (2004) use the term *furitaa* (p. 99), from the English words free time, to refer to the time that Japanese teenagers spend on their hobbies. Outside school, teenagers may spend a lot of time with friends at fast food restaurants or bookstores where magazine and manga are purchased. Other popular hangout spots are game centers equipped with the latest digital games. At home, teenagers may also spend a considerable amount of free time watching television, chatting with friends on social networks, or playing video games.

The focal point of a young South's Korean's daily life, however, is school (Dwyer, 2004). The principal goal in a South Korean teenager's life is to work toward the university entrance exam. Dwyer points out that many teenagers jokingly list sleeping as their favorite hobby (in our visual content analysis, we found that category too),

although listening to music, sports, and South Korean billiards were also popular activities. The average South Korean teenager spends 17 hours each week in front of a computer (Dwyer, 2004); we found this leisure habit also depicted in many drawings collected as data for this research.

Education has long been cherished above all else in the Chinese culture (Yi & Wu, 2004). According to survey reports, mathematics (as found in the Galactic Buddha mathematics dream, Figure 1) is Taiwanese teenagers' least favorite subject. Yi and Wu noticed that the stress placed on studying is shared by other Asian countries heavily influenced by Confucian thought. As a consequence, Taiwanese teenagers do not have much time for recreation. Teenagers in Taiwan admire Japanese culture (Yi & Wu, 2004). Proof of this admiration is a growing cosplay[14] phenomenon, as evidenced by photos we have taken of Taiwanese students (see Figure 6). "Though *cosplay* was introduced from Japan… both the public and private sectors in Taiwan have encouraged original comics and animation creations" (Tsai, 2010, para. 3). Consequently, Japanese cartoon figures, comic books, and electronic products are popular goods among teenagers in Taiwan (Chen, 2007). In addition, Taiwanese teenagers tend to emulate the dress and behavior of Japanese teenagers.[15]

Taiwanese parents often prohibit their teenage children from having access to the Internet at home (Yi & Wu, 2004). Teenagers search for access to it outside of the home; we collected several drawings depicting students in parks with computers or in wi-fi areas. When spare

Figure 6. Taiwanese cosplay by teenage girls.
Source: LiHsun Peng.

Figure 7. A drawing by a 12-year-old Taiwanese girl illustrates "Me in my favorite place: shopping."

Figure 8. A drawing by a 14-year-old Spanish girl illustrates a Japanese poem.

time is available, boys may play basketball during the afternoon or play online electronics games, while girls may shop with friends (see Figure 7) or get together at a friend's home (Yi & Wu, 2004).

Drawing Styles in a Global-Local Youth Identity

The manga style of artmaking was evidenced at all research sites, as were influences of visual codes representing games and trademarks. Prevalence of these visual influences had been pointed out by researchers in art education (such as Wilson, 2003). Toku (2001) and Koyama-Richard (2008) asserted that in a Japanese cultural context, manga styles are local and reflect traditional influences that evolved from Japanese visual culture heritage. Manga and anime (Japanese animation) styles are also global phenomena insofar as, over the past 20 years, they have spread throughout the world via television, graphic literature in Japanese and translated versions, digitized images and videos accessed through the Internet, and consoles and portable game players. If youth culture is a bricolage of different subcultures (Richards, 2011), perhaps the manga style is one of the glues that hold all the pieces together.

Global influences are expressed in the clothing styles depicted by children and teenagers in their drawings. While Western clothing has become the norm in Japan, an interesting cultural transmission and reversal has emerged in the visual representations of clothing depicted in manga and anime. The main character of a drawing produced by a female middle school student living in

Figure 9. A drawing by a 12-year-old Spanish boy. (Free artwork, made out of school.)

Madrid is shown wearing a Western style sailor uniform, which now is typically worn by Japanese female high school students. This kind of uniform is very often depicted in Japanese *shojo* and *maho shojo*.[16] The style has been imitated by Spanish teenagers, who find it aesthetically appealing (Figures 8 and 9).[17] Thus it can be observed that there is a back and forth exchange of Eastern and Western clothing cultures (Jones & Leshkowich, 2003).

Preferences for facial features and body types also might be exchanged back and forth cross-culturally. A female high school student from Spain, shown wearing a sailor uniform, is thin and has large eyes. This style may represent what Japanese youth consider to be an ideal Westerners' body shape (although it may also be seen in some traditional Eastern images), and is regularly depicted as the body form of manga characters. Kurumado (2006) indicates that Japanese artists' original use of varied "shapes and sizes of the eyes and eyebrows" (p. 9) were conventions established to convey emotion, rather than references to or preferences for ethnicity types. In either case, we see the small *kawaii*[18] girl features of Japanese manga characters in a drawing created by a female Spanish teenager.

If focus is placed only on clothing, it seems that cultural differences between Western and Eastern cultures are fading, an event that has been occurring since WWII as a movement from West to East—but the directions of aesthetic clothing style preferences are no longer one directional (Jones & Leshkowich, 2003), as indicated above. However, if focus is placed on the depiction of nature, it is often found that expressions unique to each country still remain. We will turn attention to depictions of nature next, as we address the research question regarding evidence of the local cultural consciousness of children and teenagers.

The way in which nature is depicted in drawings of a translated poem by the Japanese poet Ryokan, which were drawn by children in Madrid, definitely differed from drawings by the Japanese children that expressed their reactions to the same poem.

Suns depicted by children in Madrid were yellow. Suns drawn by Japanese, Korean, and Taiwanese children were reddish in color (see Figure 3). It is not easy to identify one reason for that red sun, but it is possible to trace artistic traditions in Western and Eastern history that may have influenced youths' depictions of the sun in these countries.[19]

Figure 10. A drawing by a 12-year-old Taiwanese boy illustrates a Chinese poem by Li-bao.

Figure 11. A drawing by an 11-year-old Spanish boy illustrates a Japanese poem from Ryokan.

The ways in which mountains were depicted also seemed culturally or geographically specific. Mountains depicted by Japanese and Taiwanese children were generally covered with green; the summits were rounded and appeared in multiple rows, one behind the other, forming a three-dimensional suggested landscape (Figure 10). We can find traditional Japanese and Taiwanese artworks that use this schema in landscape art.[20] Additionally, rivers flowing out of mountains drawn by Japanese children were drawn with a gradual curve that reflected typical ways of describing streams and rivers in Asian art. By way of contrast, mountains drawn by children in Madrid were spiky, with little green added (Figure 11), which is more typical of Western mountain landscape traditions. At times, however, influence from manga could be seen in depiction of nature by children in all the groups. Japanese children expressed a blowing wind or the

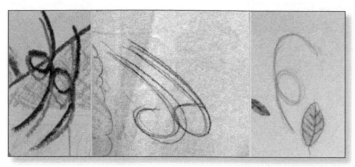

Figure 12. Several fragments of drawings made by Japanese teenagers when illustrating a Japanese poem. Motion lines are used to depict the wind with a loop shape.

Figure 13. A fragment of a drawn illustration of a Japanese poem made by a Spanish teenager. Straight-line motion lines are used to describe the wind.

movements of people and objects with motion lines, as did Spanish children, but the shapes of these lines differed. Japanese children drew motion lines using a code rooted in traditional Asian artwork, which dates back to the 12th century (Friedman & Stevenson, 1980) and is currently evidenced in manga (Figure 12). Meanwhile, Spanish children drew motion lines using another code, rooted in Western comics (Figure 13) (Saraceni, 2003).

Art Education's Role in Awakening Critical Awareness of Glocalization

Dealing with visual culture in art education classes requires attention to distinctions between local and global culture influences (Duncum, 2007). The drawings on global visual culture and heritage we have collected show the need for a new art education framework: one that considers the overtly conscious and hidden messages of older children and teenagers' art, as evidence of the social, cultural, and media influences which affect the ways they see and engage with the world. This examination of drawings by older children and adolescents in four culturally distinct regions of the world provides an intriguing glimpse into the way they make sense of local and global cultural influences. We propose that art educators and art education might play an important role in bringing students to critical awareness of global and local cultural heritages, critical distance from culture as mere consumption, and recognition of their own agency as cultural creators. In this scenario, art teachers would have updated information about popular culture—especially visual culture that is consumed by students—and become knowledgeable about the motifs, styles, and genres that older children and teenagers appropriate in their artworks.

In this way, art educators can encourage young people to critically examine certain aspects of global visual culture, be curious about the historic sources and cultural meanings of particular images, and adapt and apply non-local aesthetic forms to local contexts. Shared aesthetic forms (such as manga) and globally recognizable visual representations might serve as a common language for exchanging ideas and interactive communications between and among youth from diverse cultural backgrounds or regions of the world, while distinctively localized presentations empower youth as unique individuals within situated cultural contexts. Art educators might also invite students to distance themselves from their visual depictions of contemporary culture, question what it tells them about, and how it affects their lives, so they might be armed to make wise choices about how they spend their time in pursuit of meaningful activities. Our research tells us that teenagers are drawing in local and global motifs as they engage with their worlds; we suggest art teachers can encourage them to think critically about the contributions they are making to an interactively connected global society.

REFERENCES

Allison, A. (2000). Sailor moon: Japanese superheroes for global girls. In T. J. Craig (Ed.), *Japan pop! Inside the world of Japanese popular culture* (pp. 259–278). Armonk, NY: Sharpe.

Augé, M. (1992). *Non-lieux: Introduction à une anthropologie de la surmodernité* [Non-places: Introduction to an anthropology of supermodernity]. Paris, France: Édition du Seuil.

Banks, M. (2001). *Visual methods in social research*. London, England: Sage.

Benach, N. (2000). Nuevos espacios de consumo y construcción de imagen de la ciudad en Barcelona [New spaces of consumption and image building in Barcelona city]. *Estudios Geográficos, LXI*(238), 189–205.

Chen, J. S. (2007). A study of fan culture: Adolescent experiences with animé/manga doujinshi and cosplay in Taiwan. *Visual Arts Research, 33*(1), 14–24.

Cohn, N. (2010). Japanese visual language: The structure of manga. In T. Johnson-Woods (Ed.), *Manga: An anthology of global and cultural perspectives* (pp. 187–203). Maiden Lane, NY: Continuum International.

Diem-Wille, G. (2001). A therapeutic perspective: The use of drawings in child psychoanalysis and social science. In T. Van Leeuwen (Ed.), *Handbook of visual analysis* (pp. 119–133). London, England: Sage.

Duncum, P. (2007). What we are learning about teaching popular visual culture. In M. A. Park (Ed.), *Art education as critical cultural inquiry* (pp. 216–233). Seoul, Korea: Mijinsa.

Dwyer, E. (2004). South Korea. In J. J. Slater (Ed.), *Teen life in Asia* (pp. 205–222). Westport, CT: Greenwood Press.

Dwyer, E., & Ide, R. (2004). Japan. In J. J. Slater (Ed.), *Teen life in Asia* (pp. 87–111). Westport, CT: Greenwood Press.

Flick, U. (1998). *An introduction to qualitative research*. London, England: Sage.

Freedman, K. (2003). *Teaching visual culture: Curriculum, aesthetics and the social life of art*. Reston, VA: National Art Education Association and New York, NY: Teachers College Press.

Friedman, S. L., & Stevenson, M. B. (1980). Perception of movement in pictures. In M. A. Hagen (Ed.), *The perception of pictures* (Vol. 1) (pp. 225–255). New York, NY: Academic Press.

Gauntlett, D. (2007). *Moving experiences: Media effects and beyond*. Eastleigh, England: John Libbey.

Grigsby, M. (1999). The social production of gender as reflected in two Japanese culture industry products: Sailormoon and Crayon Shin-Chan. In J. A. Lent (Ed.), *Themes and issues in Asian cartooning: Cute, cheap, mad and sexy* (pp. 183–210). Bowling Green, OH: Bowling Green State University Popular Press.

Jenkins, H. (2003). Quentin Tarantino's Star Wars? Digital cinema, media convergence and participatory culture. In D. Thorburn & H. Jenkins (Eds.), *Rethinking media change* (pp. 281–314). Cambridge, MA: The MIT Press.

Jenkins, H. (2006). *Convergence culture: Where old and new media collide*. New York: New York University Press.

Jones, C., & Leshkowich, A. M. (2003). The globalization of Asian dress: Re-orienting fashion or re-orientalizing Asia? In S. Niessen, A. M. Leshkowich & C. Jones (Eds.), *Re-Orienting fashion: The globalization of Asian dress* (pp. 1–48). Oxford, England: Berg.

Kjeldgaard, D., & Askegaard, S. (2006). The glocalization of youth culture: The global youth segment as structures of common difference. *Journal of Consumer Research, 33*(2), 231–245.

Koyama-Richard, B. (2008). *One thousand years of manga*. Paris, France: Flammarion.

Kurumado, S. (2006). Introducing manga and animé to art educational curriculum. *Voice: USSEA Newsletter Insert of Teaching Practices, 29*(1), 8–10.

Levi, A. (1996). *Samurai from outerspace: Understanding Japanese animation*. Chicago, IL: Open Court.

Lister, M., & Wells, L. (2001). Seeing beyond belief: Cultural studies as an approach to analyzing the visual. In T. Van Leeuwen (Ed.), *Handbook of visual analysis* (pp. 61–91). London, England: Sage.

McCloud, S. (1994). *Understanding comics: The invisible art*. New York, NY: Harper Perennial.

Mirzoeff, N. (1999). *An introduction to visual culture*. London, England: Routledge.

Proser, J. D. (2008). Visual methodology: Towards a more seeing research. In N. K. Denzin & Y. S. Lincoln (Eds.), *The SAGE handbook of qualitative research* (pp. 479–496). London, England: Sage.

Prough, J. (2010). Shojo manga in Japan and abroad. In T. Johnson-Woods (Ed.), *Manga: An anthology of global and cultural perspectives* (pp. 93–108). Maiden Lane, NY: Continuum International.

Richards, C. (2011). *Young people, popular culture and education*. London, England: Continuum International.

Rose, G. (2001). *Visual methodologies: Introduction to the interpretation of visual materials*. London, England: Sage.

Sanz, E., & Romero, P. (2009). Creativity and consumption of children and teenagers' leisure: A study through the interpretations of their drawings. *Educación y Futuro, 21*, 111–128.

Sanz, E., & Romero, P. (2011). Nuevos héroes, nuevas expresiones artísticas: Niñ@s masmediátic@s [New heros, new art expressions: Massmedia children]. In R. Gutiérrez & C. Escaño (Eds.), *Critical thinking and globalization* (pp. 33–40). Malaga, Spain: Spicum.

Saraceni, M. (2003). *The language of comic*. London, England: Routledge.

Schodt, F. L. (2000). *Dreamland Japan: Writings on modern manga*. Berkeley, CA: Stone Bridge.

Shiokawa, K. (1999). Cute but deadly: Women and violence in Japanese comics. In J. A. Lent (Ed.), *Themes and issues in Asian cartooning: Cute, cheap, mad and sexy* (pp. 93–125). Bowling Green, OH: Bowling Green State University Popular Press.

Spencer, C., & Woolley, H. (2000). Children and the city: A summary of recent environmental psychology research. *Child: Care, Health and Development, 26*(3), 81–198.

Steinberg, S. (Ed.). (2011). *Kinderculture: The corporate construction of childhood*. Boulder, CO: Westview Press.

Steinberg, S., Parmar, P., & Richard, B. (Eds.). (2006). *Contemporary youth culture: An international encyclopaedia*. Westport, CT: Greenwood Press.

Sternberg, R. J. (1995). *Defying the crowd: Cultivating creativity in a culture of conformity*. Michigan University: Free Press.

Tobin, S. (2012). Time and space in play: Saving and pausing with the Nintendo DS. *Games and Culture, 7*(2), 127–141.

Toku, M. (2001). What is manga? The influence of pop culture in adolescent art. *Art Education, 54*(2), 11–17.

Tsai, J. (2010, October 25). Cosplay subculture continues to boom in Taipei. *Taiwan Today*. Retrieved from http://taiwantoday.tw/ct.asp?xitem=124723&ctnode=413&mp=9

Weber, S. (2008). Visual images in research. In J. G. Knowles & A. L. Cole (Eds.), *Handbook of the arts in qualitative research* (pp. 41–54). London, England: Sage.

Wellman, B., & Hampton, K. (1999). Living networked on and offline. *Contemporary Sociology, 28*(6), 648–654.

Wilson, B. (2003). Of diagrams and rhizomes: Visual culture, contemporary art, and the impossibility of mapping the content of art education. *Studies in Art Education, 44*(3), 214–229.

Yi, C.-C., & Wu, C. (2004). Taiwan. In J. J. Slater (Ed.), *Teen life in Asia* (pp. 223–241). Westport, CT: Greenwood Press.

ENDNOTES

[1] Digital media and the Internet play an important role in the omnipresence and ubiquity of images, since almost everyone can create and share them.

[2] In the 1990s Roland Robertson merged the terms *globalization* with *localization*, from which was derived a new term *glocalization* (Wellman & Hampton, 1999).

[3] By global visual culture, we mean the set of material artifacts such as still and moving images, toys, clothes, and so forth produced in different countries, and disseminated by the mass media and the global market.

[4] We proposed Machado (Spain, XX century), Ryokan (Japan, XIX century), Hujiwara (Japan, XII century), Li Po or Li Bai (Tang Dynasty, China, VII century), Jiang Lan and Sung Tse-lai (related to Hakka ethnic minority, Taiwan, XX century).

[5] Refers to analysis of form (shape, rendering, composition, color, and visual characteristics)

[6] Two of the researchers made a first selection of drawings to be subject to in-depth analysis, from which the entire research group chose the sample to be presented in this chapter.

[7] *Kanji* are the Chinese characters (*hanzi*) used in the modern Japanese writing system, along with hiragana and katakana.

[8] *Manga* is the Japanese word for naming comics created in Japan, conforming to a characteristic style.

[9] Cram schools, or *Juku*, are private schools specialized in training students to pass the entrance examinations of high schools or universities; lessons are conducted after regular school hours and on the weekends.

[10] *Shojo manga* is a manga comic for teenage girls (Tsai, 2010).

[11] The original *Sailor-Moon* series was written by Naoko Takuchi and published in 18 volumes by Kodansha from 1991–1997. It was made into animé television series, films, musical performances, video games, and various other franchised forms.

[12] *The Simpsons* is an animated cartoon sitcom, created for television by Matt Groening for Fox Broadcasting. The series began in 1989 and is still in production (see www.thesimpsons.com).

[13] A series of 45 manga stories featuring a robotic cat, created by Fujiko Fujio, were made into animé and merchandise (see Fujio, 1969–96).

[14] *Cosplay* is a contraction of *costume* and *play* that refers to representation of fictional characters using costumes that resemble popular culture characters (Chen, 2007).

[15] Taiwan was once under military occupation by Japan, but these youth have overcome hard feelings toward Japan once held by their elders. This might be considered as a positive side effect of globalization.

[16] *Maho* is a kind of *shojo* in which heroines have magic powers.

[17] There are many academics who have offered rationales for the psychological, sociological, or cultural appeal of these uniforms and body-type preferences (Levi, 1996; Grigsby, 1999; Allison, 2000; Schodt, 2000).

[18] *Kawaii* means *cute*, a word used in Japan with an emphasis on the girl-child subculture. Japanese *manga* heroines are usually *kawaii*, but dangerous (Shiokawa, 1999).

[19] There is an artistic tradition of depicting the sun in red in South Korea. For example, Koreans have a custom of exchanging greeting cards for a new year in which a typical greeting card depicts the red sun coming out of the sea or between mountain peaks.

[20] The Chinese traditional painting called *Shan-shui-hua* (mountains and rivers landscapes), a series of hanging scrolls with ink and light colors on silk, from the Song Dynasty, represents this kind of landscape. In the Japanese side, traditional painting of the Higashiyama period usually depicts landscapes with mountains in the same way Japanese children do.

CHAPTER 18

Living on a Bridge:
The Effects of Cultural Policy on Art Education in Turkey

FATIH BENZER
University of Minnesota, Duluth

OLCAY KIRIŞOĞLU
International Society for Education through Art

Turkey is geographically and culturally positioned as a bridge between Western and Eastern worlds, and its citizens face questions about cultural preference and identity. Anatolia, which is the culturally attributed name of Turkey, served as a cradle for many cultures from 10,000 BCE to the present era. If one examines the cultural history of Turkey, one can see that a diversity of cultural traditions have flourished in Anatolia at one time or another, and have intertwined, influenced, and affected each other. Thus, Anatolian arts and crafts traditions have developed unique characteristics.

In the 19th century, Turkish citizens began experiencing philosophical disagreements about whether to follow traditional/universal, national/international, or Western/Eastern paths toward national progress. According to some Turkish intellectuals (Eyüboğlu, 1982), being contemporary meant adopting widely accepted Western and European values, which they believed were necessary for the cultural development and progress of the nation (see Figure 1). Others[1] preferred to preserve the status quo of a unique Turkish *cultural identity*, defined as the common values, norms, and beliefs of individuals (Topuz, 1998) who represented the mainstream Turkish community. Ultimately, these latter ideas gained favor, and Turkish cultural policy was structured and implemented by the state establishments, ministries, civil associations, trusts, private organizations, and institutions to protect and improve the living cultures and cultural heritage of the country.

From the mid-1990s on, artists, art historians, curators, cultural critics, and aestheticians who dealt in international art markets noticed that questions regarding preservation versus assimilation of national cultures had become popular themes for international discussion among the European intelligentsia. These questions, which had been considered and discussed within academic circles a century earlier, attracted the renewed attention of policymakers in public institutions and the Ministry of Education in Turkey. Thus, a dichotomy of opinions regarding cultural maintainence versus integration has resulted in a confusing art education curricula for public schools in Turkey.

Motivated by concerns about what stance policymaking organizations and developers of national school curricula should take when preparing students of Turkey to be nationally and internationally competent citizens, we (the authors) developed a survey, which was presented to in-service and preservice art teachers and art students at the undergraduate level in higher education. The central focus of the survey was to determine answers to the following questions:

- How is Turkish cultural policy regarding the goals of art education reflected in art education programs in public schools?

- Should there be an integration of the art history and culture of Western civilization as a major component of art education in Turkey, or should focus stay on traditional Turkish national values and heritage?

- How can we establish a fine balance between those policies dictated by officials of the Ministry of Education in Turkey, as a national cultural policy, and independently held beliefs of artists and educators that art educational practices should encourage appreciation of local cultural traditions as well as canons of Western and Eastern arts?

Figure 1. Western influences such as three-dimensional depiction of form and space, as well as expressionism are evident in this work by a Turkish student.

A Brief History of Art in Turkish Culture

The admiration of Western culture first started during the monarchy period. Such admiration came out for the sake of modernization. Since then, this admiration caused many arguments and counter-arguments about the issue. Among intellectuals, many did not take traditional minature artists seriously and turned their face towards Western art. (Eyüboğlu, 1982, p. 32)

Critical aesthetic discussions about the roles and values of visual arts in the lives of Turkish citizens began during the Monarchy in the Ottoman Empire (1299-1923) and continue to the present day. Some early literature on art criticism, for example, which considered issues and arguments of aesthetics, were published between 1911 and 1914 in *The Newspaper of Ottoman Painters Society*. Authors of the articles in the publication provided introductions to Western art and discussed the importance of art in people's everyday lives.

From the Pre-Republican Era (1897–1923) until the 1930s, Turkish aestheticians[2] from the Pre-Republican Era argued that art should have strong and idealistic moral values in its context. In order to be able to express the purity of nature and its poetic beauty, the content of the art should exemplify moral values. Another common belief among writers and critics of the era[3] was that art should communicate certain historical subjects, so people of the Turkish nation could feel proud of their nation. In other words, the didactic significance of art was considered paramount.

Prior to the 1930s, the subjects and technical qualities of an artwork were all that were discussed in terms of its aesthetic qualities. The most important criteria for judging the success of a work was deciding if the selected subject matter was significant or "correctly" represented. According to artists like Ali Canip[4] (1918), beauty was not in the subject matter or in what an artwork looked like, but how it was expressed. In traditional Turkish art, beauty was never judged by the realistic look of the subject matter of an artwork, but by an essence which is far beyond nature's laws. The art of Anatolia, like the art of the East, was more subjective than objective. Beauty was not a concept that could be totally defined or explained. In Turkish society, beauty was understood as a spiritual quality rather than an explicit or realistic feature of art.

A Brief History of Art Education in Turkish Schools

In the middle of the 19th century, painting as a course was studied in the Turkish schools for the first time at elementary and secondary levels (Kırışoğlu, 2002). The reason for including art as a subject in school programs was that the Monarchy (1299–1923) intended to reform Turkish society by copying aspects of the Western world. The purpose of art instruction was to teach technical skills to students by having them making copies of post cards and pre-drawn images on blackboards. In the following years, from simple to complex ways of teaching drawing and painting were initiated as reforms to copyist methods, which were being criticized as lacking purpose and principles. The establishment of the Academy of Fine Arts (1883) also played a big role in preparing artists and art teachers, although because the focus of teacher education programs was knowledge of pedagogy rather than knowledge of subject content, many art teachers lacked sufficient background in artmaking to be effective studio art instructors. In the following years, a certificate program in the Academy was offered for those who wanted to teach art.

The Republican Era (1923-Present) was a bright period in Turkey's cultural history. New reforms included radical changes in the Turkish alphabet and a search for a new national identity. Atatürk (1881-1938), founder of the Turkish Republic, believed freedom of thought opened up roads for a new generations of artists who were interested in exploring borders of creativity[5] and building up citizens' self-confidence as members of a culturally rich nation. Research was conducted to find out more about traditional and folk arts and crafts. These research studies provided building blocks for a new Turkish cultural landscape that included a visual arts community. A new nation was established in 1923 when the Republic of Turkey was formed—with Atatürk as first President—from the remains of the collapsed Ottoman Empire (İskender, 1982). Education policy makers were influenced by foreign educators such as John Dewey, who was invited to Turkey as an educational consultant. Dewey's report on art education included the issues of classroom environment, educational materials, and reevaluation of the curriculum. Dewey's report on Turkey (1983) can be seen as an indication of President Atatürk's desire for the establishment of democratic culture through education. Soon after Dewey's visit, the Gazi Institute of Education was established in 1929 in Ankara to prepare teachers to teach in middle schools. Art programs in both elementary and secondary levels were rearranged, and art classrooms were designed to be more child-centered

For Further Consideration

1. How are cultural policies regarding the goals of art education reflected in art education programs in higher education in your own country?

2. Describe and discuss how your cultural experiences have shaped your perception of what art is?

3. What experiences and opportunities have you had as an art teacher or art student to learn about art from other cultures?

4. Why might be it important for art teachers to build experiences for learning about diversity and art curriculum?
   - List as many key reasons as possible.
   - Would some of these reasons be more important in some parts of the world, or some cultural contexts, than others? Explain.

5. How do you explain the role of art education in public schools with regard to dealing with issues of diversity and teaching in a pluralistic society?

6. What responsibilities do art educators have to introduce students to the arts of other countries and cultures, as opposed to teaching students artistic traditions of the local/regional/national culture?
   - Could this vary from place to place, region to region, or nation to nation? Explain.

7. What factors might make it important to emphasize one artistic tradition over another?

and responsive to the physical needs and psychological interests of students, although some education specialists continued to place emphasis on teaching skills to students because of the needs of the New Republic for labor (İskender, 1982).

The first children's art shows opened in the same period, and many Turkish art educators were sent to Europe for graduate studies. Upon their return, an Art Education Department and a Craft Department were opened in the Gazi Institute of Education (1932-1933). Eventually, these two departments were integrated into an Art and Craft Education Department, which produced many successful artists and art educators (Kırışoğlu, 2002).

Turkey's modern period since the 1920s has been one of rapid growth, in which the nation's cultural make-up and represented traditions have become more and more pluralistic. Issues of internationalization are now significant not only in terms of how to address a mutlicultural social agenda, but also in terms of how resources should be utilized to assist in art learning. The central aim of internationalization in art education, as stated by policymakers in the Ministry of Education, is to conserve and develop Turkey's national culture and heritage while also encouraging students to learn about and appreciate the cultures of other people. Consideration of ways in which contemporary art is serving to transmit and extend cross-cultural ideas and values could assist students to understand how Turkish society has been changing culturally, where it is now, and how it connects to differing cultures.

Current State of Art Education in Turkey

During the 1990s, the World Bank and Higher Education Committee in Turkey jointly sponsored a National Education Development Project that aimed at building a well-structured, comprehensive art education curricula for elementary and secondary education, which was based on a discipline-based art education model.

In 2007, officials of the Turkish government agreed to join the Council of Europe National Cultural Policy Review Program. Initiated in 1986, this program reviews and assesses policies in member states at the request of the Government/Minister of Culture in order to afford comprehensive analysis and advice regarding what policies might provide the greatest benefit to that country's citizens, while still taking into account national particularities. As of 2012, efforts to draft Turkey's National Cultural Policy Report to align with this framework are still underway. However, a group of 184 individuals comprised of representatives from arts and culture institutions, civil society organizations, and artists and experts of Turkey who did not get the opportunity to partake in the National Cultural Policy planning process embarked on an unprecedented initiative and drafted a national cultural policy framework through a collective endeavor. The resulting report is a significant case of civil society assuming initiative and responsibility on public policy issues (Ada, 2011).

The Survey

The main purpose of the survey was to find answers to questions such as how the Turkish cultural policy regarding the goals of art education is reflected in art education programs in public schools, as well as if there should be an integration of the art history and culture of Western civilization as a major component of art education in Turkey. The survey also aimed to find out how we can establish a fine balance between those policies dictated by officials of the Ministry of Education in Turkey and the independently held beliefs of artists and educators.

Description of Participants

The participants in our investigation were prospective art teachers, undergraduate students of art education and visual arts, and university department chairs/heads at three different universities in Turkey. The art education students included a wide range from freshmen to seniors. The total number of participants was 121, with 100 being students and the remaining 21 being department chairs. The percentage of subject areas that students were required to take were as follows:

	Credit Hours
Studio Courses	38.0%
Art Education Courses	6.7%
Other Art Discipline Areas (Art History, Aesthetics, Criticism)	22.0%
Education Courses (Introduction to Education, Developmental Psychology, Methods of Teaching)	24.0%
General Education (Turkish Language, Atatürk's Principles,[6] Foreign Language, and Computer Skills)	9.3%

A majority of the department chairs had backgrounds in visual arts, while a few had specialized in art education. All of the department chairs served in public universities.

Methods of Data Collection

The purpose of our survey was to find out what these participants believed should be an appropriate national Turkish cultural policy, and how this policy should be reflected in art education curricula enacted in Turkish public schools. The survey also included opportunities for participants to make suggestions for a coherent and well-structured cultural policy. As part of the investigations, art education literature from the Pre-Republican, Republican, and present-day eras of art education in Turkey were examined. Data from these literature reviews helped shed light on how art education practices of the past contributed to current developments in the field.

Findings of the Study

Data collected through the surveys, as well as the data from the literature reviews of Turkish cultural policies and art education practices of the past century, provided answers to these questions:

- What opinions do teachers and students of art education have about Turkey's cultural policy regarding:

  - How is a national cultural policy currently reflected in art education practices of Turkish schools?

  - Which cultural history should be taught in schools? Turkey's own cultural history or the cultural history of others?

- What are suggestions for establishing or improving Turkey's current cultural policy?

Opinions About Turkey's Cultural Policy

The majority of students surveyed (54%) stated that the unique Turkish national cultural identity is fading away because, as a society, we are trying to adjust ourselves to become more like societies of the Western world. Powerful influences from American and European popular culture hinder us from either teaching or learning in depth about our own unique cultural identity. Students of the visual arts are not spending a sufficient amount of time learning about Turkish cultural heritages. There is not enough being done to preserve our distinctive cultural values and heritage. Turkish youth have been alienated from our historic cultural values because of mass media and corporate/consumerist influences of Western popular culture.

Most students (78%) used the word "imitation" to express the unconditional acceptance of universal values and popular culture of the Western World

Figure 2. Western and popular culture influences, such as the three-dimensional depiction of space and forms, are evident in this work of a Turkish student.

(Figure 2). They indicated a need to avoid imitating cultural values of others and suggested there should be courses in the school curriculum to teach about our own cultural values and heritage. Nearly a quarter of the students (24%) said that the cultural history of our own nation should be taught as the primary subject. The common viewpoint of these students was that it is hard to have universal values because whatever we do reflects our own cultural influences. We should be the defenders of our own culture.

Survey respondents also expressed a belief that not enough attention was being paid to representing the cultural heritages of Turkey in the international arena. Teaching Turkish heritage only in schools is not enough to inform the general national or international public about our unique contributions to world cultures. The majority of students stated that, starting with the families of Turkish schoolchildren, more needs to be done to educate the public about contributions to global society made by Turkish artists.

While only 5% of the students emphasized the importance of focusing on universal values rather than Turkish national values, 19% of students mentioned that our cultural policy should not be limited to our own cultural heritage, but should be open to cultural values and histories of other nations. These students explained that learning about universal values and the history of world cultures gives an idea of where our own aesthetic sensibilities stand in relation to those of others in the world. Learning about other cultures also provides an opportunity for Turkish citizens to analyze their own cultural heritage from many perspectives.

Over half (60%) of those students who responded to our survey stated that it is possible to integrate Western cultural ideas without losing our own cultural identitiy. To do so, however, would require that Turkish citizens examine and comprehend their own Turkish cultural identities as much as they do the Western ideals to which they are exposed through mass media and marketing strategies of American and European corporations. These students were of the opinion that learning about our own cultural heritage in depth might provide a foundational platform from which we can critically consider, understand, and accept or reject dominant cultural values. As stated by Turkish poet Melih Cevdet Anday (1915–2002), "Let's not forget that cultures are intertwined. In fact, universal values[7] help us understand the real value of our own cultural heritage and norms" (Kırışoğlu, 2002).

Opportunities for Diversity, Individual and Unique Cultural Expression

Survey data revealed that many students perceived a *lack* of equal opportunity for diversity in the current education system. They believed the national cultural policy should not dictate that art education curricula be focused on popular culture to the exclusion of fine arts education. Other students, however, described the government's current policies as narrowly defined by traditional Turkish arts and crafts. Also, some students mentioned that the national cultural policy should not be tied to the world view of the political party in power but should be structured to meet the needs and hopes of our society over time.

These students were critical of current cultural policies advocated by the Ministry of Education or the committee for National Cultural Policy as not focusing on improving or supporting creative expressions by individual citizens, due to economical inconveniences and hardships of providing such support. Most agreed that a policy that supported uniquely Turkish cultural expression was better

established during the early years of the Turkish Republic and should have had the continuity of official govenment support from then until now. One respondent stated: "Our [current] cultural policy is an imitation of Western models. Cultural values which are not familiar to us are being promoted as if they belong to us. Twenty years from now, we might not have our own cultural identity at all." Only a small percentage of students (4%) saw current government officials and institutions as open to new ideas regarding whether or not to promote a unique cultural identity or assimilate a Westernized cultural identity. Openness was seen as a result of financial contributions from private enterprises and organizations whose financial support has the effect of imposing the organizations' agendas regarding national cultural policies on public policy.

Suggestions About Cultural Policy

The respondents to our survey recognized that cultural identities change rapidly, and thus, the national cultural policies should reflect a changing face of Turkish society in a globalized era. Additionally they suggested:

- There should be increased efforts to teach traditional Turkish arts in schools.

- Turkish cultural and educational institutions should not focus on imitating other cultures. We should protect our own unique cultural identity by not accepting Western popular cultural influences unconditionally and uncritically.

- Government officals should take more responsibility in understanding and representing the cultural history of Turkey without making the instruction of culture a matter of their political agenda.

- More private organizations (and funding resources) should be established to represent Turkey's cultural heritage on the international platform.

In general, student respondents agreed that being exposed to more cultural activities and events in schools that highlighted the traditional arts and crafts of Turkey would improve people's understanding and knowledge about our cultural heritage and aesthetic ideals. Furthermore, there should be more initiatives that would introduce our national culture to the world. We should then integrate our own hereditary arts and aesthetic sensibilities with contemporary dominant Western cultural influences.

Department chairs expressed their disappointment with the current cultural policy and how it reflects on art education curricula. As one department head indicated, "Culture policy is a very important issue not to leave entirely to the hands of state." The majority of department heads shared the same concerns as students: that prescribed curricula are vulnerable to risks of being affected by political changes and policies that propose opposing views on art and culture. They suggested that the curriculum should be designed according to universal, traditional, and also Western popular cultural values. These different views should be reflected in the studio activities as well as the theoretical subject areas. Changing attitudes toward the arts and cultural policy according to the political parties' own agendas has had a negative impact on the cultural development of Turkey. Department chairs, art educators, and prospective art teachers all agreed and claimed that the cultural policy should not be based upon the political party that is elected. Similar to students' comments, the department chairs agreed on obtaining universal values without losing our own cultural identity.

Government Policy and Public Initiatives

While a government may play a significant role in both the cultural and educational policies of a nation, policy makers and policy executors are influenced by differing agendas. Governmental ideas regarding how the culture of its people is perceived on the international stage, for example, may direct attention to policies that promote imitations of Western or universal cultural models; yet, what citizens understand of their own cultural heritage, and how they express themselves as members of a culturally unique or assimilated society, are largely reliant on how cultural traditions and aesthetics are dealt with in the educational curricula. Students and department chairs of art education programs may have concepts and ideas about the importance of maintaining a unique cultural identity, but in reality their ideas do not have much effect on the subject, so long as these policies are dependent on governmental decisions. There is a need to establish well-funded organizations of visual artists, art educators, and cultural institutions that can wield impact on cultural policy, without interference from political whims and agendas of the government.

The majority of the students who participated in our survey agreed that they had positive attitudes about the leadership roles of artists in society. The experiences of the department chairs and students have awakened a belief that art could empower ordinary people and their perspectives on a more democratic cultural policy. In the context of contemporary art schools, cultural policy and a well-structured art curriculum should allow the students to see themselves as empowered participants of a national (and international) culture. Art teacher training programs should not only focus on how to assist children to honor and maintain their cultural uniqueness, but also on how to be competitive on the international stage. Such programs may guide the prospective art teachers to respect their own national heritage while also valuing global aesthetic traditions.

Implications for K-12 Art Classrooms

An implication for art teacher education programs in culturally unique countries like Turkey is that art teachers need to be made aware of the impact of national cultural policies on education. Also, art teachers should be prepared to communicate the value of local *and* global cultures to K-12 students. Crouch (2000) suggests that art education programs, regardless of where they are located globally, should move to restructure core visual art content along these lines. Curriculum programs should honor the visual culture of a cultural group, local community, or nation in question, while looking to how these aesthetic expressions and traditions interact or integrate with dominant cultures of the national or global region. Thus visual art may be understood as reflecting unique yet multiple cultural influences upon the artist, who is situated both locally and within the larger artworld. In terms of Turkey, this means that Turkish people should release themselves from saying, "We are Western," or "We are Eastern." Instead of being ashamed of cultural dualities, duality should be the starting point for a new identity (Soysal, 1989).

REFERENCES

Ada, S. (2011). *Turkiye kultur politikasi raporu* [The report on cultural policies in Turkey]. Istanbul, Turkey: Istanbul Bilgi University Press.

Canip, A. (1918). *Milli edebiyat meselesi ve Cenab bayle münakaşalarim* [Issues in national literature and discussions with Cenab Bey]. Istanbul, Turkey: Kanaat Press.

Creativity. (2001). In A. M. Stevens (Ed.), *Merriam-Webster's collegiate encyclopedia* (p. 411). Springfield, MA: Merriam-Webster.

Crouch, C. (2000). Negotiating cross-cultural education in the visual arts. *The International Journal of Art and Design, 19*(3), 332–344.

Dewey, J (1983). Report on Turkey. In J. A. Boydston (Ed.), *The middle works: Essays on politics and society, 1923–1924* (p. 2). *Vol. 15 of Collected works.* Carbondale: Southern Illinois Press.

Eyüboğlu, S. (1982). *Sanat üzerine denemeler ve eleştiriler* [Essays and criticism on art]. Istanbul, Turkey: Cem Yayınevi.

İskender, K. (1982). *Cumhuriyet dönemi Türkiye* [Turkey during Republican Era]. Ankara, Turkey: İletişim.

Kırışoğlu, O. (2002). *Sanatta eğitim: Görmek, öğrenmek, yaratmak* [Education in art: Seeing, learning, creating]. Ankara, Turkey: Pegem.

Sen, A. (1999). Democracy as a universal value. *Journal of Democracy, 10*(3), 3–17. Retrieved from http://muse.jhu.edu.ezproxy.lib.indiana.edu/journals/jod/v010/10.3sen.html

Soysal, M. (1989, November 18). Amazement on the bridge. *Milliyet Newspaper*, p. 2.

Topuz, H. (1998). *Dünyada ve Türkiye'de kültür politikaları* [Cultural policies in Turkey and in the World]. İstanbul, Turkey: Adam Yayıncılık.

ENDNOTES

[1] Ottoman sociologist, writer, poet, and political activist Ziya Gökalp (1876–1924), whose work was influenced by European thinking and ideals, advocated the imposition of Turkish language and culture onto all the citizenry as a means of achieving nationalism and modernization.

[2] These aestheticians included Tevfik Fikret (1867–1915), a poet of the Ottoman era who is considered the founder of the modern school of Turkish poetry; Cenap Şahabettin (1870–1934), a medical doctor turned poet, whose literary work was strongly influenced by French symbolism; and Süleyman Nazif (1870–1927), a poet and historian whose literary work was critical of both the Ottoman monarchy and European imperialism.

[3] These nationalists included Mehmet Âkif Ersoy (1873–1936), who is widely revered by the Turkish people for his patriotism as well as academic and literary genius. He authored the Turkish national anthem, a framed version of which typically occupies a space on the wall of every school classroom in Turkey. Another is Yahya Kemal Beyatlı (1884–1958), poet and politician, who was influenced by French Romanticism and Turkish music, His writings emphasize Turkish and Islamic historical and cultural values.

[4] Ali Canip (1887–1967) was a poet who wrote in a plain, modern style.

[5] *Creativity* is the ability to produce something new through imaginative skill, whether a new solution to a problem, a new method or device, or a new artistic object or form. The term generally refers to a richness of ideas and originality of thinking (Creativity, 2001).

[6] Ataturk's principles are republicanism, populism, secularism, reformism, nationalism, and statism.

[7] "The claim of a universal value is that people anywhere may have reason to see it as valuable" (Sen, 1999, p. 11).

Dialogic Interactions—
LOOKING, QUESTIONING, LISTENING, AND ENGAGING

SECTION THREE:
DIALOGIC INTERACTIONS—
LOOKING, QUESTIONING, LISTENING, AND ENGAGING

Introduction

MARJORIE COHEE MANIFOLD

History has shown that when people from very different cultures meet one another for the first time, there is a tendency to liken the unfamiliarities of strangers to known phenomena of one's own experience, for humans have a need to make meaning of the inexplicable. Yet, interpreting Otherness based on an assumption that the unknown can be measured by the known is an unsound practice, because it builds on the uncertain supposition that all people share a singular worldview or template of meaning-making. While impressions of the world come to us through senses (e.g., seeing, hearing, touching, tasting, smelling) that function more or less similarly among peoples of the world, interpretations of what is seen, heard, felt, or otherwise experienced through the senses are dependent on how we have been inculcated to organize meanings and how we have been socialized to construct meanings of these impressions. This being the case, how can we know the world as others know it without having been physically immersed in the everyday cultural experiences of The Other?

This dilemma is addressed in the third section of this handbook, Dialogic Interactions—Looking, Questioning, Listening, and Engaging. Deciphering meaning of a cultural artifact out of context requires a Rosetta Stone of sorts. It requires movement back and forth between what is known and what is unknown within a neutral space, where beliefs and assumptions are suspended. As we look closely, question, and listen intently for answers within this space, new forms may emerge. We begin to see not only the outward manifestations of cultural expression but the internal foundations of these expressions; we begin to recognize the tacit beliefs people hold about the nature, meaning, and operations of the world, and how these function in everyday life. Awareness of Otherness is broadened, knowledge deepened, and understanding enlightened.

Of course, before one can meaningfully interact with others in this space, one must first listen to the self and know one's own language, heart, and mind in order to be able to clearly recognize and make distinctions between the familiar Self and the unfamiliar Other. Jeanne Nemeth introduces her preservice teacher students to contemporary artists from many global settings as examples of the aesthetic forms identity maps might take. In her chapter, "Constructed Territories: Identity Mapping," she explains how examinations of artists' images serve as a ground against which her students can consider their own mapping strategies for exploring personal geographies, memories, and identities.

In "Art Education With Migrant Hispanic Populations in Multi-Age Elementary Classrooms: Instructional Strategies Learned From Practice," author Jeffrey L. Broome provides a reflective narrative of his experience as an art teacher of children of migrant parents whose work requires them to move from place to place with the seasons. The students' unexpected responses to art lessons and methods of instructions that had served him well as a teacher of students from his own cultural background awakened him to see the uniquely grounded cultural aesthetics of these students. In looking at, questioning, and listening to explanations of local images, artifacts, and artistic practices, he came to imagine and was able to construct a program of art education for them that valued their cultural experiences and communal expressions.

Debra Donnelly and Kathryn Grushka, authors of "Enhancing Global Consciousness and Cultural Sensitivities: Digital Arts-Pedagogy in a Preservice Teacher Education Context," and Martha Christopoulou, author of "'Envisioning My Future Self': Exploring Identity Construction to Promote Cultural Sensitivity," see media-conveyed images as projective spaces in or through which students can visually examine, question, and listen to messages of others, then engage in critical considerations of images they see. Donnelly and Grushka invited undergraduate students in a teacher education program to seek out misleading or problematic cultural images that are available in cyberspace, "put themselves into the shoes" of someone whose life experiences are radically different from their own, and collaborate on creating digital images in response to this dialogical exchange. By appropriating and re-mixing iconic images, exemplars of fine art, images from life, and marketing messages in the media, the students came to a deepened understanding of how images work to construct meanings and engaged in critical examinations of how we understand ourselves and others through imagery.

Christopoulou recognized that a telenovela of adolescent life in a country half a world away provided an opportunity for her bicultural adolescent students to consider themselves in relation to influences from family, local society, and global society. Before and after watching the telenovela, she asked her students to draw images of themselves in careers they hoped or expected they might one day pursue. She found that by engaging students in discussions about expectations placed on them by family, community, and media, they were able to recognize outside influences on their self-images, consider possibilities about who they wished to become, and imagine realistic future selves.

An ability to imagine positive outcomes for present life situations may not come easily for children. Anna Kende and Anikó Illés, authors of "On the Practice of Artistic Measurement of Social Mobility and Marginalization," worked with Roma children of Eastern Europe, whose families were trapped in cycles of social discrimination and poverty. In their drawings the children described hopes and dreams for a safe and secure future that they scarcely knew how they might attain. As art educators, Kende and Illés struggled to find ways of helping these children recognize themselves as having agency in a mainstream society where their needs and potentials are too often rendered invisible.

Ava Serjouie was interested in children's "emotional responses to differing circumstances" of their families' migration or immigration from one geographic area to another, and explored this topic by listening to and looking at children's drawings of happy and sad experiences. In "Happiness and Sadness Depicted by Children of Immigrant, Migrant, and Cultural Minority Families," she presents her findings. Regardless of discrimination or other external marginalizing social factors, children who were supported by tightknit cultural communities found happiness in the presence of family and friends who they loved, and suffered sadness when cut off from loved ones due to physical separation. On the other hand, children whose families had immigrated to distant geographies, where they lacked the support of extended members of family or cultural community, experienced happiness or sadness in terms of gratification or denial of their desires to possess extrinsic "things."

Kende and Illés' work with Roma children and Serjouie's research among children of Iranian heritage reveal the importance of providing a ground where children of marginalized or oppressed groups might be freed to experience and express the richness of their cultural heritages and become full participants of the global society. Additional suggestions of how visual art education might assist in this process are offered in the next two chapters of this section. In "Marginalized Roma Children: Arts-Integration and Engagement with Learning," Kathleen Hall turns our attention back to the experiences of Roma children. In this case, however, the students are members of Roma families that have relocated to Canada. In programs specially designed to address the needs of these students, teachers have prepared welcoming environments that invite playful curiosity and explorations of learning. Acceptance within classroom communities opens spaces of opportunity; thus children can imagine their future lives differently and plot realistic paths to the future.

Lori Santos, author of "Cultural Myth and ACT-E: Reclaiming One's Past and Present Identity for a Future World," looks at how we might become empowered to imagine a narrative of ourselves living and acting in a harmonious future world. Santos suggests cultural myths and stories may be called upon to heal images of self that are incomplete or distorted by the pain of stereotyped representations or discrimination and marginalization. In her chapter, she describes conversations with Native American Michael Kabotie that led to the development of a curriculum frame she calls Awareness, Critique, and Transformative-Empowerment (ACT-E). She requires her students to model the framework in order to understand how they might use it when planning culturally sensitive art curricula for secondary-level students of any ethnicity or cultural background.

Finally, we turn attention to resources outside the educational community that might be called upon to help achieve goals of cultural maintenance and agency. Jeong Im Huh and Yong-Sock Chang remind us that nations have differing art educational needs, desires, and goals for the education of their children. Mécénat business-school partnerships, which in the Western world are controversial arrangements insofar as they promote an economically or politically advantageous agenda, provide funding for art education in traditional arts of Korea that might not otherwise have been available to rural South Korean elementary students. In "A Mécénat Collaboration Toward Appreciating a Traditional, National Art Form," they describe how the use of a traditional Korean art medium, Dok paper, when applied to doll making and contemporary storytelling, helped socially marginalized elementary students become aware and appreciative of their national identity and culture, recognize the importance of using natural resources in their creations, and discover an expressive form they might use one day to contribute to a vital local community while also enriching a global artworld.

CHAPTER 19

Constructed Territories:
Identity Mapping

JEANNE NEMETH
Indiana University—Purdue University Indianapolis

What is a map? How are maps used today? How are maps like our identities? Contemporary artists use ideas of mapping and cartography to explore a myriad of issues and ideas, such as identity, global culture, personal geographies, real or imaginary places in the world, and memories. This chapter examines how art education preservice teachers, inspired by contemporary mapping strategies, engaged in mapping personal geographies as an inquiry into Self and Others, both locally and globally. Identity mapping encourages reflective dialogue and understanding of how identities are constructed, ever changing, complex, and multilayered. In addition, identity mapping allows students to express how factors such as family history, gender, geographic location, race, age, politics, religion, and profession influence how others see us and how we view ourselves.

Sharing of personal histories and identity maps facilitates a new understanding of others and contributes to a community of learners who have insights and awareness of individual perspectives. These exercises can help students begin to deconstruct stereotypes and preconceived notions about cultural identity. Students' personal identity mapping processes, ideas, narratives, and artwork will be discussed in this chapter, along with examples of contemporary artists who utilize mapping strategies in their work. A number of possibilities for integrating an art curriculum based on mapping strategies and identity will be explored.

Understanding Others Through Understanding Self

An important aspect of training preservice art education teachers is assisting students to negotiate and assimilate emerging identities of teacher, artist, and student (Alsup, 2005; Pente, 2004; Springgay, 2004). This process is initiated by looking at oneself and understanding how one perceives or constructs a personal representation of the world. Pente (2004) notes that for the artist, teacher, and student, investigations into the self are important, but often overlooked. Students sometimes don't realize the complex and underlying nature of how identities are formed, and can benefit from intrapersonal reflections and examinations of the multitude of factors that contribute to cultural identity. Cultural identity includes linguistic and communicative patterns, belief systems, values, religious beliefs and rituals, the tools and artifacts of daily life, familial relationships, gender roles, and many other factors (Schall, 2010). Congdon, Stewart, and White (2002) remind us that teachers are influenced by their personal beliefs and assumptions when making daily decisions about curriculum content, textbook selections, class schedules, and designs for learning spaces. Consequentially, it is important for students to think critically about and become aware of values and assumptions that they bring to the classroom. Students need opportunities to explore concepts of culture and identity and how these shape their own lives and the lives of others. This is best augmented by teachers and curricula that exemplify personal and cultural curiosity and awareness.

Another goal of teacher training is to provide experiences that help students accept and become tolerant of cultural identities of other classmates and people from diverse backgrounds. Increasing diversity in the United States and many other countries throughout the world means that all students must recognize many cultural perspectives and identities. Developing an empathetic view—being able to put oneself in another person's situation—is an integral part of art education. Empathy allows students to be open to varying political, cultural, and religious perspectives. It is also crucial for understanding and teaching about the global art world (Jeffers, 2009). Most likely, students will experience global interactions throughout their lives; art offers a window into understanding different cultural symbols, values, and objects, and the world of others. Additionally, Lai (2012) reinforces the importance of a worldwide consciousness, and encourages art educators to engage students in discussions about issues associated with transnational art, such as global capitalism, tourism, and other political and social implications.

Daily sharing and listening to others' views are essential components for processing and discussing similarities and differences. Open dialogue within the classroom, and with the images and ideas of others beyond the local classroom, enables cross-cultural understanding and identity development; facilitates relationships; and is the basis for collaboration, development of empathy, and cultivation of a democratic community (Gude, 2009; Guilfoyle, Placier, Hamilton, & Pinnegar, 2002). One way to promote an insightful class dialogue about cultural experiences and histories of art students is by participating in and sharing an arts-based project centered on reflective research and personal geographies. The suggested activities described in this chapter integrate identity exploration, contemporary art, and mapmaking. Students' personal narratives incorporated into mapping projects promote discussion and thoughtful consideration of how culture impacts who they are and the way they live their lives.

Personal Geographies and Real-Life Experiences

As a teacher/educator of art methods courses in a large Midwestern university, I encourage students to explore the formation of their teacher/artist/student identities.

Students are immersed in readings, research, reflective journaling, storytelling, and art based problem solving to help gain a better understanding of themselves and others in the class (Cosier & Nemeth, 2010). A curriculum in the classroom that promotes learning based on overarching conceptual frameworks and essential questions is modeled and supported (Stewart & Walker, 2005). In this case, the idea of personal and cultural identity is directly and immediately relevant to students' lives, and may be easily adapted for instructing students of any grade level.

Identity mapping is an appropriate assignment for beginning the school year. On the first day of class I ask students to respond to a personal inventory survey about interests and expectations, which includes anticipatory questions about identity and identity construction. Student responses typically indicate a vague understanding of what key elements structure their identities. Next, I assign and adapt an in-depth Identity Mapping Project questionnaire and reading, developed and presented in a chapter entitled "Mapping Identity for Curriculum Work," by Congdon, Stewart, and White (2002). The questionnaire is extensive and includes 12 categories or identity communities: Family, Gender and Sexual Identification, Geographic, Religious, Economic, Political, Recreational, Aesthetic, Racial/Ethnic, Occupational, Health, and Body. Each identity community has three to five engaging questions that I ask students to reflect upon and write about in their visual journal.

After responding to the questionnaire, students are required to prioritize the categories, indicate the three most important identity markers at this point in their lives, and write a brief explanation of their choices. For example, many college students choose family and occupation as top priorities, and explain that becoming an art teacher is the prime focus of their immediate life as a student and that they rely on the support of family members for strength and encouragement to pursue their educational goals.

Next, students discuss a series of questions, such as: How did your understanding of identity change as a result of this exercise? What did you discover about yourself? Do you think identities remain the same over time? How can a discovery of identity help us in the classroom? How might your identities affect your choices for your students' learning? Most students feel that they have gained a new perspective about what factors contribute to *who they are*, and share valuable insights during group discussions (Congdon, Stewart, & White, 2002). The Identity

Mapping Project questionnaire, reading, and group dialogue provide the groundwork for introducing maps, identity mapping strategies, and contemporary artists. The following questions frame the investigations and classroom activities: How are maps constructed? How have contemporary artists transformed, deconstructed, manipulated, and responded to mapping? What are some ways in which we can express our identities by utilizing techniques and ideas associated with mapping strategies?

Mapping Strategies: The Map as Art

In the last 50 years, artists have produced works that are inspired by the use of maps and mapping concepts. Contemporary artists employ a broad array of approaches to making maps, redefining the established conventions of cartographers, and extending our knowledge and connection to place. Recent exhibits have featured artists working with mapping ideas in a variety of media. In some cases, the physical beauty and visual attributes of maps are compelling forces; in others the curiosity of cartographical practice is the prime appeal. Sometimes artists rely on mapping techniques as a creative strategy, or they may appropriate maps into their art. Others might conceptually play with an abstract notion of maps

as part of their artwork. Engaging both intellect and feeling, subjects range from mapping as a self-portrait or record of action to perhaps creation of an imaginative journey or futuristic place. Some artists combine fact and fiction when constructing artistic maps, using mapping strategies to mark memories and thoughts, as well as actual sites (Robertson & McDaniel, 1996).

As a visual method, maps are a particularly powerful means for the representation of place and lived experience. Maps convey a range of features related to physical landscapes as well as the psychological and social connections among people and places. Psychogeography, a new way artists explore mapmaking, plays with relationships and systems, rather than imagery. These types of maps offer the possibility of unexpected connections and have the ability to chart unique ways of viewing ideas about our place in the world (Powell, 2010).

The increase of new technologies and systems of global communications, along with access to vast amounts of information, spurred an abundance of artists interested in the subject matter. According to Harmon (2009), the Internet itself can be viewed as a cultural map existing in a holistic global culture. Many artists interested in

For Further Consideration

1. How are maps like our identity?
2. What do maps tell us about the world, our place in it, and the places of others? What can we understand from a map?
3. How can Identity Mapping promote understanding and empathy for others?
4. How can Identity Mapping encourage reflective dialogue and understanding of how identities are constructed?
5. Discuss the different mediums the artists in this article have used to make their maps.
   - How does each medium help convey the work's meaning?
   - In what ways might the media, processes, and form of the map reflect the culture of the mapmaker? Give specific examples.

The following activity might be conducted within a closed classroom or through a cyber exchange with students from another part of the world through an International Computer Technology (ICT) mode (such as Skype, blog, or Adobe Connect.)

   - Carefully select a small object that has personal meaning or reflects some aspect of yourself. Bring the object to class and share it with others. Give a clear description of what it means to you and listen to what they have to say about their objects. Reflect on what you learned about yourself and classmates by sharing personal artifacts. What can we learn about another's worldview through the artifact they select, or maps of self they share?

mapping make use of satellite maps, Global Positioning System (GPS), Geographic Information Systems (GIS), and medical imaging maps, in addition to physical maps. Additionally, in the era of globalization there is an influx of migration, international exchange, dislocation, and transition. The world is defined and redefined by contested territories and changing borders. Artists are interested in these issues and this is reflected in their work, often using maps to confront the politics of boundaries and/or comment on social and economic globalization (Harmon, 2009).

Prior to creating their own maps, students explore how contemporary artists are using the map and ideas related to cartography to construct art about identity, political issues, and other topics. They begin to see that a map can be a starting point, a form of documentation, or an end result (Harmon, 2009).

Artists Exploring Mapping Ideas

The work of a few contemporary artists who have used maps or mapping concepts within the span of their artistic careers can be incorporated into classroom instruction, as examples of the range of ways cartographic ideas can be expressed. Jasper Johns' 1960s map paintings of the United States, for example, might be a familiar starting point for a class discussion or inquiry lesson. He uses the United States map as subject, inviting the viewer to think about the difference between a map and an artwork, and to question the criteria for categorizing objects in one class or another (Robertson & McDaniel, 1996). In *Map* (1963), Johns' muddy brushstrokes blur the borders of each state, calling into question the inherent conditions of determining territorial boundaries (Harmon, 2009).

Lordy Rodriquez's maps are mixed with places he has lived, and to which he wishes to return. His family moved to the United States from the Philippines when he was a child. He remembers taking many cross-country and international trips with his family to see relatives. For several years Rodriquez has been working on a project, *New States*, drawing and remapping the boundaries and locations of the 50 United States and major cities. He has added five more states to this artwork, which include Hollywood, Disney World, The Internet (Figure 1), Monopoly, and Territory State—which is comprised of the Philippines, Samoa, and Puerto Rico. In another series of map drawings, titled *Geological*, Rodriquez eliminates text and abstracts the landscape, leaving the viewer with a feeling of dislocation, a theme portrayed throughout much of his work (Austin Museum of Art, 2009).

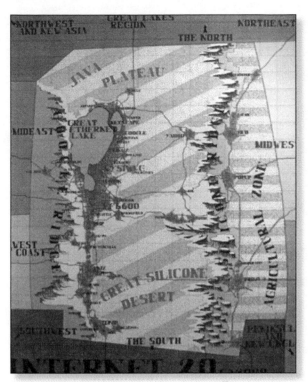

Figure 1. Lordy Rodriguez, Internet 2.0, 2007, from the series New States, ink on paper 48 x 40 inches. Courtesy of the artist and Hosfelt Gallery, San Francisco.

Ingrid Calame pushes the idea of abstraction in her mapping artworks. She traces and documents activity specific to a location, such as skid marks, stains, graffiti, and other visible markings. Layering the tracings, she creates abstract expressive patterned paintings and drawings of a site or sites she has visited. In 2007, she was invited to exhibit at the Indianapolis Art Museum and to visually respond to a local site. She spent time working at the Indianapolis Motor Speedway, tracing different types of skid marks on the track. Calame combined the Speedway lines and markings with tracings located by the Los Angeles River, near her home, to create large-scale paintings and drawings that resembled topographical maps (Karmel, 2008).

Joyce Kozloff has an interest in observing and mapping diverse cultures, examining our relationship with history. She has produced map-like images in a number of forms such as paintings, collaged map imagery, altered historical maps, modified globes, and other objects. In a gallery installation titled *Targets* (2000), Kozloff crafted a 9-foot walk-in globe (Figure 2), the interior featuring painted military maps revealing 24 countries that have been targeted by United States aerial attacks since 1945 (Harmon, 2009).

Figure 2. Joyce Kozloff, Targets, 2000, acrylic on canvas with wood frame 108 inches diameter. Photo by Jon and Anne Abbott. Courtesy of the artist and DC Moore Gallery, New York.

Figure 3. Vernon Fisher, Man Cutting Globe, 1995, lithograph 38 x 36 inches. Courtesy of the artist and Hiram Butler Gallery, Houston Texas.

Marlene Creates produced a body of work based on memory mapping, titled *The Distance Between Two Points is Measured in Memories* (1986–1988). Concerned about the increasing urbanization of the world and interested in showing the relationship between human experience and landscape, she interviewed elders about their lives in connection to places where they had lived. In northern Labrador, she worked with three different groups of people: the native Inuit, Naskapi Innu, and the Euro-Canadians. Her work for this project consisted of assemblages, which include a photograph of the person, their stories, and a memory map they drew for her of how they remembered their environment.

Part of Creates' working process is to use the memory maps to visit the places described, photograph one of the landmarks on the map, and collect an object from the landscape (Creates, 1989). Her current art practice revolves around multidisciplinary place-based art projects in Newfoundland schools. She engages students in research connected to their local environment, community, and heritage through field trips, drawing memory maps, photographing, writing recollections of their own experiences, and interviewing seniors in the community (Creates, 2008).

Through open-ended questions and thoughtful observation, students can analyze map-based artworks that are inspired from actual locations and reenvisioned by these contemporary artists. Questions can be posed regarding

how memory and perceptions of place influence understanding of the world, and students can examine the techniques and methods that established artists have used to create these interesting works of art.

Classroom Applications: Visual Thinking Strategies

Visual Thinking Strategies (VTS) is an aesthetic questioning method that can be incorporated in the classroom as a way of introducing and discussing artwork by artists using maps. The VTS inquiry strategy was developed by Abigail Housen based on her theory of aesthetic development (Visual Thinking Strategies, 2012). Vernon Fisher's image, *Man Cutting Globe*, was introduced to art education students using this VTS inquiry methodology, with surprising results (Figure 3). Discussions unfolded in which students decoded and constructed meaning about the artwork. The VTS method allowed students to learn from each other and build upon observations.

Three questions are essential to the VTS process: What is going on in this artwork? What do you see that makes you think that? What more can you find? Paraphrasing student responses is an important component, fostering a cohesive dialogue about the image. It is critical to allow time for ideas to form, evolving first from obvious observations to more in-depth, covert, and sublime meanings. The second question (What do you see that makes you think that?) prompts a student to cite evidence in the work that justifies his or her comments. The third question (What more can we find?) encourages further probing and more in-depth analysis. It is easy to engage students in 30-minute discussions and elicit responses from each member of the group using the VTS questioning method. For example, during the later part of the discussion around Fisher's image, one student pointed out that the section of the globe cut out might be a reference to strategically built United States military bases. This was an unexpected and insightful response, which contributed new meaning to the image.

Among the benefits of using the VTS inquiry technique are that students get exposed to the thinking and experiences of their peers, are actually leading the discussions, and are discovering meaning as a group. This method has been described as allowing students to participate more fully in a critical thinking studio (Housen, 2002). Introducing and selecting two or three images that have some multifaceted connections is suggested when implementing the VTS strategy. Artworks mentioned earlier in this chapter could be presented using VTS, as a way to engage students in examining artists working with mapping ideas.

Identity Mapping: Cultural Artifacts and Mapping Concepts

After investigating maps and contemporary art, students are confronted with the challenge of synthesizing ideas about identity and mapping to create a visual identity map. In order to help students generate ideas about maps and mapping concepts, students participate in brainstorming activities and an assignment utilizing a personal artifact. First, students participate in small group brainstorming sessions, answering the following questions: What is a map? What are the purposes of a map? How are maps used today? How is a map different or similar to real life? Allow time for each group to share ideas with the entire class and compile a list for future reference. Mapping terms generated by students might include: grid, compass, guide, plot, chart, life, communication, diagram, assistant, blueprint, trails, timeline, direction, survey, landmark, history, code, and topography. These words can be placed on separate pieces of paper and picked at random to use in connection with the next mapping exercise, which involves using a personal object connected to identity.

Invite students to bring to class a cultural artifact that represents some aspect of their identity. Students can sketch the object in their visual journal and write a statement describing how this object represents something

essential about who they are. After students share narratives about their personal artifacts with the class, give them the task of comparing similarities and differences about their artifacts with a partner.

The artifacts students selected in my university class contained stories that revealed interesting aspects of their lives. For example, Samantha brought in a bottle of Coke, which connected to her family identity and memories of her grandfather. She talked about how she spent many hours visiting with her grandfather, who was an artist and a positive influence in her life, stating that he always had a Coke for her when they shared time together. Shannon chose a cultural artifact with many references to her recreational identity, an important identity marker for college students. A clear plastic pouch attached to a neck ribbon, which contained a number of ephemeral items such as concert and sporting tickets and other paper documents, recorded time spent with friends and family and documented a history of these important events (Figure 4).

The second part of this lesson required students to select a random mapping term (generated in the brainstorming activity mentioned earlier) and force fit or combine this term in some manner, literally or conceptually, with their cultural artifact to create a new drawing. Force fitting

Figure 4. Cultural Artifact – Shannon.

or combining two unlikely materials, ideas, or objects is a creative strategy that can result in producing new solutions. Morgan brought a vintage dress pattern to class, which symbolized her artistic talents and interest in textiles. She randomly chose the term, "grid," and interpreted the term onto her new drawing. The image of the dress pattern and drawing (Figure 5) illustrates this process. These cultural identity objects may be shared among students in the local classroom, and an assembly of individually selected objects can be arranged to form a work of art that portrays the "identity map" of the group. Photographs could be taken of these objects to create a class cultural portrait or book for sharing with groups of students in other regions of the world.

Figure 5. Cultural Artifact and Drawing – Morgan.

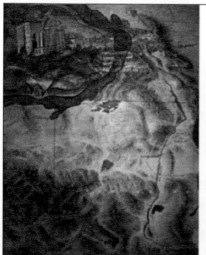

Figure 6. Identity Map – Britney.

Constructing Identity Maps

Finally, it is useful to encourage students to consider thinking about their identities in terms of a metaphor. Prompting students to think of a substitution for themselves forces them to think imaginatively. For example, ask them to respond to the following: If you were a piece of furniture or clothing, a type of map, a house, a book, a plant, a household appliance, or the like, what would you be and why? Metaphors may help students make new connections and introduce interesting perspectives that could inspire innovative map forms.

Another idea for students to consider before constructing identity map forms is to combine aspects of their outer, physical worlds and their inner worlds. Encourage them to consider their ambitions, fears, or character traits and incorporate these with geographic places of interest and community identities that they have previously written about. It is important for students to think about how to best visually represent these new items and incorporate them into their maps. An emphasis on links, pathways, roads terrains, and so forth can help students to draw previously unacknowledged connections and patterns about their lives. Finally, after creating an identity map, students could write a description or artist statement to accompany the mapping artwork.

My class completed their identity maps as artworks that would fit inside their visual journals. Mapping forms included drawings, three-dimensional pop-out constructions, multilayer collages with sewing, and other mixed media configurations. It was evident that students had gained new ideas from individual research on artists and mapping strategies. The most important aspects of this lesson included sharing artwork and accompanying narratives with small groups, taking time as a class to complete an assessment describing their mapping processes and ideas, and allowing each person an opportunity to express ideas about themselves with the class as a whole.

Student maps and identities were envisioned in a number of different formats and perspectives. Britney appropriated an old black and white topographical map from *LIFE* magazine as the background for her identity place-based work. Her geographical collage and layered drawing portrayed the relationship between her hometown and the larger urban city, where she is now living and attending school. She contrasted the physical proximity with very remote and isolated differences in culture, and used different pages of the journal to separate the two opposing worlds (Figure 6). Sam combined fact with fiction when constructing the details of his identity collage, and included a found road map and photos of himself enjoying life now. Concentrating on being present and engaged in life is vital for him. The post-it notes on the collage are handwritten statements talking about the importance of his family's support and acceptance (Figure 7). Samantha metaphorically represented her identity and chose to depict herself as a mouse, created with a cut-up map of her home county. The imaginative collage shows her altered self following a scent-induced trail, leading to a piece of cheese. She included multiple paths to the desired outcome and prize, each one filled with comments describing different aspects of her identity (Figure 8).

Students take time to complete a series of self-reflection assessment questions before they share ideas about their maps with the class. Some suggested questions include the following: (1) Describe the artwork including the medium, metaphor used, and inspiration. (2) What happened along the way? Explore the artistic process including what problems you solved, any unexpected results, or interesting anecdotes. (3) What did you learn through the art project? Reflect on what you learned about yourself, the art medium, the subject matter, and your world. (4) Give your piece a title. What does this tell the audience? (5) What did you learn about others in the class? These questions allow time to formulate ideas before presenting to their peers.

Additionally, students should reflect upon global issues portrayed through the work of artists that they studied, and discuss how mapping strategies used by artists promoted new understandings and awareness of salient world problems and concerns. Students could also compare and contrast maps in diverse mediums made by other artists from different geographic and cultural backgrounds. An extended activity could include the use of technologies such as Skype and Facebook to exchange stories and images of significant artifacts with people of other nations or regions, to compare and contrast important personal objects. Most importantly, students may discover universal truths and similarities among various cultures, which may serve to promote a broader understanding of the world.

Figure 7. Identity Map (Detail) – Sam.

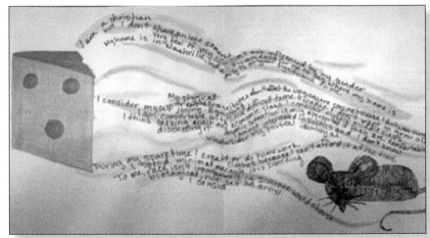

Figure 8. Identity Map – Samantha.

Conclusions and Implications

The maps and images presented in this lesson range in style and address a variety of issues, including national identity and international relationships, patterns of migration, and the potential of artistic materials. For students, mapping can be a way to revisit and critique past events or project future developments. A map can also become a form of portraiture, and a methodology for organizing the complexity of lived experience. One of the strengths of exploring personal maps and histories in the classroom is that it helps students clarify ideas about who they are and what is important to them. In addition, sharing these ideas about personal values promotes and develops working relationships with other students who may have different backgrounds and abilities. Communication and dialogue enable students to understand and accept others' assets and weaknesses, which, in turn, can cultivate an acceptance and celebration of cultural variety and differences.

The results from these classroom activities and discussions reveal the importance of creating contexts in teacher art education programs in which preservice teachers use and nurture empathetic dispositions and behaviors. Most importantly, listening to and sharing personal narratives and stories creates an art education family of others locally that could be expanded to cross-cultural/national sharing activities, which would contribute to mutual understanding.

One of the most satisfying outcomes of integrating identity mapping into courses for preservice teachers is the privilege of getting to know students on a deeper level and learning about important priorities in their lives. As a teacher, I find this information invaluable and appreciate the insights it offers into how students might approach future assignments and challenges. For students, the process of becoming a teacher and professional is not an easy journey. Self reflection and awareness of how personal and professional identities are constructed is a good place to begin.

REFERENCES

Alsup, J. (2005). *Teacher identity discourses: Negotiating personal and professional spaces.* Mahwah, NJ: Lawrence Erlbaum.

Austin Museum of Art. (2009). *Lordy Rodriquez, states of America.* Retrieved from http://amoainteractive.org/lordyrodriguez2009

Congdon, K. G., Stewart, M., & White, D. H. (2002). Mapping identity for curriculum work. In Y. Gaudelius & P. Speirs (Eds.), *Contemporary issues in art education* (pp. 108–118). Upper Saddle River, NJ: Pearson Education.

Cosier, K., & Nemeth, J. (2010). Art teachers as change makers. In T. Anderson, K. Hallmark, D. Gussak & A. Paul (Eds.), *Art education for social justice* (pp. 165–171). Reston, VA: National Art Education Association.

Creates, M. (1989). *The distance between two points is measured in memories, Labrador 1988.* Retrieved from www.marlenecreates.ca/works/1988distance.html

Creates, M. (2008). Biographical notes. *Marlene Creates.* Retrieved from www.marlenecreates.ca/bio.html

Gude, O. (2009). Art education for democratic life. *Art Education, 62*(6), 6–11.

Guilfoyle, K., Placier, P., Hamilton, M. L., & Pinnegar, S. (2002). Exploring the concept of dialogue in the self-study of teaching practices. In C. Kosnik, A. Freese & A. P. Samaras (Eds.), *Making a difference in teacher education through self-study* (pp. 96-103). East Sussex, England: Springer.

Harmon, K. (2009). *The map as art: Contemporary artists explore cartography.* New York, NY: Princeton Architectural Press.

Housen, A. C. (2002). Aesthetic thought, critical thinking and transfer. *Learning Journal, 18*(1), 99–131.

Jeffers, C. (2009). Within connections: Empathy, mirror neurons, and art education. *Art Education, 62*(2), 18–23.

Karmel, P. (2008). Field reports. In I. Calame (Ed.), *Ingrid Calame: Constellations* (pp. 34–59). New York, NY: James Cohan Gallery.

Lai, A. (2012). Culturally responsive art education in a global era. *Art Education, 65*(5), 18–23.

Pente, P. (2004). Reflections on artist/researcher/teacher identities: A game of cards. In R. Irwin & A. F. De Cosson (Eds.), *A/r/tography: Rendering self through arts-based living inquiry* (pp. 91–102). Vancouver, Canada: Pacific Educational Press.

Powell, K. (2010). Art viewing places: Students as visual ethnographers. *Art Education, 63*(6), 44–53.

Robertson, J., & McDaniel, C. (1996). Artists explore the map: 1960 to 1995. *The Midwest Quarterly, 37*(3), 302–315.

Schall, J. M. (2010). Cultural exploration through mapping. *Social Studies, 101*(4), 166–173.

Springgay, S. (2004). Body as fragment: Art-making, researching, and teaching as a boundary shift. In R. Irwin & A. F. De Cosson (Eds.), *A/r/tography: Rendering self through arts-based living inquiry* (pp. 60–74). Vancouver, Canada: Pacific Educational Press.

Stewart, M. R., & Walker, S. G. (2005). *Rethinking curriculum in art.* Worchester MA: Davis.

Visual Thinking Strategies. (2012). *What is VTS?* Retrieved from www.vtshome.org/what-is-vts

CHAPTER 20

Art Education With Migrant Hispanic Populations in Multi-Age Elementary Classrooms:
Instructional Strategies Learned From Practice

JEFFREY L. BROOME
Florida State University

66 I'd like to give you a tour of the school," the principal said as he rose from a chair in his spacious office. We stepped outside into the summer sun and headed to the art room. The principal stopped and leaned against a railing that faced the grounds surrounding the school. "Our students aren't from wealthy families that move to Florida to escape cold weather. Their families come here to work in this," he said pointing in the direction of the fence that divided the school from the surrounding rural landscape.[1]

"Most of our students come from migrant families that pass through this area to pick tomatoes and strawberries that are in-season," continued the principal. I remembered seeing several trailer camps (Figure 1) next to open fields (Figure 2) on my drive to the school. "Most of them come from Mexico and pass through Texas before making their way to us. Some stay, but others leave in the middle of the year to pick crops in the next spot. They may come again when the tomatoes are ready. Some students don't speak much English, and even fewer parents do."

"We stopped using grade levels as the system of organization in our classrooms a few years ago," said the principal. "Classes are made up of mixed-age groups that span a 3-year range. We think it promotes a sense of community and cooperative learning."

I was 22 years old and interviewing for my first position as an elementary school art teacher just after completing my bachelor's degree. I didn't speak a word of Spanish. I was far from home, where the familiar community demographic was predominantly White and African American. I had never heard of multi-age education, but I was about to accept a position at a school situated in a context with which I was decidedly unfamiliar.

Autobiographical Approach
In this chapter, I adopt autoethnographic narrative inquiry techniques (Clandinin & Huber, 2010) to describe my experiences as an art educator who worked for 8 years at an elementary school within a predominantly migrant Hispanic community. Researchers using autoethnographic methods place themselves as the subject of inquiries, focusing outwardly on a specific social situation, yet inwardly on their personal experiences in this context (Ellis, 2004). Autoethnographers often use first-person storytelling approaches that

Figure 1. Migrant workers' housing camp in central Florida.

Figure 2. Strawberry field in central Florida.

adopt the use of expressive language, and focus stories on significant events that led to personal insight. I view my years teaching at the school described above as a formative period that shaped how I teach, and impacted my development toward becoming a more culturally sensitive human. I hope that sharing my story allows opportunities for readers to consider their own professional experiences and culturally sensitive decision-making when working with diverse populations.

I begin by describing the context of my experiences at the school, and then present several stories significant to my time there. A concluding section synthesizes the emergent themes from the stories as suggested strategies relevant to teaching art to diverse socioeconomic cultural groups. In my story, I refer to the school as McCarty Elementary, as all proper names, except my own, have been replaced with pseudonyms.

Context

During my time at McCarty Elementary, the demographics of the school were approximately 65% Hispanic and 25% White; the remaining smaller percentages were students of African American, multiracial, and Native American backgrounds[2] (GreatSchools, 2012). Nearly 80% of the students qualified for free or reduced lunch programs, and the school received Title I funding for its high percentage of economically disadvantaged students.

The multi-age classes at McCarty Elementary included either team-taught groups of primary students (kindergarten, 1st and 2nd graders) or team-taught groups of intermediate students (3rd, 4th, and 5th graders). The intention of multi-age grouping was to cultivate positive community environments for students (Nishida, 2009) through an emphasis on mixed-age collaboration, rather than individualistic competition (Elkind, 1993). Homeroom teachers of multi-age classes *looped* (Ball, Grant, & Johnson, 2006), or stayed with students, for a 3-year period of time, in order to foster greater continuity in an ongoing caring atmosphere. An incoming kindergarten student would remain with a primary multi-age class for 3 years until he or she was ready to move on to an intermediate multi-age class. Students still progressed from easier to more difficult concepts, but the rate of this progress was not determined strictly by grade level (Hoffman, 2003). Administrative staff kept detailed records on transient students; when migrant children returned to our school during tomato-harvesting season, they were placed back within their originally assigned class to offer as much continuity as possible.

The centerpieces of multi-age instruction featured thematic units designed on topics of relevance to students' lives (Lolli, 1998). While the general approach was to focus instruction on big ideas of interest to all students, many teachers selected themes specifically relevant to the school population, such as units on Hispanic heroes and cultural identity. Through the efforts of the school's English for Speakers of Other Languages (ESOL) resource teacher, and in collaboration with interested homeroom, art, music, and physical education instructors, the school often held performances to celebrate cultural holidays, such as Mexico's Independence Day (Figure 3).

The multi-age classes had team names, such as the "Inquisitive Investigators" or the "Cooperative Club," and teachers did not refer to students by grade level categorization (Coyne, 2000). Students of multi-age classes tended to see themselves as unified teams, which helped

Figure 3. McCarty Elementary celebrates Mexico's Independence Day.

were easier to facilitate than I had anticipated. Students who were fluent in both English and Spanish volunteered to help new arrivals who spoke only Spanish, and I learned to rearrange seating to facilitate this process. Speaking in both languages was always allowed, and the faculty encouraged bilingual translations that helped students and teachers to understand each other.

Preservice Preparation

My undergraduate training occurred during the early 1990s, when Discipline-Based Art Education (DBAE) was the reigning model of instructional practice. DBAE focuses not just on studio art production, but also on the understanding of works of art through three additional disciplines: art history, art criticism, and aesthetics (Greer, 1984). These disciplines showcase ways that professionals in the artworld approach their work, and were to be addressed through sequential lesson plans that resembled those used by other academic areas.

to build interethnic solidarity, as conflicts along racial lines were rare. Students in these multi-age groups were eager to help one another, the general atmosphere was collaborative rather than competitive, and group projects

For Further Consideration

1. The instructional strategies described in this chapter are derived from the author's experiences working at a school within a migrant Hispanic community. Discuss the potential application of his strategies in other cultural contexts.

   • Which strategies might work well with other cultural groups?

   • Which strategies might not work as well?

   • How might these strategies be adapted to improve effectiveness in teaching students in other cultural contexts?

2. The author discusses how the school's use of multi-age classrooms was advantageous for this particular mix of ethnic minorities. However, very few teachers work at school sites where the multi-age model has been implemented. How might some multi-age instructional strategies be effectively applied to traditional graded classrooms at other schools working with culturally diverse populations?

3. The author discusses four levels of multicultural approaches to education (Banks, 2005). The fourth level, the social action approach, refers to instructional situations that allow students to make decisions and take action on issues leading to social reconstruction.

   • Other than the efforts described in the chapter, what activities could the author have planned in his efforts to reach this fourth level of social reconstruction?

   • How could he have included the local community in these activities?

4. How are multicultural approaches, such as those described by Broome, applicable to globally focused art education?

   • How could local empowerment bring students (and their community) to empowerment in global contexts?

   • What would empowerment of this type look like?

   • What might be the goal[s] of a globally focused empowerment?

Since the dominant era of DBAE, art education has undergone reconceptualization (Carpenter & Tavin, 2010), and DBAE has faced criticism for its overreliance on male-dominated canons of Western art history, its de-emphasis on creativity, and a structure that largely ignores visual culture, technology, and multiculturalism. Nevertheless, the tenets of DBAE comprised the foundation of my approach to art instruction. Furthermore, my student teaching experiences had been in upper middle-class neighborhoods. Once I accepted the job at McCarty Elementary, I still lived 30 minutes away from the school in a suburban area that was culturally and physically remote from my students' dwelling places. In terms of extracurricular experiences and my pedagogical education, I was an outsider to my students' community.

The Stories

"Mister!" called one of my students from his seat. "We need more paint, Mister!"

The students at McCarty Elementary rarely used my last name. This seemed odd, as I had always been in schooling situations where it was expected that students refer to their teachers by title and surname. At McCarty Elementary, the students just referred to me as Mister or, more often than not, Miss, since they were so accustomed to addressing female teachers throughout the week. I didn't know what to think of being called Mister at first, let alone Miss. Should I correct them? Many students were still acquiring English; were they having difficulties pronouncing my name? Or was this a coping strategy that transient students used as they moved from school to school and encountered countless new teachers? I decided not to demand that students refer to me as Mr. Broome until I had a better understanding of their reluctance to do so, but I reminded them of my name regularly during my first year of teaching.

By my second year, the ESOL resource teacher had explained that in many areas of Mexico it is respectful to refer to teachers simply as maestra or maestro (teacher) and not to use a last name. I understood that the students weren't being disrespectful, and so I adjusted my expectations accordingly (Harzing, 2010). I still corrected the students' use of Mister and Miss in relationship to gender (often to no avail), as such corrections felt more like teachable moments than cultural misunderstandings.

The Lesson That Bombed

I was excited about teaching my next lesson! I had been teaching for a couple of months, and I was ready to implement a unit I had created in a college methods course and successfully introduced to the middle-class suburban students that I worked with during my student teaching experience. The unit was on American comic strips and focused on the historical development of the art form, common aesthetic conventions of cartooning, and the production of students' own comic strips.

"Let's look at the first American comic strips from 100 years ago," I enthusiastically explained to my students. I clicked on the projector to reveal the image, which took up one entire page of a newspaper, existed within a single panel, and had no sentence bubbles. "What makes this comic different from the ones you see today?"

I was greeted with complete silence.

The seconds seemed like hours and I desperately hurled a series of poorly structured, leading questions at my students. "What's different about how they talk in this comic? Is this bigger or smaller than comics that you see today?" No one said a word.

As panic set in, I remembered a stack of newspapers in a nearby cabinet. I grabbed the comic section and held it up. "How many of you have looked at comics before?"

Still nothing.

I held up the rest of the newspaper. "How many of you have seen one of these before?" Finally someone raised his hand.

"Miss, I think my dad uses those when he paints something in the trailer."

Now I understood. These students, unlike those I had known while student teaching, did not come from print-rich home environments. They hadn't been exposed to the popular imagery of comic strips or newspapers, let alone iconic works of Western fine art that were often the centerpieces of DBAE. I began to realize that many of the curriculum building strategies I had been taught in college were going to be ineffectual in this context. I needed a new curricular design.

Local Visual Culture Icons

Although my students had not been exposed to dominant images from Western art history, they did have a love of visual art and knew about cultural artistic icons that I did not. As I continuously observed student artwork, I realized how little I knew about imagery beyond my own culture. In the stories that follow, I will detail my introduction to icons of local cultural significance, such as lowriders,[3] the Virgin of Guadalupe,[4] and cholos.[5]

1) "All my friends know the lowrider."

These art students, especially the boys, loved to draw lowriders. Although it's not unusual for boys to draw cars, my students seemed to place tremendous value on drawings of lowriders (Figure 4), especially when rendered with customized designs, hydraulics, and decorative hubcaps. The more "tricked-out," or elaborately decorated and structurally enhanced, the lowrider appeared, the better.

By the time I became conscious of the prolificacy of students' drawings of lowriders, I had largely abandoned the strategy of organizing assignments around artists, styles, or historical movements. I was finding greater success by introducing units based on themes of relevance to students' lives or that were being studied in their multi-age classrooms. I still showed artwork to students, but selected examples that were thematically relevant and represented a wider array of culturally diverse artists. Even though I tried to choose themes that appealed to a range of interests, there were always a few boys who were content to draw only lowriders. In these cases, I would find myself involved in impromptu negotiations that commonly take place between what a child might prefer to draw and the parameters that teachers establish in assignments (Hafeli, 2000).

Despite these negotiations, I felt it important to realize that lowriders were significant images in the lives of these students, and I allowed them to explore this interest when appropriate. For this purpose, I kept a book on lowrider automobile art at my book center. Indeed, scholars have identified the lowrider as a prevalent theme in contemporary Hispanic fine and popular art (Keller, Erickson, Johnson, & Alvarado, 2002).

2) Guadalupe.

A motif which frequently appeared in the voluntary work of these students was that of a woman clasping her hands in prayer, wearing a hooded cloak adorned with stars, (Figure 5) and often shown with a burst of light surrounding her; she reminded me of religious images I had seen of the Virgin Mary. Initially concerned about the challenges of discussing religion in the context of public schooling (Villeneuve & Erickson, 2006), I was reluctant to ask students about the mysterious woman. Yet after repeatedly seeing her image in their drawings, I yielded to curiosity and asked one student to tell me about her artwork.

"That's the Virgin of Guadalupe, Mister."

Figure 4. A student's drawing depicting lowriders at a local car show.

Figure 5. A student's painting of the Virgin of Guadalupe.

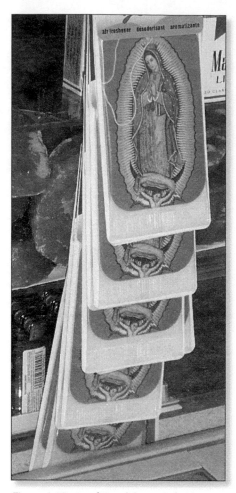

Figure 6. Virgin of Guadalupe air fresheners.

as a national holiday and a rallying point for social justice causes, including farmworkers' solidarity, feminism, anti-colonialism, and ethnic pride. Her image is prevalent in popular visual culture in Hispanic communities, and also in the work of contemporary Hispanic artists (Keller et al., 2002). Considering her significance in a variety of contexts, it was important that I understood the meanings surrounding the Virgin and the different ways that students might use her image in their artwork.

3) Cholos.

"Maria, I think that Fernando likes you." Two intermediate students were socializing as they collaborated on a larger painting. "Do you like him too?" she giggled.

"I don't think so," said Maria. "He's a little too cholo." I had heard the students use this term before, but I didn't understand its meaning.

"Maria, what does cholo mean?" I asked.

"You know, Mister. Like a homie… A little bit too gangsta."

This was a description I understood. Gangstas, thugs, and homeboys were common terms used within hip-hop culture. Through media exposure, people of non-hip-hop cultures also had become familiar with these terms. I hadn't yet been introduced to the Spanish equivalent, cholos, which appeared in the conversations and images of these students' work (Figure 7). Typical cholo garb included baggy jeans, sunglasses, bandanas, facial hair, and over-sized flannel shirts with the top button fastened. Similar to lowrider art, images of cholos represent common themes in contemporary Hispanic artwork (Keller et al., 2002). Soon after I had become accustomed to the appearance of cholos in the art of my students, I was made aware of the challenges this theme posed for me as their art teacher.

A visit from law enforcement. Our principal had called a special faculty meeting. As we filed into the media center, there was no missing the uniformed representative from our county sheriff's department. His presence set a serious tone, and the faculty sat to learn how his unit had been tracking an influx of gang activity to our area. I took careful notes as the officer explained hand gestures, colors, and imagery associated with local gangs. I realized that I had to monitor students' depictions of cholos more closely and stay informed to determine differences between harmless representations of popular imagery and depictions that might have more menacing significance.

I had never heard of the Virgin of Guadalupe, so I simply nodded and moved on to talk to another student. Avoiding conversations about the Virgin was easier than avoiding visual contact with her image. As I frequented the local community, I recognized images of the Virgin of Guadalupe everywhere: on t-shirts, flags, candles, and even air fresheners (Figure 6). I learned that the Virgin has been acknowledged as the patron saint of Hispanic Catholics since she first materialized as a vision to a converted Indian peasant, Juan Diego, in 1531 (Maätita, 2011). Appearing similarly to manifestations of the Virgin Mary throughout European history, but with darker skin and speaking the indigenous language of Nahuatl, the Virgin spoke to Diego of building a church in the hills near Mexico City. When Diego presented the request to a local bishop, a miraculous imprint of the Virgin was revealed on Diego's cloak.

Eventually, the Virgin of Guadalupe was recognized by the Catholic Church as a legitimate apparition of Mary. The date of her appearance to Diego came to be celebrated

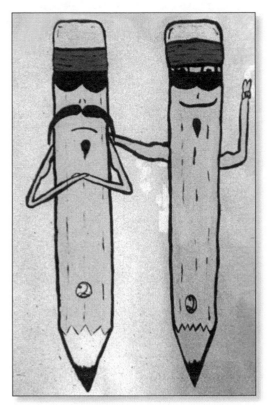

Figure 7. A student's painting of two pencils depicted as cholos.

Discussion: Strategies Learned From Practice

Rather than providing narratives as a purely descriptive endeavor, autoethnographers frequently include an analysis of the themes that emerge within their stories (Ellis, 2004). An emergent theme within my stories is that curriculum based on the assumption that students of diverse socioeconomic levels have access to the same resources and experiences prior to arriving at school is curriculum that rests on shaky foundations. Asking students to analyze the history of American comic strips was unsuccessful because most of my students had never been exposed to comics of the past or present. Yet, while it is a mistake to assume that students arrive at school on an equal playing field related to past experiences, it is just as important to assume that all students can learn at high levels regardless of their previous access to resources (Nieto, 2009).

Similarly, curriculum that over-relies on Eurocentric examples from Western history may not resonate well with students from diverse cultures. Students have a tendency to search for people like themselves in instructional content (Sadker & Zittleman, 2007). My decision to switch to a thematic approach to organizing

curricula was based on the ease with which culturally diverse examples could be woven into such units, and also my dissatisfaction with DBAE's over-emphasis on Western art historical canons.

Another overarching theme in my stories relates to instructors' willingness to learn about diverse cultures in their classrooms, and to make cultural accommodations as needed (Nieto, 2009). I was flexible in the ways that students addressed me, in the use of language in my classroom, and in learning about the significance of visual culture iconography. Although I was initially uncomfortable discussing the religious nature of the Virgin of Guadalupe in a public school classroom, I came to appreciate her significance in students' lives and the multiple meanings she represented. On the other hand, I became more wary of how students depicted cholos once I knew more about gang culture symbolism. In either case, instructors should make efforts to understand diverse cultures in their classrooms, and the role of accommodation should not rest entirely with students. When teaching a unit on the theme of identity, I understood and fostered students' use of symbolic imagery related to the Virgin of Guadalupe, lowriders, and other visual culture icons, but did not allow the use of gang-associated imagery inappropriate for school settings. Although students of other ethnic backgrounds were far fewer in numbers at McCarty Elementary, I became sensitive to their under-representation in traditional curricula as well. I made efforts to occasionally touch on these other cultural artworld traditions through similar thematic units, such as an exploration of African American quilting practices during a unit on family customs, in the belief that it was important to be egalitarian in my instructional approach and to build understanding between the different cultural groups at McCarty Elementary.

The school's use of multi-age classrooms was advantageous for this particular mix of ethnic minorities. In Nieto's (2009) synthesis of studies on different cultural groups in school settings, she asserts that teachers who emphasize cooperation over competition may provide a better fit for students who come from cultures with core values related to communal relationships, extended family, and shared responsibility. She describes the use of heterogeneous ability groups, collaborative assignments, and the presence of caring teachers as important ingredients in fostering successful global learning communities. These ingredients appeared in the multi-age classrooms of McCarty Elementary through mixed-age cooperation, an emphasis on team unity, and looping strategies that established ongoing relationships and continuity for transient students. While I'm not suggesting that all schools switch to multi-age structures, I am suggesting that multi-age strategies could be successfully adopted by schools with similarly diverse populations.

Multicultural Approaches

Banks (2005) suggests that there are four levels to multicultural approaches in education. Each level builds on the next, with the fourth level presenting the most significant changes to curricula leading to the greatest social impact.

The first level, the contributions approach, focuses on the added discussion of cultural holidays and heroes within traditional curricular structures (Banks, 2005). This approach was used frequently at McCarty Elementary, especially during student performances near Mexico's Independence Day. The second level, the additive approach, involves the addition of themes and content related to the perspectives of specific cultural groups. This approach was facilitated regularly by teachers at McCarty Elementary through thematic units developed for multi-age classrooms.

The third level of multicultural approaches, the transformational approach, requires fundamental changes in the structure of curriculum that allow students to see issues from the perspectives of other cultural groups (Banks, 2005). The use of multi-age classrooms represented a significant change in the organizational structure of schooling, and the arrangement of these groups for a 3-year period seemed to build interethnic unity between the various cultures within classes. However, the thematic units used in instruction rarely moved beyond the contributions or additive approaches in discussing diversity, and it might be a stretch to say that these units were truly transformational. Although students of different backgrounds displayed a sense of unity while in school, I could not claim to know that these students would exhibit a similar respect for diversity later in life.

The fourth level of multicultural approaches to education, the social action approach, refers to instructional situations that allow students to make decisions and take action on issues leading to social reconstruction (Banks, 2005). To some extent, I attempted to address social reconstructionism by encouraging student cultural preferences in image production. It's possible that the validation of such imagery may have helped to build student pride in community and culture, inculcated a sense of self-worth, and empowered students to be self-expressive.

Theobald and Nachtigal (1995) imply that curriculum that allows students to understand themselves and their place in local communities is socially reconstructive at some level, and that such educational approaches may increase the possibility of students making future contributions to their communities. In more direct ways, I addressed social justice through my ongoing stance on gang-related imagery and consistently monitored this issue of local concern.

Epilogue

After 8 memorable years at McCarty Elementary, I moved to a new city to pursue a doctoral degree. My experiences made me a more culturally sensitive person and teacher. I had grown from a first year teacher with few experiences with diverse populations to one that couldn't imagine working in situations without such colorful diversity. Along the way, I married the ESOL resource teacher, herself a Mexican citizen, who had helped me greatly during my initial inquiries into Hispanic culture. We continue to celebrate cultural diversity and a mix of heritages through our own two children.

I am hopeful that my stories can be used as a springboard for stimulating discussion on strategies appropriate for teaching art with all diverse socioeconomic cultural groups, not just with migrant Hispanic populations. As I have suggested, it is important for teachers to actively explore the significance of unfamiliar local cultural iconography. In order to do so, teachers may adopt student-centered approaches that give children opportunities to share imagery of cultural importance. These images can be discussed openly and critically, and may provide opportunities for teachers to connect the shared cultural icons to the global artworld. Open-ended assignments, rather than prescriptive teacher-centered approaches, can allow students to explore cultural aesthetics in their own artwork as well. The resulting artwork may stimulate additional opportunities for student artists to honor their own cultural traditions and for classmates to become more culturally sensitive and aware in an increasingly global society.

REFERENCES

Ball, T., Grant, J., & Johnson, B. (2006). Looping. In N. C. Lester & L. Constable (Eds.), *Multiage in a nutshell: Your guide to a multiage classroom* (pp. 14–17). Eagleby, Australia: Multiage Association of Queensland.

Banks, J. A. (2005). Approaches to multicultural curriculum reform. In J. A. Banks & C. A. McGee Banks (Eds.), *Multicultural education: Issues and perspectives* (5th ed.) (pp. 242–264). Hoboken, NJ: John Wiley & Sons.

Carpenter, B. S., & Tavin, K. M. (2010). Drawing (past, present, and future) together: A (graphic) look at the reconceptualization of art education. *Studies in Art Education, 51*(4), 327–352.

Clandinin, D. J., & Huber, J. (2010). Narrative inquiry. In P. Peterson, E. Baker & B. McGaw (Eds.), *International encyclopedia of education* (3rd ed.) (pp. 436–441). New York, NY: Elsevier.

Coyne, A. L. (2000). *Creating a year-long theme: A teacher's journey for multi-age and single-age classrooms.* Columbus, OH: Englefield and Arnold.

Elkind, D. (1993). Multiage grouping. In D. Sumner (Ed.), *Multiage classrooms: The ungrading of America's schools* (p. 11). Peterborough, NH: The Society for Developmental Education.

Ellis, C. (2004). *The ethnographic I: A methodological novel about autoethnography.* Walnut Creek, CA: Alta Mira Press.

GreatSchools. (2012). Dan McCarty School. Retrieved from www.greatschools.org/florida/fort-pierce/2910-Dan-McCarty-School

Greer, D. (1984). Discipline-based art education: Approaching art as a subject of study. *Studies in Art Education, 25*(4), 212–218.

Hafeli, M. (2000). Negotiating "fit" in student artwork: Classroom conversations. *Studies in Art Education, 41*(2), 130–145.

Harzing, A. (2010). What's in a name? Cross country differences in preferred ways of address for university teachers. *Academy of International Business Insight, 10*(3), 3-8. Retrieved from http://aib.msu.edu/publications/insights/insights_v010n03.pdf

Hoffman, J. (2003). Multiage teachers' beliefs and practices. *Journal of Research in Childhood Education, 18*(1), 5–17.

Keller, G. D., Erickson, M., Johnson, K., & Alvarado, J. (2002). *Contemporary Chicana and Chicano art: Artists, works, culture, and education* (Vols. 1–2). Tempe, AZ: Bilingual Press.

Lolli, E. M. (1998). Multiage magic. *Primary Voices K-6, 6*(2), 10–18.

Maätita, F. (2011). Virgin of Guadalupe. In M. Z. Stange, C. K. Oyster & J. E. Sloan (Eds.), *Encyclopedia of women in today's world* (Vol. 4, pp. 1523–1524). Los Angeles, CA: Sage.

Nieto, S. (2009). *The light in their eyes: Creating multicultural learning communities* (10th anniversary ed.). New York, NY: Teachers College Press.

Nishida, Y. (2009). *The challenge of multiage primary education in public education.* Saarbrucken, Germany: VDM Verlag, Dr. Mueller Aktiengesellschaft.

Sadker, D. M., & Zittleman, K. R. (2007). *Teachers, schools, and society: A brief introduction to education.* New York, NY: McGraw-Hill.

Theobald, P., & Nachtigal, P. (1995). Culture, community, and the promise of rural education. *Phi Delta Kappan, 77*(2), 132–135.

United States Census Bureau. (2012). Retrieved from www.census.gov/population/race

Vargas, G. (2010). *Contemporary Chicano art: Color and culture for a new America.* Austin: University of Texas Press.

Villeneuve, P., & Erickson, M. (2006). A taxonomy of understanding: Reflective art responses and issues arising from teaching of religious art. *Journal of Cultural Research in Art Education, 24*, 1–14.

ENDNOTES

[1] All personal communications detailed in this book chapter come from the author's remembrances of events that took place between the dates of 1994 and 2003.

[2] In this chapter, I use the terms preferred by the United States Census Bureau (2012) when discussing race or cultural origins. For example, *Hispanic* is the term used by the United States Census Bureau in describing people from Spanish-speaking nations or lineages.

[3] In this chapter, the term *lowrider* is used to describe a type of automobile specifically modified, often with hydraulic suspension, to cruise lower to the ground. Lowriders often feature ornate painted urban designs and accessories, and were first prevalent in Hispanic and African American communities.

[4] Patron saint of Hispanic Catholics (Maätita, 2011)

[5] Urban Spanish slang for a male with street reputation, attitude, and aesthetic appearance (Vargas, 2010)

CHAPTER 21

Enhancing Global Consciousness and Cultural Sensitivities:
Digital Arts-Pedagogy in a Preservice Teacher Education Context

DEBRA DONNELLY
KATHRYN GRUSHKA
The University of Newcastle, Australia

In a rapidly changing world made smaller by digital technologies and globalization, having an understanding of the impact of local and national policies on the world community is vital knowledge for any citizen group. Developing this kind of knowledge and understanding requires looking at different national and cultural groups through wide lenses in order to see, accept, and respect differences transculturally. The authors of this chapter are lecturers in history and visual arts education and coordinate both undergraduate and postgraduate teacher education programs at the University of Newcastle. The authors share research interests in global education and in the capacity of images as contemporary representational forms with classroom applications. We conceived, developed, and implemented an innovative preservice teacher education course for a cohort of cross-disciplinary secondary specialists. Objectives of the Information and Communications Technologies (ICT) course were to encourage students to gain knowledge and address issues of transcultural interactions and impacts, through use of digital technologies and image manipulation, to enhance global consciousness.

The course immerses secondary preservice teachers in an arts-led (Gibson & Ewing, 2011), critical global education agenda. It positions visual culture as central to the circulation of values and ideas, and sees visual images and artifacts as vital for learning in a digital ocular-centric 21st century (Rose, 2007). We believe that harnessing visual media culture through the possibilities afforded by image manipulation technologies provides a strategic foundation for student learning across disciplines. These methods can be framed to explore understandings about global issues and challenges in the context of contemporary life, and to encourage students to recognize and perceive themselves as citizens of a global community.

In this chapter we present a model, Studio Pedagogy for Visual World Learning, as a framework for pedagogical practices in the digital arts-studio environment. The model acknowledges that we are all visual subjects and that our identities are significantly shaped by how we view ourselves, how we view others, and how others view us (Mirzoeff, 1998). It identifies thinking through the cognitive and affective tools of image critique and image production. Image critique and production are both supported by the connectivity to words and other symbolic systems and an abundance of hybrid digital representations. Digital visual technologies have been identified as powerful vehicles for transformative learning (Buckingham, 2007; Walsh, 2007; Cope & Kalantzis, 2008; Barton & Levstik, 2004). Image deconstruction and manipulation supports critical insights and empathic understandings. They propel individuals to confront conflicting understandings in the resolution of new images as they come to an appreciation of the mutually dependent nature of citizenship.

The preservice teachers, who were the students in our course, were tasked with an examination of a global issue related to their subject specialization and the production of a montage of images and text that identified and countered cultural stereotypes by challenging or reconciling a view of The Other. Objectives of the course were to cultivate open-mindedness, engagement, and empathy with the diverse cacophony of global voices through digital image and text montage (Grushka & Donnelly, 2010). In this chapter, we feature student works in order to demonstrate the power of the creative process in generating intra- and inter-textual narratives, as students with little or no background in visual arts education engage in digital image and text manipulation.

The Model of Studio Pedagogy for Visual World Learning

Figure 1 offers a graphic representation of the teaching and learning cycle of this teacher education course, and provides a framework through which to unpack the pedagogical practices and illuminate its broad application to other learning environments. It is envisaged that our preservice teacher students will adapt the experience of this course and integrate it into their developing teaching practice. Indeed, a vital aspect of the course rationale is the applicability of the instruction, viewing, and production strategies to other educational settings and contexts.

The model has been divided into four quadrants. The Becoming Globalized Identities quadrant is a reflective space where images are re-represented (Bolt, 2004). The second quadrant is called Inhabiting a Problematized Global Cultural Space and views knowledge as complex, problematic, and interpretative. The third quadrant, Explicit Learning Protocols, examines the teaching, learning, and assessment configurations of the course. Finally, Digital Learning Environment and Exhibition examines the problem-seeking and problem-solving cycle

of the digital arts-studio environment. This quadrant highlights opportunities for exhibition, critique, reflection, audience feedback, and assessment of the creative process.

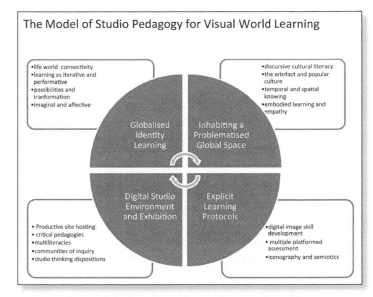

Figure 1. The Model of Studio Pedagogy for Visual World Learning.

Becoming Globalized Identities

Contemporary life may be experienced as a collage of visual and auditory events that happen in a time and spatial compression. Hybrid images from new media technologies are constantly re-forming as products of merging distinctive cultures or national identities. The blurring of these identities has given rise to the notion of the world citizen. One interpretation sees the stateless entity that results as an antithesis of a patriot and imagines a specter of world government by big business conglomerates (Gibson, 2008). However, a world citizen can also be seen as having moved to a level beyond state and national citizenship and holding trans-national concerns about global issues such as the environment, peace, trade, inequality, and cultural imperialism. This latter view of world citizenship has been linked to the notion of cosmopolitanism (Osler & Vincent, 2002), which promotes international experience, respect, and honoring of other cultures, and a concern for global issues. Cosmopolitanism is characterized by a shift away from bounded and unique cultural communities and single identities—and is now represented by an intensified mixing of the signs, symbols, and activities of compressed cultures (Held, 2004). In order to deal with these complexities, successful citizens of a globalized world need skills and attitudes that allow them to collaborate, negotiate, think critically, and gain multiple perspectives through dialogic co-construction of meaning with individuals from diverse backgrounds, interests, and cultures (Gibson & Ewing, 2011). This concept of a skilled, cosmopolitan world citizen was promoted in the preservice teacher course, which we developed and taught.

An ability to communicate about Self and Others using images, or visual communicative proficiency (Grushka, 2007), is critical to the development of a cosmopolitan world citizen. Arts-studio pedagogy is oriented toward accessing ideas and images that are grounded in the vernacular of an individual's everyday life (Dissanayake, 2008). In the production and exhibition of the artworks, our students were tasked with using imaging acts that involved selecting, editing, and reworking images to refine their intended meaning. These activities see a citizen testing his or her ideas about self with those of others as a communicative act (Habermas, 1976). The pedagogy acknowledges that identification of self often resides in the visual clues of one's lifeworld, and that it is increasingly an important place from which to explore identity (Jones, 2007).

The arts-studio also can be characterized as an embodied pedagogy (O'Loughlin, 2006), informed by our inner and outer worlds of experience. Imaging as an embodied learning act links feelings, the imagination, and the aesthetic responses of students as they connect to the world of experience and experimentation for personal agency (Semetsky, 2003, 2010). Our course sought to explore these notions and harness the process to a consideration of global issues.

In order to develop a personal and social reflexive capacity, preservice teachers need character qualities of appreciation, mastery, ethical reason, empathy, and reflection and a focus on the cognitive skills of convergent and divergent thinking (Folson, 2005). The arts-studio thinking model (Hetland, Winner, Veenema, & Sheridan, 2007) carries these attributes, along with an additional ability to envisage. This aligns with the recent work of Krznaric (2011), who presents the idea that the way society changes is by shifting the way individuals come to understand it. Krznaric (2007) argues that there is an increasing need for empathy toward others. Empathy requires that one look through the eyes of others, step into their shoes, or imagine oneself in the shoes of another. Such a perspective "extends the individual beyond his/her own ego and self-interest, toward 'outrospection' where [he/she] discovers self by learning about other people [and] finding out how they think, feel and look at the world" (p. 6).

Border Protection (Figure 2) is an example of a student who "put herself into the shoes" of a refugee, and in so doing, communicates her own ideas about Self and Others. While researching images that communicate alienation, rejection, or loneliness, the student spent time actually feeling and imagining this experience in order to select the best image for carrying this message to the viewer. The student selected a child, an innocent participant, as an affectively more powerful choice than an image of an adult might have been. Extended manipulation of the image, by playing with the scale and position

For Further Consideration

1. The artists use images in literal and symbolic ways. How do they combine these images through processes of montage to make meaning?

2. How does the artwork *Mind the Gap* comment about global citizenship and inequality? Consider irony and juxtaposition.

3. How do the images work to capture the viewers' emotional response and how does this make the works effective in communicating an idea?

4. Select an image and deconstruct how the symbols, images, and their relationships work together to tell the cultural narrative.

5. Choose an issue of global importance and investigate it using montage. Construct a learning journal that reflects on this creative process.

6. How can visual media arts promote global understanding?

Figure 2. Sherelle Murray (2010) Border Protection, *digital image.*

of the child within the overall poster message, required another level of exploration with affective, political, and social implications of the image. Exploring the position of the child in relation to a background and texts encouraged a deeper understanding of this global issue. Messages about loss of identity appear as graffiti on the brick wall: "Date of birth Unknown," "Address Unknown," "Parents Unknown." The final political message results from the simulation of an official Department of Immigration and Citizenship document stamp, "Denied." The title *Border Protection* is heavily ironic, since the innocent child can present no threat to Australia's national security, and the pervasive brick wall symbolizes a barrier reinforced through suspicion and indifference by those national citizens who would seek to guard their privilege. The work resonates with diverse aspects that inform global identities such as race, ethnicity, class, religion, nationality, territory, or inter-generational values. *Border Protection* exemplifies how reflexivity inherent in arts-studio practices involves the writing of new narratives about Self and Others in an empathic way. This aligns with Conde's (2011) idea that becoming is a socially embodied and performative system of dispositions.

Inhabiting a Problematised Global Cultural Space

Current definitions of global citizenship focus on being active members of community as political, social, environmental, and economic agents who explore and experience new modes and processes of connectedness and interdependence with the broader society (Halliday, 2001). While visual images of difference may facilitate cultural diversity and promote the development of dispositions that are more open, tolerant, and flexible, they can also present contradictory positions by revealing, for

example, rapid movement across traditional boundaries, the emergence of new borders, the homogenization of cultures, social and economic inequalities, religious intolerances, and social or political instability. Robertson (1992) has offered a useful definition of globalization as involving not only what people do but how they view the world. He proposes that globalization has brought about "the compression of the world and the intensification of consciousness of the world as a whole" (p. 8). Contemporary citizens are saturated with images and impressions from all over the world. We, the authors of this chapter, argue that if our preservice teachers are to become informed global citizens and teach their students to be informed global citizens, they must be equipped to navigate the visual transnational commodity society and its rapidly changing communication context.

The work of Case (1993) and Merryfield (2000) inspired the development direction of the course we designed and implemented. Case identified two interconnected dimensions—the substantive and the perceptual—that facilitate global perspectives. He defined the substantive elements as knowledge of cultural values and practices, global interconnections, present worldwide concerns and conditions, historic origins and patterns in worldwide events, and future directions. The perceptual dimension included five cognitive and affective attributes: open-mindedness, anticipation and acceptance of complexity, resistance to stereotyping, inclination to empathy, and gender equity. These ideas are supported by Merryfield (2000), who calls for the demolition of post-colonial knowledge structures and transformation to an understanding of the complexity of our interconnected world (Zong, 2005). Merryfield advocates giving voice to the marginalized, the omitted, and the misrepresented, and questions accepted power relationships in culture dialogues. These notions informed a course design that allowed preservice teachers to explore the intellect and affective domains of learning, and gave voice to the revelatory conclusions of these learning quests.

Camouflage Your Imperfections (Figure 3) is an example of artwork created by a preservice history teacher. It addresses the plight of first nation peoples in an Australian context. The embedded text, "Camouflage Your Imperfections" and "Assimilation," highlight the uneasy relationship between past paternalistic policies and present realities of disadvantage, alienation, and Aboriginal identity in contemporary Australian society. The metaphor of cleansing is used to imply notions of racial and power inequalities. Through the use of a visual

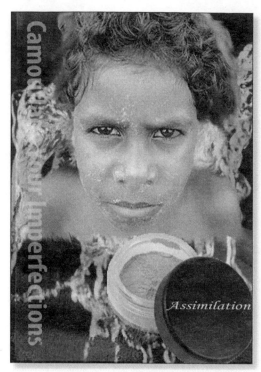

Figure 3. Michael Flanagan (2009) Camouflage Your Imperfections, *digital image.*

media convention—the "close-up" shot for intimacy with the viewer—the directness of the subject's eyes forces the viewer into a space where he or she must confront post-colonial knowledge structures and experience social connection with another. The poster effectively addresses issues of identity, conformity, and racial stereotyping, thus enhancing a disposition of critical citizenry in both its creator, who is watching and being watched, and the viewer, who is visually challenged by those questions that preoccupied the image's creator.

Explicit Learning Protocols

Explicit learning protocols were incorporated as features of our course. These draw on the work of Zammit and Downes (2002), who described creating, locating, and critiquing as essential skills in working with images for meaning. Explicit teaching occurs around these three skills. Lectures on the role of the image and design principles and a series of technology workshops were presented to students by the writers of this chapter, who were the course designers and teachers. We took a team-teaching, collaborative approach and were both present throughout the classes. Preservice teachers, who were the students of this course, were introduced to the role of images in multiple text analysis as these applied to local curriculum documents, and they were challenged to improve their digital computer competencies. The course

was delivered in a computer laboratory at our university and was developed around the World Wide Web as a communication portal, and linked to school-required learning outcomes. Other course foci were: the strong interdisciplinary approach that encouraged students to work outside their discipline area; accessing public image data sources, acknowledging the sources of their images, and attending to Copyright matters or Fair Use policies; refining image selection with regard to image size and appropriateness; digitally manipulating images; re-con-textualizing images as digital montage to make new meaning; and using narrative and disruption to trigger learning. Students were required to critically interpret a range of images as data. These might include historical images, family photographs, popular media, maps, histograms, scientific illustrations, or other evidence of the physical to inform a site study, case study, an event, or a narrative. Collins (1995) described this as the skill of *techno-textuality*, or mediation of knowledge using new media and new literacies (Anstey & Bull, 2006; Kalantzis & Cope, 2005). Posters made by students as a requirement of the course were conceived as motivational entry points to critically thinking about images, while group analysis of the posters drove extended discussion around identified key issues or problems.

The poster assessment process included two key phases. In the first phase, which was a formative assessment phase, students worked in collaborative pairs and conceptualized a curriculum topic that was problematic, such as climate change, global inequality, genocide, or genetic manipulation. In collaboration with teachers and peers, the pairs co-constructed preliminary ideas about how the problem might be addressed. These ideas were then presented to the group. During presentations, pairs of students were provided feedback about the effectiveness of their images in representing different concepts, and were inspired by the work of other pairs.

When completed, the posters were assessed in relation to conceptualization and technical refinements from the initial presentation, with a focus on the development of semiotic skills, the authenticity to the unit of work, and a refined resolution of both image and concept. A high achieving work would demonstrate a complexity of ideas, multiple interpretive possibilities, and refinement in visualization through the application of visual conventions or visual language with other selected texts. Students were also assessed on their ability to present coherent ideas and communicate how their critical and imaginative insights generated new concepts or meanings as digital artifact. Each narrative perspective reflected sophisticated use of semiotics in the creation of multiple layers of meaning through the use of images, text, and other semiotic systems that evidenced high ICT and visual digital technical skills. Overall, authentic assessment tasks, which were grounded in the media spaces of a digital world, linked personal inquiry to motivation and engagement in learning and addressed the public concern for student evaluations and accountability for curriculum implementation.

This arts-studio pedagogy approach required students to engage in an appropriation and remixing of global iconic imagery, fine art imagery, images from life, and marketing messages in the media. Using iconography or the application of visual conventions, rather than simply presenting the world illustratively, deepened their understanding of how images work to construct meanings. The work *Mona=globalised art* (Figure 4) is an excellent example of ironic appropriation of iconography, whereby the preservice visual arts teacher selected images to challenge Western cultural imperialism and the legitimization of traditional artifacts in the global marketplace. Juxtapositioning was employed to create a visual aesthetic disruption and stimulate debate about what objects hold iconic status within contemporary societies and how artworks might generate complex narratives that value several cultural heritages or challenge a dominant culture.

Figure 4. *Kirra Little (2010)* Mona=globalised art, *digital image.*

Figure 5. *Phoebe Rioden and Lauren Sullivan (2010),* Mind the Gap, *digital image.*

The narrative perspective in this student work demonstrates a sophisticated techno-textuality appropriation of images from different sources digitally. The African beaded doll body juxtaposed with the face of Leonardo da Vinci's *Mona Lisa* remixes well-known images to create multiple layers of meaning. The narrative reflects authenticity of images, digital skill, clear intent, and meaning in relation to the selected curriculum topic.

Digital Learning Environment and Exhibition

We developed and located this teacher education course in a changing landscape of digital new media and the lifeworld of today's youth. The preservice teachers were required to research images in both traditional and online contexts, and make informed judgments about the ways knowledge and information are being communicated, valued, and privileged within new media contexts. Taking this critical pedagogy approach, the students identified and evaluated effects of deep-seated societal assumptions and dominant ideologies while they also developed more nuanced critical understandings of how images might serve transformative visions of the future.

Figure 5 is the work of a pair of preservice teachers in the discipline areas of geography and economics. The two cleverly utilized the conceit of the billboard to advertise their message in a cityscape. The work subverts popular culture symbols by highlighting the plight of exploited female workers who live in developing countries, and juxtaposing images of these women against multinational companies who are shown as faceless, suited men backgrounded by a map of the world. *Mind the Gap* is strategically and aesthetically located to divide the image and to symbolize division in the global economic world. The printed text has multilayered meanings using connotation and irony. The "gap" can be understood as alluding to the gap between the rich and poor, but also refers to the clothing company of the same name that has been involved in controversy over their exploitative production methods. There also are echoes of "mind the gap" warnings commonly heard on railway platforms, and this is sustained by the bands above and below the text that are reminiscent of train lines and stress the divide between rich and poor and the gender power imbalance. The transformation of the iconic text "iPod" to "iSweat" further sustains these notions of exploitation and disadvantage, and the insertion of the famous fashion brand Gucci speaks to the trivial indulgences of the wealthy at the expense of poor. The final ironic twist is that as sweat shop workers labor to satisfy the commercial appetites of the affluent, they are themselves seduced by consumerism, insofar as they are pacified by individual entertainment devices. The team of preservice teachers who created this work successfully utilized symbol subversion, image juxtaposition, and intra and inter-textual irony to highlight and question the injustice of world trade and labor structures.

New Digital Learning Spaces

The term *multiliteracies* refers to today's literacy as having multiple forms of knowledge and functionality over a variety of platforms, requiring seamless navigation between paper, electronic, and live texts and their semiotic systems (Kress, 2003; Anstey & Bull, 2006). It is argued that skills in reading and writing paper text are no longer sufficient for future citizens, as rapid and dramatic advances in technology and the resulting globalization and social change requires a more wide-ranging set of skills and understandings (Kress & Van Leeuwen, 2006; Anstey & Bull, 2006; Lankshear & Knobel, 2006; Kalantzis & Cope, 2005). It was our intention that our preservice teachers explore multiliteracy dispositions as a side effect of synthesizing information, images, and ideas from a wide range of sources and in the emerging digital spaces of new media communication. Through construction of montage images, these students experienced authentic digital media spaces. They use self-managed learning processes across various digital platforms as a model for their own teaching practice in the communication context and knowledge technologies of the 21st-century classroom.

The independent, self-directed learning structure of an arts digital studio environment provided students with a powerful learning experience. They were empowered to learn by being provided encouragement and opportunity to explore their discipline in a way that privileged image and text literacies. Beyond simply retelling or narrating stories, the digital montage posters created viewer tension and irony. Digital technologies allowed students to create new meanings as they engaged in intellectual and emotional processes in order to understand the complexities of issues relevant to their disciplines. This work was challenging, and students were busy and lively. After short, formal lectures and technical demonstrations, each session became a workshop, and the lecturers became facilitators and mentors in partnership relationships with their preservice teacher students. Students were encouraged to critique and discuss one another's work in the open learning space. They worked at their own pace in and outside class time toward final resolution of their ideas.

In the last session of the course, students displayed their completed work and undertook a short presentation and reflection on the creative process and the product. The focus of this event was celebration of achievement and recognition of their learning journeys. This was an enjoyable and casual gathering, which culminated in students setting up the exhibition in the corridors of the School of Education. This exhibition, while the final stage in the assessment cycle, heralded a new encounter with a wider audience of peers, which saw the students re-evaluate the success of their posters; many considered further refinement at this point or ventured to new ideas for classroom implementation.

The student learning presented in this chapter provides evidence that exploration across a range of disciplines can create new images that inform learner identities. Our students moved beyond the confines of their varied discipline fields to the exploration of dynamic, global relationships across temporal, social, geographic, and semiotic domains using images. This course was developed using a model of studio pedagogy that provided our students with the knowledge and skills to deal with the ambiguity, contradictions, and dissonance of their increasingly visual media world. With today's unprecedented challenges, including sustainability and global injustices, critically minded teachers need to inspire their charges to envisage, propose, and act to bring about the imaginative human responses that our globalized future will need. This course embeds pedagogical methods with broad application across educational settings. It demonstrates that artspedagogies can facilitate encounters with global frontiers and provide opportunities for the traversing and exploration of visual lifeworlds and imagined possibilities.

ACKNOWLEDGMENTS

The authors would like to acknowledge the contribution of all the preservice teachers who ventured into this new area of learning—in particular, the following preservice teachers who gave permission for their images to be used in this chapter: Sherelle Murray, Michael Flanagan, Kirra Smith, Pheobe Rioden, and Lauren Hicks.

REFERENCES

Anstey, M., & Bull, G. (2006). *Teaching and learning multiliteracies: Changing times, changing literacies.* Kensington Gardens, Australia: Australian Literacy Educators.

Barton, K., & Levstik, L. (2004). *Teaching history for the common good.* Mahwah, NJ: Lawrence Erlbaum.

Bolt, B. (2004). *Art beyond representation: The performative power of the image.* London, England: I. B. Tauris.

Buckingham, D. (2007). Digital media literacies: Rethinking media education in the age of the Internet. *Research in Comparative and International Education, 2*(1), 43–55.

Case, R. (1993). Key elements of a global perspective. *Social Education, 57*(6), 318–325.

Collins, J. (1995). *Architectures of excess: Cultural life in the information age.* New York, NY: Routledge.

Conde, I. (2011). *Crossed concepts: Identity, habitus and reflexivity in a revised framework.* e-Working Paper No. 113/201, Lisbon, Portugal: Instituto Universitario de Lisboa. Retrieved from www.cies.iscte.pt/destaques/documents/CIES-WP113_Conde.pdf

Cope, B., & Kalantzis, M. (2008). Ubiquitous learning: An agenda for educational transformation. *Proceedings of the 6th International Conference on Networked Learning.* Retrieved from www.networkedlearningconference.org.uk/past/nlc2008/abstracts/PDFs/Cope_576-582.pdf

Dissanayake, E. (2008). The arts after Darwin: Does art have an origin and adaptive function? In K. Z. & W. V. Damme (Eds.), *World art studies: Exploring concepts and approaches* (pp. 241–263). Amsterdam, The Netherlands: Zaliz.

Folson, C. (2005). Teaching for intellectual and emotional learning (TIEL). *Issues in Teacher Education, 14*(2), 75–94.

Gibson, I. (2008). Evolving processes of global citizenship. *Ritsumeika International Affairs, 6,* 53–75.

Gibson, R., & Ewing, R. (2011). *Transforming the curriculum through the arts.* South Yarra, Australia: Palgrave Macmillan.

Grushka, K. (2007). *Identity, image and meaning beyond the classroom: Visual and performative communicative practice in a visual 21st century* (Doctoral dissertation). Retrieved from http://ogma.newcastle.edu.au:8080/vital/access/manager/Repository/uon:2799

Grushka, K., & Donnelly, D. (2010). Digital technologies and performative pedagogies: Repositioning the visual. *Digital Culture and Education, 2*(1), 83–102.

Habermas, J. (1976). *Communication and the evolution of society.* (T. McCarthy, Trans.). Boston, MA: Beacon Press.

Halliday, F. (2001). *The world at 2000: Perils and promises.* New York, NY: Palgrave.

Held, D. (Ed.). (2004). *A globalizing world? Culture, economics, politics.* London, England: Routledge, Open University Press.

Hetland, L., Winner, E., Veenema, S., & Sheridan, K. M. (2007). *Studio thinking: The real benefits of arts education.* New York, NY: Teachers College Press.

Jones, A. (2007). *1970/2007: Why does feminism still matter in the visual arts?* Paper presented at Taking a Hard Look: Gender and Visual Culture Conference, Institute for Women's and Gender Studies, University of Pretoria, Pretoria, Australia.

Kalantzis, M., & Cope, B. (2005). *Learning by design.* Melbourne, Australia: Victorian Schools Innovation Commission.

Kress, G. (2003). *Literacy in the new media age.* London, England: Routledge.

Kress, G., & Van Leeuwen, T. (2006). *Reading images: The grammar of visual design* (2nd ed.). New York, NY: Routledge.

Krznaric, R. (2007). *Empathy and the art of living.* Oxford, England: The Blackbird Collective.

Krznaric, R. (2011). *The wonderbox: Curious histories of how to live.* London, England: Profile Books.

Lankshear, C., & Knobel, M. (2006). Discussing new literacies. *Language Art, 84*(1), 78–86.

Merryfield, M. M. (2000). Using electronic technologies to promote equity and cultural diversity in social studies and global education. *Theory and Practice in Social Education, 26*(4), 342–369.

Mirzoeff, N. (Ed.). (1998). *The visual culture reader.* New York, NY: Routledge.

O'Loughlin, M. (2006). *Embodiment and education: Exploring creatural existence* (Vol. 15). Dordrecht, The Netherlands: Springer.

Osler, A., & Vincent, P. (2002). *Citizenship and the challenge of global education.* Staffordshire, England: Trentham Books.

Robertson, R. (1992). *Globalization: Social theory and global cullture.* London, England: Sage.

Rose, G. (2007). *Visual methodologies: An introduction to the interpretation of visual materials* (2nd ed.). London, England: Sage.

Semetsky, I. (2003). The problematics of human subjectivity: Gilles Deleuze and the Deweyan legacy. *Studies in Philosophy and Education, 22*(3–4), 221–225.

Semetsky, I. (2010). *Semiotics education experience.* Rotterdam, The Netherlands: Sense.

Walsh, C. (2007). Creativity as capital in the literacy classroom: Youth as multimodal designers. *Literacy, 41*(2), 79–85.

Zammit, K., & Downes, T. (2002). New learning environments and the multiliterate individual: A framework for educators. *Australian Journal of Language and Literacy, 25*(2), 24–36.

Zong, G. (2005). *Increasing preservice teachers' cross cultural understanding and global awareness via computer-mediated communication.* Paper presented at the National Association of Multicultural Education annual conference, Atlanta, GA.

CHAPTER 22

"Envisioning My Future Self":
Exploring Identity Construction to Promote Cultural Sensitivity

MARTHA CHRISTOPOULOU
139 Primary School of Athens

Due to worldwide media access and the Internet, and because of expanding patterns of migration (Meyer, Sherman, & Makinster, 2006; Barron, 2006), children in present day, post-industrial, globalized societies are more likely to meet and interact with people from diverse cultural backgrounds than were children in previous generations. However, in culturally diverse school environments, failure at interpersonal communication and misunderstandings of those from less empowered or minority cultures are quite common (Nikolaou, 2000; Barron, 2006). These conditions demand an art education that assists elementary students' understanding, appreciation, and acceptance of cultural diversity in a manner that is respectful and prepares them to function competently in familiar and unfamiliar cultural contexts. Art curricula that promote these competencies would include activities of cultural intercommunication and identity exploration. The latter is important because it provides learners with opportunities to communicate dimensions of their own cultural, religious, and linguistics backgrounds; life experiences; interests; and abilities as contributors to dialogic interaction.

Identity exploration is understood as a reflective self-examination of one's personal background. It is the foundational starting point of learning from others who are culturally different (Todd, 2003). Encouraging students to reflect on aspects of their own identity may foster greater awareness of the many factors that contribute to identity formation. It also may provide students with opportunities to challenge stereotypes and cultural assumptions they hold about themselves and others. When developing culturally sensitive art curricula for elementary school children, three important issues need to be taken into account: Which aspects of identity can readily be understood by elementary students? How can students connect their own visual and aesthetic experiences from everyday life to different facets of self-identity? How can self-identity facilitate acceptance, understanding, and respect for others?

Identity Revisited

Answering the question, "Who am I?" assumes a high degree of complexity. Answers may come from things with which a person associates—such as roles played—or explicit attributes of appearance. At an individual level, identity is grounded in personal values, goals, and self-knowledge (Cheek, 1989; Triandis, 1989) and is constructed by the person herself (Ferdman, 2000, p. 20). Age, gender, and sexuality; social and economic class; education and job; geographic location; religion and language; political status; and ethnicity are elements that construct cultural identity over one's lifespan (Ballengee Morris & Stuhr, 2001). Individual and group ethnic identities are formed by a subjective or imagined sense of common origins, common beliefs and values, commonalities in language and religion, and shared perceptions of historical continuity and ancestry, or place of origin (De Vos, 1995; Berry, Poortinga, Segall, & Dasen, 1992). At a group level, images and conventions shared with other members of a given group help individuals distinguish themselves from others (Ferdman, 2000). Individuals personalize the group to which they belong as they participate in its customs, rituals, or activities. Finally, identity is constituted from public judgments of an individual, such as popularity or reputations that are managed by others and form a sense of social identity.

Given that identity is the totality of multiple self-concepts and/or self-images constructed by particular influences under specific situations and reconstructed throughout an individual's life, it may require a high level of cognition to be totally comprehended. Elementary school children can explore and talk about their skills, abilities, feelings, and attitudes, and incorporate this information into their view of self. Children who are around the age of 12 can answer questions about self and identity that refer to physical attributes, cognitive capabilities, activities that are approved or disapproved by others, and knowledge and learned skills they have acquired in the past (Damon & Hart, 1982; Kazi & Demetriou, 2001). They become capable of answering questions about motivation, emotional states and dreams, fantasies, and desires. They can also answer questions about their social character (i.e., their perceptions of how they are regarded by others) and self-ideals, or how they would like to be in the future.

The Notion of "Future Self" in Children's Dreams and Aspirations

Visions of possible future selves are derived from representations of the self in the past and the role models and symbols provided by significant others, such as parents or peers, the media, and sociocultural experiences. Visions of future selves also are influenced by visual images, especially those from popular culture and the mass media. Visual imagery plays a significant role in the ongoing process of identity formation, as it provides people with a range of role models to emulate to create self-images and concepts (Huntemann & Morgan, 2001; Schroeder & Borgerson, 2003). Altogether, sociocultural

factors and visual imagery influence ideas about (1) physical attributes relating to body image and beauty; (2) lifestyle possibilities, such as being rich, poor, glamorous, or having an active social life; (3) general abilities, for example, being able to play an instrument or draw well; (4) occupational alternatives; and finally, (5) possibilities tied to the opinions of others, such as being appreciated, loved, feared, or unpopular (Markus & Nurius, 1986, p. 958). Thus, future self-visualizations reveal the constructive nature of identity and self and, at the same time, reflect the extent to which identity is socially determined and constrained.

A Curriculum Example From Practice

This narrative account gives a general idea of the objectives, procedures, and products of a curriculum implemented at a multicultural public elementary school situated in the center of Athens, Greece, with 5th-grade students. Demographics of the school were: 157 students, 46% of which were first or second generation immigrants mainly from Albania, Romania, and ex-Soviet Union countries. Grade 5 had 22 students consisting of 12 boys and 10 girls. Four students were from Albania, two from Romania, and one from Ukraine. Also, one was of Greek-African descent and another was Greek-Albanian. Art lessons were taught by the classroom generalist teacher with whom I, as deputy headteacher of the school at that time, collaborated in developing and evaluating aims, content, and learning activities of an art unit for these 5th-grade students. The curricular unit was delivered between October and November of 2010, and was organized into five lessons lasting 40 minutes each, during which I acted as participant observer. The teaching/learning events were documented by note-taking and tape-recording.

Students of the class were invited to imagine themselves a year from now, ten years from now, or any other future date of their choice. They were asked to discuss how they would like to grow and what they might become at some time in the future. Then they were asked to create three different self-portraits that presented how they saw themselves in the future and write comments about the features they had emphasized. Further instructions,—for example, to draw portraits reflecting parents' expectations or other significant influences—were not given at that time because both the classroom teacher and I considered these to be leading prompts. Although students were invited to use their choice of medium, most

Figure 1. One year from now: Taller and in better shape, *pen, pencil colours, and crayons, by Lambros.*

Figure 2. Fifteen years from now: Owner of a bird shop and parrot specialist, *pen and crayons, by Lambros.*

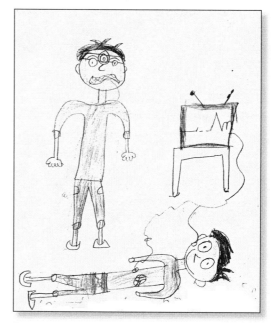

Figure 3. I want to become a doctor, *pencil and felt tip markers, by Mario.*

chose to use pens, colored pencils, and felt tip markers; a few used mixed media including crayons and/or paint.

Next students were asked to identify categories into which their works naturally fell and display them accordingly, so every class participant had a work posted for discussion. Main categories included self-portraits emphasizing changes in physical attributes, lifestyle possibilities, social status, and occupational aspirations. For example, Lambros imagined being taller and in better physical condition and, eventually, being owner of a bird shop (Figures 1 and 2), while Mario thought he might become a doctor (Figure 3).

During a follow-up class discussion, stress was placed on description, analysis, and interpretation. The students reflected on their work as they answered questions about: (1) ways their hopes, aspirations, goals, motives, fantasies, desires, fears, or threats were depicted; (2) what kinds of life experiences had influenced the particular portrayals; and (3) changes and transformations described in their portraits of self in the future. Lambros explained to his classmates that, because he was interested in birds and read books and watched TV documentaries about

them, he would like to own a bird shop. Students also were encouraged to identify family, peer, or community influences in the ways they envisioned their future selves, as well as identify influences from popular and mass media visual imagery. For example, Lambros was interested in reading and watching documentaries about animals, especially birds, as a result of early conversations with his uncle, who was a veterinarian. Finally, students were invited to examine similarities and differences in their collective works that might be attributable to gender, cultural, or ethnic background. They particularly commented on works that emphasized concerns of bodily characteristics and physical appearance. Students noted: "It seems that girls and boys want to change their appearance when they grow up," and, "But girls are more interested than boys in looking like singers and actresses because [singers and actresses] are beautiful."[1]

Influences of Media on Self-Identity

In the next lesson, the students watched a 15-minute video from a TV series broadcast on a Greek state channel. The Argentinean teen telenovela *Rebelde Way* was selected because it was considered a window into the adolescent world and life in general (Christopoulou, 2010). Its plotline revolves around the life of a group of rich and a few poor students who attend a private high school in Buenos Aires. Social class, conflict, teenage dreams of the future, and love and sexual relationships are main themes. The particular telenovela communicates values about social change at a personal level within family and society. The telenovela plots, characters, and character interactions also promote behavioral and verbal codes, lifestyle models, aesthetic standards, and gender and social class stereotypes. So, it is quite possible the images this show presents to children might influence their aspirations, desires, fantasies, dreams, and visions of future self.

Class discussion about these influences was supported by asking students their opinions through questions such as: "How and to what extent are audiences influenced by the behavior of the characters in, or the content of this telenovela?"; "How do audiences use this telenovela to get advice about events in their lives?"; "Would you want to be like one of these characters or live a similar life? Why/why not?"; "Could there be anything you dream of being in the future after watching *Rebelde Ways*? What? Why?"; and "Could this telenovela contribute in any way to your life plans? How?" Next students were invited to make a visual diary about the thoughts, dreams, desires, and fantasies generated by their favorite TV program and create a series of drawings representing these ideas of self in the future.

Drawings after watching the telenovela and written comments revealed that these students, especially the girls, were greatly concerned with bodily characteristics and physical appearance. Anna, for example, was clear about the aspects of her physical appearance she wanted to change: "Longer hair and full lips like the singer Elena Paparizou" (Figure 4). It appeared that she had already identified and appreciated the physical characteristics and qualities of this celebrated music icon in accordance with her future expectations and gender identification (Fisherkeller, 1997; Kennedy, Salisbury, & Prunty, 1997; Signorielli, 2001).

For Further Consideration

1. What and how might aspects of identity be explored by elementary students in ways that are sensitive to their concerns about the future?

2. Exploring the notion of future self was considered by the author as a type of *virtual* cultural immersion experience.
   - How is cultural immersion defined typically?
   - In what ways are the activities that are described by the author virtual cultural immersion experiences?
   - Brainstorm other examples of (real or virtual) cultural immersion activities that might be integrated into an art lesson.

3. Brainstorm: Media images frequently are created for commercial profit or to benefit political or other powerful groups. What strategies might art teachers use to help students understand how these kinds of images might influence their sense of personal identity and their understandings of others in positive, negative, realistic, or stereotypical ways?

4. How can elementary students express compassion for others and assist one another in envisioning and supporting positive goals for the future?

Figure 4. Me having long hair and full lips, *pen, pencil colours, felt tip markers, and crayons, by Anna (visual diary).*

Figure 5. My dream is to be a car rally driver, *pencil, by Costas (visual diary).*

Students identified desired lifestyles that were promoted by certain cultural icons, especially pop and sports stars. Such lifestyles were associated with fashion, fame, glamour, social status, and possession of money: "Paparizou has nice clothes. If I was [sic] pop star I would always wear fashionable clothes," and "I want to become a car rally driver like Vettel who is famous and earns lots of money so I will have a better life" (Figure 5). Fantasizing celebrity status, success, and money was informed by the glamorous way certain jobs are depicted on TV and in print media. Students' current lower socioeconomic status may possibly have influenced such dreams, particularly when there seemed to be no strong interest or parental model to counter or challenge these as potential life goals. Visual culture resources were used, therefore, to construct symbolic links among their current situations and the better lives into which several students wanted to move through visualizations of a future self (Fisherkeller, 1997).

After completing the practical task of drawing in visual diaries, the students shared their sketches and ideas through open class discussions and self-reflections, and were urged to critically analyze and interpret their visual diaries and drawings of future selves. They were encouraged to discuss issues of conflict between values and role models provided by family, community, religious and ethnic groups, or peers and those communicated by favorite TV programs. As one student noted: "My dad says that TV programs teach us that fame is the most important thing in life, but having a good job and getting good pay is much more important; and I think he may be right about this because you can have a good life [if you have a good job with good pay]." They also were asked to identify similarities and differences in the ways they appropriated values, stereotypes, and models conveyed by TV programs. Students mainly talked about similarities in the ways they learned values by observing role models, attitudes, and behaviors: "I look at what other people do or how they behave on TV programs and get ideas about what to do in similar situations." Regarding differences, gender identification was the main factor that was suggested by the students: "I choose what to look at… I basically look at women who look great and cool."

Effects of Visual Culture on Future Self Construction

The way these students described their future lives, prior to being asked to watch the clipping of a commercial telenovela, demonstrated that they had developed emerging awareness of where their personal interests might lead them and what expectations their parents and local community held for them in the future. Popular culture and media images provided additional layers of identity references, such as value patterns; stereotypes; and cultural icons of gender typologies, beauty ideals, and social role portrayals that signal who or what counts in society. The telenovela *Rebelde Way,* for example, promoted White, upper-class values; female body beauty images; and role models for upward social mobility. My observations suggested that students as consumers of such kinds of images constructed visions of future selves based on their perceptions of self in relation to these ideals, and in collaboration with members of their family or the local sociocultural groups with whom they shared or challenged these images (Schroeder & Borgerson, 2003). By examining portrayals of wealth, lifestyle, and fame contrasted to poverty and anonymity, as portrayed in television shows such as *Patty the Most Beautiful Story*,[2] or by TV show personas like Eugenia Manolides,[3] students reckoned that idealized self-images indeed stimulated their desire to be like the main characters of favorite TV programs.

Considering Sociocultural Factors

Exploring visions of future self through discussions and artmaking functioned as a way of enabling these students to recognize the role family, local culture, and mass media visual culture plays in an individual's identity construction, and to understand how they constructed and performed identities and self-concepts in their own lives (Freedman, 2003). Moreover, it was a starting point for enabling students to acquire positive predispositions towards Otherness (Barron, 2006). Most of the students acknowledged that the lives of their favorite media figures were out of the ordinary and, as such, provided them more possibilities to imagine future selves than the lives of ordinary people. It is probable that they perceived media figures as desirable Others, whose Otherness was better or superior to local expectations. They also recognized Otherness by considering how expectations of family and local community might differ from their own and the visions held by classmates like Mario, who drew himself as a doctor (Figure 3).

Mario embraced his father's aspirations about his future potential: "My dad says that doctors are more worthy because they serve ill people and earn good money." Discussing such hierarchies about people's worthiness, the students realized that family values about upward social mobility and the social status of certain professions can shape one's future dreams. Students noted: "It is like our parents dream for us and we hold these dreams," and "I think that parents want us to do something better than they did in their lives. But what happens if you don't want to study to become a doctor?" Thoughtful discussion about the future possibilities each student shared with family or other important reference groups appeared to enhance their understanding of the variation of cultural values and belief systems that played roles in the realistic or unrealistic aspirations and the construction of future selves.

The Concept of Future Self as a Virtual Cultural Experience

Exploring the concept of future self might be considered a type of virtual cultural immersion experience, insofar as it provided students with opportunities to interact and engage with their co-students from cultures different from their own. Cultural immersion usually includes activities designed to provide direct, substantial, and meaningful interactions with members of other cultures in real-life settings (Vaughan, 2005; Tomlinson-Clarke & Clarke, 2010). The art classroom served as a microcosm where such interactions took place, especially when students were engaged in both affective and consciousness-raising learning experiences. For example, while the students were engaged in examinations of and reflections on their own interests in popular culture; role models emulated; and cultural assumptions about beauty, desire, or glamour that affected the construction of future self-images, they were encouraged to consider the cultural contexts that influenced their own future self-visions. They could compare and contrast differences between their own family's expectations of them and the different expectations placed upon peers from differing family-cultural backgrounds. This gave them opportunities to gain insights into diversities of attitude and value and, thus, extend their understanding of cultural differences.

Students also had the opportunity to explore and discuss the ways global events and media bring images of distant cultures close to them and influence their desires and dreams. Yet, they did not seem to recognize that media images are manufactured to promote the commercial, political, or private agendas of their creators. One student suggested, for example: "All foreign TV series show us how people live elsewhere and we can get ideas for our lives." They appeared to have difficulties explaining how such globalized media texts might be decoded or ameliorated with expectations of parents and friends from their own cultural backgrounds, probably because TV images are subtle, seductive, and comprised of multiply layered meanings. As Gamson, Croteau, Hoynes, and Sasson (1992) and Anderson, Huston, Schmitt, Linebarger, and Wright (2001) point out, such meanings are difficult to unpack and discern, even by adults, due to rapid succession and fast alternation of TV images, which does not allow time for reflection on what is being watched. However, there was some indication from students' drawings and verbal and written comments that they could isolate, identify, and critique appropriate media-conveyed values and models that suited them; fitted into their already existing cultural norms; and were accepted by family, peers, and local communities. For instance, students appeared to appreciate individualistic values of achievement, success, and self-direction and brought a variety of examples of what these meant for them: "earning good money," "going to university in order to learn and study so we can do something important in their lives," and "all people have abilities and potential to become something special."

A productive form of cultural exchange took place as the students looked at and interpreted other students' depictions of future selves. Artistic expression as a mode of communication gave the possibility of appreciating differences among classmates within local community and considering how ideas about the future, which others expressed, were different from or similar to one's own. A description in my field-notes was that "the students were encouraged to think through and acknowledge the multiple visions of future selves drawn by their classmates." As they were guided to interpret, evaluate, and reflect on these depictions, the students deciphered meanings from diverse representations of culture and embarked on understanding what other people value, dislike, know, aspire to, or what problems they acknowledge. Finally, my observations suggested that inviting the students to tell in what way their future-self drawings made them different from everyone else in the group and similar to or different from adolescents living in another country strengthened their voices and gave them a feeling of inclusion in the local community and larger global youth group.

Summary

This instructional activity was an example of how students might be assisted in understanding themselves in relation to their society and becoming open to other's perspectives. As part of the process of evaluating student learning at the conclusion of the "Envisioning my Future Self" unit, students wrote statements about what they had learned. One student insightfully remarked, "Family, peers and TV influence our thinking about future selves." Another noted, "I understood how my co-students and I see ourselves in the future."

One such learning experience is not sufficient to bring about deep sense of self, or lasting positive changes in attitudes towards others, or even competency with culturally different people. It can be a starting point, however, for providing students with opportunities to explore identity, make connections to their cultural backgrounds, and thus develop awareness and appreciation

of their own and others' identities. It may also provide them with opportunities to recognize differences and similarities between realities of local cultural experiences and realities or ideals portrayed by TV shows that depict life in other cultures, and reflect on ways media images influence their self-concepts. It is important that teachers help students understand how media images produce meaning, reflect the values and viewpoints of media makers, project stereotypes and deceptive "ideals," and shape visions of self. This might extend to comparing the stereotypes of various cultural groups, which are projected by media, to the realities of their own lives and the lives of peers from the depicted cultures. Students may consider whether such media images accurately describe themselves and their lived experiences or the experiences they have from other cultures.

Future self is a concept that most students can fully comprehend, as they have the ability to anticipate future states and envision a variety of possible selves that derive from dreams, aspirations, fantasies, desires, and fears as well as visual culture and social influences. Critical examination of the notion of future self in art lessons has the potential to increase children's self-understanding and knowledge about others. Reflecting on the teaching and learning experience, I concluded that self-reflective art activities and discussion provided students with opportunities to consciously analyze and respond to issues of differences among others of the class. This in turn enhanced comfort level among students from diverse ethnic and cultural backgrounds and cultivated awareness and appreciation of one another's differences. Communally shared idea exchanges, interpretations, and cultural interactions encourage emotionally positive connections among the students. Follow-up art activities might include role play, re-construction of body images using Photoshop, producing short videos on one's family values, or storytelling about the fears of not fitting into local or global society (with brainstorming about how these fears might be resolved). Such activities have potential to expand understanding about identity and further cultivate tolerance and respect for diverging points of view.

REFERENCES

Anderson, D. R., Huston, A. C., Schmitt, K. L., Linebarger, D. L., & Wright, J. C. (2001). Creativity. *Monographs of the Society for Research in Child Development, 66*(1), 67–78.

Ballengee Morris, C., & Stuhr, P. (2001). Multicultural art and visual cultural education in a changing world. *Art Education, 54*(4), 6–13.

Barron, R. M. (2006). *Exploring identity through self portraiture* (Unpublished MA thesis). College of the Arts and Sciences, Georgia State University, Atlanta.

Berry, J., Poortinga, Y., Segall, M., & Dasen, P. (1992). *Cross-cultural psychology.* Cambridge, England: Cambridge University Press.

Cheek, J. M. (1989). Identity orientations and self-interpretation. In D. M. Buss & N. Cantor (Eds.), *Personality psychology: Recent trends and emerging directions* (pp. 275–285). New York, NY: Springer-Verlag.

Christopoulou, M. (2010). Telenovelas as art curriculum content. *Art Education, 63*(4), 19–24.

Damon, W., & Hart, D. (1982). The development of self-understanding from infancy through adolescence. *Child Development, 53*(4), 841–864.

De Vos, G. A. (1995). Ethnic pluralism: Conflict and accommodation. In L. Rommanucci-Ross & G. A. De Vos (Eds.), *Ethnic identity, creation conflict and accommodation* (pp. 15–45). London, England: Altimira.

Ferdman, B. M. (2000). 'Why am I who I am?' Constructing the cultural self in multicultural perspective. *Human Development, 43*(1), 19–23.

Fisherkeller, J. (1997). Everyday learning about identities among young adolescents in television culture. *Anthropology & Education Quarterly, 28*(4), 467–492.

Freedman, K. (2003). The importance of student artistic production to teaching visual culture. *Art Education, 56*(2), 38–43.

Gamson, W. A., Croteau, D., Hoynes, W., & Sasson, T. (1992). Media images and the social construction of reality. *Annual Review of Sociology, 18*, 373–393.

Huntemann, N., & Morgan, M. (2001). Mass media and identity development. In D. G. Singer & J. L. Singer (Eds.), *Handbook of children and the media* (pp. 309–320). Thousand Oaks, CA: Sage.

Kazi, S., & Demetriou, A. (2001). *Unity and modularity in the mind and the self: Studies on the representation between self-awareness, personality and intellectual development from childhood to adolescence.* London, England: Routledge.

Kennedy, D., Salisbury, L., & Prunty, M. E. V. (1997). *Reflections of girls in the media.* Report on Fourth Annual Children and the Media Conference, April 10–May 2, Los Angeles, CA, United States.

Markus, H., & Nurius, P. (1986). Possible selves. *American Psychologist, 41*(9), 954–969.

Meyer, L., Sherman, L., & Makinster, J. (2006). The effects of the Japan bridge project on third graders' cultural sensitivity. *Theory and Research in Social Education, 34*(3), 347–369.

Nikolaou, G. (2000). Ένταξη και Εκπαίδευση των Αλλοδαπών Μαθητών στο Δημοτικό Σχολείο (Adaptation and Education of Foreign Students in Primary School). Athens, Greece: Elleneka Grammata.

Schroeder, J. E., & Borgerson, J. L. (2003). *Identity and iteration: Marketing images and the constitution of consuming subjects.* Paper presented at Critical Marketing Stream, 3rd International Critical Management Studies Conference, Lancaster University, UK, 2003. Retrieved from www.mngt.waikato.ac.nz/ejrot/cmsconference/2003/abstracts/criticalmarketing/Schroeder.pdf

Signorielli, N. (2001). Television's gender role images and contribution to stereotyping. In D. G. Singer & J. L. Singer (Eds.), *Handbook of children and the media* (pp. 341–358). Thousand Oaks, CA: Sage.

Todd, H. (2003). *Learning from the other: Levinas, psychoanalysis, and ethical possibilities in education.* Albany, NY: SUNY Press.

Tomlinson-Clarke, S. M., & Clarke, D. (2010). Culturally focused community-centered service learning: An international cultural immersion experience. *Journal of Multicultural Counseling & Development, 38*(3), 166–175.

Triandis, H. C. (1989). The self and social behavior in differing cultural contexts. *Psychological Review, 96*(3), 506–520.

Vaughan, W. (2005). Educating for diversity, social responsibility and action: Preservice teachers engage in immersion experiences. *Journal of Cultural Diversity, 12*(1), 26–30.

ENDNOTES

[1] Student quotes and short conversational excerpts are from field notes and transcriptions of tape recordings taken during lessons between October and November 2010.

[2] *Patty the Most Beautiful Story (Patito Feo* in Spanish, *Ugly Duckling* in English) is a comedy telenovela for children and adolescents that revolves around the life of an unattractive teenage girl who wants to become a singer and is in love with a handsome teenaged boy. Subplots include the search for her father and rivalries with classmates.

[3] Eugenia Manolides is a former music composer and conductor who moved into show business as a hostess of popular television reality shows. She is considered by many to be a successful role model because of her public career and her marriage to Greek politician and writer Adonis Georgiades.

CHAPTER 23

On the Practice of Artistic Measurement of Social Mobility and Marginalization

ANNA KENDE
Eötvös Loránd University

ANIKÓ ILLÉS
Moholy-Nagy University of Art and Design

Nine-year-old Béla lives in a shabby house in the outskirts of Budapest, the capital of Hungary. When we asked him, along with his classmates, to make a drawing of his home, he called to us and whispered quietly in our ears that he swears he's living with his uncle, and therefore wants to make a drawing of his uncle's house instead of his parents'.[1]

This seemingly insignificant episode gave evidence that disclosing information about one's poverty—both to oneself and to others—may be far from an easy or straightforward task. It is hindered by the social norms of Béla's cultural context, where being poor and unable to provide for one's family is a shameful and stigmatizing condition.

Béla and his family are members of a Roma[2] (Gypsy) community living in Hungary, a relatively poor country in East-Central Europe. Having once been a socialist state, Hungary has been a member of the European Union (EU) since 2004. Roma people make up the largest ethnic minority group in Hungary, about 5–8% of the overall population of 10 million. They are an ethnically, culturally, and linguistically heterogeneous minority group whose members face comparable problems to those of some racial minorities in the United States (Stewart, 2001). Research shows that poverty affects both Roma and non-Roma Hungarians, but Roma people tend to be among the poorest. Reproduction of poverty across generations is extremely strong in Hungary. The most important determinant of a child growing up to be poor is the parents' low level of education and unemployment, the effect of which is stronger than in any other EU country (Bass, Darvas, & Ferge, 2007). Poverty among Roma people also is reinforced by ethnic tension (Szalai, 2005). These socio-logical and economic facts all contribute to the low levels of social mobility of the population in general in comparison to other countries of the developed world; in other words, if you are born poor in Hungary, you are likely to remain poor throughout your life (Ward, Lelkes, Sutherland, & Tóth, 2009).

Psychological Consequences of Social Marginalization in the Context of Art Education

The feedback children receive from their own families and members of their immediate communities serves as the basis of identity development. Social exclusion and disadvantage of entire communities or groups within society are potentially psychologically harmful conditions (e.g., Nunn & Thompson, 1996), which may negatively impact the identity development of children who are members of marginalized groups. Therefore, Roma children in Hungary, like any other children belonging to an excepted minority group, are at higher risk of experiencing loss of control, learned helplessness (a dissociation between one's behavior and its consequences), low self-esteem, negative identity (a sense of not belonging to a group rather than belonging to one), value conflicts, and isolation, all of which are seriously harmful and may be life-threatening conditions (Beale Spencer & Markstrom-Adams, 1990; Erikson, 1968; Phinney, 1990). Social marginalization might be reinforced by daily social interactions, encounters, and treatment by members of institutions such as schools or media that repeat or perpetrate the stereotype (Young, 1990). Inversely, negative effects of marginalization can be disputed by loved ones, teachers, and members of the child's home community who are fair, non-judgmental, and empathetic toward members of the socially excepted group (Wright, Masten, & Narayan, 2012). Social interactions that reinforce an individual's sense of belonging while positively differentiating her from other groups are a precondition to the development of an integrated identity.

Art teachers working with children from culturally marginalized and economically impoverished communities need to recognize that while the reproduction of poverty can be sufficiently accounted for by sociology and economics, this does not explain where the psychological border between having prospects for the future and hopelessness about one's prospects lies. This threshold is not only determined by hard economic and demographic data, but also by psychological processes responsible for the integrity of a person (Beale Spencer & Markstrom-Adams, 1990; Nunn & Thompson, 1996). Therefore, as researchers in fields of psychology and art education, we developed a project aimed at helping us understand something about how marginalization influences children's concepts of their own current situations and prospects for social mobility or prosperity. Our goal was to reach a better understanding of the psychological strategies children employ in a socially disadvantaged position in the process of identity development, and to point to ways in which positive strategies could be enhanced.

We focused our study on children during the pre-adolescent period, because this age group is believed to be already aware of their own social and ethnic group, yet, in contrast with adolescents, they do not yet question the authenticity of their surroundings or their own social position (Phinney, 1990). Moreover, we used artmaking as a tool for exploring the ideas these children hold of themselves and their prospects in life in relation to the experiences of dominant culture. The authority of art, or more precisely education through art, has been recognized as a powerful tool for assessing and celebrating children's creativity and cultural wisdom (Read, 1955).

We questioned how faith in social mobility or the lack thereof might appear in the drawings of children living in poverty and/or belonging to the Roma ethnic minority group in Hungary. Children's drawings have been used in many different ways to approach poverty or social marginalization by art educators, sociologists, psychologists, and psychiatrists (Coles, 2003; Golomb, 1981; McEvilley, 1992; Veale, 2005). The immediate predecessor to our study was a groundbreaking study carried out by three Hungarian scholars in 1978 (Gerő, Csanádi, & Ladányi, 1978/2006), which used children's drawings to point to the fact that even a 10-year-old child could have an understanding of the limits of social mobility of the lower social classes. Our aim was to give a social psychological interpretation of children's drawings about their own life perspectives, and at the same time, look at the potential of visual education in dealing with problems connected to social deprivation.

The Research Design: Working With Children's Drawings

Four hundred and thirty-six children (225 boys and 211 girls), aged 8 to 10, from 23 school classes participated in our study, in both urban and rural settings in Hungary. Schools were selected based on personal recommendations and demographic data provided by government statistics. The schools we chose fulfilled the following criteria: they were situated in socio-economically deprived neighborhoods, parents of the children were characterized by low levels of education and high levels of unemployment, and a large percentage of students in these schools came from ethnic Roma backgrounds. According to national statistics, nearly half of the households in neighborhoods served by these schools did not have a single employed family member (National Development Agency, 2009). Of the participants of the study, 24% lived in the capital city of Budapest, 34% lived in smaller towns in the countryside, and 42% dwelt in villages. Data collection took place between March and May of 2010.

First, the two investigators (i.e., the authors) provided each participant with a new 12-piece crayon set and A4 size papers to use. Then we asked children to make drawings on the basis of these questions:

1. Where do you live now? (The first drawing will later be referred to as the Current house)

2. Where will you live when you grow up? (Future house)

3. What is the house of your dreams like? (Dream house)

Instructions about each of the drawing tasks were given by one of two moderators, who were master's students in psychology from the local university. The children's regular classroom teacher also was present during the instruction and drawing period, which occurred during a special time apart from regular class routines.

When most children finished the first drawing, they received guidance for the second, and when they were finished with the second, they received instructions for the third one. With the exception of a couple of children, they all finished all three drawings within the allocated time, 45 to 60 minutes. Participation was voluntary and following parents' agreement. There were no pressures on children to finish quickly or to finish at all.

For Further Consideration

1. Kende and Illés asked Roma children to draw three versions of a house from the perspective of present life, future expectations, and fantastic dreams. Through these images and conversations about the images, they communicated embarrassment and anguish about their current place in society, ambivalence and yearning for what life might be like for them in the future, and puzzlement about how their lives might be transformed.

   • What kinds of conversations or activities in the art room might help students, such as these Roma children, sort through their feelings and begin to construct realistic goals and ways of attaining those goals?

2. Consider motifs other than houses that might serve as signifiers of a student's present, future, and imagined understandings of a personal and cultural place in society. Assign your students to produce three versions of the selected topic. These drawings should serve as stimuli for engaging students in discussions of perceptions about diversity, tolerance, discrimination, appreciation or prejudice.

   • How might a sharing of visual images soften entrenched stereotypical ideas about ourselves, our future lives, and one another?

After engaging in an in-depth discussion of the topic, complete one of the two following activities.

Activity #1

Working together in groups, brainstorm an outline for an art educational program that might assist students who are like these children (i.e., from isolated, economically impoverished, and marginalized groups) to gain voice, agency, and a place of respect and power in a globally connected world. Consider:

1. What historic traditions are foundational to the contemporary life experiences of this cultural group?

2. With what social/political/practical obstacles are they currently faced?

3. How might they re-envision the future through art or artmaking?

4. How might they share these communications assisted by visual art beyond their local community?

Activity #2

Plan an art class exercise that encourages K-12 children to explore issues of double-standard systems that stem from cultural discrimination and/or social marginalization. Students should address issues of diversity, as well as social mobility, within the framework of the exercise. Thereafter, students should:

1. Provide strategies that incorporate media or interactive communicative technologies as a means of sharing cultural experiences, images, and ideas with students from other regions of the world.

2. Provide strategies that take advantage of more traditional (media and communicative) opportunities to share cultural experiences, images, and ideas with students from other regions of the world.

Children participated in the research with great enthusiasm; most of them understood the instructions at once, while only a few needed a bit of additional explanation. After the completion of the drawings, group interviews were conducted with the children, during which they could explain if and why the three pictures differed. These group interviews were conducted by the same moderators who had assigned and overseen the drawings. The interviews lasted about 15 to 20 minutes, with all children participating as a group. We also made observations of these children in their regular school settings, observed the neighborhoods where the schoolchildren lived, and interviewed random parents of the children in their homes.[3]

Research Findings

Relying on house drawings seemed a promising subject matter for uncovering the students' ideas about current, future, and imagined life conditions. Valsiner affirms one's home as an important symbol of belonging. Therefore, the image one projects of his or her home is capable of pointing to a hidden dimension of identity (2000). Additionally, the interesting house is one of the four items of the Clark's Drawing Abilities Test (Clark, 1989), in which the drawing of a house has proved to be significant in revealing high ability in artmaking.

Working with children's drawings as qualitative data was a complex task. While analyzing the drawings, we paid attention to children's drawing abilities insofar as they seemed typical or atypical for this age group (Golomb, 1981; Kellog, 1969), as well as other psychodynamic influences, such as the desire to live up to expectations, social comparison, and competition between classmates (Brown, 2004; Pepitone, 1980). This basically meant we could not assign much significance to recurring themes or solutions within a group. We did not carry out the individual psychological analysis of the drawings, since our goal was not to focus on intrapsychic processes—neither did the circumstances of data collection allow this type of analysis, nor did the broadness of the research question require it. Rather, our focus was on a psychosocial phenomenon. The method of analysis we employed was based on the grounded theory approach suggested by Denzin and Lincoln (1994), which meant that the main categories of analysis were not externally established, but arose from these specific drawings. It is for this reason that we kept the units of analysis flexible enough to embrace the diversity of the phenomenon described later in this chapter.

We carried out the analysis of the pictures on three levels:

1. The pictures were arranged into vague groups based on *overall impressions*. Such impressions were determined by the comparison of the three—present, future, and dream—houses of each child. For example, we recognized if the three drawings depicted houses that were almost entirely similar, or, in contrast, differed from one another. We also noted if the picture made a cheerful impression or a depressing one, and so forth.

2. *General features* were identified, such as the use of space, size of the house, colors, level of detail, ornamentation, topics, and so forth.

3. *Specificities*, especially the presence or absence of certain features on one, two, or all three drawings (e.g., signs of wealth, a fence, a car, TV, a specific house type) were also identified.

Social Mobility as Depicted in the Drawings

Houses presented in the crayon drawings were predominantly colorful. While in reality the students' homes were often gray and rundown, there were only a dozen instances of realistic portrayal of the current house, the use of dark colors, or a strikingly different size or shape of the currently dwelt-in house in comparison with the second picture of an imagined future house. Brightly colored presentations may have suggested a learned style of drawing houses through observations of idealistically illustrated houses in children's books or other media. We suspected, however, the strong tendency for brightly colored drawings to be a wishful visual depiction of the current and future houses. Here, we recognize some of the well-known social psychological coping strategies, such as the positive distortion of one's own circumstances, the belief in a nicer future, or the capacity of progress (Comer, 2010).

Upward social mobility toward adulthood appeared on almost all pictures, most often in a highly *schematic* way, which means that the three houses were very similar to one another, with a recognizable but insignificant improvement when comparing the first to the second and the second to the third drawings, such as an additional ornament or a minor change in size, color, or shape (Figure 1).

Looking beyond the schematic drawings of three equivalent houses with insignificant improvements, or the stereotypic depiction of houses, what we come to see

Figure 1. Selected samples of upward mobility appeared in a schematic way.

Figure 2. Selected samples of dream of a middle-class life.

Figure 3. Selected samples of features of security.

is the widespread phenomena of the dream of a middle-class life. A picture on the wall, flowers in a vase, a car parked in front of the house, or a dog in a dog shed appeared not in the future house, but on the picture of the dream house. Village children made drawings of multistory apartment blocks, and city children made images of family houses (Figure 2). These do not reflect far-fetched dreams created in their fantasies, but dreams of a comfortable life.

Particularly important evidence of desire for a secure and comfortable life was indicated in the inclusion of a fence in the images. Drawing a fence around the house has particular importance in the case of village children, because their actual houses are often not surrounded by fences, but stand naked in the street, as opposed to the houses of the wealthier inhabitants of the village. A fence is needed if there is property to guard, if a family needs privacy, or

if there is a need to indicate borders between neighbors (Valsiner, 2000). Thus a fence is a symbol of security and prosperity, and a practical and realistic part of everyday life. The fact that the houses of the children often lack a fence can explain the significance of drawing a fence on any of the three drawings as part of depicting the present or implying upward social mobility in the future.

In the third picture of the dream house, where children made a drawing of the house they would most like to live in, some evidence of childish imagination occurred (such as a picture of a dragon, an architecturally interesting building, an ice-cream machine, and a slide coming down from the top of the house) and there were houses reflecting great wealth (such as a house in an exotic place or one with a swimming pool), but these imaginative dream house embellishments were far rarer than drawings that suggested dreams of middle-class lives.

Nevertheless, a castle as a dream house also appeared and was a common topic depicted in the third picture. We counted 98 castle drawings altogether. A bastion or palace is undoubtedly a schematic representation of wealth and security, and together with such features as the appearance of a fence or a dog on the future or the dream house, was interpreted as an indicator of the significance of security in children's lives. Appearance of both the castle and fence (Figures 3 and 4) may have suggested a desire for security and wishes for material goods held by many of the participating children.

Figure 4. Examples of security.

Figure 5. Selected samples of features of wealth.

Additionally there were specific features which pointed directly to economic wealth in a dreamed for future. The children's third drawings included features such as a dollar sign, a house with a sign "casino" or "poker" on it (Figure 5), and a drawing of a Playboy rabbit, all of which are associated with wealth or easy, non-conventional access to money.

Children Analyzing Their Own Drawings

Group interviews following the collection of drawings varied in depth and length, ranging from a few minutes with only a few children who finished drawing quicker than the others, or the entire class for about 15 minutes. We conducted these open-ended conversations not only to refine our interpretations of the pictures, but also because we were genuinely interested in children's analysis of their drawings. Furthermore, these conversations had the potential to show whether drawings are indeed a good starting point for dealing with issues of social marginalization. Children described what they depicted, talked about the differences between the three pictures, explained why their current house was or was not different from the future and dream house, and discussed what was necessary to achieve the life they dream of.

When children talked about their dream houses, they referred to desires for increase in size, beauty, wealth, and colorfulness compared to the current and future house. They listed wishes of things that were well-known to them but presently unattainable. Often they described what is missing from their house today, or what they would like to change in their circumstances. "We can fit better in a larger house," or the current house "is ugly." These hopes were evidenced in their artworks, as well. Also, they mentioned security as part of the change they might or would like to experience. They talked about a strong fence or a wall around their house, or a dog that could defend them. They described the castle not only as a form of wealth, but also as a sign of security in statements such as: "I made a drawing of a robot. I will live in a robot house, so that nobody can attack me," "strong wall," "a fence," "a large dog," "a job with the police," and "a guard with a crossbow."

Sometimes dream houses were dissociated from realistic opportunities, and children mentioned castles, lions, 100 children, or football fields, thus relying more on their fantasies than on everyday realities. One child stated, "I will have a golden house with a golden bed, with everything made of gold in it. I will have a golden dog and a golden swimming-pool."

When we asked children what was necessary to realize their dreams, they mentioned the lack of money as a main obstacle. "A castle costs a lot of money, that's why I will never live there." They also recited a well-internalized association that in order to have money, they needed to work, and in order to find work, they needed to study well. They mentioned some realistic difficulties in these associations, such as "It is difficult to earn a lot of money," and "In order to get my dream house, I first need to figure out what kind of work I want to do and how." Furthermore, they added alternative ways to earn money, such as "metal recycling," "winning in a card game," "gambling," "I get in an accident and receive an insurance payment," and "I will have 100 kids, and get a large family allowance."

Reimagining Self in Future Life

While there is general agreement that identity-formation is a process experienced by people of all cultures and societies, research carried out in various culturally diverse societies suggests that racial or ethnic identification occurs differently in cases of children belonging to minority and majority ethnic and racial groups (Baumann, 1996; Camilleri & Malewska-Peyre, 1997; Clark & Clark, 1947). Phinney (1990) argues that ethnic minority children are faced with particular tasks during their development as a consequence of the stereotypes and prejudices perpetrated upon them by mainstream society, and of differences in values between majority and minority members of society. People are strongly inclined to find ways to overcome psychologically harmful situations (Werner, 2001). Therefore, differences between value systems of marginalized peoples and the mainstream do not simply threaten development of positive self-imaging, but also create a situation in which a child belonging to a minority group may seek alternative ways to ensure psychological well-being and an integrated sense of identity. In some cases, however, the alternate ways of seeking well-being are so unrealistic as to result in added frustration and a sense of hopelessness in achieving meaningful goals.

The tendency to depict the present and the future in a positive way and to rely on a typical house schema created a large number of similarly drawn houses. Nonetheless, from the slight differences between the three houses drawn by each child, a sign of upward social mobility, a belief in a better future was clear. As Coles (2003) highlighted in his psychiatric work with children, the positive depiction can reflect strength of effort to overcome the psychological difficulties arising from pressing societal or individual problems. Children belonging to minority groups and/or experiencing deprivation employ various strategies to maintain the integrity of their identities. Middle-class dreams indicated the desire of assimilating and adapting to majority norms (Berry, 1996). The large

number of pleasant-looking, colorful houses on the first drawing (present house) following a previously learned pattern (from observing drawings by other children in the classroom, book illustrations, or other childlike house images) suggested to us these children may have employed a strategy of denial in overcoming marginalization (Breakwell, 1986) that protected them from acknowledging a disconnection between the reality of what their own homes look like and the schema of "house"—or as in the case of Béla, that served as a protection against other's negative opinions about the realities of their lives.

Despite these strategies, which tend to mask the experience of marginalization, what we actually witnessed was that, once the three houses were on paper, the drawings served as useful starting points for talking about the opportunities of mobility and their limitations. If the houses did not differ from one another, children had the opportunity to explain why they believe their circumstances will not change significantly in the future. If the houses were very different, they took the opportunity to talk about what they would like to achieve or change in their current situation. Our study made it clear that children are to some basic degree aware of their social marginalization, but need a crutch to be able to talk about it and verbalize how they feel about the limits of their opportunities. Visual education, the activity of drawing (Coles, 2003), gives them this crutch, as it has the potential to open a dialogue with one another and the teacher.

Both the pictures and children's explanations indicated the presence of a double value system (Phinney, 1990). This means that children proclaimed that the conditions of upward mobility and financial security were studying well and getting a job, which fulfills the norms and ideals of the majority society (i.e., individual success is dependent on the effort they make). However, they depicted and mentioned alternative ways of attaining financial success such as metal recycling, playing poker, receiving insurance payments for injuries, and child care allowances, which may be economic survival techniques they have observed at work in their communities. What this double value system indicates is that children are aware of the norms and values of the majority society, and are struggling to leverage mainstream norms and values toward success.

The values of the majority society may not serve as realistic bases of identity formation in a marginalized situation. The two different sets of norms and values are not simply different from one another, they are mutually exclusive. These children miss the connection or are not able to intuitively ascertain how a middle-class lifestyle and social integration can be achieved. The double value system is not an essential part of their culture, but the result of experiences of social marginalization is compounded by a reproduction of poverty and policies of majority institutions (school, municipality, media, etc.) that fail to recognize and account for the differing real-life experiences and lack of opportunities open to members of marginalized groups (Bass et al., 2007; Young, 1990). These children's efforts of masking marginalization and of reconciling the double value system indicate that, although these children are affected by their socially disadvantaged situation, they are actively seeking solutions and have not given up on the possibility of social mobility.

Implications for Art Education

Artmaking may present ways of reenvisioning and planning solutions to entrenched conditions. A series of case studies is presented by child psychiatrist Robert Coles (2003) about the strength of children in overcoming the difficulties presented either by the social environment (e.g., affected by the racial struggles of the '60s in the Southern US), immigration, segregation, or other social circumstances. Coles presents the long and difficult process of overcoming fear and anger and shows that drawing can be a helpful tool in this psychological process, as well as a good indicator of differing stages of healing.

Practices of art education might attend to how critical approaches to viewing images can help students make meaning of and successfully negotiate the world that surrounds them, and disentangle the multiple ways contemporary life is organized (Smith-Shank, 2011). The real message of education through art leads us to a wider context of the educational paradigm. The question of what to teach children cannot be passed by. Noddings (1995), for example, argues for the importance of learning how to live life instead of learning disciplinary contents. According to her, children have to be taught how to be useful, happy, and lovable members of their environment. Following her arguments, being able to reflect on one's own living circumstances, or more abstractly on one's social status, is inseparable from the skills and experiences of living life. Furthermore, working with children on the cognition and reflection of their world is not just a possibility but a must for visual culture art education. These children's drawings were testaments of deprivation and socio-economic situation, yet also evidenced the

power of visual art in revealing concealed understandings of a present reality, future possibility, and dreamed of or idyllic life. Follow-up classroom conversations and discussions suggested that idioms of social marginalization need not deny the possibility of positive identity development of children belonging to marginalized groups. Art educators have the potential to help children cope with their situation and find achievable ways of integrating into society. Through art images, art educators may engage children in conversations about the difficulties of psychological management of marginalization. They can employ approaches that encourage and support development of various social and cultural competencies. Through use of artistic models produced by people from many cultures, circumstances, and ways of life, they may engage children in deep conversations about how current conditions of exclusion might be bridged and how they might become empowered for lives of unlimited possibility. Finally, art educators might extend the effectiveness of in-class strategies by recognizing an obligation to find ways of cooperating with members of the culturally marginalized community, teachers of other subjects, school administrators, and policy makers in order to assist these children in imagining and realistically achieving the better futures they envision.

REFERENCES

Bass, L., Darvas, Á., & Ferge, Z. (2007). A gyermekszegénység elleni nemzeti program kimunkálása: A szegénységben élők helyzetének változása 2001 és 2006 között - különös tekintettel a gyermekes családokra. *"Legyen jobb a gyerekeknek!" Nemzeti Stratégia, 2007-2032* [National program against child poverty: Changing the circumstances of people, and especially families with children living in poverty between 2001 and 2006. *"Make it better for children!" National Strategy, 2007–2032*]. Budapest, Hungary: Miniszterelnöki Hivatal. Retrieved from https://hirkozpont.magyarorszag.hu/hatteranyagok/gyerekeknek

Baumann, G. (1996). *Contesting culture: Discourse of identity in multi-ethnic London.* Cambridge, MA: Cambridge University Press.

Beale Spencer, M., & Markstrom-Adams, C. (1990). Identity processes among racial and ethnic minority children in America. *Child Development, 61*(2), 290–310.

Berry, J. W. (1996). *Cross-cultural psychology: Research and applications.* Cambridge, MA: Cambridge University Press.

Breakwell, G. M. (1986). *Coping with threatened identities.* London, England: Methuen.

Brown, B. B. (2004). Adolescents' relationships with peers. In R. M. Lerner & L. Steinberg (Eds.), *Handbook of adolescent psychology* (pp. 363–394.) Hoboken, NJ: Wiley.

Camilleri, C., & Malewska-Peyre, G. (1997). Socialization and identity strategies. In J. W. Berry, P. R. Dasen & T. S. Saraswathi (Eds.), *Handbook of cross-cultural psychology, Vol. 2: Basic processes and human development* (pp. 41–67). Boston, MA: Allyn & Bacon.

Clark, G. (1989). Screening and identifying students talented in the visual arts: Clark's drawing abilities test. *Gifted Child Quarterly, 33*(3), 98–105.

Clark, K. B., & Clark, M. P. (1947). Racial identification and preference in Negro children. In E. Maccoby, T. Newcomb & E. Hartley (Eds.), *Readings in social psychology* (pp. 602–611). New York, NY: Holt, Rinehart and Winston.

Coles, R. (2003) *Children of crisis: Selections from the Pulitzer Prize-winning five-volume children of crisis series.* Boston, MA: Little, Brown and Company.

Comer, R. J. (2010). *Abnormal psychology.* New York, NY: Freeman & Company.

Denzin, N. K., & Lincoln, Y. S. (1994). *Handbook of qualitative research.* London, England: Sage.

Erikson, E. H. (1968). *Identity: Youth and crisis.* New York, NY: Norton.

Gerő, Z., Csanádi, G., & Ladányi, J. (2006). *Mobilitási esélyek és a kisegítő iskola* [Chances of Mobility and Special Education Schools]. Budapest, Hungary: Új Mandátum Kiadó. (Original work published 1978)

Golomb, C. (1981). Representation and reality: The origins and determinants of young children's drawing. *Review of Research in Visual Arts Education, 7*(2), 36–48.

Kellogg, R. (1969). *Analyzing children's art.* Palo Alto, CA: The National Press.

McEvilley, T. (1992). *Art and otherness: Crisis in cultural identity.* New York, NY: McPherson & Company.

National Development Agency. (2009). *Leghátrányosabb helyzetű kistérségek felzárkóztatási programja* [Compensatory program for the most disadvantaged regions]. Retrieved from www.nfu.hu/lhh

Noddings, N. (1995). A morally defensible mission for schools in the 21st century. *Phi Delta Kappan, 76*(5), 365.

Nunn, K., & Thompson, S. (1996). The pervasive refusal syndrome: Learned helplessness and hopelessness. *Clinical Child Psychology and Psychiatry, 1*(1), 121–132.

Pepitone, E. (1980). *Children in cooperation and competition.* Toronto, Canada: Lexington Books.

Phinney, J. S. (1990). Ethnic identity in adolescents and adults: Review of the research. *Psychological Bulletin, 108*(3), 499–514.

Read, H. (1955). Education through art: A revolutionary policy. *Art Education, 8*(7), 3–7.

Smith-Shank, D. L. (2011). Material culture and issues-based art education. In A. Kárpáti & E. Gaul (Eds.), *Art - space - education: Proceedings of the 33rd InSEA World Congress, Budapest, Hungary, 25–30th June 2011* [CD-ROM]. Budapest, Hungary: Hungarian Art Teachers' Association.

Stewart, M. S. (2001). Underclass, race and 'the Roma' in post-communist Eastern Europe. In C. Hann (Ed.), *Postsocialism: Ideals, ideologies and practices in Europe and Asia* (pp. 133–156). New York, NY: Routledge.

Szalai, J. (2005) A jóléti fogda [The welfare trap]. In M. Neményi & J. Szalai (Eds.), *A kisebbségek kisebbsége* [Minority of Minorities] (pp. 43–93). Budapest, Hungary: Új Mandátum Könyvkiadó.

Valsiner, J. (2000). *Culture and human development: An introduction.* London, England: Sage.

Veale, A. (2005). Creative methodologies in participatory research with children. In S. Greene & D. Hogan (Eds.), *Researching children's experience: Approaches and methods* (pp. 253–273). London, England: Sage.

Ward, T., Lelkes, O., Sutherland, H., & Tóth, I. G. (2009). *European inequalities: Social inclusion and income distribution in the European Union.* Budapest, Hungary: TÁRKI Social Research Institute.

Werner, E. E., & Smith, R. S. (2001). *Journeys from childhood to midlife: Risk, resiliency, and recovery.* Ithaca, NY: Cornell University Press.

Wright, M. O., Masten, A. S., & Narayan, A. J. (2012). Resilience processes in development: Four waves of research on positive adaptation in the context of adversity. In S. Goldstein & R. B. Brooks (Eds.), *Handbook of resilience in children* (2nd ed.) (pp. 15–38). New York, NY: Springer.

Young, I. M. (1990). *Justice and the politics of difference.* Princeton, NJ: Princeton University Press.

ENDNOTES

[1] All student anecdotes and direct quotes throughout this article are from the research field notes of the authors.

[2] We use the term *Roma*, as this is the most commonly used reference to this ethnic group in East Central Europe (in English). See: http://en.wikipedia.org/wiki/Romani_people

[3] Although the interviews and observations were both transcribed and analyzed, they do not compose part of the current chapter. Nonetheless, we occasionally refer to these results as well.

CHAPTER 24

Happiness and Sadness Depicted by Children of Immigrant, Migrant, and Cultural Minority Families

AVA SERJOUIE
Independent Art and Child Art Researcher and Artist

Immigration and migration are concerns of many contemporary educators. Due to various motivating conditions, many people are moving within countries and across national borders in search of new homes. Life in the new country or region is different in many respects from life in one's former homeland. Han (2000) believes that leaving all that is familiar to one and starting life in a new environment is like a break in the biography of one's life. Yet, people do not leave everything behind and begin entirely anew when they move from place to place. They bring first languages, customs, traditions, likes and dislikes, beliefs, and all that they have experienced in their homelands. While it may be difficult for migrating adults to learn a second language and adjust to different sociocultural contexts, it is also stressful for children of immigrant and migrant families, who must adapt to expectations of parents and elders from the Old World and requirements of fitting into a new social community.

I am interested in the extent to which children's emotional responses to differing circumstances of immigration versus migration might be similar or dissimilar, and as an art educator, I am interested in the extent to which these differences might be evidenced in children's drawings. Because I am an educator from an Iranian background, who is familiar with Iranian language (Farsi) and culture, I decided to examine differences between the drawings made by Muslim Iranian children who live with their families in Tehran; children whose parents are of an Iranian religious and ethnic minority group (and are therefore insulated within the mainstream Iranian society) or who migrated from one area of Iran to another; and the drawings of children of Muslim Iranian immigrants to a country with very different aesthetic, religious, and cultural traditions from those of the home country.

Children and Immigration, Migration, or Cultural Exclusion

For more than a century, children's works of art have been studied by psychologists, sociologists, and art educators for evidence regarding children's artistic cognitive growth and development (Gardner, 1973, 1980; Goodnow, 1977; Kellogg, 1969; Lindstrom, 1970; Piaget, 1969, 1977; Piaget & Inhelder, 1967, 1971). Also, several studies have provided insight about how children use symbols to express ideas about their everyday lives (Aronsson & Andersson, 1996; Aronsson & Junge, 2000; Wilson & Wilson, 1984; Winner & Gardner, 1981). However, children's drawings have rarely been explored as a means of understanding feelings about what it is like to negotiate differences between the cultural backgrounds inculcated by the child's parents and the sociocultural realities of their experiences outside the family. This understanding would be helpful to educators in planning programs and curricula to assist students from diverse cultural backgrounds, immigrant experiences, and migrant experiences to bridge old and new cultural circumstances.

I sought to compare the art and ideas of three small groups of 6- and 7-year-old children (six girls and six boys in total) who were all born to middle-class parents from Iranian backgrounds living as immigrants, long-term residents, or sequestered or migrant minorities within larger mainstream societies. The first group consisted of three children born to Iranian (Muslim) parents who had immigrated to and were living in Munich, Germany. These children visited a Saturday school to learn how to read and write Persian; it was in this school setting that I was able to work with them. The second group was comprised of six Muslim Iranian natives living in Tehran, who were attending summer classes in English and art.[1] The school administrators and teachers allowed me to work with this group of children after school.[2]

The third group included one boy whose ethnic (Kurdish) family had migrated from Northwest Iran to Tehran in search of employment and security, and two children from a Christian community within Tehran. Christians are a large minority in Iran who immigrated to Iran from Armenia more than four hundred years ago; however, due to their religious beliefs there is a cultural gap that still separates them from the Muslim majority. For this reason, the circumstances of these latter two children might be somewhat similar to that of migrants from one region to another, when the migrants' cultural traditions are distinguishably different from those of the entrenched society.

Since the Iranian revolution, Christians have been allowed to practice their religion and cultural traditions. It is forbidden, however, that they allow Muslims into their community, since this could be interpreted as proselytizing or trying to persuade Muslims to convert to Christianity. Nevertheless, through a trusted friend I was allowed into the Christian community and attended church prayers with them every Sunday, which gave parents time and opportunities to get to know, accept, and trust my intentions as a researcher. Eventually, I was given permission to visit their children's art and music class, which was conducted every Sunday by one of the parents while other adults attended Mass.

Methods

For this study, I worked with each child subject separately in one room for two sessions, while other children of their respective groups were taking English, art, or music lessons elsewhere. The focus of each session was on one of two drawing themes, *happiness* or *sadness*. For example, I would ask the child: "What makes you happy [or sad]? What is happiness [or sadness]? Why does that make you happy [or sad]?"

It was important to get psychologically close to each subject and establish a warm connection between us, so the child would feel safe about honestly expressing thoughts, feelings, or personal experiences of happiness or sadness. Therefore, because I was meeting most of these children for the first time, I arranged to interview them and have them produce their drawings in a school environment that was familiar to them. Some of the children might have felt cultural pressure to please me by saying or drawing that which they perceived me to want from them, and all were obliged to sit through a session, answer questions, and draw while having a video camera focused on them. Yet, nearly all the children appeared to respond comfortably to these unfamiliar situations; some even expressed joy at being photographed, or demonstrated other forms of appreciation for the special one-on-one attention.

Listening to and Looking at Children's Ideas

Neuß (1999) clearly emphasizes the importance of an interview or a dialogue with a child in conjunction with artmaking as a way of understanding the child's expressions. Trautner and Milbrath (2008) iterate the importance of observing the whole drawing process and making note of what the child says during drawing. Being interviewed before drawing prepares children to reflect upon what they intend to draw and how this might be visually represented in response to the interview; during the drawing process, nonverbal interpersonal communication and reflection upon the experience being described takes place (Neuß, 1999). Thus, dialogic conversation with children before and as they draw can grant us insight into the way they view their world; their ideas, feelings, and opinions of things happening around them; and what factors influence or affect their views.

Following my interview with each child, the child was asked to draw what he or she had described or explained during the interview. Children in all three groups were provided the same drawing materials, which were a

For Further Consideration

Serjouie found that the children from marginalized and/or migrant backgrounds whose families lived in close-knit communities within a larger (mainstream) national culture experienced human interactions and celebrations as primary sources of pleasurable situations, similar to their peers in the mainstream. Children of immigrant parents may have experienced situations of pleasure differently from their parents, and tend to be more materialistic than other groups of this study.

1. Discuss possible explanations for Serjouie's findings.

2. What other research supports or refutes Serjouie's findings?

3. What implications does this have for the art education of children from immigrant, migrant, or marginalized backgrounds?

4. What might be appropriate goals of art education for these students?

An Exploratory Activity

Invite students to explore how children in different parts of the world respond to a particular universal situation. Begin by having students chose a phenomenon that might be experienced as pleasurable by children within *any or all* culture communities—such as playing games, celebrating a wedding, eating a meal, singing or playing music, or helping with chores. Focus on situations whereby pleasure might derive primarily from either social interaction, acquisition of or interaction with an object, or from a solitary self-fulfilling activity.

Having determined the focusing topic, direct students to online galleries of child art, such as Artsonia,[1] Crayola Connects Us,[2] the International Children's Art Exhibition (ICAE),[3] or USSEA/InSEA Child Art Exchange,[4] where they might find examples of art by children from many regions of the world.

Many of the images posted on these sites were selected by teachers as examples of work in response to an assignment. For this reason, direct students to select no more than two student examples from a single school site or web page, but instruct students to find 10 to 20 works altogether from a variety of global locations (regions, nations, or cultures) from this or a combination of gallery sites. Download examples of artwork that focus on the selected topic, and include any pertinent information about the artist (i.e., location, age, title of the work, explanation of the work, etc.).

Looking at clues within the work, decide if the child artist visual describes the source of pleasure derived from the phenomenon as:

1. focusing on or resulting from *social interaction*;

2. based on acquisition of, interaction with, or possession of a *special object* or objects;

3. resulting from a *self-rewarding activity* such as singing or playing an instrument, playing a video game, reading, making art, or creating something; or

4. other (none of the above).

Organize all images into the above categories indicating the source of pleasure fulfillment. Then, examine information about the artists of the images. Add notations that indicate the national, regional (for example, rural, urban, tropical, or desert region—if known), or cultural background of the child artist.

Plot on a chart the countries or cultures of the child artist associated with each artwork and overlay this atop the works that have been organized into categorizes.

1. Do any patterns emerge from this exploration?
   - Do the children of some nations or cultures favor one type of relationship over another?
   - If so, what does this generally tell you about cultural experiences of children from these areas?
   - Are individuals within each country more alike than they are different, or more different that they are alike?

2. Prior to asking the children to draw, Serjouie interviewed the children who were the subjects of her study.
   - What information might interviews with child artists contribute to your understanding of the images you examined?
   - What questions might you ask children about their experiences—before or after they create their drawings—that would help you make meaning of these expressions?

3. How might child artists use artmaking as a focal point from which to engage children of other cultures in conversations about universally shared experiences?
   - What questions might child artists ask of one another before they create their artwork?
   - How might these questions be expanded by viewing the artworks of peers from other nations, regions, or cultures of the world?

Endnotes

[1] www.artsonia.com
[2] www2.crayola.com/theArtOfChildhood/gallery/
[3] www.pentel.com/icae
[4] www.insea.org/childartexchange.html

box of 24-color oil pastels and a blank white sheet of A3 paper. Each was told he or she could turn the paper in any direction that best suited the drawing theme. When it seemed appropriate, children were prompted by questions such as, "How would you like to draw what you described? What colors would you use?" Proceedings of the interviews and drawing sessions were videoed to examine nonverbal aspects of the child's behaviour, interactions between the child and me during the process, and as a reference during the analysis phase of the investigation. Observing the children while they were drawing granted me an opportunity to glimpse their thought processes without the pressure of verbal narratives. Listening to their explanations and conversations about their work contributed additional information to my investigation.

Looking at the Data

After conducting two interviews and collecting two drawings from each child, analysis followed a step-by-step procedure of coding and categorizing concepts that organized these data into content analytical units (Lichtman, 2006). Concept units were derived from an analysis of images, as well as information provided during the interviews and conversations during artmaking. They corresponded with the four qualitative categories suggested by Neuß (1999):

- *Representation*, which refers to the colors, lines, textures, and other formal qualities of the image.

- *Imagination and Fantasies* of the child as expressed through his drawing. In this study, the children's drawings were examined for evidences of cultural inferences that might have triggered their imaginative renditions.

- *Action and Communication*. Viewers tend to link single picture elements with one another to form a harmonious whole. However, before I could determine how or if certain visual elements had been linked together according to the intentions of the child, it was necessary to ask about what was happening in the child's picture from his or her perspective.

- *Symbolisation and Biographical Background*. This was determined from information the child provided verbally about his or her drawing and intentions. (p. 87)

Concept units were then examined in order to determine similarities and differences attributable to each child and all the children of each group.

Sadness and Happiness in the Life of a Child

Happiness and Sadness were chosen as themes to be addressed because these are human emotions that even very young children are likely to have experienced. Therefore, the subjects could reflect upon their personal experiences when speaking about or drawing examples of these themes. All the children who were living in Iran, regardless of their religious or ethnic backgrounds (i.e., Muslim, Kurdish, or Christian), mentioned shared family and community experience as conveying happiness. These included attending weddings (Figure 1), going out with others, visiting Mecca, or other religious or social events that occasioned interactions with family, relatives, or friends. They described doing things with one or more relatives and family members. In their interview responses, social and communal life was iterated as a core of happiness. On the other hand, when talking about sadness, all but two of these children (one girl and one boy) referred to personal experiences or the experience of being deprived of the company of loved ones. For example, sad themes included staying at home, not visiting grandmother, or the death of a family member (Figure 2). They interpreted happiness and sadness based on social interaction or social deprivation in context of family and human relationships. These children are used to growing up and living in close, supportive, and caring family units, and this was reflected in their verbal and visual expressions.

Figure 1. The drawing is by a 6-year-old Iranian girl living in Iran. The happiness theme shows her uncle's wedding. Included details are the bride and the bridegroom, a car on the left, and coloured bulb lamps on the top of the page. The child told stories about the bride's hairdresser and how the bride wore a tiara, but in the end, the child forgot to draw it. Iranian weddings are important, elaborately celebrated events.

Figure 2. The 6-year-old boy living in Tehran shows the burial of a family member as an example of what makes him sad. He had been to a burial and found it very sad; he paid attention to every detail of the event, such as the way Muslim women mourn.

Figure 3. A drawing by a 7-year-old Iranian girl living in Germany based on a theme of sadness shows that she is sad because her mother will not allow her to eat chocolate. Both figures are depicted wearing tiaras.

By contrast, the children of Iranian immigrants living in Germany mentioned *personal* experiences as sources of happiness, but did not make any reference to family members or relatives. Friends were mentioned but only in relation to one's self, such as in contexts of playing together. *Nature* and *things* were described as sources of happiness, as, for example, when a child stated that flowers made her happy. When talking about sadness, only one child referred to conflict or deprivation from social or communal life as a source of sorrow. In this instance, the child mentioned an argument with friends as a sad experience. All others of this group talked about obstacles to their personal desires as sources of sadness (Figure 3).

Although the sampling of children is too small to draw sweeping conclusions about this difference, it may be that, having little contact or losing contact altogether with relatives still living in Iran, the Iranian-German children may have replaced the comfort of human contact with comfort of things, or grown less dependent on families for emotional support. Additionally, due to their young age and lack of ability to communicate easily in the language of their host country, the children may not have had ample opportunities to connect with German children of their age. Therefore social life did not comprise the core of these children's joy, although discord with others might have triggered unhappy feelings.

This may be compared and contrasted to studies of German nationals, who generally place a very high value and status on friends and friendships. In an empirical emotion-study of happiness [or] "what makes [German people] happy" it was found that 54% of Germans associate happiness with interactions with friends. (Viviano, 2007). On the other hand, Pflug (2008) acknowledged that

> Most German respondents did not make explicit reference to their families in their essays, as according to them this has no prominent status in their social lives. A related point was made by some respondents who stated that they wanted to 'select' friends with whom they were 'in tune' (p. 557)

This conception of friendship stresses the flexible nature of social relations. Friends are chosen if they "fit with one's own character" (p. 557). In this sense, it may be that people living in Germany, which is a more capitalistic society than Iran[3] (Mayer, Albert, Trommsdorff, & Schwarz, 2005), may come to view friendships as commodities. Thus, it may be that children of Iranian immigrants to Germany, when talking about or referring to social life, were entering into and appropriating this aspect of the German culture.

Motifs and Symbols in Children's Drawings

Iranian children living in Tehran drew images of human figures, the sun, houses, cars, trees, flowers, and other symbols in ways that were descriptive of the national mainstream culture. For example, a car was shown decorated for a wedding (see Figure 1), and mountains, which can be seen to the North (Figure 4) by people living in Tehran, appeared in drawings by three Iranian children. Kaaba (Figure 5), the most important religious symbol for Muslims, was drawn by one of the boys.

Figure 4. A drawing by a 6-year-old boy from Tehran. He has drawn his grandmother. We see her wearing a scarf. On top of the page we see the mountains in the north of Tehran.

Figure 6. A drawing by a 7-year-old Kurdish boy living in Iran, showing sadness. The boy was saddened "when someone becomes a martyr." The evening prior to drawing this image, he had watched a television show about war.

who may have experienced sorrows of having lost family members or friends to martyrdom during earlier national conflicts; his references to these tragic events seem to have been inspired by images and media presentations of the subject.

Scenes drawn by children living in Iran also referenced elements and understandings of mainstream Iranian culture, such as a funeral scene drawn by one boy, which depicted the deceased person wrapped in a white cloth. He drew soil on both sides of the grave and showed people with hands raised to their faces. He said that the people in the drawing had come to cry. I asked him how a viewer might know this just by looking at the picture, and he pointed to the women's arms raised to their faces as signs of weeping (see Figure 2). This contradicts Golomb's (1992) conclusions that children of this age seldom describe emotion through gesture of body parts. She found that 1st graders in Western contexts expressed happiness by depicting faces with turned up lips or sadness by faces with turned down lips. Yet, the Muslim children living in Iran did not express emotion through curvature of lips, although one girl of this group drew tears as indication of sadness. On the other hand, expressing emotion through lips was seen among children from Iranian backgrounds who lived in Germany and among the Christian-Iranian children living in Tehran.

Figure 5. A 6-year-old boy living in Tehran explains that "visiting Kaaba with his family" makes him happy. Kaaba is the most important shrine for Muslims.

Tanks and aeroplanes were a reference to war and the unstable political situations of the Middle East. Although war has long been over between Iran and Iraq (1980–1988), murals of the martyrs and films about the war, as well as documentaries on the Iranian national TV, keep the memory of those sad days alive in the minds of the Iranian people. When talking about what makes him sad, a 7-year-old boy, who has never personally experienced war,[4] mentioned martyrdom as representing sadness (Figure 6). In response to my question regarding how he knows this, he explained that he had seen stories about martyrdom on national TV. Previous research has determined that children are sensitive to the political views of those around them, even when these are only indirectly articulated through nonverbal messages (Coles, 2000). Yet, this child gave no indication of having gained this knowledge from members of his Kurdish community,

Details that suggested attention to local culture by children living in Iran included colored light bulbs as decoration for weddings, and women shown with scarves, which referenced the traditional dress code of Islamic rule. Iranian-German children drew symbols of Western popular culture, such as princess-like crowns on the heads of two figures and a rainbow drawn to express intense feelings of happiness. One girl from this latter group eagerly described the figure of her St. Nicolas doll in great detail. St. Nicolas, who is a Christian and also German subject, was carefully included in both her happy and sad drawings (Figure 7 and 8). The reuse of Nicolas's image to communicate opposing emotions, however, did not suggest that the girl lacked flexibility in selecting motifs to convey her ideas. She was quite aware that her drawing was a means of transferring information to me. This was made evident when she drew one St. Nicolas image from the front and another from the back (Figure 9); she rationalized the lack of detail in the latter drawing by explaining that because she had drawn him once from the front, I should know what he looks like. She did not want to repeat what had already been visually articulated.

Depicting St. Nicolas may have been an example of this child's flexibility in adapting a Christian/German symbol for her own purposes. On the other hand, since St. Nicolas is depicted in visual form and story as a loving grandfather-figure who gives gifts of toys (i.e., *things* that are desired) to children; perhaps he was embraced as a metaphoric substitute for loss of cultural community (e.g., extended family) that the child unconsciously sensed but was unable to consciously articulate. The absence of support from elders of a close cultural community may have been replaced by a symbolic substitute that offers desirable things in place of real, caring social contact.

Evidence of a disconnect between her parent's and her own current cultural experiences also was suggested by this girl's clumsy efforts to draw a Persian carpet and her comment, "My carpet is very difficult, even adults can't draw it" (personal communication, n. d.). As a national-cultural group, Iranians are very proud of their carpets and almost every Iranian home includes a Persian (Iranian) carpet. This child mentioned and attempted to represent the carpet in both of her drawings, just as she had done with the Nicolas figure. Yet, she complained that she could not easily draw the carpet in her bedroom. The patterns on these carpets are complicated and require keen observation and concentration to be accurately copied. Drawing these patterns from memory would be exceedingly difficult. Her observation of the complexity of the carpet pattern and awareness of the way these artifacts are valued by the adults in the Iranian community may have intimidated her drawing efforts. She lives between two worlds, with symbols presented from both cultures in her life, and she was trying to bring these

Figure 7. A picture drawn by an Iranian girl living in Germany in response to a question about what makes her happy. She describes happiness as being able to play with her friends. Above the wardrobe she carefully colored an image of her St. Nicolas doll. Also she drew a green carpet on the floor but did not include the details of its pattern, saying these were too difficult even for adults to draw.

Figure 8. In the second session she drew St. Nicolas from the back and excluded all the details. This second drawing depicts a sad experience.

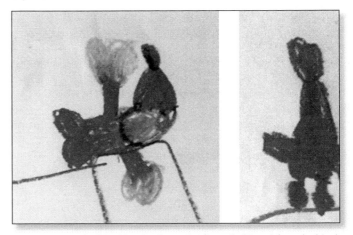

Figure 9. Detail of St. Nicolas from the front (left) and from behind (right).

cultural concepts together in her drawings. Because Persian carpets were uncommon in German homes or other building interiors, she may not have worked out an altogether satisfactory schema for their depiction. Additionally, she implicitly may have understood that remembered images of these artifacts had begun to fade for her parents and, like her, they also would have had difficulty replicating the carpet patterns.

Symbols and Signs in Relation to Sociocultural Environment

Some of the differences observed in the drawings of these three small groups of children may be attributed to the fact that children learn to draw from other children (Vygotsky, 1978). For example, the children of Iranian immigrants living in Germany may have indicated emotion through the facial feature of lips because children in Westernized cultures tend to draw smiling or frowning mouths on their figures. Also, Christian children living in Iran, who experience education in a different context than their Muslim peers, may have appropriated a more Westernized way of representing emotion, whereas Muslim children living in Iran may not have been socialized to draw in this way. Children, regardless of the cultural backgrounds of their parents, might learn and come to identify with the traditions and cultures to which they are exposed outside the family in their everyday lives. Therefore the boy who was born a member of a religious minority group living in Iran drew the Kaaba and an Islamic burial ceremony that is typical of Muslim Iranian culture. A girl who was born to and raised by Iranian immigrants living in Germany appropriated the German cultural motif of St. Nicholas—a grandfatherly figure who gives gifts of toys and other *things* to children—as her own. She frequently talked about her St. Nicolas doll. She drew the figure carefully and described him in verbal and visual detail. Yet, she declared a Persian carpet difficult to draw, due to its complex patterns. Neither she nor other children of her local (Iranian immigrant and German national) peer group have developed a schema sufficient to the task of accurately conveying a notion of this physical artifact.

Sources of Happiness and Sadness

In his studies of children living in traumatizing or economically impoverished situations, Coles (2003) found that poorer children were more likely to reference human interactions in their artwork than they were to describe material objects. Yet poverty may not be the only explanation for this phenomenon. Fazelli (2011), writing about happiness in Iran, declares that happiness has a different meaning in each social structure. He believes that middle-class families in Iran still enjoy performing religious ceremonies, participating in family gatherings, and engaging in social and cultural rituals. His conclusions were supported by the references of both groups of children who were from middle-class communities and living in Iran to religious ceremonies and family gatherings as sources of happiness. Also, they described sadness in relation to losing or being separated from social interactions with families and others of their community. Social closeness was an important factor in the emotional well-being of children who lived in Iran, regardless of whether they were offspring of parents from the mainstream community or of migrant or culturally segregated minority parents living within the majority Iranian society.

On the other hand, children of immigrant parents living in Germany did not seem to experience or value family ties or the local community bond as strongly as children living in Iran. This could be due to lack of contact with some family members who were still living in Iran or obstacles in developing close associations with peers in the host country, due to language deficits or perceived differences in appearance or cultural expressions. The Iranian-German children looked to outer things and inner desires as a means of constructing a place for themselves. In this matter Coles (in Woodruff & Woodruff, 1992, p. 58) stresses that children of immigrant parents, who frequently draw objects, might do so out of a need to recall people or objects that have been lost or that they fear losing. They also might flexibly mix second hand memories of their parents' homeland (as in the case of the attempt to include a Persian carpet in a drawing) with their own understandings of the immediate everyday world.

Conclusions and Implications

It is worth noting that children of this study did not necessarily behave in ways predicted by Golomb. Unlike her supposition that young children would not use bodily gesture to expression emotion, those living in Iran seemed quite able to do so. On the other hand, Coles' observation that immigrant children draw objects as substitutes for people or things that have been lost or left behind, and that second-hand memories become entangled or confused by current experiences, may have been borne out in the explanations and drawings by children of immigrant parents. This group of children described and presented acquisition or deprivation of *things* and *personal desires* as sources of *happiness* or *sadness*. In this case, children who—due to the immigration of their parents to a distance geographic and cultural place—did not experience a sense of belonging to large extended families or close knit communities, seemed to have substituted a valuing of things and personal fulfillment of desires for caring or cooperative interactions with others. On the other hand, it seemed evident that the support of caring extended families and communities, along with exposure to local media stories about histories of people like themselves, assisted children from the ethnically different or religiously isolated groups to experience a sense of cultural connection to those of the larger, national society.

Because this study included an overall sampling of only 12 children, no firm predictions of the behaviors of other children from other differing migrant, culturally marginalized, or immigrant children can be assumed. Because immigrating and migrating parents might bring culturally specific ways of understanding the world with them and pass these along to their children, and because they and their children may appropriate some cultural behaviors and beliefs of those in the new environment, the meanings each child makes of these circumstances will be unique. No content-specific curriculum might be designed that will fit the needs of *all* children of immigrant, migrant, or nonmainstream local communities.

Implications for art educators would focus on the importance of preparing classrooms as caring communities where teachers and children share images and stories with one another. While these experiences of dialogic communication are important to the well-being of all students, it is especially important to immigrant or migrant children who may have been cut off from close ties with extended families or find themselves torn between cultural customs carried over from previous family experiences, and unfamiliar or incongruent customs of their current everyday environments. Just as strong supportive family interactions seemed to aid children of marginalized groups living in Iran to make harmonious connections to the mainstream Iranian society, a supportive classroom might assist children of migrant or immigrant backgrounds to bridge differences between the cultural messages they receive from their families and those they are experiencing in the new environment.

Exposing children to a wide diversity of images depicting the human condition from many cultural points of view, and engaging children in conversations about the feelings of joy or sorrow these circumstances elicit, may assist children in making meaning of their own personal experiences and situating themselves in larger human landscapes. Additionally, instructing children in histories and traditions of cultural artifacts from their Old World *and* new world cultures (i.e., for example, Persian rug designs and St. Nicolas figures) may help children see why these were important to the people who have made and used them in the past, how meanings and purposes of artifacts may change over time, and the meanings these works may hold in the present.

Observations, comments, and drawings created by all the subjects of this study made it evident that young children have clear ideas about what situations produce feelings of happiness or sadness in their lives. They are observant of their surroundings and their contacts, and they bring these unique experiences and expressions with them into the art room. Symbols, themes, and motifs from their living environment are presented in their drawings; feelings about experiences are mentioned in their comments and also emerge in their drawn images as desires, thought, and feelings that they sometimes cannot articulate clearly in words. In order to understand the felt experiences of young students, teachers must observe their images and listen to the stories they tell about these pictures. Together, stories and images may enlighten teachers about effective ways of guiding students whose biographies have been broken or complicated by migration or immigration to make sense of and integrate differing cultural influences of their lives.

REFERENCES

Aronsson, K., & Andersson, S. (1996). Social scaling in children's drawings of class-room life: A cultural comparative analysis of children's drawings in Africa and Sweden. *British Journal of Developmental Psychology, 14*, 301-314.

Aronsson, K., & Junge, B. (2000). Intellectual realism and social scaling in Ethiopian Children's Drawings. In L. Linstrom (Ed.), *The cultural context: Comparative studies of art education and children's drawings* (pp. 135-159). Stockholm, Sweden: Stockholm Institute of Education Press.

Coles, R. (2000). *The political life of children*. New York, NY: Atlantic Monthly Press.

Coles, R. (2003). *Children of crisis*. New York, NY: Back Bay Books.

Fazelli, H. (2011). شادی در گذشته ایران باستان [Happiness in the Old Iranian culture]. Retrieved from www.mehremihan.ir/iranian-culture/976-shadi-iranbastan.html

Gardner, H. (1980). *Artful scribbles*. London, England: Norman.

Gardner, H. (1973). *The arts and the human development*. New York, NY: Wiley.

Golomb, C. (1992). *The child's creation of a pictorial world*. Berkeley: University of California Press.

Goodnow, J. J. (1977). *Children drawing*. Cambridge, MA: Harvard University Press.

Han, P. (2000). *Soziologie der migration: Erklärungsmodelle, fakten, politisch konsequenzen, perspektive* [Sociology of migration: Explanatory model, facts, political consequences, perspectives]. Stuttgart, Germany: Lucius & Lucius.

Kellogg, R. (1969). *Analysing children's art*. Palo Alto, CA: National Press Books.

Lichtman, M. (2006). *Qualitative research in education*. London, England: Sage.

Lindstrom, M. (1970). Children's art. Berkeley and Los Angeles: University of California Press.

Mayer, B., Albert, I., Trommsdorff, G., & Schwarz, B. (2005). Value of children in Germany: Dimension, comparison of generations, and relevance for parenting. In G. Trommsdorff & B. Nauck (Eds.), The value of children in cross-cultural perspective: Case studies from eight societies (pp. 43–65). Lengerich, Germany: Pabst Science Publishers.

Neuß, N. (1999). *Symbolische verarbeitung von fernseh erlbnissen in kinderzeichnungen: Eine empirische studie mit vorschulkindern* [Symbolic works from children's television watching experiences: An empirical study with pre-schoolers]. München, Germany: Kopäd.

Pflug, J. (2008), Folk theories of happiness: A cross-cultural comparison of conceptions of happiness in Germany and South Africa. *Social Indicator Research, 92*(3), 551–563.

Piaget, J. (1969). *The mechanisms of perception*. New York, NY: Basic Books.

Piaget, J. (1977). The role of action in the development of thinking. In W. F. Overton & J. Mac-Carthy Gallagher (Eds.), *Knowledge and development* (pp. 17–42). New York, NY: Plenum Press.

Piaget, J., & Inhelder, B. (1967). *The child's concept of space*. New York, NY: Norton.

Piaget, J., & Inhelder, B. (1971). *Mental imagery in the child*. New York, NY: Basic Books.

The World Bank. (2012). Doing business: Measuring business regulations. *Economy rankings*. Retrieved from www.doingbusiness.org/rankings

Trautner, H. M., & Milbrath, C. (2008). Children's knowledge about pictures, drawing, and art. In C. Milbrath & H. M. Trautner (Eds.), *Children's understanding and production of pictures, drawings, and art* (pp. 3–19). Boston, MA: Hogrefe.

Viviano. (2007). *Glücksstudie: Was Deutschland glücklich macht* [Happiness study: What makes Germany happy]. Retrieved from www.viviano.de/ak/Magazin-Partnerschaft-Ratgeber/glueecklich-9224.shtml

Vygotsky, L. S. (1978). *Mind in society: The development of higher psychological processes*. Cambridge, MA: Harvard University Press.

Wilson, B., & Wilson, M. (1984). Children's drawings in Egypt: Cultural style acquisition as graphic development. *Visual Arts Research, 10*, 13–26.

Winner, E., & Gardner, H. (1981). The art in children's drawings. *Review of Research in Visual Arts Education, 14*, 18–31.

Woodruff, J., & Woodruff, S. C. (Eds.). (1992). *Conversations with Robert Coles*. Jackson: University Press of Mississippi.

ENDNOTES

[1] In Iran children are separated into single sex schools right after kindergarten; therefore I had to visit both the boys' and girls' schools in order to have children from both genders as participants of this study.

[2] Since the revolution in 1979, Christians have gone to a separate school from Muslims.

[3] See also a 2012 report of global finance, which ranked Germany as 20th and Iran as 145th in terms of ease of doing business (i.e., business friendly) in the world (The World Bank, 2012).

[4] His family had come to Tehran in search of work. In Iran the memories of the war are kept alive by the films and documentaries that are shown on TV; also on the walls we see murals of the soldiers killed in war. The revolution took place 33 years ago and the conflicts go back to over 25 years ago at least. The boy was 7 at the time I did this research; just one day before our conversation and his drawing of themes based on happiness and sadness, he had seen a televised film about the war.

CHAPTER 25

Marginalized Roma Children:
Arts-Integration and Engagement With Learning

KATHLEEN HALL
Canadian International School of Egypt

The Roma are the largest ethnic minority in Europe. However, until recently, very little has been known about their history or culture. Among outsider members of dominant Western societies, *Gypsy* is a term that has been applied to the Roma. Originally it was a shortened version of the word *Egyptian*, in reference to the place from which the Roma were mistakenly believed to have migrated. Many Roma now consider the term Gypsy to present a negative stereotype of their culture, and prefer to be called Roma. The word *Roma* is an adapted word derived from *Dom*, which means "person" or "human being" in Sanskrit, a language of Northern India, from where the Roma actually originated (Lee, 2011). The Roma are descendents of the Rajput (sons of kings) warriors who left India in the 11th century AD (Rishi, 1996). Their migratory path wound through Russia, Eastern and Central Europe, then onward through other European countries to England and Ireland. The Roma language, derived from Sanskrit, has now been worked into its own and varied dialect, with many words and phrases adopted from other languages (Smith, 1997). The Roma have a rich culture resulting from centuries of being skilled artisans, craft persons, musicians, dancers, and storytellers. Throughout their nomadic past, much of Roma history was handed down from generation to generation as oral tradition; consequently until recently there has been little recorded history about the Roma.

The Roma Situation

Although historians now have a clearer idea of the origins of the Roma, they are currently "one of the most misunderstood, marginalized, and discriminated-against ethnic groups" in Europe (Tamas, 2001, p. 1). Many Roma suffer extreme poverty, living in mahalas (quarters or neighborhoods) within makeshift houses without water, electricity, or sewage; they experience high unemployment and lack of health care, and often their children are denied rights to public education. These conditions of poverty are a direct result of centuries of discrimination carried over into contemporary society. Roma living in East-Central Europe have frequently endured attacks against their persons and neighborhoods, which authorities have failed or been unwilling to prevent (Gokcen, 2011; Hungarian Watch, 2011; Silverman, 1995/2010). Consequently many Roma children live unsettled lives and have known the effects of prejudice and discrimination from early childhood; in many cases it has severely diminished their educational experiences and opportunities. Those Roma children who attend school in their country of origin may be treated poorly by prejudiced classmates, teachers, and educational systems that segregate them and put them in classes designated for the mentally challenged (Greenberg,

2010). Many Roma parents feel reluctant to send their children to school, perceiving it as "a hostile place that offers little of value for their children" (UNICEF, 2011, p. 21). Roma children who immigrate with their families to North America may also face social and educational challenges. Often these children enter schools in Canada or the United States dispirited and manifesting low self-esteem, with little confidence in their own academic abilities. Children of Roma refugee families may live in constant fear of being sent back to their countries of origin, and therefore may not feel an urgency to attend school, or may attend irregularly. Authors of a report on Roma refugee families in Hamilton, Ontario, Canada (Walsh, Este, Krieg, & Giurgiu, 2011) write, "The problems Roma refugees have with establishing relationships with institutional systems must be understood within the context of their long history of racism, marginalization and social exclusion… Roma culture features a mistrust of institutional systems and doubts about provider compassion and competence" (Walsh et al., 2011, p. 9). With many Roma coming to Canada and the United States as refugees seeking asylum from grave poverty and life threatening persecution, it is important for North American educators to gain an understanding of the Roma and be sensitive to the cultural and psychological needs of Roma children who are enrolled in their schools. Building trust is essential, for without it, very little engagement with the teacher, peers, or learning environment will occur.

Arts-Integrated Learning and Best Practices in Roma Education

My study of Roma culture and experiences in working with Roma children in Kosovo became the foundation on which I have based research into arts-integrated learning as best practices in education for marginalized Roma children. While a graduate student at the University of Victoria (British Columbia, Canada), I had the opportunity to become involved with an educational program for Roma children who were living in Kosovo. Balkan Sunflowers (BSF) is a non-governmental organization (NGO) that came to help Roma, Ashkali,[1] and Egyptian (RAE) children after the Kosovo war of 1999. They provide out-of-school educational support to help marginalized children in the surrounding communities of Prishtina, Kosovo. Children come to the centers for preschool, language club, homework help, enjoyment and support, lunch, and school materials. Through the support of BSF, school dropout rates among these young people are reduced, children gain confidence as learners (Figures 2 and 3), and parents are given the opportunity to learn about the value of school (Figure 4).

Figure 1. School House, Gračanica, Kosovo. Photo by Kathleen Hall.

Figure 2. Guided imagery painting, Gračanica, Kosovo. Photo by Kathleen Hall.

Figure 3. Children and their paintings, Shtime, Kosovo. Photo by Kathleen Hall.

Figure 4. Roma parents attend their children's art show, Plemetina, Kosovo. Photo by Kathleen Hall.

As a volunteer instructor for the program, I drew upon my background as an art educator to develop an art curriculum to be used in their summer program, which was implemented by BSF youth leaders who were older teenagers who themselves had benefitted from BSF educational programs. I initially had very little knowledge about RAE peoples, Kosovo, the language or background experiences of the children involved, or the educational difficulties they faced. I found that most of the children enrolled in the summer program were engaged, attentive, and had some self-confidence in their abilities. Their lives of poverty did not seem to dim a bright enthusiasm for learning. Yet, I was soon to learn that this enthusiasm for learning was atypical for many Roma children and, in this case, was likely due to the fact that these children did not experience discrimination, abuse, or segregation at the centers, but were accepted members of the learning environment. They were trusted, and they trusted the leaders and educators in return. Children voluntarily came to the centers every day and were actively involved in the activities offered there; they were engaged with and experiencing success with learning. Coming to know that this learning

For Further Consideration

1. When teaching about other cultures, what strategies might you use to verify the cultural information you are presenting?

2. Identify and reflect on three main issues that might challenge Roma students' learning in traditional classroom settings.

   - To what extent do you think that these issues are specific to Roma populations, versus other cultural groups that may be marginalized or discriminated against by a hegemonic mainstream society?

   - Discuss how the "Human Relations" theory might be used in a classroom to support learners from Roma or other students from marginalized cultural backgrounds.

3. Discuss and evaluate why Jan Sajko's visual art program was successful in engaging Roma students with learning.

   - What can be concluded about the most important factors contributing to the educational success of Roma students?

4. What images or artifacts might people who have experienced attacks against their persons and/or neighborhoods use to communicate with authority groups, policy makers, or others, in order to attract attention, open conversations, and ameliorate situations?

   - What messages would they convey?

   - How might dialogue between marginalized and mainstream cultural entities be invited in a way that would assure or increase possibility of mutual participation?

5. Brainstorm ways that members of isolated, socioeconomically disadvantaged or marginalized groups might gain access to, participate in, and become a visible presence in global contexts. Consider the role art education might play in this process.

6. **Studio Activity:** Using cultural variance, develop a studio activity that goes beyond merely celebrating The Other by inviting dialogue between marginalized and mainstream cultural entities.

environment was in direct contrast to what most Roma children experience in traditional school settings throughout many East-Central Europe led me to some thoughts that formed the basis of my inquiry into ways of addressing the needs of marginalized Roma children in traditional classroom settings. Reflecting upon the mainly arts-based structure of the summer program, and the inclusive, accepting culture of the learning centres, I began to consider how arts-based education and other strategies would help Roma children successfully engage with learning.

Roma Culture and the Arts

From my observations and experiences in working with Roma children, I have concluded that a primary challenge for educators is to find ways to engage children of this little-understood and severely marginalized group in learning that is in accord with their cultural experiences. Roma children are generally quite knowledgeable about their customs and traditions by the time they reach school age. They have been culturally educated by observing adults in their community and being actively involved with community life (Enguita, 2004; Levinson, 2005; Monaci, Trentin, Zanon, & De Lumè, 2006; Tauber, 2004). Prior to the mid- to late-20th century, Roma children grew up knowing the arts as an integral part of their community life; visual art (traditional crafts and material culture), music, and dance were integrated with and almost inseparable from everyday life. A life rich in these traditions still remains for many Roma families and communities, but poverty is so entrenched in some severely economically disadvantaged Roma communities that traditional arts activities, except perhaps music and dance, are no longer commonly practiced. It also has been difficult for Roma visual artists to emerge in contemporary society due to the fact that "no attention is usually paid to artistic skills of children in the Romani families bringing up a lot of children and often struggling to make ends meet. Hence the children's talent that is not nurtured is gradually stunted and wasted" (Museum of Romani Culture, 2010, para. 11). Additionally, traditional curriculum models[2] adhered to by many East-Central European schools do not support arts education, and policymakers—who largely consist of people from dominant sociocultural groups—do not consider support of Roma culture an educational priority. In rare instances when individual art educators develop programs that respect the customs and traditions of Roma cultures, however, the expressive abilities and artistic skills of Roma children flourish.

In Slovakia, art teacher Jan Sajko developed a unique and exemplary art program in a school for Roma children. The program, which does not follow a traditional Slovakian curriculum, has been hugely successful and has gained international acclaim. Sajko understood that "these children need more individual attention," and urged teachers to "work with them from their starting place… using their experiences and points of reference as themes… [There is] great scope for drawing on the richness of Romany culture" (Figure 4). Through his visual art program, Sajko teaches lessons in "Romany history, traditional crafts, and musical instruments… [and] students are invited to illustrate Romany songs and folk tales" (Sajko, 2000, para. 2).

Jan Sajko developed an original teaching methodology for the Roma children in his school by encouraging the students to draw upon the experiences of their real life situations, by communicating with his students about their lives and culture, and through the use of playful activities that encouraged the students' creative responses to art (Figure 5) (Europa, 2009). Sajko's methodology helps to "release the artistic potential of Roma children and develop their personality" (Europa, 2009, p. 2). The children's artworks from Jan Sajko's program are exquisite; their visual stories of Roma culture offer profound insights into the lives of Roma children (Figures 6 and 7). Although Sajko's art program in Slovakia is an exception in East-Central Europe, it is proof of the great power of visual art for Roma children to experience engagement with learning through connections with their inner, creative selves and their rich, cultural heritage.

Two Canadian Programs Using Arts-Integration With Roma Children

My interest in working with Roma students led me to investigate two Canadian educational programs that point to arts-integrated learning as best practices in education for marginalized Roma children. Both programs were developed in the large and culturally diverse city of Toronto. One program is called "LEAP" and addresses the considerable gaps in refugee children's learning that are attributable to such factors as: discrimination, war, migration, or personal psychological or situational factors. The second program, "Roma Experience" curriculum, was developed to teach both Roma and non-Roma students about the cultural heritage of the Roma, educate about similarities and differences, erase stereotypes, and dispel feelings of mutual distrust or intolerance. When paired with Human Relations approaches to instruction, these programs have been found to be an effective means of assisting immigrant Roma children's educational progress.

Figure 5. Student work from http://ematusov.soe.udel.edu/jano. Used with permission of Jan Sajko.

Figure 6. Pupils working together on the big size portrait/paper collage—workshop—Stobrawa. From http://128.175.34.249/ RomaArt/Photos%202004/Forms/slideshow. aspx?ViewStyle=slideshow. Used with permission of Jan Sajko.

Figure 7. Cinka Panna, teamwork (12–14). From http://ematusov. soe.udel.edu/jano. Used with permission of Jan Sajko.

The LEAP Program

LEAP (Learning Enrichment Academic Program) was developed by The Toronto District School Board (TDSB) in response to the influx of immigrant and refugee children who arrive in Canada with considerable gaps in their learning. Some of the contributing factors to the educational limitations of LEAP students have been due to life experiences that may have limited their access to formal education due to distance, war, migration, or personal factors (Regier, Goossen, DiGiuseppe, & Campey, 2005). While LEAP was not specifically developed as an arts-integrated program, I was directed to an exemplary LEAP teacher, Susan Heagy,[3] who uses the arts and visual art in particular to engage her students with learning.

The LEAP class that I observed was in an elementary school located in one of Toronto's poorest and most culturally diverse neighborhoods. Children attending this school come from over 200 different countries; many speak first languages other than English. Several students, including the Roma children, are refugees.

In the LEAP class that Susan Heagy teaches, there are typically 12 to 14 students per year. Prior to their involvement in LEAP, the students are tested for multiple intelligences and their preferred learning modes are identified. Heagy is then able to consider what manner of teaching will best suit the child's learning needs. Thereafter, the children are brought together in a learning environment that features trust, respect, laughter, and encouragement of individual creativity and uniqueness, with the use of "differentiated instructional strategies" to accommodate individual learning styles (S. Heagy, personal communication, November 14, 2011); visual images and artmaking activities also are used as a means of engaging all students with learning.

For one of their first lessons, students are invited to draw upon their own cultural knowledge in creating an artwork, and share this with other students. In this way students identify the similarities and differences among the diversities of their cultural experiences and become aware that perhaps they are more alike than different. Art is used extensively to teach concepts in science and math (Figures 8 and 9), encourage language and literacy (Figure 10), and as a stand-alone subject where children learn about art terminology and artists while developing their aesthetic abilities. All students are engaged in class projects that focus on teaching the prescribed grade level curriculum. While the class itself is comprised of students from different countries and cultural backgrounds, aspects of multicultural education such as respect for diversity, promoting human rights, and equality are not taught as separate subjects but are dealt with constantly throughout the day, as Heagy targets teachable moments when these issues present themselves within the class. Heagy also models the respectful behavior she expects of the students, and takes every opportunity to point out to students how their actions and attitudes affect

Figure 8. A boy explaining his painting of Gears and Motion (Susan Heagy's class). Used with permission.

Figure 9. Roma children studying gears in Susan Heagy's classroom. Used with permission.

Figure 10. A boy's painting is inspired by a study of gears and pulleys. Used with permission.

others. Her students quickly learn that expected behaviors within the class include tolerance, acceptance, and mutual respect.

At the conclusion of the school year, Roma students in Susan Heagy's arts-enriched LEAP class, which I observed as a site of a research investigation, had measured learning gains in language and numeracy consistent with the other minority children within the class. Language gains were assessed using the *Burns Roe Informal Reading Inventory* (see Roe & Burns, 2010)[4] for word recognition/accuracy and comprehension. The Roma students all progressed one grade level on the Burns Roe scale, which is significant considering that among all these students, English was not their first language. Numeracy was measured for knowledge of computation, and on average the Roma students gained 2.5 grade levels (Heagy, personal communication, July 22, 2012).

While it appears the differentiated instructional strategies and integrative arts approach to curriculum promoted by LEAP addressed the academic needs of the students, it is difficult to discern if the arts-enriched program was solely responsible for the gains measured in the Roma students' learning. Nevertheless, both Edwin Ziegfeld and Viktor Lowenfeld (see Corwin, 2001), among others, laid out a strong case for the democracy-shaping benefits of art education and described ways it supports appreciation of one's own culture and the cultures of others. Heagy's successful approach to instructing children of Roma and other immigrant backgrounds was based on modeling fairness and acceptance in her daily interactions with the class, and making students aware of their behaviors in terms of tolerance and respect for the human rights of others. This approach aligns with what Sleeter and Grant define as the "Human Relations" theory of multicultural education; the "goals of this approach are to create positive feelings among students and erase stereotypes, thus promoting unity and tolerance in a society composed of different people" (Sleeter & Grant, 2007, p. 77). Human Relations theory focuses on the affective level and is aimed at helping students to feel good about themselves and their own cultural background, while learning to communicate with and accept others who come from different cultural groups. Group learning is often used by Human Relations educators; as the students work together on various cooperative learning projects they learn more about each other and begin to understand people who are different from themselves, which helps to challenge stereotypes (Sleeter & Grant, 2007). Heagy often uses group work within her classroom to encourage collaboration and help students to work cooperatively with each other and assist each other in achieving academic goals. However, the ground rules of respecting each other's opinion and allowing each other's voice to be heard are clearly established prior to working together on learning projects.

The "Roma Experience" Curriculum

Another program used by the TDSB for the education of Roma students was the "Roma Experience," which consisted of a curriculum specifically designed in response to an influx of Roma students into the district. Because teachers and students were unfamiliar with the Roma people and had very little knowledge of their history or culture, members of the TDSB Equity Department, with the assistance of members of the Toronto Roma Community Centre, put together a curriculum that introduced both Roma and non-Roma students to the unique and often unknown heritage of the Roma Nation (Toronto District School Board, 2000). Through the use of visual art, photography, music, poetry, stories, and drama, students gained a basic understanding of the Roma experience. The curriculum also focused on human rights issues through the introduction and study of *The Universal Declaration of Human Rights* (United Nations, 1948) and *The Declaration of the Rights of the Child* (United Nations, 1959).

The learning experience concluded with a mural, which was created by the children in collaboration with a visiting Roma artist, Lynn Hutchinson Lee. The mural presented the children's perspectives and understandings of Roma life and history in relation to issues of human rights. Thus, the arts became the vehicle through which both Roma and non-Roma children learned about Romani history and culture and were able to develop empathetic connections with one another. While there were no formal assessments of the learning experience from the Roma curriculum, teachers indicated that both they and the students gained a greater understanding and appreciation of Roma culture, and the violation of human rights issues that Roma people have been battling for centuries. Powerful images presented in the curriculum and created by the children in their collaborative artwork was a very effective way to help students engage with learning, both on affective and cognitive levels (Lynn Hutchinson Lee, personal communication, February 27, 2012).

Multicultural education and critical consciousness. The TDSB Roma Curriculum could be defined as a "Single-Group Study" in multicultural education, where the aim is to "empower oppressed groups and develop allies" (Sleeter & Grant, 2007, p. 111). By focusing on the history of the Roma people through human rights issues, and their cultural strengths, students gain a sense of what Paulo Friere calls "critical consciousness," and "as students learn about their group, they grow in pride and knowledge about themselves, and as others learn about their group, they too, will change in relationship to their new knowledge" (Sleeter & Grant, 2007, p. 123).

Research Studies: Support for Arts-Integrated Learning

Three recent studies, one from Canada and two from the United States, discuss the benefits of learning through the arts, with two revealing the significance of arts-integrated learning for marginalized students. A study conducted in Canada, *Learning Through the Arts: Lessons of Engagement* (Smithrim & Upitus, 2005), documented the academic benefits gained by students involved in a 3-year arts-integrated program; the study concluded with the statement: "Our analysis provided strong indications that involvement in the arts went hand-in-hand with engagement in learning at school" (p. 120). The longitudinal study determined that an arts education approach increased student engagement in school, and speculated that the general academic gains which apparently resulted may have been due to a greater sense of attention to learning that was developed through the students' experiences with arts education.

An American study funded by the U.S. Department of Education: Arts in Education Model Development and Dissemination Program, *Rochester Arts Impact Study 2006–2009* (United States Department of Education, 2010), also documents the effects of arts-integrated learning, citing increases in academic achievement and engagement with learning, with the greatest improvement in learning and engagement occurring among younger students, those with disabilities, English language learners, and students living in communities marked by severe poverty (United States Department of Education, 2010).

A study titled "A+ Schools: North Carolina's Experiment with Art in Education" (Thomas & Arnold, 2011) explored the effects of an instructional model that employed "innovative interdisciplinary teaching strategies using creative projects and activities to stimulate learning" (p. 96). The model drew upon Howard Gardner's "Multiple Intelligence Theory" and other research done by Eisner,

Efland, and Duncum, which support the use of the arts in developing cognitive abilities. Although no significant improvements in academic development were evidenced in the testing of students as a result of the application of this model, researchers felt that "students may experience an intangible benefit that is not immediately discernible in the EOG [End of Grade test]" (Thomas & Arnold, 2011, p. 102). The "intangible benefit" was a positive interaction between the cognitive and affective domains.

These three studies lend some support for the use of arts-integration as a curriculum model for Roma education, as Roma students are typically English language learners, experience high poverty, and have difficulty engaging with learning. The number one measurable benefit of learning through the arts in all three of the studies was the engagement with learning that marginalized students, in particular, experienced. Teachers involved in teaching immigrant Roma and non-Roma children through LEAP and the "Roma Experience" curriculum described the students as being actively engaged with learning through art, becoming aware of human rights issues, and developing greater appreciation and tolerance for cultural differences. Learning through the arts engaged multiple intelligences and emotional learning, and it is possible that greater motivation for learning in general was developed, as learning in one area overlapped into other areas. This greater motivation for and engagement with learning seemed the predominant observable academic effect of arts-integrations in both LEAP and the "Roma Experience Curriculum" programs.

Conclusion

I am not suggesting that visual art education, artmaking experiences, or integrative art curricula alone are the answer to solving all the challenges of Roma education, such as negative stereotypes, false perceptions, and rampant discrimination. However, practices of art education within an arts-integrated curriculum are useful tools for encouraging positive experiences that foster imminently necessary cultural understanding.

> Given the challenges of a diverse global civilization, the opportunities provided by art education to expand students' cultural horizons can help to bridge a cultural or generational divide, deepen their comprehension of world history and events, and foster empathy and communication amongst diverse groups. (Thomas & Arnold, 2011, p. 103)

Modelling and treating children with respect sets the tone for a culturally sensitive classroom: Presenting art education through lesson content that engages children

with the art of their own and others' cultures through the making and sharing of personally expressive art, and through creating art in collaborative contexts, helps to develop attitudes of tolerance and deep appreciation for one's own and other cultures. The teaching strategies that both Jan Sajko and Susan Heagy use with their students embody building trust and mutual respect through personal communication and sensitivity to students' cultural backgrounds. Their approach is not a celebration of Otherness so much as it is an acknowledgment that all students have diverse ways in which they learn, influenced by their personal life experiences and cultural backgrounds. This strategy also encourages the sense of community, which John Dewey (1916) described as a goal of education. By enabling students as a community of people who live, learn, and support one another's artistic expressions and academic achievements, the structure may become a process that empowers these students to work together toward positive goals in their everyday lives. Additionally, programs such as LEAP and the "Roma Experience" curriculum, while encouraging academic success, more specifically help to develop a sense of self-empowerment and self-voice amongst Roma children. In return, these children feel valued and valuable and are more likely to succeed academically, if for no other reason than they gain a sense of hope that academic knowledge may benefit them in the future.

Thus, it is my belief that cultural sensitivity arts-integrative approaches would help both Roma and non-Roma children come to honor and appreciate one another's cultural experiences and would facilitate a positive educational environment wherein they may come to experience greater academic successes in school and more harmonious interactions within the mainstream society.

ACKNOWLEDGMENTS

I would like to thank Gina Csanyi-Robah and Susan Heagy for facilitating my research and sharing their time and knowledge with me. Through their compassion and dedication, both of these women are improving the lives of marginalized children.

AUTHOR NOTES

Excerpts in this chapter have been previously published in: Hall, K. (2011). The Roma: Education and Marginalization. *BCATA Journal for Art Teachers, 53*(2), 46–51.

Throughout this chapter, the term "arts-integration" (and its interchangeable terms such as "arts-enriched" or "learning through the arts") refers to curriculum that includes teaching through one or more of the arts: visual, theatre, dance, music.

REFERENCES

Corwin, S. K. (2001). *Exploring the legends: Guideposts to the future*. Reston, VA: National Art Education Association.

Dewey, J. (1916). *Democracy and education: An introduction to the philosophy of education*. New York, NY: Macmillan.

Enguita, M. F. (2004). School and ethnicity: The case of Gypsies. *Pedagogy, Culture & Society, 12*(2), 201–216.

Europa. (2009). Arts in a Roma school (Slovakia). In *Compilation of Good Practice on Fostering Creativity and Innovation in the fields of Learning and cultural awareness*. Retrieved from www.create2009.europa.eu/fileadmin/Content/Downloads/PDF/Projects/National_projects/SK_Arts_in_a_Roma_school.pdf

Gokcen, S. (2011, October 11). Ukranian police must stop targeting Roma. *European Roma Rights Centre*. Retrieved from www.errc.org/article/ukrainian-police-must-stop-targeting-roma/3937

Greenberg, J. (2010). Report on Roma education today: From slavery to segregation and beyond. *Columbia Law Review, 110*(4), 919–1001.

Hall, K. (2011). The Roma: Education and marginalization. *BCATA Journal for Art Teachers, 53*(2), 46–51.

Hungarian Watch. (2011, March 18). *Roman citizens under Neo-Nazi siege: So where's the press?* Hungarian Watch Archives. Retrieved from http://hungarianwatch.wordpress.com/2011/03/18/neo-nazis-terrorize-roma-in-hungarian-village

Lee, R. (2011). *Roma self identity*. Retrieved from www.romatoronto.org/facts_identity.html

Levinson, M. P. (2005). The role of play in the formation and maintenance of cultural identity: Gypsy children in home and school contexts. *Journal of Contemporary Ethnography, 34*(5), 499–532.

Monaci, M. G., Trentin, R., Zanon, O., & De Lumè, F. (2006). Scholastic integration of gypsies in Italy: Teachers' attitudes and experience. *School Psychology International, 27*(1), 79–103.

Museum of Romani Culture. (2010). *Roma visual arts in the former Czechoslovakia* (Translated from Czechoslovakian). Retrieved from www.rommuz.cz/en/visual-art/

Regier, S., Goossen, T., DiGiuseppe, M., & Campey, J. (2005). *Renewing Toronto's ESL Programs… charting a course towards more effective ESL program delivery*. A Report from the Community Social Planning Council of Toronto 2005.

Rishi, W. R. (1996). *Roma: the Panjabi emigrants in Europe, Central and Middle Asia, the USSR and the Americas*. Patiala, India: Punjabi University.

Roe, B., & Burns, P. C. (2010). *Informal reading inventory: Preprimer to twelfth grade*. Belmont, CA: Wadsworth.

Sajko, J. (2000). *Notes on the experiences of a Slovak art teacher in a Romany school*. Retrieved from http://ematusov.soe.udel.edu/jano/#_Toc491628113

Silverman, C. (2010, March 19). *Persecution and politicization: Roma (Gypsies) of Eastern Europe* [Article reprinted from (1995, Summer). *Cultural Survival Quarterly, 19*(2)]. Retrieved from www.culturalsurvival.org/publications/cultural-survival-quarterly/albania/persecution-and-politicization-roma-gypsies-eastern

Sleeter, C., & Grant, C. (2007). *Making choices for multicultural education: Five approaches to race, class, and gender*. Hoboken, NJ: John Wiley & Sons.

Smith, T. (1997). Recognising difference: The Romani 'Gypsy' child socialisation and education process. *British Journal of Sociology of Education, 18*(2), 243–256.

Smithrim, K., & Upitis, R. (2005). Learning through the arts: Lessons of engagement. *Canadian Journal of Education/Revue canadienne de l'éducation. 28*(1/2), 109–127.

Tamas, J. (2001). A hidden minority becomes visible: Romani refugee children in the schools. *Childhood education*. Retrieved from FindArticles.com: http://findarticles.com/p/articles/mi_qa3614/ is_200101 /ai_n8947775

Tauber, E. (2004). Sinti Estraixaria children at school or, how to preserve 'the Sinti way of thinking.' *Romani Studies, 14*(1), 1–23.

Thomas, R., & Arnold, A. (2011). The A+ schools: A new look at curriculum integration. *Visual Arts Research, 37*(1), 96–104.

Toronto District School Board. (2000). *The Roma experience: Curriculum unit for the junior level*. Toronto, Canada: Toronto District School Board, and The Roma Community and Advocacy Centre.

UNICEF. (2011). *The right of Roma children to education: Position paper*. Retrieved from www.unicef.org/ceecis/UNICEF_ROE_Roma_Position_Paper_Web.pdf

United Nations. (1948). *The universal declaration of human rights*. Retrieved from www.un.org/en/documents/udhr

United Nations. (1959). Declaration of the Rights of the Child. *UN General Assembly Resolution 1386*. Retrieved from www.un.org/cyberschoolbus/humanrights/resources/child.asp

United States Department of Education. (2010). *Rochester arts impact study 2006–2009*. Arts in Education Model Development and Dissemination Program.

Walsh, C., Este, D., Krieg, B., & Giurgiu, B. (2011). Needs of refugee children in Canada: What can Roma refugee families tell us? *Journal of Comparative Family Studies, 4*(4), 599–613.

ENDNOTES

1. An Albanian-speaking ethnic minority of Kosovo and Albania.

2. To clarify and make distinct what is meant by "traditional school" and "traditional methods of teaching" in East-Central European countries I am referring to both the structure of classrooms that have rows of desks and limited student movement, accompanied by the delivery of curriculum that tends to be teacher-centered and rote-learning-based, as well as the traditionally discriminatory views of the Roma that are held within education.

3. All quotes and information from Susan Heagy were in the form of personal communications, September 2011–July 22, 2012.

4. www.learnalberta.ca/content/ieptLibrary/documents/RATI_burns_and_roe.pdf

CHAPTER 26

Cultural Myth and ACT-E:
Reclaiming One's Past and Present Identity for a Future World

LORI SANTOS
Utah Valley University

Soul and face and body, words and action contribute to our identity. We invent ourselves. We are invented by others. I'm not sure what I look like; I just know I don't look like "one," at least according to cultural definitions of what constitutes "Indianness." (Merskin, 1996, p. 281)

The question "Who am I?" is something to which we can all relate. Today's youth encounter multiple past and present influences that impact the sense of self or identity they will carry with them into the future. While students consciously align most with the present—often without questioning how and why their concepts of identity have come to be—it is by looking into the past and toward the future that art educators have the opportunity to engage students in active processes of identity construction.

This chapter draws upon the work of Michael Kabotie (Hopi) to explain a culturally sensitive approach to art education curriculum design. The aim of the approach is to stir awareness, engage critique, transform imagination, and empower students through discourse about how cultural myth and story inform past and present identity, and project a future identity. By modeling the approach, my preservice art education students were able to move past paradigmatic thinking about Native[1] art and cultures while broadening understanding of their own cultural identities. Consequently, they were able to apply the design when developing art curriculum units for secondary-level students that focused on images of culture and cultural identity in global contexts.

Art, Artists, and Art Education of Living Cultures

Cultural imaging is a serious concern of art education. Bringing students to recognize authentic representations of diverse cultures is not achieved by merely assigning process-based art projects, with the assumption that global awareness will be stimulated through incidental exposure to diverse cultural arts or crafts. Such practices rely on a heroes and holidays curriculum approach that trivializes cultural understanding and emphasizes a Eurocentric lens (Banks, 2000). This approach does little to bring students to an understanding of culture within a dynamic of contemporary life experience. Furthermore, popular art lessons such as creating cardboard Indian shields or toilet paper kachina dolls[2] do not teach meaningful relationships of art to life and are not respectful of the deep beliefs and cultural practices of a people. As representatives of a field that teaches the art and culture of others, art educators have a duty to engage students in culturally responsive and respectful curricula (Knight, 2000) that reach beyond a frozen past or trivialized present to reflect postmodern perspectives of living cultures (Desai, 2000; Efland, Freedman, & Stuhr, 1996).

Perceptions of Indianness

Teaching students about contemporary Native cultures is problematic, since what is visualized as *Indian*[3] is a loaded conception of image, media, and form. Conceptualizing definitions of *Indianness* is equally challenging, whether teaching about Native American arts and artists to students of Native or non-Native backgrounds. Art historians Berlo and Phillips (1998) stated that defining a Native American person entangles diverse considerations of time and place, material and function. Often, a Native artist's self-identity (and others' perceptions) of Indianness become linked to stereotypical notions about media choices, modes and purposes of artmaking, and historic traditions. Understanding what constitutes authentic Native art requires an ability to weigh distinctions between objects produced for personal or tribal cultural uses versus those intended for market events.[4] Objects intended for cultural uses, for example, require attention to historical and contemporary aesthetics within changing life contexts. Native artifacts intended for market must attend to the expectations and preferences of non-Native consumers without trivializing or dishonoring the diverse aesthetic traditions of Natives. So long as there is disparity between these various elements, there is a need for healing of broken or disconnected cultural knowledge in order that a viable identity of Indianness be formed, recognized, and appreciated by people from both Native and non-Native backgrounds.

During the 1960s, in a movement aimed at reclaiming the Indian image, Native artists associated with the American Indian Arts Institute in Santa Fe began revisualizing themselves in their artworks via contemporary media and styles. While seemingly bearing little imprint of the traditional *Native aesthetic* as recognized or defined by many non-Natives, new generations of Native artists became actively engaged in complex issues of Indian identity within a postmodern world. Notable examples included such works as James Luna's *The Artifact Piece* (1987)[5] and Vivianne Gray's *But, You Don't Look Indian* (1989).[6] These artists blended their traditional beliefs (i.e., the past) with mainstream knowledge, experiences, and media (i.e., the present) to empower and reclaim a visualization of the Native by the Native (Archuleta, 1994; Mihesuah, 1998; Pearlstone, 2005) that might enlighten and guide future generations of Natives and non-Natives. Cultural myth and story were integral to this process.

Relationship of Myth, Story, and Identity Construction

Barthes (1984) gives a definition of myth as a system of communication and mode of signification that helps us make sense of our experiences within the world. Whether conveyed linguistically or through image, myths serve as discourses about that which has been shared, interpreted, and reinterpreted throughout time. Gill (1990) stated,

> Myth should be thought of as a story on which truth is based, rather than thinking of myth as a true story.... Myths function as a means by which human beings can articulate... [fundamental things about themselves and culture] through the revision and recreation of their stories. (p. 138)

Myths explain the workings of the world within specific cultural contexts. Myths provide frameworks for constructing self, but do not exclusively define self. This is because, as we recall stories of the past in relationship to the present, and as we look to the future (Clandinin & Connelly, 2006), we individually choose from the tools of our experiences to create who we are. In this process, sociocultural experiences inform our mini (individual) stories, while myths as metanarratives serve as metaphors of possibilities. Thus, myths may be understood as dynamic stories, which inform changing identities.

Yet, there is another commonly held definition of myth as a story that has been so changed and distorted in the telling and retelling that it no longer contains the ability to reveal truth; rather, it presents a generalized version or inflexible stereotype of a culture and a fragmented or broken understanding of cultural self. A critical examination of myth and story allows one to distinguish between transformative myth and limiting stereotype—between that which *is healing* and that which *requires healing*. In the space between healing and being healed is a middle ground; we are able to distinguish distinctions between these processes, not only as they pertain to our own cultural identities, but also as they relate to the cultural identities of others.

It is within this concept of identity construction that I discuss my conversations with Hopi artist Michael Kabotie and his work, which were ultimately the impetus for my envisioning and enacting the ACT-E (Awareness, Critique, Transformative-Empowerment) curriculum approach in my teaching. The model, which I developed and will describe, may be used by art teachers when designing culture-centered curricular units for students of all cultural backgrounds, since it encourages transformative construction (or reconstruction) of the student's personal identity and respect for the identities of others.

Michael Kabotie: Journey to the Middle Ground of Healing Identity

Michael Kabotie referred to the construction of his own identity as a mythic "journey" that included a battle between "healed and unhealed" aspects of self in the search for a "middle place" (M. Kabotie, personal communication, 2009). Along the way, he explored ties to his Hopi identity and paralleled these with a Hopi understanding of cultural myth. He was guided by stories of his people. These stories, as they have been retold through time, demonstrate how Hopi art from the past to the present is a continuum of ceremonial prayers in support of healing influences; the intent is to quicken a harmonious future for the world. The Hopi concept of a middle place is not simply a poised position between past and present, but a place of healing that is not for Hopis alone, but for all humankind.

Kabotie believed art deals with the human spirit. He often said, "In order to be enlightened we must first be endarkened" (M. Kabotie, personal communication, 2009). It is in our darkest moments that the deepest healing can emerge. Kabotie's art enacted this healing process by exploring and tying together cultural myths, real histories, and personal experiences in a visual story of past, present, and future. A premiere representation of this appears in a five-panel kiva mural, created by Kabotie in

For Further Consideration

1. One popular definition of myth is of an imaginary or fictitious story. People often use the term to discredit or belittle a story as superstitious or untrue. What alternate definition does Santos propose?

   - Discuss the differences between these concepts.

   - Might both be applicable to myths of past or present? How?

   - How might both definitions be at work in processes of healing?

   - What does Santos describe as requiring healing, and how does healing take place?

2. What might be a "middle ground" of a student's experiences in art learning and making when topics other than self are addressed?

   - List some of the big ideas that might be addressed using the ACT-E model as demonstrated in this chapter.

   - Outline how mythic past and present might be explored—and future might be envisioned—in these alternately suggested big ideas or topics.

   - How could an ACT-E approach to curriculum design assist in awareness, critique, and transformative-empowerment relative to these ideas?

To further investigate the applicability of the ACT-E approach to curriculum design and implementation, select and complete one of the following suggested activities:

1. Identify three different cultural or national groups with which you are unfamiliar. Examine works by contemporary artists from these cultural groups. How do they creatively address issues of identity? Describe your findings in a visual journal.

2. Reflect on your own life experiences: What features of your life are currently undergoing transformation? What role within your identity has changed the most dramatically? Using the ACT-E model as a framework, write about this in your visual journal. Also consider:

   - In what area of your life do you feel you want to see a greater change, or what area of your life do you feel is still in its infancy? Using the ACT-E model, define how it might transform and empower you.

   - Maybe there is a place that you feel you do not have any power. How might ACT-E lead you to transformative-empowerment?

   - How might ACT-E and revelations about your own transformation-empowerment inform a pedagogy that considers and draws connections between students in diverse national or cultural contexts?

collaboration with fellow Hopi artist Delbridge Honnanie. The mural, which is housed at the Museum of Northern Arizona in Flagstaff, narrates a holistic concept they referred to as "the journey of the human spirit" (M. Kabotie, personal communication, 2009).

After extensively researching ancient Hopi kiva murals at Awat'ovi[7] and recalling their own childhood memories and adulthood experiences, Kabotie and Honnanie presented a journey of contemporary human experience that is symbolically paralleled by myth. Through the mural, which rests in the mock kiva[8] within the museum, they explored key historic events of contradiction such as "a weaving of the shadow side (the unhealed) and the light side of our lives" (M. Kabotie, personal communication, 2009).

Their visual narrative begins with a panel depicting the emergence of the Hopi people into this world of plants, animals, clouds, lightning, and stars—all life forms (Figure 1). The artists explained, the Hopi creation myth describes humans as emerging from darkness beneath the Earth into light of the world, but bringing a shadow of unhealed sorrows with them.

In the second panel (Figure 2), the artists depict a historic period of conflict between people of Awat'ovi and the early Spanish church of San Bernardo that sparked the Pueblo Rebellion of 1680. Pueblo people from as far

Figure 2. Second panel, kiva mural. Michael Kabotie and Delbridge Honnanie. (Courtesy of the Kabotie family and the Museum of Northern Arizona.)

Figure 3. Third panel, kiva mural. Michael Kabotie and Delbridge Honnanie. (Courtesy of the Kabotie family and the Museum of Northern Arizona.)

away as Taos, New Mexico (over 300 miles), joined in this rebellion "of forced conversions and forced labor imposed by the Spanish" (Museum of Northern Arizona, n.d., para. 6). Gray-faced figures emphasize the violent conflict as a historic experience that still represents—for many Hopi—an unhealed sense of loss and suffering.

The central panel (Figure 3) articulates an understanding of "the middle place" which is the essence of the emergence myth. It represents the rebirth of Hopi consciousness through images of three women, the Katsinam[9] (i.e., spiritual messengers and moral teachers of the Hopi people), and Buddha of a non-Native American culture placed in close proximity to one another. Following a critique of the past, the figures in this panel are shown "seeking a common ground or pursuing a middle place of harmony" (M. Kabotie, personal communication, 2009).

Progress in the guise of of industry, modern technology, and quests for wealth and power has adversely impacted the traditional lives, health, and ways of being of the

Figure 1. First panel, kiva mural. Michael Kabotie and Delbridge Honnanie. (Courtesy of the Kabotie family and the Museum of Northern Arizona.)

Hopi. This is shown in the fourth panel (Figure 4). Also appearing are the mythic trickster twins, as abandoned or discarded children.

The final mural segment (Figure 5) "represents the re-education of the brother and sister twins of Hopi mythology" (Museum of Northern Arizona, n.d., para. 9). Here, after engaging in a heroic journey, the once-lost twins have become "bearers of new ritual knowledge" (Geertz, 1994, p. 75). They have found transformative-empowerment in healing stories of the past and present, and can now imagine and influence a future. Symbols of a changing and empowered world rest on a serpent, which represents knowledge. A computer with www and apple motifs is enveloped by ancient petroglyphs and traditional Native symbols of healing. The apple makes reference to a popular brand of modern technology, but also makes symbolic reference to widely held associations of the apple with knowledge and power.

Figure 4. Fourth panel, kiva mural. Michael Kabotie and Delbridge Honnanie. (Courtesy of the Kabotie family and the Museum of Northern Arizona.)

Figure 5. Fifth panel, kiva mural. Michael Kabotie and Delbridge Honnanie. (Courtesy of the Kabotie family and the Museum of Northern Arizona.)

Kabotie spoke of how storytelling as an aspect of Hopi culture influenced his desire to set out upon his own exploratory journey of self and share his art with the wider world.[10] In *The Journey of the Human Spirit* mural, which was inspired by stories told by Kabotie's family and members of his community, he draws parallels between his life experiences and the story of the Hopi people. Layered by interplays of visual culture and processes of self-identity, the mural stands as powerful testimony to how cultural stories and art might contribute to identity construction. His inspirational work also provided impetus for development of ACT-E, the curriculum approach I developed and will describe.

ACT-E: A Model of Curriculum Development

Kabotie's search for a sense of cultural self through explorations of past and present myths, toward future possibility, inspired me to develop the Awareness, Critique, and Transformative-Empowerment (ACT-E) model of curriculum development for use by teachers of diverse students in secondary and post-secondary art educational settings. I use this model in my instruction of undergraduate art teacher education students at the large university in the Northwestern United States where I am a member of the faculty of the Art Education program. I require my preservice teachers to *enact* features of the model as they *apply* it as a guide for developing curricular units for secondary (7-12) level art students.

An ACT-E approach to art curriculum is based on a notion that students may come to a deeper understanding of their cultural self-identities by overlaying their actual life experiences against *myths*—both as ancient stories that relate the fundamental worldviews of a people and as the stereotypical stories others tell of a people. As students engage in comparisons of mythic archetypes, fictitious stereotypes, and personal experiences, they become aware of inconsistencies and misconceptions we hold of ourselves and others. They begin to see how these incongruities have caused hurts, conflicts, and miscommunications in past and present relationships. As a result, they are motivated to seek and claim a middle ground wherein they might reenvision myths of the past and stories of the present to envision empowering narratives of who they might become and how they might interact in the future.

Awareness: Identity in the Art Classroom

The ACT-E model begins with learning experiences aimed at bringing students to an *awareness* of the complex social and cultural systems that influence sense of cultural self.

My students approached the awareness phase of the ACT-E model by studying current articles about cultural, multicultural, and global art education; culturally relevant pedagogies; visual culture; and Native art. For example, the art of Hopi artist Michael Kabotie served to focus student discussions about works of art as stories of identity. They became aware of the influences of myth and story as visually articulated by Kabotie and Honnanie.

Following this discourse, a key assignment for these preservice students is the creation of a personal mind-map that *enacts* features of the model while engaging them in their own stories of identity. Through personal identity maps (Figures 6 and 7), students considered realms (social, familial, political, religious) and roles (artist, teacher, woman, husband, daughter, son) that comprise the warp and weft of identity. They were directed to articulate words and symbols connected to realms and roles they identified as key components of their maps (Figure 8). The process opened students to personal meaning making and brought them to a deeper awareness of how concepts of self are actively constructed. The identity mapping process also provided support for the second ACT-E stage of discourse, *critique*, as they compared and contrasted ideas, experiences, and contexts that informed their identities, and examined their feelings about identity.[11]

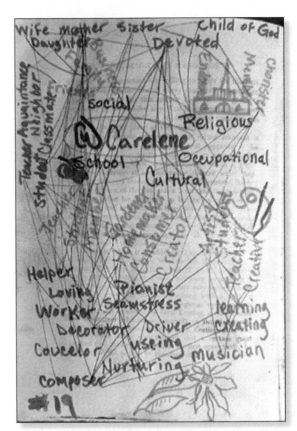

Figure 7. Awareness. Identity mapping: "My mind map was not meticulously planned out. I wrote down what roles that I played, built on that, and found connections. I discovered that everything connects. The entire page became a jumble of lines. Adding images made it more interesting and more personal to me." (Courtesy of preservice art education student).

Figure 6. Awareness. A student's identity map. (Courtesy of preservice art education student).

Figure 8. Awareness. "I chose to focus on religion for the ACT-E portion. Religion has always been a big part of my life but it is also shadow that obscures identity when others force personal preference of the application of religion. Religion was always meant as a way to make a person better but too often it has become a reason to force others to change. In a patriarchal society it makes women cry, become broken or deeply angry." (Courtesy of preservice art education student).

Figure 9. Critique. "The words are a bit obscured but they say, 'if this is the kind of life you wish.' As I became aware of where I came from I was torn between wanting to keep to tradition and wanting to break tradition. I was alarmed and puzzled and confused and angry and fiercely loyal all at the same time. I was still the little child looking to daddy but lost in the maze of finding my own way. My piece is childlike for that reason." (Courtesy of preservice art education student).

Figure 10. Transformation. "Transformation is a very long process. I'm not sure it really ever ends. I added I few images that represent some of the goals I had in mind, recognizing that I was still feeling my way but the path was becoming more ordered. I was aware that the way it looked and the way it really was were two different things." (Courtesy of preservice art education student).

Critique: Myth as a Meta-Narrative of Identity

The term *critique* often carries a negative connotation. However, art educators understand that critique allows opportunity for exploring visual form and content in art. When students are engaged in critiques of their artworks, the goal is to expand their understanding of the visual choices they have made, clarify how these choices support meaning, and discuss ways they might enhance their artistic skill.

The ACT-E model applies critique as a way of reaching beyond foci on formalistic properties of art by deconstructing expressive concepts and content of art (Figure 9). ACT-E emphasizes critique as a method of questioning and deconstructing how big ideas in art—such as identity—are informed by and understood against myths and stories of who we were, are, and might be in the future.

Critique strategies of ACT-E include asking essential questions that guide students to deeper explorations of "who I am." Also, students are encouraged to draw from myths and stories from their own cultural backgrounds, which seem to parallel personal experience with larger models of being. In this way, students begin to see how their personal identities, which are bound by time, place, social interaction and cultural stereotypes, are situated within larger shared myths or metanarratives (grand stories) of the human experience.

By critiquing the phenomenon of identity construction through mind mapping and revisiting the relationship between geography, social experience, cultural myths, and identity, students were able to see how processes of visual representation and critique can play an essential role in the identity construction process. This led them to the transformative-empowerment phase of ACT-E.

Transformative-Empowerment

To address the concept of storying the mythic self at the *transformative-empowerment* phase of ACT-E, students were directed to create self-portraits that focused on sections of their mind maps that they found especially

Figure 11. Empowerment. "In the end I have come to realize how religion can be integrated into my life without forcing me into a cookie cutter mold. I believe it can give me many possibilities, connections to the world and greater love and patience for people even those who want me to be in the cookie cutter mold. I am at peace with me and other. Green is the color of growth." (Courtesy of preservice art education student).

Figure 12. High school student participating in collaborative puzzle mural. (Courtesy of author.)

important (Figure 10). The self-portraits were to include symbolic imagery that represented their newly awakened and critically informed notions of self (Figure 11).

Additional assignments included a cross-cultural approach to making a class quilt, a collaborative mural, and a group puzzle project, all oriented around a core theme of cultural identity and diversity (Figure 12). These shared visual spaces provided ways to locate common ground and celebrate differences in identity among individuals of the class. It permitted students to listen to the voices of those who might previously have been silent (e.g., those who, due to the marginalization of their cultures, had not felt empowered to participate in mainstream aesthetic conversations) and to see them represented along with the voices and imagic representations of more outgoing or culturally mainstream students. Invisible cultural influences were brought into view; stereotypes of culture were broken; elements of the unhealed past and present yielded to healing ministrations within the group and through processes of artmaking together. The experience transformed students' understandings of themselves and empowered them to see themselves in a collaborative way, as parts of a whole.

ACT-E: A Model for Secondary-Level Art Curriculum

Students of my methods courses in art education were instructed to use the ACT-E model as an overarching framework when aligning unit goals with state and national standards, posing essential questions about big ideas (Stewart & Walker, 2005), and developing sample art lessons for secondary-level (7–12) students of art. Modeling an ACT-E approach while exploring issues of a Native American and personal cultural identity provided students an opportunity to reevaluate the ways culturally based art curricula might be developed.

Additionally, the modeled experience served as a resource; students were able to refer to their own maps and artworks in search of big idea concepts—such as family, collaboration, power, health, harmony, and religion—as themes for additional curriculum units that would utilize cross-cultural artist exemplars and address global themes of our human stories. These units could be extended to focus on how cultural identities of individuals or groups are situated and interact within a larger, global context.

Middle Ground: Past Into the Future

The ACT-E approach to art education curriculum design is intended to bring invisible, overlooked, or misunderstood cultural influences into focus; transform students' understandings of themselves; and empower them to see self in a collaborative way, as a part of a whole. Through exploration of Kabotie's experiences, students could see how identity is embedded in myths of the cultural past, and how individuals in the present experience their cultures differently. They were able to identify with Kabotie's understanding of self as Hopi among a diversity of Hopis. He stated that while he saw things through Hopi eyes, his vision did not provide an inclusive portrait of Hopi. By modeling the curriculum unit, these preservice teachers were experiencing how students from *any* cultural background or experience might reclaim personal identities from a mythic past and present, while becoming more deeply appreciative of the complexly multidimensional identities of others.

Furthermore, students began to see how one's present and future cultural lives are and may be enriched through interaction. Kabotie engaged with and responded to the world outside of the Hopi culture on a regular basis. He researched and read literature by non-Hopi scholars, communed with artists of diverse cultural backgrounds, listened to a variety of musical genres, and then filtered these phenomena back through his Hopi experience. By exchanging cultural ideas and images with non-Hopi artists and reflecting upon how this new knowledge made meaning in his own life, Kabotie was actively engaged in cultural jamming (i.e., the combining of diverse ways of knowing) beyond the Hopi reservation. Ultimately, his experiences outside Hopi culture helped him to understand himself as Hopi—as human—as a part of a changing world as it moves into the future.

Conclusions

Andrus (1995), Banks (2000), Biggers (1997), and Desai (2000) have pointed out the importance of examining and coming to terms with our own cultural identity as a prerequisite for appreciating differences and similarities with others. Although identity is commonly perceived as a sense of individual self, we are the sum of experiences couched in personal and cultural histories, myths, and stories. We must first know where we have come from, and where we are, before we can know where we are going.

The work of artist Kabotie presents an example of the role myth and story play in this identity construction. As we move in and out of temporal moments of memory, we identify the stories of our lives contextualized in relationship to people, places, things, and the mythic tales we imagine or others tell of us. Kabotie instructs us to seek a middle ground, where imaged pieces of past and present may be reconciled in order to move toward a place of harmony. This would compel teachers and students to seek out and project images of themselves and of others globally that are respectful of our past histories and present contexts, with the goal of envisioning harmonious interactions among diverse peoples in a healthy world.

Using myth and identity as centering themes in art, my students strove to understand the ACT-E approach by examining Michael Kabotie's journey through myth and narrative as a model of a search for authentic cultural identity, and by exploring their own identities through cultural myth and personal story. In the end, they came to a "middle place." They grew to awareness of the power of cultural myths and stories of the past, critiqued the constructed present, and were transformatively empowered to design culturally sensitive art curricula for secondary-level students, which might enlighten all our futures.

REFERENCES

Andrus, L. E. (1995). *Discipline based art education projects in the university classroom.* Orlando, FL: Harcourt Brace.

Archuleta, B. (1994). *The Native American fine art movement: A resource guide.* Phoenix, AZ: Heard Museum.

Banks, J. A. (2000). *Multicultural education: Theory and practice* (4th ed.). Boston, MA: Allyn and Bacon.

Barthes, R. (1984). *Mythologies.* New York, NY: Hill and Wang.

Berlo, J. C., & Phillips, R. B. (1998). *Native North American art.* Oxford, NY: Oxford University Press.

Biggers, J. (1997). Exploring cultures: A conversation with John Biggers. *ArtsEdNet Offline, 6,* 4-9.

Clandinin, J., & Connelly, F. M. (2006). *Narrative inquiry.* San Francisco, CA: Jossey-Bass.

Desai, D. (2000). Imaging difference: The politics of representation in multicultural art education. *Studies in Art Education, 41*(2), 114–129.

Efland, A. D., Freedman, K., & Stuhr, P. (1996). *Postmodern art education: An approach to curriculum.* Reston, VA: The National Art Education Association.

Geertz, A. M. (1994). *The invention of prophecy: Continuity and meaning in Hopi Indian religion*. Berkeley: University of California Press.

Gill, S. (1990). Mother Earth and American myth. In J. A. Clifford (Ed.), *The invented Indian: Cultural fictions and government policies* (pp. 129–144). New Brunswick, Canada: Transaction.

Hopi Cultural Presentation Office. (2009). *Katsina dolls*. Retrieved from www8.nau.edu/hcpo-p/katsina.html

Kabotie, M. (n.d.). *Artist Hopid (1973-1978)* [Website]. Retrieved from www.kabotie.com/Pages/artisthopid.html

Knight, W. B. (2000). *Preparing preservice teachers to work with diverse student populations: Implications for visual art teacher education* (Unpublished doctoral dissertation). Ohio State University, Columbus, OH.

Merskin, D. L. (1996). What does one look like? In S. Bird (Ed.), *Dressing in feathers: The construction of the Indian in American popular culture* (pp. 281–284). Boulder, CO: Westview Press.

Mihesuah, D. (1998). *Natives and academics: Researching and writing about American Indians*. Lincoln: University of Nebraska Press.

Museum of Northern Arizona. (n.d.). *The Kiva gallery* [Website]. Retrieved from http://musnaz.org/plan-your-visit/what-to-do-here/tour-the-exhibits/hopi-kiva-gallery/a-modern-hopi-kiva-mural/

Pearlstone, Z. (2005). *About face: Self-portraits by Native American, First Nations, and Inuit artists*. Santa Fe, NM: Wheelwright museum of the American Indian.

Stewart, M. G., & Walker, S. R. (2005). *Rethinking curriculum in art*. Worcester, MA: Davis.

Voth, H. R. (1905). Traditions of the Hopi. Retrieved from www.sacred-texts.com/nam/hopi/toth/toth002.htm

Wikipedia. (2013). *Hopi kachina dolls*. Retrieved from http://en.wikipedia.org/wiki/Hopi_Kachina_dolls

ENDNOTES

[1] In this chapter, *Native* refers to the full range of Native American artists, and is not characterizing or grouping people of different cultural knowledge and sensitivities.

[2] Kachina or katsina dolls were traditionally used in ceremonies and as a means of educating Hopi children about characteristics of various spiritual messengers or guardians. Since the late 19th century, several new forms have evolved or been created in response to tourism market demand for them (Hopi Cultural Preservation Office, 2009; Wikipedia, 2013).

[3] The use of the term *Indian*, *Native American*, or *American Indian* is highly debated within indigenous academia and tribal communities. Due to the historical misuse of the term *Indian*, many individuals of indigenous American heritage prefer to emphasize their tribal association.

[4] Market events include exhibitions where art or craft objects are displayed and sold as art-for-art's sake, or situations whereby Native arts that have been made for commercial purposes are sold to tourists or non-Native consumers as decorative items.

[5] See www.jamesluna.com/oldsite

[6] View image at www.columbia.edu/cu/arthistory/courses/Multiple-Modernities/essay.html

[7] Awat'ovi is a 500-year-old ruin located Navajo County, Arizona. Prior to its destruction in the 18th century, it was one of the largest and most important of the pueblo villages.

[8] A kiva is an underground room, entered from the center of its ceiling, which is used for ceremonial purposes by people of Pueblo tribes. Symbolic significance of the structure suggests an analogy to the creation myth, which indicates the first people emerged from an underground womb into life (Voth, 1905).

[9] Katsina refers to spiritual beings and messengers important to daily activities and life of the Hopi (Hopi Cultural Preservation Office, 2009).

[10] See additional examples of Kabotie's work at www.kabotie.com/Pages/paintings.html

[11] During a secondary art methods course, art education students keep visual journals that included mind mapping, sketching, and journaling related to ACT-E activities. Quotes within this chapter are from student visual journals created for course assignments during the 2012–2013 school year.

CHAPTER 27

A Mécénat Collaboration Toward Appreciating a Traditional, National Art Form

JEONG IM HUH
Pusan National University of Education
YONG-SOCK CHANG
University of Illinois at Urbana-Champaign

At the 2010 UNESCO World Conference on Arts Education in Seoul, speakers observed a need for cultural/arts education in response to particular negative effects of globalization (UNESCO, 2010). Specifically, speakers referred to economic pressures and political agendas that make it difficult for schools in many areas of the world to implement arts curricula without outside financial assistance (Huh, 2009). Additionally, concern was expressed that mass-media produced, globally conveyed culture might subsume unique cultural traditions.[1] Consequently, children who are not provided opportunities to engage with the aesthetic traditions of their ancestors would lose connections to their cultural heritages and be deprived of distinctive models upon which to build a sense of self in local and global contexts.

In South Korea, where art currently is not regarded as important a subject as mathematics, science, or English (Huh, 2007), children might not be provided opportunities to learn about their historic, national traditions were it not for arts education partnership programs supported by the Korean Business Council for the Arts (KBCA). *Mécénat* is a term created in France to describe a type of relationship whereby arts programs are supported through private business funding (Korean Business Council for the Arts, 2012). Through KBCA, Mécénat funds cultural and arts education for students of elementary schools located in isolated South Korean areas (Huh, 2009).

KBCA support reflects beliefs held by business leaders and policy makers that, just as it is necessary that South Korean citizens be educated in mathematics, science, and English so as to remain globally competitive, cultural art education stimulates the production of creative works, which are a "key factor in… economy and society" (Florida, 2002, p. 4). Business leaders are motivated by desires to have students and future citizens exposed to and capable of artistic expressions that contribute to the growing economic vitality of the nation and well-being of South Korean society. Therefore, art programs that encourage culturally distinctive artistic expressions align with the Mécénat idea of creativity in art production. Recognizing KBCA's support of creative expression as a feature of art education, the authors of this chapter developed a plan for engaging three small rural populations of South Korean children in artmaking that taught appreciation for traditional Korean art forms and sustainable local resources, while also encouraging artistic self-expression.

An Issue of Creativity in Art Education

There has been an explicit or implied concern among Western scholars such as jagodzinski (2009) and Gude (2009) that business support of art programs promotes creativity as an economic commodity for a political agenda. In this regard, creativity in art would be defined as imaginative work leading to the production of innovative objects, technologies, or entertainments, rather than expression of unique ideas or feelings about the human experience. As jagodzinski (2009) stated,

> The World Bank imitative echoes throughout the majority of post-industrialized countries… Art education does not escape from this imitative… It has (once more) found its *raison d'etre* as it did after the post-World War 2 recovery. Art education is now placed in the services of the well-known "creative industries." (pp. 24–25)

Gude argues that focus on art as commodity raises social questions about business-school collaborative relationships. She feels art as a humanizing process may be challenged and creative talent usurped for commercial interests if art education is situated for social purposes. However, this is largely a Western debate. Both jagodzinski and Gude are operating from a Westernized viewpoint. The experience of Asian countries has been different, particularly post-World War II.

In an Asian context, artistic creativity that marinates national tradition provides a means for people to express and communicate an idiosyncratically differentiated aesthetic from globally predominate Western aesthetic ideals. Therefore, the negative Western hypothesis about business-school collaborations does not reflect our experience; it does not take into account the desires of artists from Eastern nations that their aesthetically distinctive artistic products be recognized in global marketplaces and the mainstream art world.

Art Education and Identity With National Community

As an art education faculty member at a Korean university and a Korean art educator/academic who currently is a graduate student at an American university, we had the opportunity to secure financial support from private business for an after-school cultural/visual art program that we designed and implemented in three isolated public elementary schools outside Pusan, South Korea. Students of these schools are marginalized by poverty and rural isolation within the larger national mainstream. We sought to inculcate a sense of identification with traditional, Korean art culture while empowering students to construct identities relating to their contemporary communities.

Wenger (1999) provides a view of learning that places it "in the context of our lived experience of participation in the world" (p. 3). Learning is a communal practice and results in social participation. The program we designed offered three dimensions of practice as community property detailed by Wenger: shared repertoire, mutual engagement, and group leadership. The results of sharing cultural history through artmaking and social interaction demonstrated Fletcher's (2009) assertion that successful practices and preservation of culture result from communal resonation with locals.

Participant Schools and Communities

In South Korea, where KBCA actively promotes and funds art education, emails are sent throughout the year to faculty at South Korean universities and the Korean Art Education Association requesting proposals for funded projects. Knowing that KBCA funders give preference to programs that stress traditional cultural education, upon receiving a KBCA invitation we proposed an after-school traditional cultural/visual art program to be offered to children of rural schools. Our proposal was accepted and we were granted funds for enacting the program.

The schools we selected for implementation of our program were rural branches connected to larger elementary schools in southeastern South Korea. The branch schools had very low enrollments of 13, 13, and 17 students respectively. Because these small numbers comprised the entire student populations of the schools, all students within each school were combined in single mixed-aged classrooms, and instruction was provided similarly to the ways students were taught in one-room schoolhouses of 19th-century rural United States. Of the students who were enrolled in these three target branches, many lived in single parent or grandparent guardianship homes and were considered marginalized by their economic and social status. Although Korean schools are required to include art content in the curriculum, these branch schools had neither community support nor resources for implementing art programs. Therefore, children enrolled at these sites were underexposed to the aesthetic and philosophical concepts provided through such traditional Korean and/or Western Fine Art focused curricula as might be available to students in larger schools (Huh & Lee, 2009).

The three central goals set forth were that the program: (1) encourage honoring and understanding of a national traditional art form, (2) assist students in grasping and expressing the relevancy of that tradition in their everyday lives (e.g., self-expression), and (3) assist in development of art skills and concepts relevant to traditional art forms in a contemporary context. We gathered an educational team to facilitate classroom activities. The team included teachers of each school and our university personnel, which comprised art education faculty, graduate students, and artists. We ensured that all team members of the initiative understood the concepts and philosophy underlying our program and could appropriately implement the activities according to our design and goals. The first priority was to encourage student identification with and aesthetic appreciation of their Korean heritage in order that cultural and communal traditions might be maintained for a new generation. The second priority was to provide students with a means of artistic self-expression through traditional media of Korean cultural history.

Students of each branch elementary school received instruction in our after-school program once a week for a 2-hour session, for a total of 30 weeks, each school receiving 60 hours of the art program. Altogether there were 43 students who participated in our program. In order to respect students' differing grade and ability levels within the one-room schoolhouse-type setting, the program could not be applied according to specific grade level expectations.

The program instructors were two Korean professional artists/guest visual art lecturers. These teachers had ample experience working in the traditional Korean art processes being taught, were knowledgeable and skilled in the program's content, and were able to adapt instruction for diverse student needs. Students chose the level of project difficulty, and the artist-teacher's job was to encourage students to challenge themselves in expressing more deeply considered ideas and bettering their artmaking skills with increasingly difficult tasks.

Two obstacles that had to be overcome in order to initiate a successful after school program were an initial lack of interest among some local classroom teachers, who may have seen an after-school program as unessential to core curriculum, and parental beliefs that their children should focus on "important" academic subjects, like math, English, science, and other academic subjects they believed to be valued by globally competitive nations. Nevertheless, the fact that our program was free, having been paid for by our Mécénat partner, encouraged high attendance, and nearly all students in each school participated in the program. Furthermore, as local classroom teachers began to see students' interests in learning sparked by activities of the program, their appreciation of its benefits increased.

Program Design and Methodology

Many art programs implemented in Korean schools emanate from a Western perspective in terms of media choices, subject content, and images or artifacts presented as exemplars. A crucial aspect of our art program was that it provided students with a uniquely traditional Korean approach to art. The aim was to inculcate a sense of respect for Korean aesthetic culture through art and evoke a desire to preserve these cultural forms. However, we authors of the program are art educators who have knowledge of inquiry-based learning methods, as well as belief in the importance of relevance and in the value of art as self-expression. We encouraged students to see each traditional art form presented as a vehicle for expressing ideas about themselves and their everyday lives. This was accomplished by organizing activities into categories that addressed the program objectives. First were tasks focused on student exposure to and research about various traditional Korean art forms. This extended to activities that encouraged students to draw relevance between these traditions and their lives, by choosing personally relevant themes and creating stories or otherwise making connections that were integrated into the art forms.

Figure 1. Cheongsachorong. *Traditional Korean lantern with a red and blue silk shade (Cho, 2012).*

Figure 2. Coloring One's Fingernails with Balsam *(Cho, 2012).*

Together these activities provided students with artistic experiences that introduced them to national and local aesthetic traditions and situated their personal interests within these traditions. The learning activities also were designed so students would be required to develop and apply greater technical artmaking skills, depending on age or ability level, and have opportunities to appreciate each other's artistic ideas and abilities.

Although experiences in several traditional Korean art forms and processes—such as drawing, painting, cloth dying and calligraphy—were included in the program, we will describe only one activity in depth: Dak-paper doll making. We focus on this art form because dolls are useful tools of cultural storytelling. Through listening to stories about Dak-paper dolls, students might gain information about and an appreciative sense of their cultural heritage; by telling stories through dolls they might preserve cultural knowledge in a contemporary context. Importantly, Dak-paper dolls also allow students to imbue their work with personal relevance, and express and share meanings with others in the social environment of their schools.

For Further Consideration

1. How might art education encourage unique self-expression and maintain distinctive cultural expressions, while also being viewed as important for economic progress? Give specific examples when answering.

2. Discuss the ways and extent to which traditional arts education might provide a foundation or template for student expressivity.

3. Compare definitions of creativity in art put forth by Florida (2002) and Gude (2009).
   - What purposes for art education does each author advocate?
   - How are these definitions and purposes similar or different from those suggested by Huh and Chang?
   - How might the needs of a nation influence the goals for art education embraced by citizens of that nation?
   - What are primary goals for art education within your nation or region?

4. What types of financial support are available to art teachers in your nation or region?
   - What types of art educational programs do they advocate and/or support?
   - Where can you find out more about accessing these funds?
   - How might you use this funding to support culturally sensitive art education for your students?

References

Florida, R. (2002). *The rise of the creative class: And how it's transforming work, leisure, community and everyday life.* New York, NY: Basic Books.

Gude, O. (2009). Questioning creativity. In N. Addison & L. Burgess (Eds.), *Debates in art and design education* (pp. 37–42). New York, NY: Routledge.

Dak-Paper, a Korean Traditional Art Media

Korean paper or Dak-paper is a form of handmade paper used by ancient Korean artists and craftspeople (Cho, 2012). Dak-paper is made from mulberry bark, a native tree that flourishes in Korea's mountainous terrain. The traditional making of Dak-paper, also known as *Hanji*, can be traced to 105 A.D. in China. Today the paper is lauded for its very high quality. Dak-paper pieces located in Korean museums have been determined to be over 1,200 years in age. When lacquered they have endured almost twice as long. Dak-paper comes in hundreds of various shades, tints, and hues, usually derived from natural color agents. This property, when coupled with its durability,[2] makes it popular to use in many kinds of artifacts and household items, like sculptured objects, cups, bowls, trays, and paper windows. Dak-paper doll construction is one traditional way of using Dak-paper. Dolls and other items made of Dak-paper were present in Korean homes from as early as the 4th century. They can still be found in Korean homes, although some are produced in factories by machines and are not made following traditional practices (Lee, 2012; Kim, 1999). Dolls made in the traditional way can be as small as 5 centimeters or as a large as an adult human (Kim, 1999).

Besides introducing Dak-paper as a traditional medium for Korean doll-making, we focused student attention on the "green" (i.e., environmentally safe) features of the material; it makes use of renewable and locally available natural resources, and fulfills other requirements of sustainability. For example, we modeled sustainable and ethical practices by insisting students use only traditional dyes and colors when constructing their dolls. Additionally, we led students to recognize that many world traditions in art and craft draw from locally indigenous natural and renewable resources, and we encouraged consideration of the impact media choices have upon the local and global environment.

Students' Responses to the Arts Program

Chang's Response

Initially, as we began teaching the Dak-paper unit, we found that presentations of ancient Dak-paper-made crafts were not appealing to students. They thought Korean art traditions were too old, tedious, and out of fashion to be relevant to their everyday lives. Chang,[3] for example, did not listen to the art lecturer's presentations about the history, processes, and aesthetics of Dak-paper

artifacts. He complained, "I don't understand why I have to take this kind of art class" (personal communication, April, 19, 2012). This reaction was somewhat understandable, since Chang's participation was involuntary; at the school administrator's urging, his parents had enrolled him in the program. Chang was easily distracted at this stage of the learning experience; he was vocal about his disinterest, and would often tell everyone that he found these history lessons boring or irrelevant.

On the day he began working on his Dak-paper doll project, however, Chang's interest in developing the dolls as characters to be set in stories of his imagined or real world was piqued. Subsequently, the activities of making Dak-paper doll figures occupied his attention for weeks. He contributed positively to session discussions including those that made reference to historic and contemporary aspects of the art form, demonstrated an active interest in the artmaking process, assisted other students with their projects, and gradually became a leader of others involved in this work. Although his technical art skills did not improve significantly, the art he created interested him conceptually. He also recognized that his ideas intrigued other students and teachers. Through this activity, therefore, he became more positive about artmaking as social experience and personal expression.

The pleasure Chang experienced in making Dak-paper dolls as media for storytelling led him to appreciate the connection between a historical-cultural tradition and his present-day world. Praise from teachers and classmates provided support that contributed to his sense of being a valued part of the school community and his sense of self-efficacy as a leader in the community. This praise and recognition encouraged him to situate himself in context of a local and national community. Theobold and Nachtigal (1995) stated in *Culture, Community and the Promise of Rural Education*, "The more students understand their community and its environs—its social structure, its economy, its history, its music, its ecology—the more they become invested in that community" (p. 9).

Initially, Chang demonstrated a resistance to "history" that is quite common to children. They are immersed in the present and rarely concerned with or interested in the past unless that past appears relevant to the present and future. Yet, in arts programs like Clark and Zimmerman's (1997) *ProjectARTS* (Arts for Rural Teachers and Students), it was found that children who could be engaged in community histories would develop honor and respect for their communities. When youth come to appreciate

Figure 3. Experiencing a traditional Korean artmaking process.

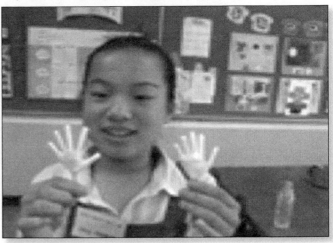

Figure 5. Making the hands.

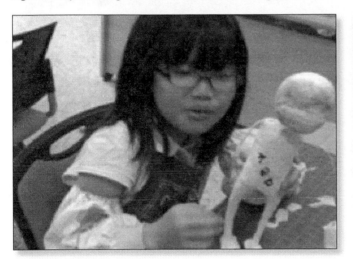

Figure 4. Making the Dak-paper doll head.

Figure 6. Making the body.

and understand the history and culture of their communities, they are more likely to stay in or return to their home communities (Hudec, 2012). Throughout Korea's long national history, emphasis has been placed on respect for one's elders and ancestors; Koreans believe this leads to healthier societies in general. Therefore, art education that inculcates appreciation and respect for the national community, and might eventually inspire contributions to local-community well-being, could be perceived as socially beneficial.

Kim's Experience

Importance of local sociocultural community was demonstrated by Kim's participation and experience in the program. Kim had been afflicted with poliomyelitis as an infant. His left hand was curled into a fist by muscle and carpal tendon damage. He had the use of his thumb

and one finger on his left hand, but barely any use of his right hand. In the beginning, his parents had not wanted him to participate in the program. They feared his handicaps would prevent him from using the materials and tools necessary to complete projects. Additionally, they were concerned that the experience would be uncomfortable for him, because he was extremely shy and did not interact well with his peers. After the principal explained to Kim's parents that all of the school's students were required to participate, the parents relented and the boy joined in program activities.

At first Kim had difficulty using materials like clay, knives, and scissors, or mixing the powdered glue required for creation of the dolls. He would drop the scissors or use two hands, awkwardly manipulating the two sides of the scissors. Sometimes a classmate would help

Figure 7. Being Caught in a Shower.[4]

him if he became frustrated. He eventually learned to handle the scissors competently. However, he continually found it difficult to mix powdered glue, and made messy efforts to blend it without lumps. Observing his struggles, his classmates worked the lumps out of the glue. This unsolicited help became an enjoyable aspect of his working with the materials. He would do most of the work in preparing his materials, and his classmates would help him when it looked like he was having problems finishing some part of the process. As the weeks progressed, his parents and teachers noticed he gained mobility in two of his left fingers, as well as developing strength in both hands. The program activities seemed to provide physical therapy for the boy and also helped him overcome shyness and develop friendships with classmates.

Unfortunately there is often a trend in Korea of marginalizing or excluding students like Kim who are different or do not fit into the norm (Park, 2009). This program provided Kim with a means of gaining social acceptance and classroom inclusion, in addition to serving as a vehicle for his self-expression. It may be said that less tolerant sociocultural traditions were assuaged as others of the class developed acceptance and appreciation of Kim as a valued member of the school community.

On the last day, when the program exhibition was held, Kim's mother affirmed that our program had made a large difference in her son's perception of himself as a member of an inclusive school-cultural community. Although we do not claim that the traditional cultural content of our program was entirely responsible for Kim's positive experiences, the studio atmosphere, which encouraged collaborative efforts of artmaking, and working in a media that reinforced group ties to a common historic repertoire, contributed to development of a classroom community in which he was able to thrive.

Acceptance of and willingness to assist, support, and collaborate with those who are different within a local community are necessary prerequisites to becoming accepting of and open to collaborations with others globally.

Community Response

Much like Clark and Zimmerman's ProjectARTS, which served rural American students, our program sought to reach marginalized rural students. Manifold (2009) wrote,

> During the initial phases of ProjectARTS, they came to realize that not only outsiders to the rural communities serving as sites for the projects, but also some of those who had intimate knowledge of the communities—including some teachers and parents of student participants—had not previously recognized these communities as having unique cultural expressions worthy of notice. (p. 89)

Manifold's statement agrees with our observations regarding the results of this Mécénat supported program for rural South Korean children. As they perceived the program's benefits to their students, teachers and parents began to show respect for the program, its goals, and the results. Parents' and teachers' initial resistance to the art program, which was grounded in a concern that education should be geared to preparing children with useful skills for future careers in a global economy, gave way to approval that their children had participated in an art education program that introduced them to Korea's aesthetic heritage. They recognized the respect this content demonstrated toward their ancestral heritage and the way artmaking processes reinforced their children's social well-being, sense of belonging, and leadership in community. Teachers saw that it increased student interests in other academic subjects. Students experienced pride in their personal accomplishments and satisfaction in both local social interactions and the common cultural heritage they shared. While arguably, some of these personal and social benefits could be attributed to the inculcating behaviors of studio artmaking in general, we observed the cultural attributes of the program to be of special importance to this population of students and their community.

Mécénat Support, Art Education, and Community

Mécénat-like programs have been criticized by some art educators who are concerned with maintaining the autonomy of public schools. However, it was the authors' experience that, beyond providing financial support, our business partner did not dictate, censor, or otherwise interfere with the educational project we designed and implemented for children of three small rural South Korean communities. The Mécénat provided a financial means, but art-interested experts and communities directed the design and implementation of the program. Both are critical to a program's success in terms of its benefits to students and communities locally and beyond.

The UNESCO concern that globalization might negatively affect the diversity of cultural expressions and unique characters of small local communities presents a dilemma to parents in places like rural South Korea. These parents want their children and nation to be successful in a competitive world, but they also wish to honor the distinctive traditions of their ancestral heritage. Our program demonstrated how a Mécénat-supported cultural art education program could provide opportunities for children to experience social success and make connections between contemporary life and traditions of community, while also leading students and their parents to recognize and value how indigenous, readily available, and inexpensive materials, when applied to a popular artistic form, might contribute unique aesthetic expressions to the global art world.

By funding cultural arts programs such as the one we designed and implemented, Mécénat partnerships encourage student self-expression and social integration, promote pride and interest in ancient cultural traditions, and inspire adaptations of those traditions in ways that are culturally distinctive, yet innovative and relevant to contemporary globalized society. Mécénat-school partnerships thus contribute to art-rich communities, and these are places where people want to work and live (Florida, 2002). If these communities are located in rural or semi-rural areas, the flight of rural people to urban centers is slowed. The production of culturally unique arts by rural people contributes to tourism and eco-tourism. This benefits local and national economies. When children respect and honor the local communities, they are likely to see their home communities as places worthy of attention when they become adults. Research shows that children who are engaged in research of the local are more likely to expand their interests beyond the local and also more likely to contribute to the sustenance and well-being of their home communities (Theobald & Nachtigal, 1995). This is important to a culture whose traditions demand the honoring of one's ancestors. Thus, support of arts through school-business relationships can be mutually beneficial to the well-being of individuals and local communities, as well as national and business interests.

Artistic traditions that are being lost to globalizing effects of mass-media conveyed popular culture may be revived and made visible to others of the global society. Artists who seek distinctive aesthetic identities in a world dominated by Western cultural influences may call upon cultural heritage as foundation for idiosyncratic expression. Art education that emphasizes cultural heritage as a vital tool for maintaining diversity contributes variety to global art worlds and encourages cultural understanding between nations. Within this framework, engaging South Korean students in a traditional Korean art form may be viewed as nurturing artistic development and self-expression in ways that support the personal well-being of young citizens, and potentially contributing to local and national economies, while also aesthetically enriching the global community (Brannan, 2005).

Conclusions

When business interests support arts education initiatives, it suggests a valuing of arts by business CEOs. Arguments can be made that this valuing is directly related to needs that 21st century workers have art-based skills and proficiencies—both culture-specific and universal—necessary for filling job markets. These Mécénat goals of assuring educational programs that prepare students with skills that will contribute to a future Gross National Product (GNP), however, are not inconsistent with the aims of art educators and community members. Recognizing how to make healthy and respectful uses of natural resources, being able to share stories that are personally relevant, developing attitudes of inclusiveness, and working with those who are different are skills that open students to participation in global art worlds and marketplaces. Nurturing students to make connections between traditions of the past and needs of the future may increase their ability to conceptualize and create innovative products that are respectful of that which deserves consideration, such as community maintenance, respect for unique cultural expressions, and the environment. Experiences of artmaking that respect the maker's cultural heritage, encourage self-expression, and provide skills that contribute toward a successful future may be deeply satisfying for both the maker and his or her community.

We took advantage of a Mécénat-school partnership in offering students of three rural South Korean communities an opportunity to reconnect with their heritage/

traditional culture through artmaking. The experience helped strengthen students' self-esteem, permitted self-expression, encouraged cooperative learning, and supported social integration and leadership development. It situated them in a national aesthetic tradition and helped to engender a sense of themselves as members of a larger Korean culture. Parents and teachers recognized and appreciated these benefits of the program for their children and the community. Program designers and instructors foresee potential for impact within and beyond the local community.

We believe there is a global benefit in nations valuing local cultural arts and sharing these arts with other cultural groups. The goal of UNESCO and the KBCA Mécénat program are to allow for creation of traditional cultural/arts education in the wake of globalization and a gradual loss of knowledge and appreciation for traditional art culture. Culturally unique stories and artifacts may supply marketplaces with desirable variety; yet, more importantly, learning about and honoring the arts of one's cultural heritage provides a ground for unique self-expression that contributes to the rich diversity of human experience.

REFERENCES

Brannan, M. A. (2005). *The importance of incorporating local culture into community development*. Retrieved from http://edis.ifas.ufl.edu/fy773

Cho, K.-S. (2012). *Dak-paper dolls* (Blog). Retrieved from http://blog.naver.com/skwmom

Clark, G., & Zimmerman, E. (1997). *ProjectARTS, Programs for ethnically diverse, economically disadvantaged, high ability, visual arts students in rural communities: Identification, curriculum, evaluation*. Bloomington: Javits Gifted and Talented Students Education Program and Indiana University.

Fletcher, R. (2009). Ecotourism discourse: Challenging the stakeholders theory. *Journal of Ecotourism, 8*(3), 269–285.

Florida, R. (2002). *The rise of the creative class: And how it's transforming work, leisure, community and everyday life*. New York, NY: Basic Books.

Gude, O. (2009). Questioning creativity. In N. Addison & L. Burgess (Eds.), *Debates in art and design education* (pp. 37–42). New York, NY: Routledge.

Hudec, C. (2012, July 18). *University fights rural 'Brain Drain' with new program*. Retrieved from http://blogs.edweek.org/edweek/rural_education/2012/07/texas_university_launches_program_to_combat_rural_brain_drain.html

Huh, J. I. (2007). An aesthetic exploration of the relation of art and morality in art education: Focused on Dewey and Deutsch. *Art Education Research Review, 21*(1), 275–294.

Huh, J. I. (2009). *A study on development of an intensified arts and cultural education program connected with arts activity* (KACES-0940-R019). Seoul, Korea: Korea Arts Culture Education Service.

Huh, J. I., & Lee, E. J. (2009). A study of teaching methods using Buddhist pagodas in elementary art education. *Art Education Research Review, 25*(1), 163–185.

jagodzinski, j. (2009). The hijacking of creativity: The dilemma of contemporary art education. In N. Addison & L. Burgess (Eds.), *Debates in art and design education* (pp. 23–34). New York, NY: Routledge.

Kim, M. S. (1999). *Dak-paper dolls*. Seoul, Korea: Jong-Eun Nara.

Korean Business Council for the Arts (2012). 메세나란? (What is Mécénat?). Retrieved from www.mecenat.or.kr/mecenat/about_mecenat.jsp

Lee, S. C. (2012). *Hanji: A beautiful Korean paper*. Seoul, Korea: Hyum Am Sa.

Manifold, M. C. (2009). Envisioning invisible cultures. In F. R. Sabol & M. C. Manifold (Eds.), *Through the prism: Looking into the spectrum of writings by Enid Zimmerman* (pp. 89–99). Reston, VA: National Art Education Association.

Park, C. E. (2009). *The genesis of multicultural education*. Seoul, Korea: The Borderless Village.

Theobald, P., & Nachtigal, P. (1995). Culture, community, and the promise of rural education. *Phi Delta Kappan, 77*(2), 132–135.

UNESCO (2010, May). *Outcomes of Second World Conference on Arts Education*. Retrieved from http://portal.unesco.org/culture/en/ev.php-URL_ID=39949&URL_DO=DO_TOPIC&URL_SECTION=201.html

Wenger, E. (1999). *Communities of practice: Learning, meaning, and identity*. New York, NY: Cambridge University Press.

ENDNOTES

[1] See http://whc.unesco.org/en/wheducation

[2] This form of paper is stronger and lasts longer than many Western papier-mâché-like counterparts.

[3] Students' names throughout this chapter are pseudonyms.

[4] Image retrieved from http://shop.jejun.com/ej/tour/simple_tour.html?mode=seogwi&list_id=%B4%DA%C1%BE%C0%CC%C0%CE%C7%FC%B9%DA%B9%B0%B0%FC&tuid=1148365246

Selected Resources

About the Contributors

Selected Resources for Art Teachers and Educators

There are a number of resources that provide lesson ideas, images, and communication platforms for designing culturally sensitive art curricula or researching topics of culture in global contexts. The following are a partial list of some of useful resources or resource sites.

Books

Addo, A. O. (2012). African education through the arts. In O. N. Ukpokodu & P. Ukpokodu (Eds.), *Contemporary voices from the margins: Educators on African and American Education* (pp. 29–66). Charlotte, NC: Information Age Education.

Boughton, D., & Mason, R. (Eds.). (1999). *Beyond multicultural art education: International perspectives*. Münster, Germany: Waxmann Verlag GmbH.

Bresler, L. (Ed.). (2007). *International handbook of research in arts education*. Dordrecht, The Netherlands: Springer.

Buntinx, G., Rassool, C., Kratz, C., Szwajam L., Ybarra-Frausto, T., & Kirshenblatt-Gimblett, B. (Eds.). (2006). *Museum frictions: Public cultures/global transformations*. Durham, NC: Duke University Press Books.

Cahan, S., & Kocur, Z. (1996). *Contemporary art and multicultural education*. New York, NY: Routledge.

Chapell, S. V., & Faltis, C. J. (2013). *The arts and emergent bilingual youth: Building culturally responsive, critical and creative education in school and community contexts*. New York, NY: Routledge.

Chung, S. K. (Ed.). (2012). *Teaching Asian art: Content, context, and pedagogy*. Reston, VA: National Art Education Association.

Davis, J. W. (2009). *Image as idea: The arts in global cultures*. Dubuque, IA: Kendall/Hunt.

Delacruz, E. D., Arnold, A., Kuo, A., & Parsons, M. (2009). *Globalization, art, and education*. Reston, VA: National Art Education Association.

Eca, T., & Mason, R. (2008). *International dialogues about visual culture, education, and art*. Bristol, England: Intellect.

Freedman, K., & Hernandez, F. (Eds.). (1998). *Curriculum, culture, and art education: Comparative perspectives*. Albany: State University of New York Press.

Grande, J. K. (2007). *Dialogues in diversity: Art from marginal to mainstream*. Pari, Italy: Pari.

Harding, J., & Pinsent, P. (2008). *What do you see? International perspectives on children's book illustration*. Newcastle upon Tyne, England: Cambridge Scholars.

Kauppinen, H. (1995). *Trends in art education from diverse cultures*. Reston, VA: National Art Education Association.

New Museum. (2010). *Rethinking contemporary art and multicultural education*. New York, NY: Routledge.

Park, C. C. (2009). *Creating with reverence: Art, diversity, culture and soul*. Charleston, SC: BookSurge.

Smiers, J. (2003). *Arts under pressure: Protecting cultural diversity in the age of globalization*. London, England: Zed Books.

Spivak, G. C. (2012). *An aesthetic education in the era of globalization*. Cambridge, MA: Harvard University Press.

Young, B. (2011). *Art, culture and ethnicity* (2nd ed.). Reston, VA: National Art Education Association.

Books of Identity and Arts of Diverse Cultures

Ankori, G. (2006). *Palestinian art*. London, England: Reaktion Books.

Bartra, E. (2003). *Crafting gender: Women and folk art in Latin America and the Caribbean*. Durham, NC: Duke University Press.

Belting, H., Buddensieg, A., & Weibel, P. (2013). *The global contemporary and the rise of new art worlds*. Cambridge, MA: The MIT Press.

Berry, J. K. (2011). *Personal geography: Explorations in mixed-media making*. Richmond, VA: North Light Books.

Frishman, M., & Khan, H-U. (Eds.). (2002). *The mosque: Architectural development and regional diversity*. London, England: Thames and Hudson.

Harmon, K., & Clemans, G. (2010). *The map as art: Contemporary artists explore cartography*. Princeton Architectural Press.

Jani, V. (2011). *Diversity in design: Perspective from the non-Western world*. New York, NY: Fairchild.

Laddaga, R. (2004). *Shifting map: Artists' platforms and strategies for cultural diversity*. Rotterdam, The Netherlands: nai010 publishers/Rijksakademie van Beeldende Kunsten/Rain Artists' Initiatives.

Lloyd, F. (2002). *Contemporary Arab women's art: Dialogues of the present*. New York, NY: I. B. Taurus.

Logsdon, G. (2007). *The mother of all arts: Agrarianism and the creative impulse*. Lexington: The University Press of Kentucky.

Longenecker, M., & Gardiner, L. (Eds.). (1989). *Folk art of the Soviet Union: Reflections of the rich cultural diversity of the 15 republics*. San Diego, CA: Mingei International Museum of the World.

McEvilley, T., & Buchloh, B. (2013). *Making art global: Volume 2 / Magiciens de la Terre 1989*. Stuttgart, Germany: Walther König, Köln.

Monem, N. (2009). *Contemporary art in the Middle East: Artworld*. London, England: Black Dog.

Morgan, D., & Promey, S. M. (2001). *The visual culture of American religions*. Berkeley: University of California Press.

Raven, A., & Demonte, C. (2000). *Women of the world: A global collection of art*. Portland, OR: Pomegranate Communications.

Tatum, C. M. (2001). *Chicano popular culture: Que hable el pueblo*. Tucson: University of Arizona Press.

Books for Children

Ajmera, M., & Ivanko, J. D. (2005). *To be an artist*. Watertown, MA: Charlesbridge.

Asael, A., Rabemiafara, S., & Veneman, A. M. (2011). *Children of the world: How we live, learn and play in poems, drawings, and photographs*. New York, NY: Universe.

Atkin, S. B. (2000). *Voices from the field: Children of migrant farmworkers tell their stories* (reprint edition). New York, NY: Little, Brown and Company.

Blohm, J. M., & Lapinsky, T. (2006). *Kids like me: Voices of the immigrant experience*. Boston, MA: Nicholas Brealey.

DK Publishing. (2005). *A life like mine: How children live around the world* (reprint edition). New York, NY: DK Children.

Ehlert, L. (2002). *Market day: A story told with folk art*. Boston, MA: HMH Books for Young Readers.

Flanagan, A. K., & Flanagan, R. (1999). *Mrs. Scott's beautiful art*. New York, NY: Children's Press.

Flatt, L. (2011). *Art and culture in the early Islamic world*. New York, NY: Crabtree.

Fulbeck, K., Cher, C., & Soetoro-Ng, M. (2010). *Mixed: Portraits of multiracial kids*. New York, NY: Chronicle Books.

Garza, C. L. (1990). *Family pictures/Cuadros de familia*. San Francisco, CA: Children's Book Press.

Garza, C. L. (2000). *In my family/En mi familia*. San Francisco, CA: Children's Book Press.

Goldman, D. (2007). *On my block: Stories and paintings by fifteen artists*. San Francisco, CA: Children's Book Press.

Hamanaka, S., & Ohmi, A. (1999). *In search of the spirit: The living national treasures of Japan*. New York, NY: HarperCollins.

Kindersley, A., & Kindersley, B. (1995). *Children just like me: A unique celebration of children around the world*. New York, NY: DK Children.

Kindersley, A., & Kindersley, B., Gavin, J., & Hall, A. (1997). *Children just like me: Our favorite stories*. New York, NY: DK Children.

Mazer, A. (1993). *American street: A multicultural anthology of stories*. New York, NY: Persea.

Menzel, P., Mann, C. C., & Kennedy, P. (1995). *Material world: A global family portrait*. San Francisco, CA: Sierra Book Club.

Meredith, S., Hickman, C., Rogers, K., Kirkby, J., Le Rolland, L., & Bhachu, V. (2010). *The Usborne encyclopedia book of world religions* (Internet Linked Encyclopedia). London, England: Usborne.

Morris, A., & Heyman, K. (1995). *Homes and houses* (Around the World Series). New York, NY: HarperCollins.

Muller, J. (2006). *Changing countryside*. Alhambra, CA: Heryin Books.

Noel, N. (1998). *Joy in simplicity: An artistic & poetic journey into Amish country, featuring original art by Nancy Noel*. Zionsville, IN: Noel Studio.

Otfinoski, S. (2011). *African Americans in the visual arts*. New York, NY: Facts on File.

Paley, N. (1995). *Finding art's place: Experiments in contemporary culture and education*. New York, NY: Routledge.

Raczka, B. (2008). *Where in the world? Around the globe in 13 works of art*. Minneapolis, MN: First Avenue Editions.

Rochelle, B. (2000). *Words and wings: A treasury of African-American art and poetry*. New York, NY: Amistad.

Rohmer, H. (1997). *Just like me: Stories and self-portraits by fourteen artists*. San Francisco, CA: Children's Book Press.

Rohmer, H. (1999). *Honoring our ancestors: Stories and paintings by fourteen artists*. San Francisco, CA: Children's Book Press.

Rolbin, C. (2011). *Art and life in rural Japan: Toho Village through the eyes of its youth*. London, England: New Generation Press.

Rotner, S. M., & Kelly, S. M. (2010). *Shades of people* (reprint edition). New York, NY: Holiday House.

Smith, D. J., & Armstrong, S. (2009). *If America were a village: A book about the people of the United States*. Toronto, Canada: Kids Can Press.

Smith, D. J., & Armstrong, S. (2011). *If the world were a village: A book about the world's people* (2nd ed.). Toronto, Canada: Kids Can Press.

Students of Cunningham Elementary School. (1996). *We are all related*. Vancouver, Canada: Raincoast Books.

Touba, J., Ale, C. B., & Glasser, B. (1998). *Nepal: Chandra Bahadur Ale's painting: "Simple Living"* (Young Artists of the World). New York, NY: Powerkids Press.

Touba, J., Forconesi, M., Glasser, B., & IACA World Awareness Children's Museum. (1998). *Argentina: Marianela Forconesi's painting; "My Father's Farm"* (Young Artists of the World). New York, NY: Powerkids Press.

Touba, J., Glasser, B., Lin, L., & IACA World Awareness Children's Museum. (1998). *Taiwan: Lisa Lin's painting; "Mooncakes"* (Young Artists of the World). New York, NY: Powerkids Press.

Touba, J., Heinonen, A., Glasser, B., & IACA World Awareness Children's Museum. (1998). *Finland: Anne Heinonen's painting; "Life at Home"* (Young Artists of the World). New York, NY: Powerkids Press.

Touba, J., Kotyenko, S., Glasser, B., & IACA World Awareness Children's Museum. (1998). *Ukraine: Sasha Kotyenko's painting; "Embroidery Time"* (Young Artists of the World). New York, NY: Powerkids Press.

Touba, J., Ngome, P., Glasser, B., & IACA World Awareness Children's Museum. (1998). *Gabon: Phillippe Ngome's painting; "My Family Goes to Market"* (Young Artists of the World). New York, NY: Powerkids Press.

Zhang, S. N. (1998). *The children of China: An artist's journey*. Toronto, Canada: Tundra Books.

Zim, J. (1975). *My shalom, my peace: Paintings and poems by Jewish and Arab children*. New York, NY: McGraw-Hill.

Journals and Magazines

Art Education (www.arteducators.org)
> *Art Education* is an official journal of the National Art Education Association, and is available to members of that professional organization. It includes articles on a wide variety of topics, which are of interest to art educators at all levels and in diverse contexts of art education.

Canku Ota (www.turtletrack.org)
> An online newsletter for and about Native life and traditions in North America. Materials appropriate for all ages are included.

Chandamama (www.chandamama.com/index.htm)
> Originally aimed at teaching elementary-level children of India about the nation's richly diverse cultural traditions, this magazine offers myths, folktales, histories, graphic stories, art, music, interactive games and activities, and stories of everyday life in India. Issues are published in English and six Indian dialects. The website offers links to audio texts of stories.

ChildArt (www.icaf.org/childart)
> This publication of the International Child Art Foundation features articles written for children from ages 10-12, and may be used by art educators in a variety of contexts.

Denizen (www.denizenmag.com)
> *Denizen* is an online magazine for children who have lived, for a variety of reasons, in more than one country. Articles address the struggles to find, and joys of cultivating, a sense of identity as a global nomad. Appropriate for secondary-level students and above.

Faces® : *World Cultures for Grades 5-9* (www.cobblestonepub.com/magazine/fac)
> Published by Cobblestone & Cricket, each issue of this themed magazine shows children from around the world in contexts of their daily lives. Photographs, articles, and activities focus on art, culture, animals, geography, and language. Teacher's guides are available from the website.

Iguana Magazine for Kids ages 7-12 (www.cricketmag.com/IGA--IGUANA-Magazine-for-Kids-ages-7-12)
> This Spanish language magazine for children offers fictional stories, biographies, and cross-disciplinary activities that introduce children to Latino culture. It may present useful background information and resource materials when teaching to or about Latin American cultures.

International Journal of Education Through Art (IJETA) (www.insea.org)
> A publication of the International Society for Education through Art (InSEA), IJETA features research studies and essays by academics and art educators from all over the world, and addresses art educational topics of global interest and concern.

Journal of Cultural Research in Art Education (JCRAE) (http://ussea.webhost.uits.arizona.edu/JCRAE.html)
> Published by the United States Society for Education through Art (USSEA), this journal focuses on topics related to issues of cultural diversity and art education within the United States, with some attention paid to global cultures and art education.

Museum International (http://portal.unesco.org/culture/en/ev.php-URL_ID=2356&URL_DO=DO_TOPIC&URL_SECTION=201.html)
> This journal, which is published by UNESCO, presents a forum for information about cultural heritages globally. Issues of policy, ethics, and practices at national and international levels are addressed in contexts of art, archeology, cultural heritages, and other fields of relevance to global societies and cultures, philosophy, and economic sustainability.

Skipping Stones Magazine, An International Multicultural Magazine (www.skippingstones.org)
> Stories, poems, artwork, and photos contributed by children from all over the world are featured in this magazine. Each issue also contains articles, teaching guides, and instructional resources for designing learning experiences based on topics of the issue. The multilingual contents include English translations.

Teaching Tolerance (www.tolerance.org/magazine/archives)
> Subscriptions are free to teachers. Issues are themed by topics relating to cultural awareness and acceptance. The magazines are aimed at student audiences and are appropriate for classroom use.

The UNESCO Courier (www.unesco.org/new/en/unesco-courier/the-magazine)
> Geared to adult audiences, this downloadable, full-color journal includes articles that might be used as discussion starters for older teens and young adults. Issues are themed and available in six languages (Arabic, Chinese, English, French, Russian, and Spanish). Back issues are available.

Visual Culture & Gender (VCG) (http://vcg.emitto.net)
> This online multimedia journal includes articles and materials that consider "how visual culture constructs gender in context with representations of race, age, sexuality, social units, (dis)ability, and social class" (VCG website), and encourages international dialogues of these topics.

Journal Articles and Book Chapters

Ballengee Morris, C., & Taylor, C. (2005). You can hide but you can't run: Interdisciplinary and culturally sensitive approaches to mask making. *Art Education, 58*(5), 12–17.

Bastos, F. M. C. (2006). Border-crossing dialogues: Engaging art education students in cultural research. *Art Education, 59*(4), 20–24.

Brown, S. L. (2007). Using visual art as a bridge to our cultural heritage: Roy Strassberg's "Holocaust Bone Structures" series. *Art Education, 60*(2), 25–32.

Chandler, R. (2007). Colorquest: A museum pedagogy on ethnic self-identity, representation, and cultural histories at the Boston MFA. *International Journal of Education through Art, 3*(3), 173–184.

Chin, C. D. (2011). Critiquing commonly available multicultural art education resources. *International Journal of Education through Art, 7*(3), 299–313.

Chung, S. K. (2009). Presenting cultural artifacts in the art museum: A university-museum collaboration. *Art Education, 62*(3), 33–39.

Coleman, A. (2006). Integrating human rights and the visual arts: A peace summer education project for Israeli and Palestinian students. *International Journal of Arts Education, 2*(1), 43–49.

Hubbard, K. (2009). Immersion required: An art teacher living, teaching, and studying art in an unfamiliar culture. *Art Education, 62*(1), 40–45.

Hwang, R.-L. (2006). Integrating Buddhist doctrine into arts education. *International Journal of Education through Art, 2*(2), 93–103.

Lai, A. (2012). Culturally responsive. *Art Education, 65*(5), 18–23.

Lopez, V. (2009). The hyphen goes where? Four stories of the dual-cultural experience in the art classroom. *Art Education, 62*(5), 19–24.

Manifold, M. C. (2000). Valuing a rural aesthetic. *Art Education, 53*(4), 18–24.

Mendoza, H. R., & Matyók, T. (2013). Designing student citizenship: Internationalised education in transformative disciplines. *International Journal of Art & Design Education, 32*(2), 215–225.

Pepin-Wakefield, Y. (2010). Beyond the veil: Learning to teach fine arts in a Muslim culture. *Art Education, 63*(6), 13–18.

Radcliffe-Thomas, N. (2007). Intercultural chameleons or the Chinese way? Chinese students in Western art and design education. *Art, Design, and Communication in Higher Education, 6*(1), 41–55.

Smith-Shank, D. L. (2002). Community celebrations as ritual signifiers. *Visual Arts Research, 28*(2), 57–63.

Tavin, K., & Hausman, J. (2004). Art education and visual culture in the age of globalization. *Art Education, 57*(5), 47–52.

Willis, S. (2012). Quadratic pedagogy. In L. Campbell and S. Simmons III (Eds.), *The heart of art education: Holistic approaches to creativity, integration, and transformation* (pp. 133–140). Reston, VA: National Art Education Association.

Yi, S. D., & Kim, H. S. (2005). A movement towards Eastern ethnocentric art education: The value of Korean art and cultural heritage. *Art Education, 58*(5), 18–24.

Resource Guides: Art Units and Lesson Plans

Archuleta, M., Meyers, M., Nahmias, S. S., Woodsum, J. A., & Yorba, J. (1994). *The Native American fine art movement: A resource guide.* Phoenix, AZ: Heard Muscum. Retrieved from www.heard.org/pdfs/fine-arts-web.pdf

Asher, R. (2009). Advocating peace and global art education: Two quilts, one world. *The International Journal of Learning, 16*(2), 435–448. Retrieved from http://ijl.cgpublisher.com/product/pub.30/prod.2044

Asia Society. (2013). *Attitudes towards nature in Daoist art.* Retrieved from http://asiasociety.org/education/resources-schools/elementary-lesson-plans/attitudes-towards-nature-daoist-art

Asia Society. (2013). *Best Web 2.0 sites for global learning.* Retrieved from http://asiasociety.org/education/resources-schools/partnership-ideas/best-web-20-sites-global-learning

Asia Society. (2013). *Twice upon a time: Multi-cultural Cinderella.* Retrieved from http://asiasociety.org/education/resources-schools/elementary-lesson-plans/twice-upon-time-multi-cultural-cinderella

Bardeguez, C., & Kocur, Z. (1996). American identity. In S. Cahan and Z. Kocur (Eds.), *Contemporary art and multicultural education* (pp. 233–254). New York: The New Museum of Contemporary Art.

Children's Museum of Indianapolis. (2009). *Take me there Egypt: Become a traveler. A unit of study for grades 3-5.* Retrieved from www.childrensmuseum.org/sites/default/files/files/uos_takemethereegypt.pdf

Culture 2000 Programme of the European Union. (2000). *A Europe of tales* (Animated video). Retrieved at www.europeoftales.net

Downs, D. (2005). *Patchwork: Seminole and Miccosukee art and activities*. Sarasota, FL: Pineapple Press.

Eiteljorg Museum. (2002). *Mihtohseenionki (The people's place): Teachers resource guide*. Retrieved from www.eiteljorg.org/learn/resources

Glenbow Museum. (2013). *Honouring traditions: Reframing Native art*. 21st century learning. Retrieved from www.glenbow.org/programs/school/21C/honouring/index.cfm

Higgins, R. (2010). *Teaching world cultures*. Retrieved from www.learnnc.org/lp/pages/6390?ref=search

Hirschfelder, A., & Beamer, Y. (2000). *Native Americans today: Resources and activities for educators grades 4–8*. Westport, CT: Libraries Unlimited.

Philadelphia Folklore Project. (2009). *Resources for folk arts education*. Retrieved from www.folkloreproject.org/programs/education/Resources%20for%20Folk%20Arts%20Ed.pdf

Shabhas, A. (2002). *Medieval banquet in the Alhambra Palace*. Berkeley, CA: AWAIR, Arab World and Islamic Resources & School Services.

THIRTEEN (Producer). (2009). *Art through time: A global view* [Video Series and Teaching Materials]. Annanberg Learner. Retrieved from www.learner.org/resources/series211.html

Tiller, C., & Clifford, S. (2011). *Artists in creative education: Unlocking children's creativity—A practical guide for artists*. Newcastle on Tyne, England: Creativity, Culture and Education. Retrieved from www.artistsincreativeeducation.com/page/1/main.aspx

UNESCO. (2013). *Journeys to school*. Retrieved from http://publishing.unesco.org/details.aspx?&Code_Livre=4973&change=E#

UNESCO. (2013). *Why teach about the holocaust?* Retrieved from http://unesdoc.unesco.org/images/0021/002186/218631E.pdf

Willis, S. (2013). *Diversity in the classroom*. AP central. Retrieved from http://apcentral.collegeboard.com/apc/members/courses/teachers_corner/44360.html

Zimmerman, E. (1999). *Teaching art from a global perspective*. ERIC Digest. Retrieved from www.ericdigests.org/pre-9219/global.htm

Websites

AfriPOP! (http://afripopmag.com)
Older teens and young adult students would find this an interesting resource for studying the cultural achievements of contemporary African artists in areas of music, fashion, art, and film. Editors of the online site describe it as "specifically geared to sophisticated Afropolitans all over the globe. We speak to an audience who grew up with African values but aren't afraid to think of themselves as global citizens" (http://afripopmag.com/about).

Al Makan (www.almakan-syria.org/english)
Cultural website of the Syrian NGO Al Makan Art Association, the site offers news, multimedia presentations of art events, online art galleries, and resources for teaching to and about art and artists of Syria and other nations of the world.

Appalshop (http://appalshop.org)
Appalshop is the multimedia result of a US War on Poverty initiative of the late 1960s. Operators of the site focus on documenting the cultural riches of their community and disseminating information about Appalachians arts, crafts, and folkways to the world. Appalshop serves as an example of a cultural community being empowered to participate in global art worlds.

Artsedge (http://artsedge.kennedy-center.org/educators.aspx)
The Kennedy Center offers lesson plans, teaching guides, and visual materials for teaching a broad range of art-related topics in culturally respectful ways.

Asia Society: Education (http://asiasociety.org/education)
Provides links and resources for teaching to and about Asian cultures, and reports on model cross-cultural programs that integrate media and the arts.

ChinaVine (http://chinavine.org)
Read more about this web resource in Congdon and Blandy's chapter of this text, "It's About Them, It's About Us: Using ChinaVine as an Educational Tool."

¡Colorín Colorado! (www.colorincolorado.org/web_resources/by_type_of_organization/publishers_childrens_books)
Links are provided to publishers of bilingual and multilingual children's picture books and texts that promote cultural respect and appreciation.

¡Del Corizon! Latino Voices in American Art: Profesores (http://americanart.si.edu/education/corazon/profesores_home.cfm)
Includes links to lesson plans and units created by the Smithsonian Art Museum for use in teaching to and about people and artists of Chicano, Latino, and Hispanic cultures.

Fowler Museum at UCLA, Teacher Resources
(www.fowler.ucla.edu/teacher-resources)
This museum website offers downloadable resources
and curriculum units for teaching about traditional
and living cultures around the world.

Global Project Based Learning Resource List
(http://my-ecoach.com/online/webresourcelist.
php?rlid=6499)
Created by Linda Ullah, this website includes links
to interactive communication technologies, online
databases, and software platforms that facilitate cross-
cultural projects.

The J. Paul Getty Museum
(http://artsedge.kennedy-center.org/educators.aspx)
Presents art educational materials for English-speaking
as well as ESL and multilingual students.

Japan Society: About Japan, A Teacher's Resources
(http://aboutjapan.japansociety.org/page/
japaneducation_home)
Units and lessons on topics related to Japanese life
and culture, which are available on this website, were
created as collaborations between art specialists and
teachers.

A Journey through Slavic Culture
(http://russianculture.wordpress.com)
Appropriate for secondary and postsecondary students,
this blog site presents visual, literary, and documentary
information and links for teaching about Eastern
European/Russian cultures, from antiquity to the
present day.

LASER: Latin American School and Educational
Resources (www.laser.msu.edu/teachers.php)
Educators can search for teaching units and lesson
plans by country/region, level, discipline, and subject.

Learn About Hmong (www.hmongnet.org)
This multimedia website of the Hmong Cultural
Center of Minnesota provides links to visual and audio
materials and resources useful to teaching the cultural
arts of Hmong people.

Learn NC (www.learnnc.org)
A website that is sponsored by the University of North
Carolina at Chapel Hill, School of Education, offers kits
and lesson materials for teaching to and about world
cultures and cultural diversity.

Museum of International Folk Art
(www.internationalfolkart.org/eventsedu/curricula.html)
Offers free curricula guides for teaching about historic
and contemporary folk cultures from South America,
Central America, and the Southwestern United States.

National Art Education Association
(www.arteducators.org)
The home site of NAEA, a national professional
organization for art educators, provides access
to extensive resources and information about art
educational practices, policies, and research.

National Museum of Africa Art (http://africa.si.edu/
education/classroom-resources/)
Free downloadable teaching guides, art images,
primary source materials, and lessons are available
on a range of topics from contemporary African art
and artists to historic and traditional crafts of diverse
African cultures.

Native Online (www.nativeonline.com)
Designed and maintained by First Nations people, this
website provides links to and information about the
artwork of living Native artists.

NativeWeb (www.nativeweb.org)
NativeWeb is hosted by a consortium of Native and
indigenous groups world-wide. Information is not
strictly limited to art or art educational materials. The
site serves as an excellent database for student research
regarding issues of concern or relevance to indigenous
peoples in many nations.

Oyate (www.oyate.org)
This website is operated by a board of Native
Americans whose goal is to insure that Native peoples
are respectfully treated in educational and media
contexts. The website features lists of picture books,
texts, and teaching materials that have been approved
as portraying accurate information about various
Native groups.

Smithsonian Education
(www.smithsonianeducation.org/educators/index.html)
Provides links to vast repositories of lesson plans and
educational resources, including units and lessons of
cultural history, diversity, art, and design, prepared by
educators from various Smithsonian Museums.

Teaching Tolerance (www.tolerance.org)
A project of the Southern Poverty Law Center, the site
offers free downloadable teaching resources in the form
of kits, teaching units, lessons, magazines, posters, and
other educational resources, to teachers in the United
States and Canada. The educational resources cover a
wide range of topics relevant to diversity and cultural
tolerance.

UNESCO: United Nations Educational, Scientific and Cultural Organization (http://en.unesco.org)
A wide variety of reports and resources is available through this website. Included are curricular guides, teaching kits, units, lessons, and other instructional materials, as well as research data and news about peoples in all parts of the world. Particular focus is upon marginalized and endangered cultural groups.

World Digital Library (www.wdl.org/en)
This website gives free access to hundreds of primary cultural materials from nine regions of the world.

Youth Media Reporter (www.youthmediareporter.org)
While much of the information in this source is dated, the website offers inspiring examples of visual media projects created by youth and refugees living in impoverished regions and countries of the world. The website is sponsored by the Family Health International and Academy for Educational Development (fhi 360).

Child Art Exhibitions

The Arts Olympiad (www.icaf.org/artsolympiad)
Organized by International Child Art Foundation (ICAF), exhibitions are held every four years, in a cycle that mirrors the International Olympics for athletes. Artworks are guided by lesson plans made available to teachers from the website.

Artsonia (www.artsonia.com)
Artsonia is advertised as an online "Art Museum." Teachers submit digital versions of students' artworks for posting in online galleries. Artworks are organized by school, state, or nation.

Crayola Connects Us (www2.crayola.com/theArtOf Childhood/gallery/)
A commercially sponsored website of high quality.

International Child Art Exhibition: Kshitij (www.kshitij.org)
Kshitij, an art society based in India, has organized annual international child exhibitions since 2003. Each focuses on a theme. Entry fees are required and awards are given to outstanding entries.

International Children's Art Exhibition (ICAE) (www.pentel.com/icae)
ICAE was founded in Japan and is sponsored by Pentel. Thousands of entries by children around the world are judged according to criteria of originality, content, and cultural expression. Winning artworks are included in exhibitions that are displayed in various sites throughout the world.

International Children's Exhibition of Fine Arts Lidice (ICEFA) (www.mdvv-lidice.cz/en)
This themed exhibition/competition was established in 1967 to honor children lost in war during and since WWII. Of thousands of entries, 1,400 are selected annually for exhibition in various locations on six continents. Information about entry is available on the website.

International Exchange Exhibition of Children's Art: Narita City (www.narita-childart.jp/file/index_e.html)
International art entries and art by children of Narita City, Japan, are selected for exhibition annually. Awarded works are posted online.

Kanagawa Biennial World Children's Art Exhibition (www.earthplaza.jp/biennial/English/index.html)
Every other year since 1979, children's artworks from all over the world are selected and exhibited in Kanagawa Prefecture, Japan. Grand prize winning works are organized by country and posted on the website.

London International Gallery of Children's Art (LIGCA) (http://ligca.org/our-collection/)
This online-only gallery features artworks by children internationally.

Paintbrush Diplomacy (http://paintbrushdiplomacy.org/programs/international-art-exchange)
Artworks and writings based on themes or personal preferences may be sent to organizers of this program, who will arrange exchanges with teachers from other participating countries.

USSEA/InSEA Child Art Exchange (http://ussea.net/child-art-exchange/)
Teachers are invited to submit digital images of student artworks, which may be based on annually suggested themes or personal preference. All submissions are posted on the USSEA website.

About the Contributors

About the Editors

MARJORIE COHEE MANIFOLD is Associate Professor of Art Education in the Curriculum and Instruction Department, School of Education, Indiana University. In her research, Manifold has studied the aesthetic sensibilities and artistic practices of folk artists in dynamic interaction with their local communities. This includes explorations of the artmaking practices and products of adolescents and young adults in online communities. Based on findings from these inquiries, she has developed curricula for teaching studio art online to students across national and international boundaries. She has presented at national and international conferences and served on numerous review boards of journals in art education, new media, and comparative studies in education; her numerous publications have appeared in peer-reviewed journals and as book chapters. Additionally, Manifold served as President of the United States Society for Education through Art (USSEA) from 2009–2011, has served two terms as a North American World Councilor to the International Society for Education through Art (InSEA), and is currently InSEA Vice-President.

STEVE WILLIS taught art in public schools for 23 years prior to joining the faculty at Missouri State University in Springfield, where he is Professor of Art Education. He is a member of the Cherokee of Western Missouri and his research interests include: indigenous knowledge, issues of equity, Native American practices, tribal cultural construction, issues of arts assessment, service learning, community engagement, and spirituality in art. As an International Baccalaureate (IB) examiner, he has traveled nationally to conduct Visual Arts examinations and has evaluated IB *Extended Essays* from Europe, Africa, the Middle East, Asia, and the Americas. He is a member of the National Advisory Committee for the Praxis II Art Education Examination; has served as a consultant for various schools, school districts, and community arts organizations; has presented at national and international conferences; and has published in and served on the editorial boards of several national and international journals. Steve is active in both the International Society for Education through Art (InSEA) as a World Councilor (2014–2017) and the United States Society for Education through Art (USSEA). He served as USSEA President (2013–2015). As a contemporary artist, he creates images concerning spirituality (www.stevewillis.org).

ENID ZIMMERMAN is Professor Emerita of Art Education and current Coordinator of High Ability Programs at Indiana University. In her research, she focuses on art talent development, creativity and art education, art teacher education, feminist art education, leadership and mentoring, global art education, and curriculum and policy issues. She has authored over 35 articles, 20 book chapters, and 25 books and monographs and has taught or conducted workshops in more than 25 countries. She was the first NAEA Research Commission Chair and is presently an NAEA Research Commissioner. Zimmerman has received numerous university, national, and international awards; the NAEA Elliot Eisner Lifetime Achievement Award (2014) is the most recent. She also served two terms as a North American World Councilor for the International Society for Education through Art. She co-edited *Connecting Creativity Research and Practice in Art Education* (NAEA, 2015) and had a leading chapter published in the *Handbook of Research on Creativity* (Edward Elgar, 2013). In addition, Zimmerman served as editor of 14 NAEA Advocacy White Papers (2011–2012) and wrote one of them. She presently is involved developing and evaluating leadership programs for NAEA. *Through the Prism: Looking at the Spectrum of Writings of Enid Zimmerman* (NAEA, 2009), co-authored by Robert Sabol and Marjorie Manifold, summarizes her influences on art education through her own writings and those of her former students and colleagues.

About the Authors

JONI BOYD ACUFF, PhD, is an Assistant Professor of Art Education in the Department of Arts Administration, Education and Policy at The Ohio State University. Critical multicultural art education is the core of her research. For Acuff, critical multiculturalism is the lens through which she analyzes varying formal and informal modes and avenues of art educational dissemination, practices, and interpretations. Her research and scholarship also includes critical race theory in art education; community-based art education; and culturally responsive teaching, pedagogy, and curriculum development. Acuff has over 14 years of art teaching experience in both traditional and non-traditional classrooms. She has worked extensively with diverse populations of learners, including students with special needs (cognitive and physical), student who identify as LGBTQ, and students from varying racial backgrounds and socioeconomic levels.

HYERI AHN is Assistant Professor in the School of Fine Arts and the Head of Graduate Program in Art Education at Kookmin University in Seoul, Korea. She is a former chief-editor of *Art Education Review*, the official journal of Society for Art Education of Korea. Her research interests include technology, integration, visual culture, and community in art education. She received her PhD from the University of Missouri at Columbia.

DOUG BLANDY is Professor in the Arts and Administration Program and Senior Vice Provost for Academic Affairs at the University of Oregon. His research and teaching focuses on art educational experiences in community-based settings and addresses the needs of all students within a lifelong learning context. He also concentrates on the relationships between art, education, gender, community, and place. Blandy's research defines, describes, critiques, and analyzes the implementation of community arts programs that are participatory, community focused, community-based, and culturally democratic. His research has been published in *Studies in Art Education, Art Education,* and the *Journal of Multicultural and Cross-Cultural Research in Art Education,* as well as other academic journals. Most recently Blandy co-edited, with Paul Bolin, *Matter Matters: Art Education and Material Culture Studies,* published by the National Art Education Association in 2012. Along with Kristin G. Congdon he is co-principal investigator of ChinaVine, an interactive web-based project with a mission to interpret China's cultural heritage for English reading/writing audiences.

JEFFREY L. BROOME is Associate Professor of Art Education at Florida State University. His interests include multiage art education, cultural diversity, and humanistic approaches to art curriculum. He delivers presentations at national and state conferences, international symposia, and at school district workshops. Broome's manuscripts have been accepted for publication as book chapters as well as articles in *Studies in Art Education,* the *Journal of Cultural Research in Art Education, Visual Arts Research,* the *Journal of Multiage Education, Art Education Australia, The Journal of Art for Life, Arts Education Policy Review,* and *Art Education.* Previously, he worked for the University of North Texas, the University of Georgia, and for 8 years as a public school art teacher.

MARTHA CHRISTOPOULOU is currently Headteacher at 139 Primary School of Athens, Greece. She holds a BA and Postgraduate Diploma in educational studies and an MA and PhD in art education. Christopoulou's research focuses on visual culture education, critical pedagogy, identity formation, and reflective practice. At present, she is researching the impact of the Greek financial crisis on children's lives and ways of developing art/visual culture curricula that promote resilience. Her work is published in several journals including *Art Education, International Journal of Art and Design Education, International Journal of Education through Art,* and *School Arts Magazine.* Christopoulou has presented papers in international and national conferences including the International Society for Education through Art conferences in Viseu, Portugal, and Heidelberg, Germany.

KATHRYN COLEMAN is an artist, researcher, and teacher in Melbourne, Australia. She is active in the Association for Authentic, Experiential and Evidence-Based Learning (AAEEBL) as a Board Member and Conference Committee Member. Her research specifically focuses on the use of digital portfolios, open badges and digital learning spaces in education, and the arts for lifelong and life-wide learning. Coleman has many years of experience teaching both secondary and higher art and design education. She has been a casual Academic in Art and Design History and Art Administration at the University of New South Wales (UNSW, Australia), and is a PhD candidate at the Melbourne Graduate School of Education, The University of Melbourne. The working title of her thesis is *Creativity, Artistic Identity and Digital Portfolios: Exploring Artist Identities Through Stories and Art as Researcher-Teacher.*

SUSAN COLEMAN is an experienced visual arts educator who has taught in southwestern Sydney, New South Wales, Australia schools for 32 years. She believes in creating experiences for students that are rich and engaging through Visual Arts programs that present carefully planned sequences, which allow teachers to innovate, experiment, and challenge, but provide a clear framework of assistance for all students. Coleman is highly experienced in the development, design, and production of student resources and programs for ArtExpress and has a Master of Education (Gifted and Talented) from the University of New South Wales. She works with primary school and secondary students in creating interesting artworks in many media, organizes artist-run workshops in schools and at district level, and regularly provides professional development for her staff and other members of the school in Visual Arts and other discipline areas.

KRISTIN G. CONGDON is Professor Emerita of Philosophy and Humanities at the University of Central Florida. She has published extensively on folk art, community art, multi-cultural art education, and feminism, in an effort to celebrate artists who have had little visibility in the art world. Her authored or co-authored books include *Happy Clouds, Happy Trees: The Bob Ross Phenomenon* (2014), *American Folk Art: A Regional Reference* (2012), *Just Above the Water: Florida Folk Art* (2006), and *Community Art in Action* (2004). She has also been senior editor of *Art Education* and *Studies in Art Education* and is a principal co-investigator of ChinaVine, an interdisciplinary project that documents China's cultural heritage.

GLEN COUTTS is part-time Professor of Applied Visual Arts and a Docent at University of Lapland in Finland. He was Reader in Art and Design Education at the University of Strathclyde in Glasgow until April 2010. He writes regularly about issues in art education and is currently Vice-President of the International Society for Education through Art and Principal Editor of the *International Journal of Education through Art*.

MELANIE DAVENPORT is Associate Professor of Art Education at Georgia State University. Previously, she taught art in Fulton County Public Schools as an elementary art teacher and as an adaptive art specialist. Her research interests focus upon international-comparative and intercultural approaches to art education, media literacy and visual culture, and indigenous education. From 2007-2009, she taught visual communication strategies to Huichol youth in Mexico, toward the production of stop-motion animated shorts that present their traditional stories in their own languages. Davenport has also studied middle school art education in Japan and collaborated on projects with art educators in many countries. She has an extensive record of presentations and publications in the field, at the regional, national, and international level. She is an active member and formerly served on the boards of both InSEA and USSEA.

MARIT DEWHURST is Director of Art Education and Assistant Professor of Art and Museum Education at City College of New York, where she also directs City Art Lab, a community arts project. She has worked as an educator and program coordinator in multiple educational settings, including the Museum of Modern Art in New York, where she coordinated afterschool Teen Programs. Dewhurst's work on the role of art in social justice education, culturally relevant pedagogy, and community development has been published in several books and journals, among them *Equity and Excellence in Education*, *Journal of Art Education*, and *International Journal of Education Through Art*. She works closely with Museum Teen Summit, a youth-led research and advocacy program for museum teen programs in New York City. Her recent book, *Social Justice Art: A Framework for Activist Art Pedagogy*, was published by Harvard Education Press in 2014.

DEBRA DONNELLY is a history educator in the School of Education at the University of Newcastle in Australia, where she works with preservice teachers in both undergraduate and postgraduate programs. She has a secondary school background with extensive classroom, school administration, and welfare experience across a range of educational settings in New South Wales and internationally. Donnelly's research interests center on the role of the visual and media in the development of historical and global consciousness in an age of ever-increasing access through modern technology; she seeks to clarify the relationship between teachers' conceptual frameworks of understanding, problematic knowledge, and pedagogical practice. Donnelly has been the recipient of numerous teaching awards, including the University of Newcastle's Vice-Chancellor's Award for Outstanding Contribution to Student Learning (2011) and Teaching Excellence Award (2010), and she was a semi-finalist, with Kathryn Grushka, in the Adobe Design Achievement Awards in 2011.

LAURIE ELDRIDGE is an art educator in the Phoenix valley area public school district in Arizona. She teaches art to students in kindergarten through 8th grade. Her research interests include issues of teaching sensitively and responsibly about indigenous peoples and their arts. She believes that sensitive teaching about diverse populations benefits all by affirming the value and dignity of every human being.

MARY ERICKSON earned her BFA in Art Education from the University of Illinois and her MA and PhD in Art Education from Ohio State University. She taught at the high school (Indiana), community college (Illinois), and state college (Pennsylvania) levels before joining the faculty of Arizona State University's School of Art in 1990. She is the online curriculum developer for the Gallery at the Tempe Center for the Arts, which has adopted her inquiry approach for K-12 student lessons, for docent training, and for teacher workshops. She served as co-curator for Mixing it Up, a Mexican American art exhibition at the Tempe Center for the Arts. She is also co-author of *Chicano Art for Our Millennium* and *Contemporary Chicana and Chicano Art: Works, Culture and Education*, both published by Arizona State University's Bilingual Press.

KATHRYN GRUSHKA is currently Senior Lecturer at the University of Newcastle's School of Education, and is a nationally recognized Visual Arts & Design Educator, visual art education researcher, curriculum writer, and artist. She is known especially for her work on the performative role of artmaking, imaginative becoming, reflective practice, adaptive knowledge, and transformative learning. In teaching and learning, Grushka's research is centered on ensuring the most explicit links between research insights into cognition, embodied visual knowing, and subjectivity insights. Her research links the fields of visual art, design, visual digital technologies, critical and performative pedagogies, and knowledge as visual representation. She has been the recipient of numerous awards, including the New South Wales Institute for Educational Research Doctoral Award. She received the University of Newcastle prestigious awards for Teaching Quality in 2005 and Student Learning in 2010.

KATHLEEN HALL has been an art educator in public school systems within Canada and the United States. She received a PhD in Educational Studies: Art Education, from the University of Victoria, British Columbia, Canada. Her research focused on the role of arts-based learning as an aspect of best practices in education for marginalized Roma children. Her research interests in Roma education began while doing volunteer work in a summer arts program in Kosovo where she became aware of the educational challenges many Roma children face in East-Central Europe. This opportunity led her to question how these challenges affect the school experiences of Roma refugee children who flee the rampant persecution of their home countries and seek asylum in Canada. Kathleen has presented her research at conferences within both Canada and the United States, and has written articles on Roma education and art that have been published in print and online formats.

JEONG IM HUH is a Professor in Art Education at Pusan National University of Education in South Korea and teaches courses in traditional Korean art. She was the president of the Korean Elementary Art Education Association from 2001 to 2002, and is currently the Chairperson for the Arts Education Research Institute of Pusan National University of Education. She is an editor of *Journal of Art Education* in Korea. Huh has presented her work and research in local and international professional conferences in Korea, Japan, and Hungary. Her research—which focuses on creativity, aesthetic education, traditional Korean art, and integrated education centered in art activities—has been published in numerous publications in South Korea. She also is a prolific artist and has had several solo and group art exhibitions.

ANIKÓ ILLÉS is Associate Professor at the Department of Pedagogy and Psychology, Moholy-Nagy University of Art and Design, where she is responsible for the visual art teacher training programs. Her research interests are connected to several topics of art education such as creativity, education through art, and appreciation of art.

TIMO JOKELA is Professor of Art Education and Dean of the Faculty of Art and Design, University of Lapland. He also worked as Visiting Professor of Art Education and Environmental Art at the University of Strathclyde, Glasgow, Scotland (2006–2011). He has been responsible for several international and regional action research projects in the field of art education. Jokela works actively as an environmental artist, often using natural materials and the local cultural heritage as a starting point for his works. He has realized several exhibitions and environmental art and community art projects in Finland and abroad. Jokela has published several articles and books.

ANNA KENDE is Associate Professor in the Department of Social Psychology, Eötvös Loránd University, Budapest, Hungary. Her research focuses on processes of social inclusion and exclusion, on differing forms of prejudices, and on the effects of social marginalization on children's identity formation.

ANGELA M. LA PORTE is Associate Professor of Art Education at the University of Arkansas in Fayetteville. She has presented numerous papers at state, national, and international conferences and has published on intergenerational, social, and multicultural issues in art education. She edited and contributed writings to a book published by the National Art Education Association (NAEA), *Community Connections: Intergenerational Links in Art Education*. La Porte recently contributed a chapter to a 2nd edition of the NAEA publication *Art Culture and Ethnicity* ("Building Community in Harlem"), an article in *The International Journal of Education Through Art* ("Older Adult Responses to Art Curriculum and Self-Directed Learning"), and an article in *Studies in Art Education* ("Beyond Traditional Art Education: Transformative Lifelong Learning in Community-Based Settings with Older Adults," co-authored).

FOTINI LARKOU is currently working for the Cyprus Ministry of Education and Culture as Assistant Headmistress, Art Advisor in Primary Education, and Advisor for the National Art Curriculum. She has 20 years' experience in teaching art to primary students, 10 of which have been involved in advisory work and designing and implementing educational programs in art museums. As Art Advisor and Advisor of Educational Programs in Primary Education she organized art seminars for primary teachers, undertook teacher training for professional development in art teaching/learning, carried out Museum Education Seminars for primary teachers, and delivered sample lessons and practical workshops in the field of Art Education for primary teachers. She also took part in the design and development of a new national art curriculum and supported teachers to implement it. She obtained her PhD in 2010 under the supervision of Professor Rachel Mason. Since then she has had the opportunity to work part-time as a visiting lecturer in two private universities in the education department. She is a committee member of Cyprus Society for Education through Art (CySEA) and a founding member of Hambis Printmaking School-Museum.

JEANNE NEMETH is Associate Professor of Art Education at Herron School of Art at Indiana University—Purdue University Indianapolis. She holds a PhD in Curriculum and Instruction from Indiana University Bloomington with a minor in Museum Studies, and a MFA in Photography and Digital Media from the University of Cincinnati. Her research interests include material culture studies, contemporary art practices, and environmental psychology. Nemeth studies the relationship between contemporary collecting and art practice, focusing on the collecting practices of artists, art educators, and students. A recently published chapter, "The Practice of Collecting: Private Worlds of Youth Culture and a Rationale for Art Curriculum," examines the interplay between children's personal space and their collected objects, exploring how objects represent personal and communal experiences in time and place. Her current research revolves around preserved collections of artists whose homes, workspaces, and gardens have been converted into museums. These investigations have contributed to critical inquiry into better understanding how our constructed environments influence everyday creative processes, identity formation, and psychological states—and affect emotions and behavior.

LI-HSUN PENG is an Associate Professor in Creative Design Department, YunTech, National Yunlin University of Science and Technology, Taiwan. His research interests are related to the connections between design, visual culture, and post-colonial theories, with particular reference to identities of the Taiwanese. His PhD research was entitled "Crossing Borders: A Formosan's Postcolonial Exploration of European Art Deco Women Designers," and his research papers have been presented in journals, international congresses, and symposia.

ANTONIO PABLO ROMERO GONZÁLEZ is Assistant Professor of Art Education in the Department of Art Education in the UAM (Universidad Autónoma de Madrid, Spain). His research interests are of cultural pedagogies, creativity related to cultural diversity, contemporary Asian Art, and comparative Art Education.

JOCELYN SALAZ received a BFA in Art History and an MA in Art Education at the University of New Mexico. She has taught art in rural New Mexico's Cuba Independent School District and is currently teaching art at Puesta del Sol Elementary School in Rio Rancho, New Mexico. As an Art21 Educator, she is interested in using contemporary art, artists, and themes as a basis for curriculum. In addition to working in the schools, she has worked with teenage witnesses of domestic violence at a non-profit organization that provides services to Spanish-speaking domestic violence victims. Her interests include multicultural art education and social justice.

LORI SANTOS is Assistant Professor and Program Coordinator of Art Education at Utah Valley University. Her career spans over 20 years of service in schools and museums across Kansas, Texas, Arizona, New York, Nebraska, and Utah. She received her PhD in art education from the University of North Texas, with a specialization in Native American and Latino art history. As an art educator she examines contemporary applications of culturally and socially inclusive philosophies of art education in curriculum and instruction; as an artist, she explores the complex connections between culture and art. Multicultural discourses in art education and Native American art and cultures are her primary research foci. She was recently awarded the 2012–2013 Utah Art Education Association Higher Education Educator of the Year award.

ESTEFANÍA SANZ LOBO is Associate Professor and Head of the Department of Art Education in the Universidad Autónoma de Madrid (UAM), Spain. Her research interests are in international and comparative art education, creativity, and visual culture.

AVA SERJOUIE received her MA from Alzahra University, and her PhD from Erfurt University. Prior to receiving her PhD, she taught art and worked at the Museum of Contemporary Art in Iran. Currently, she teaches in a German high school and works as an independent child art researcher. Her inquiries focus on children's production and understanding of images, their interpretation of themes of sadness and happiness in the work of other artists, and the role of environment, culture, and media on children's inference making. Serjouie is also an artist whose personal artworks are influenced by dreams and emotions aroused by contemporary Persian poetry intertwined with childhood memories. Her paintings have been widely exhibited throughout Europe, Iran, and the United States.

JONATHAN SILVERMAN is the Chair of the Education Department and Coordinator of the Arts in Education Program at Saint Michael's College in Colchester, Vermont. His favorite courses to teach include Heroes, Art, and Social Justice; Arts: The Creative Process; and Teaching Art and Social Studies for the K-8 Classroom. He has published articles and led workshops at various professional conferences on creativity, aesthetics, innovative curriculum, teaching English Language Learners through the arts, and school reform. He has acted as a consultant to school districts that seek to develop learning in and through the arts. His EdD was earned at the University of Vermont's Program in Education Leadership and Policy Studies with a focus on aesthetic education. He maintains his artistic identity through watercolor, theater, and chorus.

JEN SONG is the Associate Director of Education of the New Museum of Contemporary Art in New York City, where the mission is to promote new art and new ideas. In addition to overseeing programs for diverse audiences at the New Museum, she works directly with high school teachers interested in using contemporary art to explore issues of social justice in their classroom. Song has worked on various museum education programs, including school partnerships and access programs, at the Museum of Modern Art and Brooklyn Museum. She has also taught museum and art education classes in graduate programs around New York City, including Bank Street College of Education, New York University, Teachers College, Teacher U, and City College of New York.

JOANNE E. SOWELL is Professor Emeritus at the University of Nebraska at Omaha where she taught ancient, medieval, and cross-cultural art history. Her publications have been in the areas of medieval Cistercian architecture and the pedagogy of art history. She has published pedagogical articles in *Art Education, Art Journal, Multicultural Prism,* and *College Teaching.* Sowell has been working with K-12 art teachers for over 20 years in conjunction with Nebraska's Prairie Visions Summer Inservice Institute. She developed and taught a cross-cultural art history course for teachers working on a master's degree in arts integration. In 1995 she received the NAEA Western Region Higher Education Art Educator of the Year award. Recently she has been working with colleagues to write curriculum materials for teachers that focus on public art in the Omaha, Nebraska/Council Bluffs, Iowa, metropolitan area.

PAMELA STEPHENS, President's Distinguished Teaching Fellow and Professor of Art Education at Northern Arizona University (NAU), began her teaching career in pK-12 public schools. She earned a Doctor of Philosophy from the University of North Texas, where she also served as a project coordinator for a national initiative known as Transforming Education through the Arts Challenge. During the past decade Stephens has focused on preparing highly qualified art educators and developing teaching materials for art classrooms. Graduates of the NAU art education program now teach in schools across the United States, in Europe, the Middle East, and Asia. Instructional materials that Stephens has created include a series of art history books and animated videos for children, *Bridging the Curriculum through Art* (a book for teachers), and numerous articles. She serves on the editorial board of *SchoolArts,* is an active member of the National and Arizona Art Education Associations, is a frequent presenter at conferences, and has won multiple teaching awards.

DOUGLAS STEVENS is Lecturer of Music Education at Georgia State University. An eclectic professional background—including military music, pedagogy, composition, and small business, as well as symphony and opera—led Stevens, a graduate of Carleton College, to attend Georgia State University for Music Education Certification. Later he taught elementary strings and classroom music for Fulton County Schools. He earned his Master's in Music Education in 2004 and became Assistant Project Coordinator for the Center for Education Partnerships, where he co-developed the curriculum for nationally renowned *The Sound Learning Program*. He has taught this integrated art and music course for over 7 years, and has presented nationally and internationally about this and other projects.

JENNIFER STOOPES-MOKAMBA earned a BFA from Minneapolis College of Art & Design, MN, and an MAT from Kennesaw State University, GA. She currently teaches art to K-12 students in the rural community of LeRoy, MN, after having taught on the Fort Berthold Reservation in Mandaree, ND. She is particularly interested in the use of authentic artifacts and the role culture plays in art teaching and learning. Her own art focuses on the wide open spaces of the rural landscape.

ATSUSHI SUMI is Professor, Faculty of Human Development, University of Toyama (Japan). He is an instructor of arts education and teacher education. His research interests are in art education theory and assessment. His work has been published in the *Art Education* journal. He has presented at InSEA and UNESCO conferences.

MARISSA VIDRIO earned her AA in fashion design from the Fashion Institute of Design and Merchandising in Los Angeles, a BFA in textiles from California College of the Arts in Oakland, and an MFA in fibers from Arizona State University. After completing her post-baccalaureate certification, also at Arizona State University, she began teaching in the Cartwright School District in Phoenix, Arizona, where she is in her 19th year. Vidrio was raised in a Mexican/Jewish family in Los Angeles and takes inspiration from having lived 3 years in western Norway. She is a desert dweller, artist, educator, mom, and wrangler of two K-9 delinquents.

COURTNEY WEIDA is Associate Professor of Art Education at Adelphi University in Garden City, New York. She has taught pK-12 within schools and community programs in Boston and New York. She is licensed in Visual Art, English, and Elementary classroom teaching. She completed her doctorate in Art and Art Education at Columbia University Teachers College. Her research primarily explores craft and gender issues in art education.